HS 150 Б2500

'Til The Echoes Ring Again

'Til The Echoes Ring Again

A Pictorial History of Boston College Sports

Jack Falla

A Terry Catchpole Book

The Stephen Greene Press

BRATTLEBORO, | LEXINGTON,
VERMONT | MASSACHUSETTS

To Barbara, for your support, much of the credit and most of the royalties. To Brian and Tracey, a father's gratitude for your understanding that the speed of the typewriter is in inverse proportion to the volume of the stereo.

First Edition

Text copyright © 1982 by Jack Falla

Illustrations copyright © 1982 by Boston College

This book is manufactured in the United States of America. It is designed by Irving Perkins Associates and published by The Stephen Greene Press, Fessenden Road, Brattleboro, Vermont 05301.

Library of Congress Cataloging in Publication Data

Falla, Jack, 1944–
'Til the echoes ring again.

Includes index.
1. Boston College—Athletics—History.   I. Title.
II. Title: Until the echoes ring again.
GV691.B67F34   1982   796'.07'1174461   82-20929
ISBN 0–8289–0486–3

"For Boston, for Boston,
We sing our proud refrain!
. . . .
For Boston, for Boston,
'Til the echoes ring again."
    For Boston
    THOMAS J. HURLEY,
    Boston College, Class of 1888

Pride goeth before an explanation:

Boston College men have ever been criticized or
praised for their college spirit . . . A college woman
once said to me, "You Boston College people are all alike."
If this be so, it is not unnatural nor is it a fault.
Boston College men, having had the same basic training, naturally
should react in much the same way . . . We are deeply
interested in the welfare of Alma Mater. If we talk
Boston College, it is because we love her.

Dr. Nathaniel J. Hasenfus, (deceased)
Boston College, Class of 1922

On recruiting for a Catholic college in Boston:

"I think I'll go to Harvard"
  Schoolboy football star
  Joe McKenney in 1922

"You'll go to Boston College or you'll go to work"
  Mother of Joe McKenney,
  1926 Boston College football captain

Acknowledgments

SPECIAL THANKS: NATHANIEL J. Hasenfus '22 (Deceased)

I never knew the late Nat Hasenfus. When I first saw his name and the designation "Athletic Historian" listed on the roster of Boston College's Hall of Fame, I wondered what a non-varsity athlete—a writer no less—had done to merit such honor. It was at about this time that Bill Flynn loaned me his copy of Hasenfus's 1943 book, *Athletics at Boston College,* a meticulous season-by-season recounting of the history of Boston College football and hockey up to World War II.

In addition to this published work, Hasenfus had also compiled, in similar painstaking season-by-season format, an unpublished history of Boston College basketball from its beginnings to 1976 and an update of his football and hockey histories from the forties. Such was Hasenfus's fervor for his Alma Mater that he had also compiled a series of scrapbooks for the academic years 1942–1943 to 1975–1976, containing newspaper clippings covering football, hockey, basketball, baseball, and track and field. These various works were of such great help in the researching of this volume that it may be fair to say that, without Nat Hasenfus, this book would not exist. He worked hard for his niche in the Hall of Fame.

There are others without whose willing support this history could not have been researched and written. My particular thanks to Boston College President the Reverend J. Donald Monan, S.J., for his approval of this project and to Athletic Director Bill Flynn for his initial support of the book and the generous amount of time he devoted to interviews, identifying photo subjects, and supplying missing facts.

Director of Sports Publicity Reid Oslin and his staff cheerfully and competently handled the author's almost daily requests for information, photographs, and general background.

Additional photographs were borrowed from the Boston College archives, where university archivist Father Paul A. FitzGerald and his assistant, Angelina Graham, provided author and editor with work space, guidance, and access to the archives' invaluable materials. Father Fitz-Gerald is co-author with Boston College historian Father Charles F. Donovan, S.J., of *Boston College: A Pictorial History,* a useful reference.

As Boston College is not in the photography business, however, the photo files in both the archives and athletic department were understandably sparse, especially in the pre-World War II years. So please accept this explanation if a photo of your favorite player, favorite play, or favorite game is not included.

Many coaches and former athletes gave generously of their time, files, and memories in support of this project. Constraints of time and space—and the ever-present risk of an omission—do not allow an exhaustive list (virtually all are mentioned in the text), but I would like to acknowledge the considerable contributions and continuing interest of former hockey and golf coach John "Snooks" Kelley and assistant basketball coach Frank Power.

Thanks also to several persons outside of the Boston College community: to my editor Terry Catchpole, not one to let friendship stand in the path of a nicely grooved swing with a number two pencil; to publisher Tom Begner of The Stephen Greene Press/Lewis Publishing Company for maintaining considerable composure as the author hurtled past deadlines with hardly a wave of acknowledgment; to my father, who once made the Boston College–Holy Cross game an autumn ritual; to my son, Brian, a walking media guide of college hockey statistics since 1978; and to my aunt, Mary Sweeney of Manchester, New Hampshire, who typed the football chapter and who thirty years ago (with my uncle, James F. Sweeney, BC '43) took me to my first Boston College athletic contest, a 13-0 football loss to Clemson—but it's the thought that counts.

Jack Falla
Chestnut Hill, Massachusetts

Contents

Acknowledgments   xi

Introduction by William J. Flynn   xv

1 | Beginnings   1

2 | Football   6

3 | Ice Hockey   53

4 | Basketball   86

5 | Baseball, Track, and Field   124

6 | Women's Sports   158

7 | Soccer, Golf, and Tennis   167

Appendix I Year-by-Year Major Sports Team Records   175

Appendix II Major and Minor Sports Letterwinners   198

Appendix III Major Sports Team Records   212

Appendix IV Boston College Hall of Fame   215

Index   217

Introduction
BY WILLIAM J. FLYNN

For Boston, for Boston
We sing our proud refrain!
For Boston, for Boston
'Til the echoes ring again!

To THOUSANDS OF people, these words are the catalyst for thousands of stories. For many, myself included, they send a tingle up the spine. I can recall hearing the famous lyric many years ago as a young Boston schoolboy, as vividly as I can recall the Boston College band serenading our basketball team during the 1982 NCAA championship playoffs.

Even though these words celebrate our pride in the entire University, they have become a theme of the tradition of success that is Boston College athletics. It is that tradition which is captured so well in Jack Falla's history of athletics at Boston College.

To preserve in words and pictures the history of any great organization or institution is an important task; to capture the spirit, dedication, and accomplishments of our student-athletes and coaches over the years is priceless.

I have always envied the universities that had the talent and resources to record their athletic deeds and accomplishments in a formal way, and

I hope that all members of the Boston College family will be proud of this chronicle of our long and storied tradition.

Dr. Nat Hasenfus '22 was known as the historian of Boston College athletics since almost the beginnings of formal athletic competition at this University. He wrote a hardcover history of Boston College football and hockey that was published in 1943. I remember receiving a letter from Nat, my former high school English teacher, asking for contributions to underwrite initial publication costs. Even though I was away from home and didn't have a lot of money in those days, the nostalgia and interest that I had in the project prompted me to assist as best I could. To this day, I am quietly proud to have been listed as a sponsor of that monumental effort.

Dr. Hasenfus never ceased collecting every box score, press clipping, program, and publication concerning Boston College sports. He filed every one of them so that someday he could fulfill his dream of writing an updated second edition of his Boston College sports history. Sadly, that dream never came true, as our beloved sports historian passed away in 1976. However, his years of collecting and sorting news items about Boston College athletics were not in vain. His son, David Hasenfus, turned his father's material over to the Boston College Archives, and a great deal of the information contained in this book was culled from Dr. Hasenfus' research and work.

When Terry Catchpole approached me in February 1982 to ask if the Stephen Greene Press could look into publishing a new history of Boston College athletics, I thought that I had been visited by a messenger from heaven. I was similarly thrilled when I learned that Jack Falla had been selected as author of the work, as I had just finished reading his scholarly and informative book, *NCAA: The Voice of College Sports.*

It is most difficult to even attempt to put on paper the lifetimes of memories that our athletes, coaches, students, alumni, and fans have so long enjoyed; but I feel certain that Jack has accomplished this extraordinary task—capturing the excitement, color, thrills, victories, and even the occasional heartaches of this long saga of athletic activity.

Our university historian, Reverend Charles F. Donovan, S.J., and university archivist Reverend Paul A. FitzGerald, S.J., recently published a pictorial history of Boston College. I was frankly amazed, as I read this outstanding work, just how important a part athletics has played in the history and development of our great university. To me, athletics is an integral and vital part of all that is Boston College, and I think this book vividly captures this unique and proud attribute.

In closing, I want to thank all of the men and women who have contributed so much to our shining athletic tradition, both on the playing field and through their long and unwavering support of the Eagles' teams. Without them, the echoes would not have rung again, and again, and again.

Athletic Director Bill Flynn (inset) as a young Eagle back in the late 1930s; and (right) receiving a momento from Governor Edward J. King (BC, '47) at the dedication of the William J. Flynn Student Recreation Complex in 1979, with college president Reverend J. Donald Monan, S. J., looking on at right.

1

Beginnings

IT HAS NOT been an easy nor wholly pleasant journey. Once the abused, unwanted academic orphan of nineteenth-century Yankee Boston, Boston College has risen to become one of the largest Jesuit universities in the world, a school of unassailable academic merit and, to come to the point, the leader in New England college sports.

Boston College is the only school in once athletically dominant New England that still schedules the nation's foremost football powers, places football and basketball games on network television, and regularly produces hockey and basketball teams of national tournament calibre. And, exemplifying the peculiar phenomenon that occurs at a handful of schools—Notre Dame, Alabama, UCLA among them—Boston College manages to produce more fans than graduates. "Boston College is *Boston's* College," a college official says.

Indeed, Boston College is Alma Mater to 72,000 living alumni. More than this, she is the adopted darling of untold legions of subway alumni, primarily Boston Catholics, many of Irish, Polish, and Italian descent, whose fathers adopted the great Boston College football and hockey teams of the 1940s and whose children know by heart the words to *For Boston*. This spontaneous popular adoption is particularly satisfying to a school that, a century ago, was struggling for its institutional life—combating social and religious prejudice and coping with its own poverty. Sports was a part of that struggle.

But this all came long after the cannonball.

Sir Inigo de Onoz y Loyola was a Spanish knight and, by his own admission, not a lovable fellow. He was, he confessed, "a man given to the vanities of the world, whose chief delight consisted in martial exercises, with a great and vain desire to win renown."

A shot from a French cannon changed that. The ball broke his right leg and tore most of the calf muscle off the left leg on May 20, 1521, while Sir Inigo (later St. Ignatius Loyola) was unsuccessfully directing defense of a Spanish citadel at Pamplona. Convalescing in the Spanish town of Loyola, Ignatius read the hospital's only two books, a life of Christ and a volume on the lives of the saints. Of the saints he concluded,

1

St. Ignatius Loyola founded the Company of Jesus, later the Society of Jesus, in 1538, and the first Jesuit college—in Messina, Sicily—in 1548. Three hundred years later, the Jesuits' organized presence first appeared in Boston, followed by the founding of Boston College in 1863.

"These men were of the same frame as I; why then should I not do what they have done?"

After seventeen years of study, being of the opinion that an educated man could accomplish in a short time what an uneducated man could never accomplish, Ignatius and a few followers founded the Company of Jesus, later the Society of Jesus, whose members were popularly, and at first derogatorily, called "Jesuits." The label endured, as did the order. The Jesuits, pledged to the Pope's service, soon expanded their missionary work to include the establishment of schools and colleges. Ignatius founded the world's first Jesuit college at Messina, Sicily, in 1548.

The order came to North America in the early seventeenth century and, by 1769, it had established the first American Jesuit college, Georgetown (now Georgetown University), near what was to be Washington, D.C. The Jesuits came to Boston in 1847 in the person of sixty-five-year-old Irish-born Reverend John McElroy, S. J., who became pastor of St. Mary's parish in the North End.

McElroy arrived in the city amid a massive flood of Irish-Catholic immigration, a result of the Irish potato famine. Between 1840 and 1860, Catholics became the single largest religious denomination in Boston, an influx that went unappreciated, though by no means unnoted, by Boston's Yankee establishment.

Historian Richard D. Brown writes of Yankee-Irish relations in Boston in the 1840s: "Yankees widely regarded (the Irish) as fundamentally 'different' from other white people, and believed that the Catholic church was the embodiment of tyranny and corruption." During the decade before McElroy's arrival, bigots had rioted against Catholics, destroying a convent in Charlestown. In other cases, Catholic schoolboys were flogged for refusing to read aloud from a Protestant version of the Bible.

While an expanding Massachusetts economy absorbed the incoming Irish as low-paid mill workers, tenant farmers, and menials, the door to better jobs—and to the higher education that would help secure them—was firmly closed. The Irish, writes Brown, were the "mudsill" of society.

The public and parochial elementary schools of the day were adequate to train youths in the fundamentals of arithmetic and English grammar, but they did not provide the classical education needed for entry to Harvard, Williams, or Amherst. Latin schools and private academies were the vehicles by which wealthy or ambitious parents—that is to say white, American-born, Protestant parents—set their sons on the road to careers as doctors, lawyers, and ministers. Even putting aside anti-Catholic sentiment, without the money for a proper secondary education the children of Irish Catholic families could hold little hope for the future.

Immediately upon his arrival in Boston, Father McElroy sought to overcome this adversity by establishing a Catholic preparatory school and Catholic college. He first purchased a lot on Leverett Street in the city's West End in 1856, but he was prevented from realizing his ambition by anti-Catholic residents and he eventually had to sell the property.

A year later, Boston Mayor Alexander H. Rice intervened to help McElroy purchase a site on Harrison Avenue in Boston's then developing South End. And in 1858, at age seventy-six, the priest broke ground for three structures—a residence for Jesuits, the Church of the Immaculate Conception, and a preparatory school and college to be called "the Boston College."

The Massachusetts Legislature chartered the Boston College (which almost immediately became known simply as Boston College) in 1863 and, a year later, the new school opened its doors under the presidency of Father John Bapst. Bapst was a Swiss who, a half-dozen years earlier, had been seized by an anti-Catholic mob in Ellsworth, Maine, and had been stripped, tarred, feathered, and ridden out of town on a rail.

The first Boston College students, all boys, pursued the traditional college preparatory curriculum, a classical and highly structured course derived from the old Jesuit *Ratio Studiorum*. Sport was not a part of the curriculum, as almost all college administrators at the time felt that sport

was strictly an extracurricular student affair, to be endured, though not encouraged or organized, by the faculty. One of the games popular with preparatory school boys of the mid-1860s was called football, a bloody rough-and-tumble combination of soccer and rugby, that bore little resemblance to the game we see today; though it did call for use of the feet and a ball.

The only form of physical education encouraged at Boston College in these post-Civil War days was military drill, and let it be noted that Boston College's first drill team was a good one. Called Foster's Cadets, named after its commander, the blue-and-gold-clad company became so proficient that, in the late 1860s, it challenged other corps to competition. There were no takers.

Boston College grew slowly and remained desperately poor. It was not until 1876 that enrollment exceeded 200 and, of these, 140 were in the preparatory school; a year later the college granted its first diplomas, with eleven students receiving A.B. degrees.

In the 1870s, with football growing in popularity among students, athletics gained a margin

In the late 1850s, the Society of Jesus purchased land on Harrison Avenue in Boston's South End, and began construction of the Church of the Immaculate Conception (left) and an educational facility that was to become the original Boston College. This photo was taken in the early 1870s by essayist-poet Oliver Wendell Holmes.

BC's first athletic facility was a gymnasium erected on the South End site in the late 1870s, outfitted with a running track and gymnastic equipment. This would be the limit of the college's sports facilities until after the campus was moved to Chestnut Hill in 1913.

of faculty acknowledgement when representatives of Rutgers, Yale, Princeton, and Columbia met in 1873 to try to agree on a common set of football rules. At Boston College, meanwhile, the administration raised money to add a gymnasium to the college, a modest facility equipped with a pair of rings, a trapeze, a set of parallel bars, and two upright posts with a crosspiece. *Mens sana in corpore sano*—but only four men at a time, please.

In warm weather, pickup baseball games and informal track competitions were staples of student picnics at Miller's Field, Roxbury, near what is now the Dudley Street MBTA station. (Star of the early baseball games was Dennis J. Sullivan, Class of 1877, a catcher who later played for the professional Boston Nationals.) By 1883, students were beginning to pressure the faculty for

formal support of athletics, with the following plea published in the first volume of the *Stylus*, Boston College's literary magazine, in May of that year: "We are pleased to notice the interest displayed this year in baseball. Already Second Grammar is about to follow suit. Why could we not have a College Nine?"

Apparently, the request was granted, as the July 1883 issue of the *Stylus* published this cryptic report: "The College Nine was punished rather severely by the Jamaicas on May 19th, not so badly by the Holy Cross Nine on May 24th. Courage boys!"

But the decisive step in faculty support of sports at Boston College came in the aftermath of the publication of an anonymous letter in the *Stylus* of September 19, 1884. The letter, signed "Cripple," was written in support of an earlier letter by "Athlete '85" urging formation of a Boston College Athletic Club. "Cripple" wrote:

The suggestion to form an (Athletic Association) is a movement in the right direction. The most casual observer would say we have already made good athletes in the college. The conduct of our baseball club at Worcester last spring was ample evidence of what it might be if only it possessed a little training. All that is needed is concerted action. An A.A. would insure this.

"Cripple" got his wish. In October 1884 a three-man student committee called on the college's new president, Reverend Edward V. Boursaud, and received permission to form the Boston College Athletic Club. A large majority of Boston College students joined the club and elected as its first secretary Thomas J. Hurley, the student who would later write the school's fight song, *For Boston*. A year later, Leo J. Brand, S. J., was appointed by Boursaud to be the first Faculty Director of Athletics.

Among the Boston College Athletic Club's first acts was raising funds to refurbish the gymnasium. By 1890, the facility was outfitted with new equipment, wired for electric lights, and served as Spring training site for the Boston Nationals baseball team.

Predictably, given the growing popularity of football among students across the country in the 1890s, the Boston College Athletic Club was soon agitating for a college football team. But, with scarcely enough money to keep the doors open, the administration was not about to underwrite football, and Boston College students had to content themselves with a series of class games, the biggest of which reportedly was "Rhetoric vs. Poetry," a "classic" of sorts.

Even if the college had not been poor, the students may not have gotten their football team because football, while popular with students, was falling into widespread disfavor elsewhere.

The football of the 1880s and 1890s was a brutal game in which punching an opponent was punishable by no more than a warning. Across the Charles River in Cambridge, the Harvard Athletic Committee called football, "brutal, demoralizing to teams and players, and extremely dangerous."

"There is no sport outside of a bullfight," wrote the *New York Herald,* "that provides the same degree of ferocity, danger, and excitement as shown in an ordinary intercollegiate game of football."

No matter. By the 1890s, at Boston College as at 119 other colleges throughout the country, excitement was to prevail over ferocity and danger.

2

Football

The James Street Era: 1893–1912

STUDENTS WOULD SELL but the administration would not buy.

Twice, once in 1889 and again in 1890, student delegations sought and were refused administrative sanction for intercollegiate football. Students were instead advised to concentrate on their studies. After all, Boston College was still struggling to establish itself as an alternative avenue of opportunity for a class that desperately needed it and not as another football team in a game already dominated by the Big Three colleges of the Yankee-Protestant establishment— Harvard, Yale, and Princeton.

In 1891, a group of students received permission but no money from President E. I. Devitt, S. J., to form a Boston College football team. The students were led by Joseph F. O'Connell, '92, who, because of his previous playing experience with the Dorchester Combination Football Club, was also elected captain of this first semi-official football team.

Otherwise, there was no coach, no equipment,

no uniforms, and only a small playing field near the college building on James Street. And because The Boston College Athletic Club did not play college varsities, there was no newspaper coverage. However, thanks to the late Dr. Nathaniel J. Hasenfus, '22, voluntary Boston College sports historian, who talked with some of the players and spectators in this era, we have an idea of what the earliest days of Boston College football were like.

The schedule consisted of games with local high schools, academies, and minor colleges. Among the first men out for the 1892 team was one who was forced to play under a Greek name ("Plinthos") so as to escape detection by parents who, presumably, had not sent him to college to play football. The player's name was Frank Brick, and he would later play four consecutive years of varsity competition after Boston College officially inaugurated football in 1893.

Twenty-two men reported for practice in the fall of 1893, among them fullback Bernie

Boston College's first official football team contained players with assumed names and was "managed" by Joseph C. Drum.

Wefers, a fleet-footed transfer from Holy Cross who briefly held the world's record (9.8 seconds) for the one-hundred-yard dash.

The team's first game was a 4–0 win over St. John's Institute, an amateur power in these days (touchdowns were then worth only four points). The first intercollegiate game, though not a *varsity* game, was played October 25, 1893, when Technology 1897 (a class team at MIT) beat Boston College 6–0 in a game which lasted only the first half because a Harvard *class* team had a game scheduled on the same field. There followed a 10–0 loss to Newton, a 10–6 win over Somerville High School, a 6–0 loss to West Roxbury High School, and then the first *varsity* game ever played by Boston College—a 10–6 win over natural rival Boston University. Frank "Plinthos" Brick scored the winning touchdown. Dr. Hasenfus reported that, at the game's conclusion, "Boston College students went wild."

The most popular play of these days was the infamous "flying wedge," a play first used by Harvard against Yale in 1892 and which typified the brutality then rampant in intercollegiate football. In the flying wedge, two five-man "V" formations smashed their way downfield, the first driving an entering wedge into the defensive ranks, the second providing a moving escort for the ball carrier. The most successful method of stopping the play called for defenders to throw themselves at the legs of the onrushing blockers. It is not surprising that about this time college players first began to take protective measures, wearing leather noseguards, and letting their hair grow out in the skull-protecting "crysanthemum" haircut.

In 1894, Boston College hired its first full-time coach, William Nagle of Mt. St. Mary's college, who fielded a losing team (1–6), and adopted maroon and gold as the college's athletic colors. These are, of course, the Papal colors, and as such, reflect the school's Jesuit origins.

This was also the year in which the *Stylus* offered a five dollar reward to the student who wrote the best "Boston College yell." In this era of increasing popularity of college football, big games, particularly those involving Harvard, Yale, Princeton, and Columbia, drew crowds upwards of 10,000, and college cheers were a new phenomenon—simple and ordinary to a 1980s ear, perhaps, but effective in giving vent to undergraduate enthusiasm. Winner of the *Stylus*

7

The sensible player of the early 1900s (here, Joseph Kenney, captain of BC's 1901 eleven) wore a protective leather nose-guard and heavily padded pants.

competition, for example, was a cheer called "Boston College Rah":

> Boston College Rah! Boston College Rah!
> B-o-s-t-o-n, B-o-s-t-o-n
> Boston! Boston! Boston!
> Rah-Rah-Rah-Rah-Rah-Team-Team-Team!

By the turn of the century, colleges everywhere were adopting "fight" songs. Boston College, however, would have to wait until after it had moved to its new Chestnut Hill campus, before it got a song of its own. Written by alumnus Thomas J. Hurley, *For Boston* has since become the most recognizable fight song in New England:

> For Boston, for Boston,
> We sing our proud refrain!
> For Boston, for Boston,
> 'Tis wisdom's earthly fane.
> For here men are men
> And their hearts are true,
> And the towers on the Heights
> Reach to heaven's own blue.
> For Boston, for Boston,
> 'Til the echoes ring again.

While cheers and songs, occupied the thoughts of its fans, the Boston College football teams of the nineties, coachless again in 1895 and 1896, continued to struggle with lack of a proper playing and practice field, with inability to draw up an all-college schedule, and with the school's general poverty. One bright spot was that among the high schools, prep schools and the occasional college opponent, the 1896 schedule included a two-game home-and-home series with the Jesuit college in Worcester, Holy Cross. While Boston College vs. Holy Cross would go on to take its place as one of the great traditional rivalries of the East, the first games had little appeal: only five hundred fans watched the 1896 home game with Holy Cross, which Boston College won 8–6 (Boston College also won the earlier game at Worcester 6–2), as compared to the three thousand fans who turned out to watch Boston College beat Boston University 10–0.

The rivalry with Holy Cross would not begin in earnest until 1897, when Boston University withdrew from its traditional Thanksgiving Day game and Boston College had to scramble for an opponent. Since that year's second Holy Cross game had been rained out earlier in the season, the idle Crusaders accepted the Thanksgiving slot as a rain date. Boston College won 12–0. More important, a tradition was born.

In 1898, Boston College named a new president, Father W. J. Read Mullan, S. J., who shared the not unpopular belief that college dollars and student time might be better spent on pursuits other than football. Consequently, he refused to allow a team to play under the school's name in 1900. After Boston College players, led by quart-

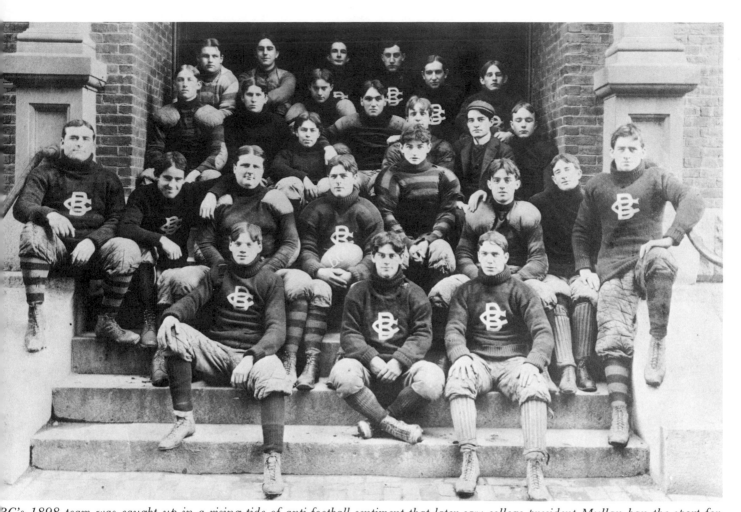

BC's 1898 team was caught up in a rising tide of anti-football sentiment that later saw college president Mullan ban the sport for a season.

erback John Kelly of Dorchester, proceeded to put together an independent team playing under the name "Boston Combination," Father Mullan relented, and in 1901, Boston College once again fielded an official team—financed by student fundraising efforts. The season ended with Boston College winning two and losing seven, all the losses shutouts.

An even worse (0–8) season in 1902, combined with continued financial problems and a louder national public outcry against the growing violence of college football, resulted in Boston College football being suspended by the administration from 1903 to 1907. This was an era in which carnage on gridirons across the country was so outrageous (18 deaths and 149 serious injuries in college football games in 1905) that President Theodore Roosevelt summoned the college game's leaders to the White House and issued an ultimatum: clean up the game or see it legally abolished.

Roosevelt's threat prompted formation of the Intercollegiate Athletic Association, predecessor to the National Collegiate Athletic Association—(NCAA)—which Boston College would join in 1914. Concurrently, there occured dramatic changes in football's rules: the forward pass was legalized; loose balls could no longer be kicked; hurdling—literally throwing a ballcarrier over the defensive line—was outlawed; mass momentum plays were prohibited; and first down yardage was increased from five to ten yards to force teams into some other offensive strategy than a relentless series of line smashes.

The rules changes worked. College football was a safer and more open game when it resumed at Boston College in 1908 under the approving gaze of President Father Thomas Ignatius Gasson.

Unfortunately, on the playing field Boston College picked up where it had left off—losing. New and unfamiliar football tactics, lack of experienced players, and the necessity of using a Harrison Avenue practice field that was nothing more than a hard-packed strip of dirt and cinders, were hurdles too high for a parade of coaches to leap. Coaches Joseph Reilly and Joe Kenney (1908), Charlie McCarthy (1909), Jim Hart (1910), Joe Courtney (1911), and Bill "Hiker" Joy (1912–1913) stumbled and bumbled through five consecutive losing seasons, including two, 1910 and 1911, in which the team did not win a game and another, 1912, during which the team had no home field.

But while the battles were being lost on the field, the war was being won in the president's office. Father Gasson, often called the "second founder" of Boston College, was a man who could keep one eye on the horizon and the other on the accounting ledger, traits that saved Boston College and secured the future of her teams.

From The Iron Major to the Sugar Bowl—1913–1941

Two months after his appointment as college president, the former philosophy professor announced his seemingly fatuous intention of purchasing for the college, "a magnificent site on Commonwealth Avenue in Brighton," a property then known as the Lawrence Farm, for the purpose of erecting new buildings and otherwise creating a spacious suburban campus. Price tag: a staggering $10 million, to be raised largely from that formerly downtrodden Irish Catholic population that was only beginning to make its still-modest fortune in the worlds of commerce and politics.

A Boston Irish Architect, Charles Donagh McGinnis of the firm of McGinnis and Walsh, won the competition to design the site and plan the imposing Gothic buildings later to become Gasson, Devlin, and St. Mary's halls, and the Bapst Library. Huge alumni lawn parties, the theme of which was "Send Your Boys to Boston College," raised enough money for Gasson to begin construction. In 1913, the freshman class became the first to attend classes at Chestnut Hill. By 1914, Gasson was welcoming all Boston College students to the campus he had begun calling "the Heights."

There was as yet no playing field at the new college. Coach Hiker Joy's 1913 team was forced to use the reservoir grounds, today known as Cleveland Circle, and otherwise "the football team was still poor," according to Father Maurice Dullea, a player from 1913 to 1916 and captain of the 1916 team. "We'd be out there sometimes without a football to practice with, so we'd get a helmet and use that as a ball. You could say we felt poor but not deprived." Whether it was because of the new surroundings, the presence of a coach who lasted more than one season (Joy lasted two), or because the team was finally catching up with the tactical advances of "open" football, the 1913 squad restored the credibility of Boston College football by playing the biggest game in the school's brief history; ironically, it ended in a tie.

The Fordham Rams were a national power when Boston College met them in New York in 1913. The game should have been little more than a tune-up for Fordham, but Boston College halfback Jim Linnehan, playing with one ankle encased in a steel brace, put Boston College ahead 27–20 late in the fourth quarter. Fordham came back to tie the game on its final possession, but Boston College had made its point—it had played a major team to a standstill and established itself as a regional power. From this base, Boston College would vault to national prominence during the next six years.

Playing on a municipal field a half-mile from its campus was hardly in keeping with the college's new-found reputation. The team finally got its own home in 1915, after alumni donated sufficient funds to erect a football stadium and cinder track in the stately shadow of Gasson Hall. On October 30 of that year, Father Charles Lyons, Gasson's successor, christened the stadium "Alumni Field" before a crowd of 5,000 at the Holy Cross game. Boston College lost 9–0 that afternoon, but a week later upset Fordham

Halfback Jimmy Fitzpatrick (right) was BC's first great passing star, while diminutive Lou Urban was a frequent target.

3–0 in what might fairly be called the team's first real "home" win after seventeen seasons of sponsoring varsity football.

While Boston College teams were struggling to establish a modest regional reputation in these pre-war years, the great Harvard teams of coach Percy Haughton were already established—as Notre Dame would be in the 1920s—as *the* dominant national football power. It was natural, therefore, that when Boston College went searching for a coach to replace Steve Mahoney, who left in 1915 after compiling an 8–8–0 record, it would look to Haughton and Harvard for a man who could fulfill its football ambitions. The choice was Charles Brickley, a former Harvard All-American whose reputation was such that news of his selection was enough to attract two New England schoolboy stars to the Heights, halfback-kicker Jimmy Fitzpatrick of Meriden, Connecticut, and receiver Louis Urban of Fall River, Massachusetts.

Fitzpatrick was a speedy runner who could pass left- or right-handed (halfbacks passed under the Brickley system), punt seventy-five yards (his career average is a school record sixty-five yards), and dropkick field goals from almost any angle inside the fifty.

Urban was a small (5'7", 165 pounds) end, with good hands developed in his three other varsity sports: baseball, basketball, and hockey. In a three-game stretch in 1919, Urban caught twenty-nine passes, most of them from Fitzpatrick, and he still holds the Boston College record for receptions in one game, with twelve against Rutgers in 1919. Brickley's first two teams turned in identical 6–2 seasons, but none of the wins came against a team of national reputation.

By 1918, American guns were booming in Europe and Boston College, as with United States colleges everywhere, felt the effects of wartime. Students—741 of them—were training daily in the Student Army Training Corps; Coach Brickley was called to the service; and the football team, allowed only one hour of daily practice, faced a schedule made up of the likes of Fort Devens and Bumpkin Island Naval Air Station. Across the country, college sports programs were pared to the bone. The official posture of the National Collegiate Athletic Association was that athletics were to be "subservient to military preparation," and that member colleges, of which Boston College was one, were to reduce travel, eliminate pre-season practice, and use volunteer coaches where possible.

At Harvard, President LeBaron Briggs cancelled some of the school's away games, saying, "Our bigger games . . . have been great public spectacles such as we do not like to be responsible for in times like these." As a result, Boston College and Harvard took advantage of their geographic proximity and open schedules to play a game at Harvard Stadium—then the Mecca of college football—on November 23, 1918. Boston College lost the game 14–6, but by playing well and proving it could be competitive with one of the Big Three, the upstarts from Chestnut Hill unwittingly set the stage for what was to be the school's most important upset win.

With the signing of the Armistice, American troops returned to the nation's campuses and 1919 became a year of athletic renaissance. At Boston College it was a year in which the football team reaped the reward of its good showing in Harvard Stadium by scheduling Harvard *and* Yale: Boston College was in the Big Time.

Brickley did not return to Boston College, his

HOME FROM "THE DUMP"

Classrooms took priority over playing fields when the Jesuits opened Boston College in the South End in 1863. If the boys needed space for their pick-up baseball games or informal track meets, they could go down to the old Miller's Field in the Roxbury section near what is today the Dudley Street MBTA station. And good luck to them and their games; Boston College was a community of scholars, not ballplayers.

That faculty hard line softened quickly as students' interest in athletics grew. By the 1880s, Boston College class teams were playing football games on the nearby Walpole Street grounds. Biggest of these interclass games was *Rhetoric* vs. *Poetry*. By 1893, Boston College students had gained administrative sanction to play intercollegiate football games—as long as they were *away* games. Boston College had no marked field on which to host a game. Practices had to be held on a short and narrow grass strip that ran between the college buildings and Newton Street. The space was adequate for the practice of running plays, but a long punt would as likely be caught by a pedestrian as by a player.

At the turn of the century, Boston College President Reverend W. J. Read Mullan, S.J., if not a man wholly sympathetic to college football, did recognize the need for a playing field and had the college purchase a nine-acre tract on Massachusetts Avenue with the intention of turning it into a combination baseball, football, and track facility. Urgent need notwithstanding, improvement of the land was delayed

for years because the desperately poor college could not raise the $25,000 required for the project. Even when the field was put to use, it was a far cry from first-class. Joe Lynch, a player on the 1908 team, in a letter to Boston College sports historian Nat Hasenfus, writes of the Massachusetts Avenue field: "Our first home game in 1908 was played on the Massachusetts Avenue grounds (The Dump). On the morning of the game the squad cut the weeds and marked the lines. The caretaker had erected the goal posts and had marked the four corners of the field and had set out a barrel of lime. . . ."

"The Dump" was sold to the Edison Company in 1911, leaving Boston College once more without a home field as new college President Reverend Thomas Ignatius Gasson, S. J., proceeded with his plans to move Boston College out of the city and onto a spacious campus in Chestnut Hill. Again, classrooms took their proper priority over fields, and the Boston College teams of 1913 and 1914 found themselves playing and practicing on a municipally-owned field beside the Chestnut Hill Reservoir near Cleveland Circle.

The football, baseball, and track teams finally got a proper home field in 1915 when alumni contributions enabled the college to install a combination gridiron, diamond, and cinder track (with a seating capacity of 5,000 for football) located near Gasson Hall. The football/baseball arrangement called for the annual removal and storage of about one-quarter of the grandstands. Parking, or lack of it, was also a problem.

By 1936, Boston College had shifted most of its

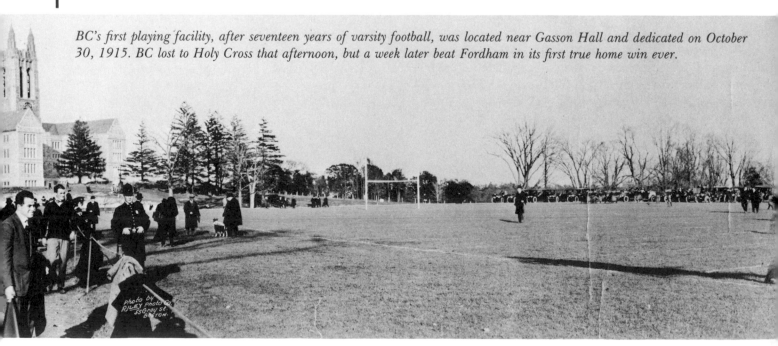

BC's first playing facility, after seventeen years of varsity football, was located near Gasson Hall and dedicated on October 30, 1915. BC lost to Holy Cross that afternoon, but a week later beat Fordham in its first true home win ever.

For one memorable 1975 game, BC pulled out all the stops: 61,000 people packed into mammoth Schaeffer Stadium, the Goodyear blimp, a national television audience on ABC— and a tough, emotional loss to Notre Dame.

major football games to Boston locales, mostly to Fenway Park which could seat about 40,000 for football. (The Eagles also on occasion used Braves Field, now called Nickerson Field and home of the Boston University Terriers.) This off-campus arrangement ended December 1, 1956 when the Red Sox closed the park to college football because of the players' devastation of the turf. Many fans and alumni thought Boston College would drop football because of lack of a stadium.

The college did indeed consider dropping the sport. Instead, college President Reverend Joseph R. N. Maxwell, S.J., alumni secretary and soon-to-be athletic director Bill Flynn, and volunteer Stadium Committee chairman Joe McKenney (1926 football captain and coach from 1928 to 1934), mobilized a special fund-raising drive that quickly raised the money needed to construct a stadium by the start of the 1957 season.

In order that all athletic facilities be grouped, and because the administration was already thinking about future construction of a gym, rink, and baseball field, Father Maxwell and Flynn decided to locate the stadium and any future athletic facilities on land near the reservoir, much of which was under water at the time of the decision.

The new stadium went up in the remarkably short span of 156 days, earning contractor John King of the

Bowen Construction Company the nickname, "The Big Steam Shovel." King's incredible 1957 timetable:

April 15—One crane and four men dismantle stands at old site.

May 13—Specially built tractors move sections of old stands down Beacon Street and set them on new footings.

June 3—Bulldozer digs into existing blacktop to prepare for sodding of the new field.

June 6 to 10—Playing surface covered with four-inches subsoil, four inches topsoil and graded.

June 17—Field sodded.

June 18—All stands from old field in place and bolted together.

July 8—Plumbing in.

July 25—Crews begin to build press box and paint stands.

August 19—New stands put on the filled end of the field which had been under water on June 20.

On September 21, 1957, Boston College dedicated its 26,000–seat (since increased to 32,000) "Alumni Stadium" in a game against Navy. The Eagles lost the game 46–6 but had at last won a permanent home.

While many Boston College football players donated their efforts during the five months of the stadium's construction, none had to cut weeds.

For twenty years BC played its big-draw football games in 33,000–seat Fenway Park, until Red Sox owner Tom Yawkey in 1956 grew tired of re-sodding his turf. Yawkey's ban almost ended football at Boston College.

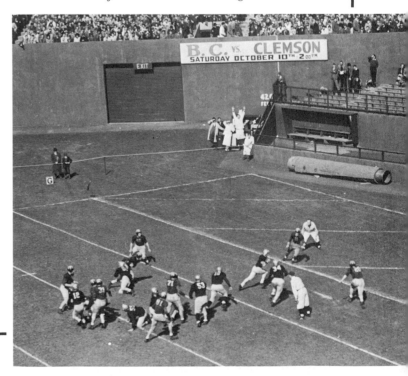

place as coach was taken by a retired major whose personality and war record were to make him a national hero and the subject of a Hollywood movie *The Iron Major*. Francis W. Cavanaugh— "You can call me coach or you can call me Major"—graduated from Dartmouth in 1901 and coached that team from 1911 to 1916 when, at age 41, he left his wife and six children to enter the service. He almost made it through. Armistice Day was less than three weeks away when Cavanaugh stepped from his dugout command post at the Battle of San Mihiel, France, to direct the fire of American field artillery against German positions. That step was almost his last. Cavanaugh disappeared in the smoke and shrapnel of a German 210 shell. When medical corpsmen found him, most of the right side of his face had been blown away and he was holding his right eye, still barely connected to the socket, in his right hand.

Medics thought he was mortally wounded and summoned a priest to administer last rites. The priest's services were not needed. After months of recuperation and reconstructive surgery, "the Iron Major" returned to the United States to make national football powers of first Boston College and then Fordham.

Ten months after being hit by the German shell, Cavanaugh was hired by then Boston College athletic director Frank Reynolds. At his first team meeting Cavanaugh set forth his philosophy of football: "Men of Boston, football is a game that should be played to the uttermost limits of respectability." Then Cavanaugh an-

Coach Frank Cavanaugh (shown, center, with assistant Bill "Hiker" Joy, right, and team manager Frank Reynolds) was a former war hero who gave BC its first taste of big-time football.

nounced his definition of the perfect football player: "He is the absolutely unspoiled fearless fellow with a quick start and an intelligent mind. Given those, the rest will take care of itself. It doesn't make any difference what race or nationality he comes from. But he must remain unspoiled. As soon as he starts looking for his place in the limelight, his playing suffers."

Cavanaugh's Boston College teams were aggressive—some said intimidating—and exceptionally well conditioned. His first team brought Boston College instant national recognition with one of the most shocking upsets in the history of college football, a 5–3 victory over Yale. The win was sealed with Fitzpatrick's forty-seven-yard, left-footed, drop kick field goal with two minutes to play, a play made possible by a twenty-seven-yard Fitzpatrick-to-Urban pass. The next day the Boston College student body snake-danced its way from Chestnut Hill to Boston in celebration, and *The New York Times* published a game account which, in the hyperbolic sports reportage of the day, hinted at the football establishment's shock over this embarrassment of one of the game's Big Three:

> The fighting football eleven of Boston College placed an indelible blot on Yale's football escutcheon this afternoon in the Yale Bowl when Frank Cavanaugh's maroon-jerseyed team staged the gridiron's sensation of the season by beating the Elis in a bitterly fought battle . . . . Yale's downfall before this scrappy crowd of Bostonians came as a severe shock to the 10,000 Yale supporters who came out expecting to see only another practice game for the big football games still to come . . . . The crowd filed out of the sunken amphitheater silently, not even waiting to see the Boston players dancing on the field like a lot of Comanches and carrying Captain Jimmy Fitzpatrick away on their shoulders.

This game, more than any other, established the Cavanaugh coaching legend. It also established a misconception. In the movie "The Iron Major," Cavanaugh, played by Pat O'Brien, gives his team an emotional fight talk before the game at Yale. In reality, according to Boston College center Jack Heaphy, defensive star of the game, Cavanaugh, recognizing that a game with Yale

BC back James Liston sweeps around right end for valuable yardage during the Eagles' stunning 1919 upset of Big Three power Yale. This victory confirmed the Cavanaugh coaching legend and put BC on the path to national sports prominence.

was motivation enough, kept his voice down, saying only: "You've read about the mighty Bulldog. You're playing before 30,000 people [it was one-third of that]. Yale has five times as many players as we have, but remember this: no matter what they do, they can't have more than eleven men on the field at the same time. That's all. Get out there."

The Yale win was no fluke. The next season, 1920, Cavanaugh produced the best team of Boston College's first twenty-nine years of football. Fitzpatrick and Urban were back as seniors, and they led an undefeated (8–0–0) team—for the first time officially called "the Eagles"—that outscored opponents 181–16 and won the Eastern College Championship. The closest game on the schedule was a 21–13 win over Yale.

More than just attracting national recognition, the 1920 team was box office. Cavanaugh knew team support began with the students, and by force of his uncompromising will, he stopped just short of making football game attendance compulsory. These were his words at a student rally before a Holy Cross game:

Men of Boston—your team plays Holy Cross tomorrow. They've done their best to get ready. I've done my best. Will you be with them when they take the field tomorrow? When those maroon and gold warriors line up for the kickoff, to do or die for the school that's yours and theirs, will you be with them? Will you? When they offer their all, so that the whole world will know that up there on the Heights we still breed men, men who can fight, men who can win—men of Bos-

ton, will you be with them? Will you? When that referee raises his arm and asks: 'Are you ready, Holy Cross? Are you ready, Boston?'—Men of Boston, will you, indeed, be ready? Will you?

In response, the next day 40,000 jammed Braves Field (then home of the National League Boston Braves, now Boston University's Nickerson Field). Boston College beat Holy Cross 14–0, though without the services of Fitzpatrick, who saw his football career end with a broken shoulder in the Georgetown game.

In the early twenties Cavanaugh and Boston College learned that when you beat up all the bullies on the block, word travels fast to distant blocks and other bullies. In 1921 it was powerful Texas' Baylor University inviting the Eagles to come down to Texas and help dedicate its new stadium in Dallas—the Cotton Bowl. The Eagles obliged, travelling 2,400 miles to play Boston College's first intersectional football game and beat the Baylor Bears 23–7 behind the quarterbacking of Steve Patten and the running of Walter Matthews.

By 1921 it was obvious that Boston College's success rested with Cavanaugh and his ability to replace one great player with another. After Fitzpatrick's graduation, Chuck Darling, a man who could play quarterback, halfback, and fullback, emerged to lead Boston College to a three-year 19–6–2 record. Like Fitzpatrick, Darling punted for a sixty-five-yard average, was the best runner on the team, and in 1923, was All-America as a quarterback and fullback. It did not hurt Dar-

15

Eagles of 1921 left South Station for a 2,400–mile train trip to Dallas and a landmark game against Baylor University.

ling's standing in the eyes of the Jesuits that he was equally strong in the classroom, with a four-year cumulative average of ninety-five.

It passed with little notice at the time, but, in 1922, Boston College acquired the services of 29-year-old trainer Frank Jones. While "Jonesy" would never receive the public acclaim accorded coaches and athletes, he would, over his 40-year career at Boston College, ending with his death in 1962, become a beloved father figure to thou-

sands of Boston College athletes. "It's like we lost one of the buildings here," said former athletic director John Curley when Jones died a few weeks before the athletic department was to honor him with "Frank Jones Day."

By 1923, the year Cavanaugh took Boston College to wins over powerful Georgetown, Fordham, and Villanova, the team had attracted such a following that a record 47,000 were at Braves Field to watch the Eagles beat Holy Cross

16–7 to put the glittering cap on a 7–1–1 season. There followed two winning years (6–3–0 in 1924; 6–2–0 in 1925) before the Iron Major closed his Boston College coaching career with an undefeated 6–0–2 season in 1926.

By this time Boston College faced the dilemma of being too strong for the smaller colleges, but because of its relatively late rise to prominence, it still had difficulty finding vacancies on the long-established schedules of such traditional powers as Harvard, Yale, and Army. This difficulty, plus a new Boston College administrative policy of offering only one-year contracts (in 1926 Cavanaugh was in the final year of a five-year contract) helped induce the coach to accept Fordham's offer of a $15,000 three-year contract. Cavanaugh took the money and the security, but his legacy to Boston College lived on in the twenty former high school football captains he attracted to the Heights as incoming freshmen before he left.

An NCAA rule kept freshmen ineligible for varsity play, leaving 1927 coach D. Leo Daley—1913 Boston College captain who had agreed to coach the team while on a one-year leave from a teaching job at Boston English High—to struggle to a 4–4 season. The Boston College freshmen, meanwhile, went undefeated. It was twenty-three-year-old Joe McKenney, 1926 Ea-

gle captain and 1927 assistant coach, who would inherit the Cavanaugh legacy and parlay it into a seven-year reign during which Boston College never had a losing season. McKenney's tenure is a long and important arc of the historical curve linking two great Boston College coaching geniuses, the revered Frank Cavanaugh and the legendary Frank Leahy.

McKenney's first Cavanaugh-recruited team proved that the Iron Major knew he could play the football futures market. The 1928 team went undefeated, untied (9–0–0), and won a second Eastern College Football title. Al Weston, a quarterback who called signals from the halfback slot and a star on the last Cavanaugh team, emerged as the best running quarterback of his day. Weston, with halfback Patrick Creedon and All-American end Charley Murphy, led an offense that outscored its opposition 263–39.

In the team's biggest upset win since the 1919 Yale game, a 6–0 blanking of Navy, Weston ran thirty yards for a touchdown, and Creedon at one point made eleven consecutive tackles. In those days a team that could play with a service academy could play with anyone, and the win brought national recognition to Boston College as one of the strongest teams in the East. But the next logical steps—to a high-profile intersectional schedule, and the bowl invitations that could accompany it—were temporarily blocked by the exigencies of the Great Depression.

The economic collapse that began in 1929 had a predictably debilitating effect on a school like Boston College. A tuition-supported, unendowed institution that drew the bulk of its students from working class families was in no shape to withstand economic hard times. There was no money available to underwrite the cost of a major intersectional football schedule or to offer the financial guarantees that would have brought the big west coast or mid-west teams to Boston. Consequently, McKenney's teams rode out the Depression retaining the advances of previous years (winning teams playing a good regional schedule before respectable, if dwindling, crowds) but assaulting no higher plateaus.

Stars of the Depression years were punter and All-America end Johnny Dixon, captain of the

BC's glamour star of the Roaring Twenties was Chuck Darling, a three-way pass-run-block threat who was also an academic standout.

Dour Gil Dobie, already a coaching legend at North Dakota, Washington, and Cornell, set the stage at BC for the spectacular teams of the early 1940s.

5–5–0 1930 team and All-America center Harry Downes of the 6–4–0 1931 team. In 1933, McKenney produced his own great Boston College team, a club that went 8–1–0, losing only to the Fordham team built by Frank Cavanaugh, who had died the previous season.

After a 5–4 season in 1934, the thirty-year-old McKenney retired from coaching to accept the position of associate director of physical education for the Boston School Department. His replacement was another Boston College alumnus, John R. "Dinny" McNamara, who was forced by illness to resign after four games; though not before his team beat Rose Bowl-contending Michigan State 18–6. The remainder of the 1935 season was guided by twenty-five-year-old ex-player Harry Downes, the last in this series of graduate coaches.

Meanwhile, opinion at the Heights was divided between those administrators and alumni who favored continuation of the use of graduate coaches and the playing of a good if not glittering schedule, and another group that wanted to see Boston College raise its national profile by hiring the best (one might say "most famous") available coach and arranging the strongest possible schedule. The latter philosophy was triumphant, and its leading proponent, Boston College athletic director Jack Curley, set about trying to make Boston College a truly national power. The result was a five-year golden era that began with the arrival of the dour-faced Scotch Presbyterian Gil Dobie in 1936 and ended with the controversial departure of the Rockne-like Irish Cath-

olic Frank Leahy; in between were two bowl appearances and a national championship.

At the time Curley hired Dobie the latter had acquired a national reputation as lustrous as that of any active coach in the country. An All-American at Minnesota in 1901, Dobie went on to coach the North Dakota Aggies to undefeated seasons in 1905 and 1906, to take the University of Washington to an incredible 58–0–3 nine-year stretch, to coach three winning teams at Navy, and become an Ivy League legend at Cornell by producing three unbeaten teams in sixteen seasons. "We have tried to secure the best man for the position and we are confident that Mr. Dobie is the man," said Jack Curley. No one disagreed.

The fifty-seven-year-old Protestant Gilmour Dobie must have been a curiosity in the Jesuit community, as he absentmindedly called priests "parson" and referred to the Mass as "services." By no accounts was he a barrel of laughs. One of Dobie's players, Dave Lucey, recalls that "when Dobie got mad he used to ask us if we were getting any scholarship aid. 'Yes Sir,' we'd say. 'Well in your case those parsons up there are wasting their money,' he'd say, pointing to the Jesuit residence, St. Mary's Hall."

But Dobie got the job done, taking Boston College to 6–1–2 seasons in 1936 and 1938, and to a relatively subpar 4–4–1 in 1937. More to the point, Dobie fulfilled alumni dreams with reputation-enhancing wins over big-name intersectional opponents such as Kansas State, Kentucky, Indiana, Florida, Western Maryland, and Detroit, as well as a 13–13 standoff with revenge-minded Michigan State.

Off the field, the shrewd Scotsman's dabblings in the stock market had made him a millionaire long before he came to Boston College. Because he was financially secure, his interest in coaching was non-mercenary and, therefore, all the more intense. In 1938, for example, Dobie held practice while the infamous hurricane of that year tore through eastern Massachusetts.

Dobie refused to recruit or play "tramp" athletes—men, some in their mid-twenties, who would drift from college to college, playing wherever the under-the-table money flowed fastest.

Like Frank Cavanaugh before him, Dobie con-

18

fined his recruiting to regional high school youngsters, most from the Boston area. When he retired after the 1938 season, he left behind a team that in two years would be the equal of any in the country and number more immortals than any other team in the history of New England college football. Among the Dobie-recruited stars were Charley O'Rourke, Chet Gladchuck, Henry Toczylowski, Gene Goodreault, and John Yauckoes.

On February 6, 1939, while his wife completed a novena and he babysat for their two children, Frank Leahy, then a thirty-year-old Fordham line coach who had just about given up hope of ever being a head coach, got a phone call from Boston College athletic director Jack Curley.

"Frank, I won't string you out. Would you be interested in coaching Boston College?"

"As line coach?" asked Leahy.

"Oh, no, Boston College wants you to be our head coach."

That night, reports sportswriter Wells Twombly in Leahy's biography, *Shake Down The Thunder,* Leahy took a hammer to the hollow bell that served as Frank Junior's piggy bank, and scraped together the train fare to Boston. Next day the Irish Catholic native of Winner, North Dakota, met with Curley, Boston College President Fr. William J. McGarry, S.J., and faculty athletic representative Father Patrick Collins. In his direct but curious way of talking (Leahy was given to imitating his college coach, Rockne, by punctuating his sentences with long, reflective "ooohs" and "aaahs"), the would-be coach laid it on the line. "Gentlemen, Holy Fathers, I am very interested in becoming a head football coach. I believe that I can bring something important to Boston College and to the young men that you bring to your school. I am the very best football coach you could hire. I promise you that. Oooh, but I have other matters in the back of my mind."

Leahy wanted to hire his own assistants, wanted assurances of alumni cooperation in recruiting, and wanted to know what kind of players Gil Dobie left behind.

He was pleased with the answers.

"I think we have our man," said Curley.

There were nine hundred Boston College football fans at South Station to greet Leahy when he arrived in mid-February for his first press conference. Leahy's Irish charm instantly melted the hearts and warmed the typewriters of Boston's normally cynical sporting press. "This man isn't coming here to lose," raved *Boston Post* columnist Bill Cunningham. "They say that Leahy is a little arrogant. That remains to be told. If he is, that's exactly what Boston College needs to win games. It's always better to have

Frank Leahy took BC fans to the heights of football ecstasy—a major bowl victory, national championship—and then left them for Notre Dame.

a man who has too much confidence than a man who stumbles around looking for it."

Later, on his first day on campus, just before start of spring practice, Leahy asked to address the Boston College student body. With his assistant coaches arrayed behind him and the football team sitting reverently in front, Coach Leahy set the tone of his uncompromising reign:

> "This is not going to be one of those stale pep talks, lads. There is genuine apathy toward not only the football team but Boston College as a whole. That will end. My assistant coaches are passing out instructions to the members of the football team. Copies will be distributed to non-football playing students on the way out. Football is going to be fun at Boston College. It will also be hard work. It will be a source of inspiration to the *entire* group of students."

He listed his rules for the players: "First, don't report late for practice. Second, there will be no insubordination. No dirty play will be tolerated. Slugging is absolutely cowardly. There will be no loafing. Aaaah, am I going too fast? And, oh yes, non-football playing students are expected to attend practices whenever possible."

There was no escape from the Leahy football crusade (though the coach did use a lighter touch when addressing a gathering of alumni, greeting them as "my fellow coaches").

In his first talk with alumni, Leahy went on to cleverly wrap himself in the revered shroud of the legendary Knute Rockne: "Boston College has a tradition of great coaches," he said. "I have come here to succeed and to win football games. My only regret is that my old coach from Notre Dame is not here to see one of his tackles step into such an important job. Somehow, I feel that he is with me in spirit. I can almost feel his hand touching my shoulder."

Boston bought the act. "Knute Rockne lives again in Frank Leahy," raved the *Boston Globe*.

Leahy's teams were as good as his words.

On the morning of September 30, 1939, Leahy awoke, vomited from anxiety, rode to Chestnut Hill with sports publicity director Billy Sullivan (later founder and owner of the professional Patriots), and directed his team to a 45–0 romp over Lebanon Valley State. The man who was becoming known as "Chuckin' Charley" O'Rourke passed for 462 yards, and a black running back—the first Leahy had ever coached and the first at Boston College, Lou Montgomery—ran forty-five yards for a touchdown.

Even a 7–0 home loss to Florida in the third game of the season (for which Leahy blamed himself for not preparing his team to face a five-man defensive line) did nothing to dampen the rampant optimism for the future of Leahy's Notre Dame-style single-wing team. "Just because Boston College lost a 7–0 verdict, don't quit on the Eagles," wrote Bill Grimes in the *Boston Evening American*.

After the Eagles rolled over Temple, St. Anselm's, Auburn, and Detroit, Boston sportswriter Col. Dave Egan wrote:

> Boston College football has always been important, but it has never had that fanaticism usually associated with Notre Dame. You will note that the good Colonel is getting behind Boston College football early this year. The suspicion here is that Frank Leahy is going places and Frank Leahy is on his way to becoming the greatest coach the game has known since Rockne died in a Kansas wheat field.

A bowl bid rested on the outcome of the 1939 Holy Cross game. By now, Frank Leahy had come to understand the New England psyche and to comprehend the true meaning of Boston College vs. Holy Cross. He told biographer Twombly:

> They were the two largest Catholic colleges in New England, an area founded by Protestants and still largely dominated by Protestants. There was Yale vs. Harvard in those days, but those Ivy League schools had a strong Protestant image, as well they might. But Boston College-Holy Cross was the Catholics' answer to the Ivy League and, ooooooh, it was not wise to lose this game.

Boston College won the game 14–0 in a raging snowstorm in front of 41,678 at Fenway Park.

On December 9, 1939, Boston College accepted an invitation for the eleventh-ranked Eagles to play the twelfth-ranked Clemson Tigers in the Cotton Bowl. Thus Boston College became the first New England team to appear in a bowl game since Harvard won the Rose Bowl in 1920.

By his own later admission, the young, intense, and overly eager Leahy might have blown the game. Instead of going to Dallas a week or two early, as is now standard practice for bowl teams, Leahy kept Boston College home where they practiced either outdoors in the cold and snow or inside in an armory where it was impossible to get good footing. "I made a stupid move," confessed Leahy. "Oooooh, I was young then and learning a great deal about my profession. We arrived on Wednesday, four days before the bowl. It was almost like spring in New England. I should have been there two weeks ahead."

A thousand alumni, students, and well-wishers boarded the ten-car train from South Station to Dallas. One man who should have boarded but did not, could not, was Lou Montgomery. This was 1940, and the south was rigidly segregated. When he was interviewed on the subject by the *Record's* Murray Kramer, Montgomery said, "Don't kid yourself. Boston College doesn't need a climax runner to win the football game. The Eagles can't miss with Toczylowski and O'Rourke. Sure, I hate not being there. But I know there isn't a man on the team that doesn't hate the fact that I can't be there."

Montgomery was wrong on one point: His open-field running *would* have helped the team. Boston College lost 6–3 and managed to score only once on a twenty-five-yard field goal by Lukachik. After the game, Boston College players wept openly in the locker room but, back in Boston, several thousand fans and a brass band would later greet the team upon its return to South Station. Among the first up on the train platform was the exiled Lou Montgomery.

"Lou, if they had let us bring you along we wouldn't have lost," said Leahy.

"I'm always going to believe that, coach," Montgomery said.

Leahy learned fast and adjusted accordingly. Football was still evolving from a game of push-and-shove to one of speed-and-motion. In his second season, Leahy accelerated and opened up the Boston College offense. He installed flankers

Halfback Lou Montgomery, first black gridder at BC, was compelled to remain behind in Boston after seeing his teammates off to the 1940 Cotton Bowl in segregated Dallas.

and men-in-motion; linemen drove off of an unset stance; and Boston College ran and passed out of a forerunner of the T-formation, with a tailback instead of a quarterback over the center. The season would prove that Leahy not only had the right idea, but that he had the right people to make it work.

O'Rourke returned at quarterback along with veteran backs Frank "Monk" Maznicki, Montgomery, and Toczylowski; they were joined by a big power-running newcomer, a blond, curly-haired Polish kid who would lunge and smash his way into New England football history, Mike Holovak. The backs who saw less action would have been starters on any other Boston College team: Harry Connolly, Adolph Kissell, Carl Lucas, Bob Jauron, Walter Beaudreau, and Ralph Nash. The line had 6′5″, 232-pound Chester Gladchuk at center, George Kerr and Joe Zabilski at guards; John Yauckoes and Joe Manzo at tackles; and as good a group of receivers as any Boston College team would ever have: Ed Zabilski, Al Lukachik, Henry Woronicz, Don Currivan, and Gene Goodreault, the latter a tackler of such reputation that *Life* and *Saturday Evening*

The offensive stars who took BC to football glory in the 1940 season included((first row, left to right) Gene Goodreault, John Yauckoes, George Kerr, Chester Gladchuck, Joe Zabilski, Joe Manzo, and Henry Woronicz; and (back row, left to right) Frank Maznicki, Henry Toczylowski, Mike Holovak, and Charlie O'Rourke.

Post tapped him as a pre-season All-American.

After crushing Center College 40–0 in the home opener, Boston College travelled to Louisiana, where they demolished Tulane 27–7. Wrote Fred Digby, *New Orleans Item* sports editor, "I've just seen this year's Sugar Bowl team and it has to be Boston College."

Leahy's team, in the time-honored you-have-to-roll-it-up-to-get-a-bowl-bid tradition, went on to beat the likes of Idaho (60–0) and Auburn (33–7) before eking out a 7–0 win over Holy Cross when substitute end Currivan, making his first start, stole the ball from a Crusader back on the Cross five; Kissell scored, Maznicki converted, and Leahy persuaded his team not to throw him in the shower because his suit was "the only one I own and it might be best not to shrink it before the Sugar Bowl game."

In fact, a few minutes after the Holy Cross game, Abe Goldberg of the Sugar Bowl Committee called Boston College's Jack Curley to ask if the Eagles would meet the Tennessee Volunteers in the 1941 Sugar Bowl. Curley said yes.

This time Leahy took his troops South two weeks early. A believer in the lean-and-hungry approach to big games, Leahy drove Boston College unsparingly with a result best interpreted later by Charley O'Rourke: "That particular young coach and that particular young football team were meant for each other. Gil Dobie had recruited an outstanding team, but he was at an age where he was past caring. Along came Leahy like a man trying to spread the gospel in a heathen land. He took us on a holy war of conquest. He was a real messiah figure as far as we were concerned."

Tennessee was a slight favorite, though sports editor Digby wrote, "Nobody has a passer like O'Rourke. The Eagles have the most incredible morale I have ever seen. And they are in such excellent shape, they will be strong when the fourth quarter comes."

Digby called it. With three minutes left in a 13–13 tie, O'Rourke, who had brought his team from its own twenty to the Tennessee twenty-four, ran twenty-four yards for the winning touchdown and staked Boston College's claim to the national title.

A crowd estimated at between 75,000 and 100,000 stood in the snow at South Station to greet the team on its return. (This time Lou Montgomery had made the bowl trip, albeit he was not permitted to play and had to watch the game from the press box.)

Later, 1,700 filled the Hotel Statler ballroom for a testimonial to the team that, even five decades later, still stands as having won the greatest sports victory in the college's history. Leahy was up to the occasion: "I told these lads at halftime that they were upholding the honor of dear old New England. I told them that they had a permanent friend in their head coach . . . . I would always be with them. I love Boston College and I will never leave it. That is my pledge and my promise." A month later he was gone to South Bend, Indiana, and the applause had turned to acrimony.

After the Sugar Bowl, Leahy had turned down several lucrative coaching offers from other colleges and pro-football teams. He had, in fact, signed a five-year agreement with Boston College, a contract that he later claimed had as its only escape avenue an "Alma Mater clause." Notre Dame was the only other football team in the world that Frank Leahy wanted to coach. If the torch of Rockne were passed, Leahy knew he could not have resisted grabbing it. It was and he didn't.

Boston College football had reached its high-water mark. With Leahy's departure the flood tide of success slowly, almost imperceptibly, began to recede.

Early Sugar Bowl action finds BC halfback Mickey Connolly (24), taking a handoff from O'Rourke (12) and outdistancing eight Tennessee pursuers for the Eagles' first touchdown. Running interference for Connolly is back Henry Toczylowski (22).

Leahy successor Denny Myers was a solid X's-and-O's strategist whose teams relied on the popular T-formation for their frequent successes.

1941 to 1959: The Denny Myers and Mike Holovak Years

After interviewing eighty candidates for Leahy's job, Curley and Boston College faculty moderator of athletics, Father Maurice Dullea, selected thirty-six year-old Brown University coach Denny Myers. He was a less emotional man than Leahy though a charming speaker and an expert in the then fashionable T-formation. Myers had established a reputation as a winner at West Virginia, Yale, and Brown.

Leahy didn't leave much for Myers. In fact, Leahy took with him to South Bend at least a dozen—some estimates go as high as twenty-seven—prep school stars who had been headed for Boston College, among them the soon-to-be Notre Dame great Angelo Bertelli. But with a fast and flexible offense and the power running of Holovak, Myers took Boston College to a respectable 7–3 season in 1941.

By the time the next season rolled around, the country was at war again, and 1942 would be the last "normal" football season before three war years; meanwhile, players were to leave for service duty and schedules were to once more feature such opponents as the Melville PT Boats. By season's end, Myers himself would be in uniform—but not before he came within one Holy Cross game of a possible national title. Despite having lost seventeen players to the service, Myers' team—led by the running of Holovak, line play of Fred Naumetz, and the receiving of Don Currivan—humbled West Virginia 33–0 in the season's opener and found itself ranked 11th in the nation. The Eagles climbed to sixth after subsequent wins over Clemson and North Carolina and were rated first in the nation by The Associated Press in mid-November. Another Sugar Bowl bid was all but in the maroon and gold bag when Holy Cross handed Boston College its worst beating in the history of their rivalry, 55–12. Holovak was the only Boston College player up to his standards in that game, grinding out 146 yards to finish the season with 965 yards and All-America honors from AP and UPI.

The intense disappointment of the defeat prompted many Boston College alumni and fans

24

to cancel a planned celebration at Boston's famed Coconut Grove nightclub on the Saturday night when fire destroyed the nightclub and killed 490 people in one of the worst tragedies in Boston's history.

Instead of going to the Sugar Bowl, Boston College accepted a bid to the then slightly less prestigious Orange Bowl, where they lost to Alabama 37–21 despite another Holovak show. With Boston College fans chanting, "Give it to Mike. Give it to Mike," the big fullback ran for all three Boston College touchdowns, two on runs of sixty-five and thirty-four yards, and played the entire game on defense.

A month after the Orange Bowl, Coach Myers enlisted in the Navy and left the job of coaching the war-year teams to his assistant, Amerino "Moody" Sarno, a native of Everett, Massachusetts, and a former All-East tackle at Fordham. In his three years, Sarno was 11–7–1 against an abbreviated schedule composed largely of military training base teams and college teams dominated by servicemen.

The exigencies of war-time schedule-making put Harvard back on the Boston College schedule in 1943 for the first time since 1919. "In these years," recalls Father Maurice Dullea, "Harvard was not interested in playing Boston College, partly because they had a lot to lose but also because they felt—and a lot of Boston College officials agreed—that the game could take on overtones of a religious war with Catholics on one side and Protestants on the other. I think we were both afraid of starting a riot."

The war hit Boston College particularly hard. Enrollment dropped from a pre-war high of 1600 to a low of 250; but, of those 250 men, ninety came out for football.

America's involvement in the Second World War brought an end to a turbulent era in American college football, an era in which the foundations of collegiate football had been shaken to its waspish roots. Boston College players and coaches did more than a fair share of the shaking. The Boston College record from the last Dobie year (1938) to the second Myers year (1942) was 41–7–2, second only to Tennessee and ahead of Notre Dame. Yet, in this same era, the one-time Big Three lords of the gridiron—Harvard, Yale, and Princeton—did not break into the nation's top fifty. The old order had changed. Indeed, it had been turned upside down.

With the Allies victorious over Germany and Japan, in 1946 the nation's campuses returned to normal. Denny Myers returned to the head coaching job, Moody Sarno returned to coaching the line, and the popular Mike Holovak returned to his Alma Mater as freshman coach.

Meanwhile, Jack Curley had put together the toughest schedule in Boston College football history. The 1946 Eagles beat Michigan State, Georgetown, and Rose Bowl champ Alabama, and they lost only to Tennessee, Wake Forest, and Holy Cross in a 6–3–0 season. Among Myers' players was one Edward J. King, later to become governor of Massachusetts but in these days just another grappling, dirty-shirted tackle, and one of many Boston College players who would later take part in the post-war pro-football boom. Between 1946 and 1948, Myers coached several future professionals, among them: King; Art Donovan, Art Spinney, Ernie Stautner, John Kissell, Butch Songin, and Mario Gianelli.

Myers' first postwar team drew a total home-game attendance of 211,000, confirming Curley's belief in the financial worth of a big-name schedule. In 1947 the throngs kept coming to Alumni Stadium and Fenway Park, their collective imagination fired by 5'8", 160-pound halfback Joe Diminick. His open-field running awakened echoes of the Holovak years, as crowds shouted: "Go, go, give it to Joe."

Diminick's speed was one of the factors prompting Myers to install the more flexible winged-T attack in 1948, a season that also saw Ed "Butch" Songin of Walpole establish himself as one of the nation's top passers. After Myers converted him from fullback, Songin was the top-rated passer in the East and fifth in the nation with 1,172 yards for thirteen touchdowns—including five to another local, Medford's Al Cannava. Boston College finished the 1948 season a respectable 5–2–2 and a box office success with record home attendance of 192,000. But the tide was about to go out and to take Denny Myers with it.

Thirty-odd years later, 1947 BC lineman Edward J. King (flanked by teammates Angelo Nicketakis, 54, Jim Benedetto, 21, and Mario Giannelli, 66) would score an upset win in another popular Massachusetts sport.

The 1949 team opened a dismal season with a 46–0 humiliation at the hands of Bud Wilkinson's Oklahoma Sooners, after which Boston College struggled to a 3–4–1 record. The season was but partially redeemed by a face-saving we-learned-it-from-Bud 76–0 rout of Holy Cross, in which fullback/kicker Ed Petela scored a Boston College record thirty-four points on four touchdowns, one field goal, and ten conversions.

The bottom fell out in 1950. After a deceptively encouraging opening day tie against Wake Forest, Boston College lost nine straight while its average home-game attendance dropped from 19,000 to 12,000. Myers decided it was time to leave—a feeling shared by Boston College alumni and fans—and accepted a job in private industry. The Boston College administration then took the advice that fans had been shouting since it was third and goal in the 1943 Orange Bowl: they gave it to Mike.

Holovak, the Boston College legend out of Lansford, Pennsylvania, had knocked around a bit since scoring those three touchdowns in the Orange Bowl. Fifteen months of his three-and-a-half-year Navy hitch were spent in the Pacific Theater, while his last four months saw him as head coach of the Melville PT Boats training base team. He then played a season for the Los Angeles Rams and two for George Halas' Chicago Bears, before returning to Boston College in 1949 as freshman team coach. While Denny Myers caught the heat for the varsity's shortcomings, Holovak was lauded for leading the freshmen to two undefeated seasons. After the 1950 disaster, Holovak was a logical choice to be handed the shattered fragments of his college's once great football program.

Holovak was a quiet, intelligent man inclined to take the burdens of coaching onto his own shoulders rather than delegate a lot of authority

College hall-of-famer Mike Holovak (here with assistant Bob Richards, on the headphones) was in the midst of an eclectic career when he took over as BC head coach in 1951, having served in the wartime Navy and played pro football; later he would coach and scout for the Patriots.

to his assistants. He began his rebuilding around quarterback Jimmy Kane of Weymouth who, by the time he was a sophomore, was being touted as the best Boston College passer since O'Rourke. Freshmen were once again eligible for varsity play in 1951, and Holovak knew he had a couple of good ones in Kane and another local, Tommy Joe Sullivan of South Boston. In the last minute of the last game of Holovak's first year as head coach, Kane hit Sullivan with a game-saving pass to give Boston College a 19–14 win over Holy Cross. Tommy Joe would leave school for the Navy, not to return for four seasons; but Kane's performance and Boston College's wins in three

of its final four games salvaged an otherwise poor (3–6–0) season, an indicator of the Holovak football renaissance.

The turn-around was slow but satisfactory, as the Eagles went 4–4–1 in 1952 to 5–3–1 the next year and set the stage for an 8–1 1954 season in which the team would come to within a minute-and-a-half of a bowl bid. Kane was playing his final year in 1954 and he, with running backs Dick Gagliardi and Edward DeSilva and All-East tackle Frank Morze, began the season by leading Boston College to consecutive wins over Detroit, Temple, VMI, Fordham, and Springfield. But dreams of an undefeated season were then shat-

Weymouth's Jimmy Kane (number 20, here throwing against Boston University) was one in a succession of outstanding local BC quarterbacks that included Charlie O'Rourke (Malden), Jack Concannon (Dorchester), and Doug Flutie (Natick).

tered when Xavier pulled out a 19–14 upset in the final minutes.

By the mid-fifties the small seating capacity of Alumni Field and the general reluctance of major inter-sectional opponents to travel to New England for less than the substantial financial guarantees they could get in the football-mad South and Midwest, conspired to force Boston College into an eastern-oriented schedule made up of lesser football powers. In 1954, Boston University was back on the Boston College schedule for the first time since 1942 and Brandeis was added in 1955. Boston College teams won, but 44–0 over hapless VMI in 1954, and 27–0 over Brandeis in 1955 was a far cry from the games against Tennessee, Auburn, Tulane, and Clemson that dotted the Boston College schedule during the bowl era. The old glories were already fading when, in 1956, the college took a near-fatal blow to the heart of its football program.

Fenway Park had always been vital to Boston College football. It could, with added bleachers, accommodate crowds in excess of 40,000, giving Boston College the capacity it needed to make good its guarantees to visitors and make a profit for itself in the bargain. But before the 1956 season began, Red Sox owner Tom Yawkey decreed that there would be no more football tearing up the prized verdure that was his Fenway Park turf. Boston College's 7–0 loss to Holy Cross, December 1, 1956, would be its last game at Fenway.

"We could drop football," suggested college President Father Joseph R. N. Maxwell to Bill Flynn, who was by then college alumni secretary as well as football line coach.

"Or we could build a stadium," said Flynn.

Rumors persisted that Boston College would abandon intercollegiate football and the *Record American*, acting on what it supposed was inside information, went so far as to have a headline set—"Boston College Drops Football"—when, on January 23, 1957, Maxwell, responding largely to alumni wishes, announced a $250,000 Alumni Stadium Fund drive to be organized by alumni secretary, varsity line coach, and soon-to-be-athletic director Flynn and chaired by 1926 captain

and former coach Joe McKenney. Maxwell made a point of expanding the drive to include "subway alumni" as well as graduates.

Alumni response was so prompt and generous that within two months of announcing the drive Maxwell, acting on Flynn's advice, had expanded the goals to include a hockey rink and new gymnasium. "Athletics is most essential for every graduate and undergraduate and plays a vital role in community life. We intend an aggressive and wholesome program," he said, sounding like a man who never seriously entertained other thoughts.

By June, alumni had raised $370,000. It is interesting to note that by this time the one-time "mudsill" of society—Irish-Catholic Americans—was statistically on its way to becoming what in the 1970s would be the most financially successful gentile ethnic group in America. It is reasonable to surmise that, as the pledges rolled in, some people were paying their dues.

"We couldn't expand the existing field because future buildings were planned for that part of the campus," recalls Flynn, "so we went down to the lower campus next to the reservoir. We picked out a rectangular section of a parking lot and all we did was dig out the asphalt, put in loam and move our old stands down around the new field."

It was nothing fancy, but the addition of new bleachers increased seating capacity to 23,000 and the payout was immediate. Navy announced it would meet Boston College in the 1957 dedication game. Florida State was also added to the 1957 schedule. Pittsburgh, Army, Syracuse, Clemson, and Miami were signed up for future years. And Maxwell was saying, "We are on the threshold of a new era for Boston College athletics."

A standing-room crowd of 30,000 filled the new stadium for the September 21 opener against Navy, only to see the midshipmen romp 46–6. But Boston College would win three of its five remaining home games and finish a respectable 5–4–0 in a season that saw the emergence of three local stars: quarterback Don Allard of Somerville, halfback Jim Colclough of Quincy, and center Cliff Poirier of Waltham.

These three, plus running back Al Miller and 1957 sophomore starter Larry Eisenhower, took the 1958 Eagles to a first-in-New England ranking and a 7–3–0 record. The only problem—and it would remain a problem for several years, probably costing Mike Holovak his job—was that the three losses were to three of the biggest "name" teams on the schedule: Syracuse, Clemson, and Villanova.

Holovak was up against it in 1959. Several members of the outstanding 1958 freshmen team were rendered ineligible by reason of scholastic failure; Allard, Colclough, and Miller had graduated, and the team had to open the season with games against Navy and Army.

Alumni and administration grumblings grew louder after the service academies beat Boston College badly, Navy winning 24–8 with two touchdowns by Winchester's Joe Bellino and Army laying it on 44–8. A late season loss to Boston University did nothing to help Holovak's cause nor, surprisingly, did the fact that the Eagles were 5–4 winners on the season thanks largely to the .534, 1,200-yard passing of junior quarterback John Amabile. Still, there was a yearning on the part of some for a recapturing of the glory years of Frank Leahy.

Though he had won at South Bend, the controversial and increasingly outspoken Leahy had fallen into disfavor with the Notre Dame administration (in part because his teams were sometimes publicly accused of illegally working the clock by faking injuries) and the great coach had been forced to resign in 1954. In a standoff in which personal and institutional pride played a part, Leahy never directly approached Boston College for a job, though, according to several college sources, Leahy had dropped hints that he would come back if asked and had, in the words of one Boston College official, "come close to apologizing to us for leaving in 1941."

Yet Boston College never directly approached Leahy nor did Leahy ask for his old job. Nevertheless, there was a change of coaches.

Athletic Director Flynn, once a line coach under Holovak, had the disagreeable job of firing his old boss. "I didn't think we should fire him," said Flynn of Holovak's final season. "I thought

he had been a winner and he deserved another year. But the administration wanted a change."

By Christmas, Ernie Hefferle, offensive line coach of the NFL's Washington Redskins and, before that, an assistant for eight years at Pitt, was the Boston College coach. Hefferle turned out to be an assistant as much by nature as by employment record.

Once again Boston College opened the season with losses to Navy and Army (in the 22–7 Navy loss, soon-to-be Heisman Trophy winner Bellino figured in twenty of his team's points), then stumbled winless through its first six games (0–5–1) and closed out a 3–6–1 season with a loss to Holy Cross. By now the pro-Holovak fans were howling with vindicated wrath and Hefferle was thinking about how happy he had been as an assistant coach. After another losing season (4–6–0) in 1961, Hefferle gladly gave up his brief tenure to return to an assistant's job at Pitt, and Boston College turned to Jim Miller, a tough midwesterner from Massilon, Ohio (a town which bills itself as "Touchdown City USA"), who had been a winner for three seasons as coach at the University of Detroit.

Miller gave Boston College fans what they wanted, a wide-open, pro-type offense at a time when professional football was establishing itself as America's *de facto* national pastime.

Two years before Miller's arrival, the upstart American Football League had been founded (in part through the efforts of Frank Leahy) and former Boston College sports-publicity director under Leahy, William Sullivan '38, had bought a New England franchise, the Boston Patriots. The Patriots signed Larry Eisenhauer following the 1960 college season, beginning a trend that in the early years of their financially precarious existence saw the Patriots become a virtual postgraduate school for Boston College's better football players, among them Art Graham, Jim Colclough, Jim Whalen, Ross O'Hanley, Butch Songin, and Harry Crump (see box).

Unlike the self-reliant Mike Holovak—who by 1962 was head coach of the Patriots—Miller was one of the new breed of organization men unhesitatingly parceling out responsibility to a staff of gifted assistants that included Boston College alumni John McCauley '53 and Cliff Poirier '59. Miller was also a little bit lucky, arriving the same year that quarterback Jack Concannon of Dorchester began to pass himself into Heisman Trophy contention. The triumverate of running back Harry Crump of Westboro, receiver Art Graham of Somerville, and Concannon gave the Eagles an outstanding passer-runner-receiver combination.

On the first play of Boston College's first game under Miller, the 6'3", 200-pound Concannon ran fifty-eight yards on a keeper for a touchdown in a 27–0 romp over Detroit. The following week he threw a first-play seventy-eight-yard scoring bomb to Graham in a 28–13 win over Villanova. In a season in which he would rank eleventh in the nation in passing, with 97 completions for 1,456 yards, Concannon had only one bad day: one completion vs. Navy and Roger Staubach, the man who would beat out Concannon in the following year's Heisman voting.

The *Globe's* Jerry Nason claimed that the 8–2 Eagles team was playing "bowl quality ball." The promoters of New York's Gotham Bowl apparently agreed and issued an invitation, but Boston College administration officials, over the outraged protests of the student body, rejected the offer to play in what they perceived to be a bowl of the second rank.

Jack Concannon was 1963. It didn't matter that Graham had graduated to the Patriots; Concannon simply redirected his attack, throwing twenty-six of eighty-five completions to Jim Whalen as Boston College rolled to a 6–3–0 year. Yet along with the Concannon glitter—All-America, All-East, Heisman candidate, NCAA press guide cover boy, draft choice of the Philadelphia Eagles—came three losses to important opponents: Syracuse, Air Force, and Holy Cross. But 1963 was only the beginning, as Miller's teams never again recaptured the success of the 1962 season. 1964 and 1965 brought teams that some thought had good talent but a better schedule, and they gradually fell to 6–3–0 and 6–4–0 records before turning in consecutive 4–6–0 seasons in 1966 and 1967.

Athletic Director Flynn stood behind the need for an uncompromising schedule. "Boston is a sophisticated and highly competitive sports market; people will only pay to see the best," maintained the architect of a schedule that saw Boston College playing Penn State, Tennessee, Syracuse, and the three major service academies. "We've surveyed our fans and we find these are some of the teams they want to see Boston College play. We feel we can win more than we lose against 70 or 80 percent of the teams on our schedule. As for the others, well, you can't beat the country's top teams if you don't play them."

Maybe it was a case of "on any given Saturday" or maybe the Eagles proved they really could handle Flynn's iron when the 1964 team turned in one of the biggest and most crowd-pleasing home upsets in its history. Disdaining what would have been a tie game "moral victory" over the nationally ranked Syracuse Orangemen, Boston College quarterback Larry Marzetti threw a last-minute "Hail Mary" pass to Bill Cronin on the fifteen. Cronin caught the prayer and drove into the end zone to give Boston College a 21–14 victory, its biggest triumph since the 1941 Sugar Bowl.

The football program picked up one of its best off-field victories the same year when Miller out-recruited 204 other football-playing colleges to sign high school All-America running back Brendan McCarthy of Washington, D.C. (It no doubt helped that McCarthy's father, Bill, played football at Boston College in the 1930s.) The power-running fullback so much reminded Eagle fans of Mike Holovak that "Give it to Brendan" became the soundtrack of Boston College home games from 1965 to 1967, as McCarthy ran for a career total of 2,060 yards, and first place among all Boston College backs, forty-nine yards ahead of Holovak.

While the country slipped deeper into the morass of Vietnam and American college students took to the streets in protest, football—a game built on power, "the bomb," "the blitz," and territorial control—inevitably came to be viewed as the ultimate athletic metaphor for war. It is not surprising that the changing times and declining won-lost records conspired to drastically reduce Boston College football attendance, culling out disillusioned students on the one side

Quarterback Jack Concannon was a Heisman Trophy runner up and top-round pro draft choice.

Against highly-ranked Syracuse in 1964, end Bill Cronin caught a last-minute desperation pass to win an upset victory, 21–14, and a kiss from coach Jim Miller.

Fullback Brendan McCarthy was a much-coveted Washington, D.C., schoolboy stand-out who opted for BC and the chance to eclipse Mike Holovak as the Eagles' top career rusher.

and disappointed alumni on the other. Between 1964 and 1967, home attendance dropped from an average of 23,900 per game to an average 12,771, the second lowest average since records began being kept in the 1940s and only a few more than the team averaged in the winless 1950 season. Something had to change and, as usual, it was the coach.

"He could have stayed," Flynn says of Miller. "But he didn't want a one-year contract, and under the circumstances, that's all we were going to offer him." Under the circumstances, Miller decided to give up coaching and accept an executive position with George Steinbrenner's American Shipbuilding Company.

Early in 1967 Boston College hired a proven program rebuilder, a management-by-objective type of coach, who referred to his players as "personnel" and to his defensive alignments as "looks." Joe Yukica was nothing if not methodical.

The Modern Era: 1968 to 1982

Joe Yukica was an end at Penn State (1950–1952) under Rip Engle before joining Engle's staff in the instructive, if obscure, job of assistant coach of the freshman team. In the mid-fifties, Yukica flew the safety of Alma Mater to make his reputation in the competitive Pennsylvania coal country high school leagues; later, as an assistant at Dartmouth in the early sixties, the thirty-year-old Yukica absorbed head coach Bob Blackman's "winning is a habit" attitude as the Big Green won three Ivy League titles and the 1965 Lambert Trophy (best in-the-East). Yukica proved he could practice what Blackman and Engle preached when, as head coach, he made a winner out of a University of New Hampshire team that used to whoop it up after a tie. On December 21, 1967, Boston College got itself a little bit of Engle, a little bit of Blackman, and a whole lot of Joseph Michael Yukica, picking the sidelines veteran as the college's twenty-seventh head football coach.

Spring drills were brutal. Pads every day and head knocking every minute. "We wanted to find out who could hit and who wanted to play football," explained Yukica.

While around him dawned the "Age of Aquarius"—peace, love, and do your own thing—Joe Yukica searched for and produced one of the most endangered species of the late sixties: self-disciplined young adults. "To me, character is self-discipline—pushing yourself when you're tired, not letting up when you know you don't have a chance, and respect for other people. That's the kind of boy I want for my football team."

Yukica disdained, or perhaps was incapable of, the inspirational rhetoric of Cavanaugh or the passion of Leahy. Instead he resorted to straightforward underscoring of the work ethic. Under his tutelage, Boston College football was to be ten games and fifty-two weeks of preparation.

The first dramatic public evidence of the worth of Yukica's methods came in what Nat Hasenfus called "the most tremendous victory in twenty-five years." He referred to 1968's 49–15 opening day rout of Navy. "I, who had missed but four Boston College home games since 1914," wrote the historian, "had never seen a more blistering attack than that which carried the ball from the Boston College twenty to the Navy end zone in ten plays, eight yards to the play without once resorting to the air. The victory did as much for Boston College fortunes as had (the wins) over Yale in 1919 or the Sugar Bowl game of 1941." Senior quarterback Joe Marzetti was the on-field hero, running for one touchdown and passing for three (two to Dave Bennett and one to Joe Catone). But it was Yukica that the Boston College players carried from the field.

Three consecutive but more or less predictable mid-season losses to Tulane, Penn State, and Army led to an eventual 6–3–0 record. Not the stuff of bowl bids, it was nonetheless Boston College's first winning season in three years. Also,

Coach Joe Yukica, plagued by quirky quarterbacks and midseason upsets, was under constant pressure despite nine winning seasons and a 68–33 record at BC.

in the otherwise forgettable 58–25 bombing by Army, Yukica found his quarterback for the next three seasons in sophomore Frank "Red" Harris of nearby Malden. With Marzetti injured, and the Eagles forced to play catch-up ball, Harris set two still-enduring single game team records—most passes attempted (fifty-seven) and most completions (thirty-seven).

Yukica's second edition finished a disappointing 5–4 in 1969, a season chiefly notable for an interruption in the Holy Cross series and for the rising star of junior running back Fred Willis of Natick.

An epidemic of hepatitis stopped the Holy Cross season, forcing the team to disband. Nothing stopped Willis. Or at least nothing stopped him until he gained an average 4.5 yards for each of his 128 carries. In 1969 and 1970, Willis ran ahead of Mike Holovak and Brendan McCarthy as Boston College's all-time rushing leader, accumulating a career total of 2,115 yards.

From the first game of his junior year, Willis showed he had the speed and power of which great tailbacks are made. He gained one hundred sixty-eight yards in an opening day win over Navy and the next week scored three touchdowns in a 28–24 victory over Tulane. But a recurring hip pointer and some mid-season inconsistency held him to six hundred ten yards for the season, a creditable total but not an indicator of the great things to come.

Yukica went into 1970 looking for the payout for his system. "We . . . tried to build team confidence by letting the kids know we believed in

what we were doing, that we were sure it would work. But players never really buy your program until you win on the field," said the coach.

In 1970 the Eagles won big, as big as any Boston College team since 1962, going 8–2 against a schedule that included the three major service academies and the Pennsylvania "iron," Pittsburgh and Penn State.

Willis scored two touchdowns and ran for more than one hundred yards in an opening day 28–21 win over Villanova, then repeated the feat the next week, adding a touchdown pass reception in a 28–14 win in a 97-degree steambath at Navy. Willis and Harris continued to roll the next week with Willis running for three touchdowns (eight in three games) and 147 yards, and Harris completing thirteen passes, six to another local player, Jim O'Shea of Lynn. The season's only losses came at the hands of an undefeated Air Force and a Penn State team led by future Pittsburgh Steelers Franco Harris and Jack Ham.

The losses were consecutive mid-season defeats, especially annoying because they reinforced a trend of Yukica's early years. His teams lost three in a row in the middle of his first season, four in a row the next year. Alumni Stadium boo birds were in fine voice for the fifth game of the season, raining their displeasure upon Yukica and quarterback Harris, the latter being one for six and two interceptions in the first half against Army and the former showing a disinclination to remove his quarterback from the field. The decision seemed stubborn and stupid. It also made the season.

33

The Boston College mascot, a golden eagle, was one of the last of the acquired trappings of American college sport. In 1920, a mild public embarassment along with a strong reaction by one Father Edward J. McLaughlin, 1914, changed an alleycat into an eagle.

After the Boston College track team won the 1920 Eastern Intercollegiates, a Boston newspaper cartoonist portrayed the team as a smug alleycat licking clean the dishes of the other teams. Father McLaughlin didn't go for that image. "This sort of thing is hardly elevating," he wrote to the student newspaper *The Heights*, "but, still, we must trust to the imagination of the artist unless we offer him the idea ourselves." Father McLaughlin went on to suggest that " . . . it is important that we adopt a mascot to preside at our pow-wows and triumphant feats. . . . And why not the eagle, symbol of majesty, power, and freedom? Its natural habitat is the high places. Surely, the Heights is made to order for such a selection."

Were that not argument enough, Father McLaughlin presented the socio-ethnic clincher: "Glad would a [Boston College fan] feel to see his mascot grasping the Yale pup . . . or soaring triumphantly over the Stadium walls, bearing John Harvard's toppiece to the trophy room at Chestnut Hill."

That did it. Boston College officially adopted the eagle as its mascot. Nation-wide publicity attending that announcement prompted one Captain Welch of Texas, a fishing boat skipper, to send Boston College what he took to be an eagle. The bird was actually a hawk that had landed, exhausted, on the boat's deck. No matter. Students kept the bird in a cage in the tower of the administration building. Prophetically, the bird broke free and flew away on October 26, 1923, the day before a 7–6 loss to Marquette.

The first real eagle, nicknamed Herpy, was captured on a New Mexico ranch and sent to the college by Reverend John A. Risacher, S.J., a former teacher at Boston College High, who was then working in El Paso, Texas. At Boston College, Herpy was placed in a large cage near the science building, an accomodation which so ill-pleased him that, in his efforts to bite through the cage, he injured his beak and had to be given to the Franklin Park Zoo where he spent the rest of his days. Father Risacher also sent the college a stuffed and mounted golden eagle, which resided in the athletic department offices for some forty years and which, until 1961, served as the official Boston College eagle.

In the spring of 1961, a committee of three students, unhappy that Boston College had been without a live mascot since the late twenties, launched "Project Mascot." John D. Provasoli of Natick, Robert Hart of Lowell, and James McLaughlin of Elsmere, New York, began efforts to secure a live golden eagle. Provasoli called his friend, former Natick resident Neils Colby of Longmont, Colorado—eagle country. Colby said he could get the "finest species of *Aquila chrysaetos* in the nation," but first, Boston College would need special federal and state permits and the bird must then have inoculations and special housing. The college was helped in this regard by Franklin Park Zoo superintendent Walter Stone, who agreed to have the zoo house and care for the bird.

Colby came through. In August 1961, a two-month- old, ten-pound golden eagle taken in the mountains above Longmont arrived at Chestnut Hill. There to greet the bewildered bird were Provasoli, Stone, and football coach Ernie Hefferle. In Septem-

For forty years, official BC mascot was a stuffed and mounted golden eagle (held here by, among others, 1920s football star Chuck Darling, second from left) which had been donated by an alumnus in Texas.

Star of BC games during the early 1960s was a live golden eagle named Margo (short for maroon and gold) who died in 1966 and was not replaced due to heightened public sensitivity toward the eagle as an endangered species.

ber, a student-run name-the-eagle contest produced the winning suggestion, "Margo," a name taken from the first letters of maroon and gold and one appropriate for a bird that was, in fact, a female.

For five seasons, Margo was brought to every home football game and even made the travelling team for trips to West Point, Holy Cross, and Syracuse. Margo was scheduled to accompany the team to Annapolis for a September 17, 1966, game against Navy, but in August, the bird was struck by a virus and died at Franklin Park.

More stringent government restrictions against the taking of eagles—by now an endangered species—made it impossible and undesirable for Boston College to obtain a new live mascot. Instead, the college soon joined what has since become a national sports trend toward the use of costumed human mascots cavorting along the sidelines and across the basketball courts, acting less as a symbol and more as a supplementary free-style cheerleader.

When Boston College's popular human eagle, Eddie "the Eagle" Rovegno—whose repertoire included exaggerated signs of the Cross and solemn genuflections to the hoop gods—graduated in 1982, students announced campus-wide auditions to find a suitable replacement. The winner, it was said, would not have to live in Franklin Park.

The live-eagle tradition was supplanted at BC by use of non-endangered humans, a succession of acrobatic students (most recently the talented Eddie Rovegno, '82) whose sideline antics combined comedy and cheerleading.

"I continued to believe in him," said Yukica, recalling halftime of the Army game with Boston College down 13–0. "At no time did any of us lose confidence in him and I think he knew it."

In the second half, Harris delivered on his coach's confidence. In one of the most versatile performances ever by a Boston College quarterback, Harris completed twelve of thirteen second-half passes, ran for a pair of touchdowns, threw a twenty-one-yard scoring pass to John Bonistalli, and engineered scoring drives of fifty-seven, sixty-four, and sixty yards. With Boston College hanging on 14–13 and worrying about Army's long-range field goal kicker Arden Jensen, Harris went sandlot to put away the game.

"I noticed whenever we ran Willis on a dive, Army zeroed in on him and completely ignored me," said Harris. "So I told the guys I was going to keep the ball this time and try to bootleg it." Harris ran ten yards for a touchdown that would have counted were the teams playing two-hand tag.

Harris and Willis sat out a 65–12 mercy killing of the last football team ever fielded by the University of Buffalo; but both returned for a 21–6 upset of Pittsburgh that saw Willis gain one hundred thirty-nine yards and score two touchdowns, one on a pass from Harris.

There followed a defeat of UMass 21–10, and a 54–0 publicity-making pounding of Holy Cross.

The Holy Cross game will be most remembered as the one in which Willis' ninety-six yards gave him a record 1,007 and made him the first Boston College runner to gain more than a thousand yards in a season. It also brought his career total to 2,107, breaking Brendan McCarthy's mark of 2,060. Willis' career record 180 points also broke the forty-three-year-old scoring record of 155 points held by Al Weston. Though his team could not wangle a bowl invitation, Willis got two, playing in the Blue-Gray game and Senior Bowl and winning the Bulger Lowe Award as New England's outstanding football player.

Amidst further trappings of "big time"—synthetic turf, enlarged press box, 6,000 additional seats—Yukica took his 1971 team to a height neither he nor they would regain. In the talent-

Fred Willis (here running through Navy in 1970) was the first Eagle back to break the 1,000–yard-per-season barrier, and his 2,115 career yards placed him ahead of Brendan McCarthy and Mike Holovak.

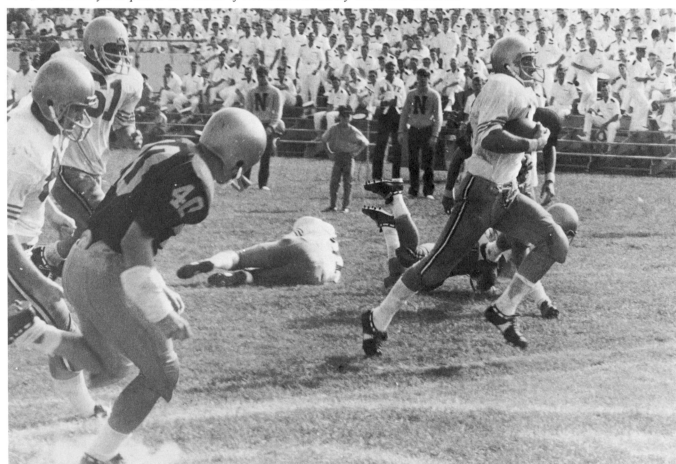

behind-talent tradition that separates a football *program* from a football *team,* Yukica fielded a backfield in which the flanker and two running backs would be drafted by NFL clubs: back Tom Bougus broke Willis' single-season rushing mark by carrying for 1,056 yards (215 of them in a 23–7 win over Villanova) and was drafted by Denver; back Bill Thomas was drafted by Dallas and flanker Eddie Rideout of Medford was signed by the Patriots. That backfield and a defense led by end Greg Broskie recorded a 9–2 record and the New England championship. Only losses to West Virginia and Texas Tech spoiled a season in which the Eagles crushed major eastern opponents, Pittsburgh (40–22) and Navy (49–6). Yukica was named "New England Coach of the Year" by UPI. The eagle was in her nest and all was well with the football world—until 1972.

"These past six weeks have been the worst of my life," junior quarterback Gary Marangi said after his intercepted passes were instrumental in consecutive losses to Navy, Air Force, and Pittsburgh. (The team had earlier lost to Tulane, and defeated Temple and Villanova.) As a sophomore, Marangi had played behind senior Ray Rippman but, in his few appearances, had performed well enough to attract favorable, pressure-producing pre-season raves. "What he knows now," wrote Peter Gammons of the *Globe* halfway through the season, "is that being Boston College quarterback means . . . every mistake [is] taken on Chestnut Hill far more seriously than the bombing of Washington and that you will be compared to Charley O'Rourke when you start to win."

Though in the midst of the first and only losing season of his Boston College coaching career (the Eagles would finish 4–7), Yukica stayed cool and stuck with Marangi, as he had earlier stuck with Red Harris. "Believe me," said the coach, "Gary Marangi is going to open a lot of eyes when this team turns."

Yukica was at least half right. The turnaround did come, but when it did, the credit went less to the quarterback and more to the greatest running back in the then eighty-year history of Boston College football.

Mike Esposito was a 5'11", 180–pound curly-haired, broad-faced, sleepy-eyed, speed-and-power runner who naturally drew the nickname, "Espo" after the fashion of Boston Bruins hockey star Phil Esposito, no relation. Esposito was another of the Boston College local kids, in this case from Wilmington High School, where he set a Massachusetts high school scoring record and otherwise comported himself like some prototypical All-American good kid. He starred in hockey and track, dated a cheerleader captain named Lee Ann (whom he later married), went to church on Sunday, and ignored scholarship offers from dozens of football-factory colleges to enroll at Boston College and remain near his widowed mother.

Mike Esposito seemed too good to be true. While Gary Marangi was taking the heat, Espo was taking the spotlight. In 1972 he gained 930 yards on 182 carries, both sophomore records, and led all Boston College scorers with nine touchdowns. At first, Espo had to share the spotlight and the ball-carrying duties with junior running back Phil Bennett, who, in one of 1972's few bright spots, set a team single-game rushing record of 253 yards in a 49–27 win over Temple. But 1973 would belong to Mike Esposito the way 1962 had belonged to Jack Concannon.

Beginning with a 159-yard, two-touchdown game in the 45–0 methodical destruction of Temple, Espo ran, crunched, caught, and occasionally blocked his way to All-East, All-New England, and the Bulger Lowe Trophy, marking the first time in three decades that that trophy had been awarded to a junior. He set two major single season team records, most carries (254) and most yards (1,293), and brought his career total to an all-time 2,223, breaking by seven yards the record it took Fred Willis *three* seasons to set.

Espo's running, Marangi's passing (mostly to Mel Briggs and sophomore starter Dave Zumbach), and the left foot of German-born soccer-style kicker Fred Steinfort (who would kick a team record fifty-five-yard field goal vs. Tulane) reversed Boston College's record from 4–7 to 7–4 but did not reverse some stereotypes. Losses to big-name foes Tulane, Miami (Florida), Syracuse, and Pittsburgh disappointed fans and

Mike Esposito was an all-American boy whose performance lived up to his image, eclipsing Fred Willis' career rushing record in just two seasons and leading BC to a number-three ranking in the East for 1974.

Quarterback Mike Kruczek set a national collegiate career-completion record—66.7 percent—but is also remembered for the passes he did not throw, in a controversial loss to Notre Dame in 1975.

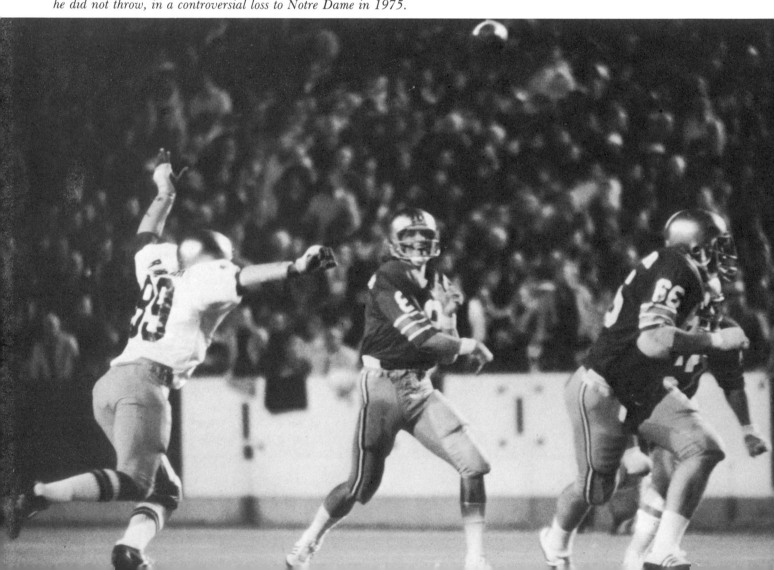

sportswriters who believed the team had the horses to do better. Even an early season victory over Texas Tech, Boston College's first win in the deep South since the 1941 Sugar Bowl, was taken in stride while a loss to a Pittsburgh team, led by future Heisman Trophy winner Tony Dorsett, drew the *Boston Herald* comment that "Boston College must have picked up a Patriot's game plan for yesterday's meeting with Pittsburgh. Behind a non-existent offense, the Eagles did their annual flopperoo in Alumni Stadium . . . ."

Minutes after the season ended with a 42–21 win over Holy Cross, Gary Marangi struck back, speaking what was on a lot of players' minds: "We played top teams and we won two games down South [Texas Tech and West Virginia] and then we get wrecked all the time in the papers, and so did the coach, and this is wrong . . . . I don't see any justification for [the criticism] we got back here in New England. We completely turned last year around; I think we proved that we should be respected."

Undaunted by the sometimes excessively high hopes harbored for its team, Boston College continued to seek top-quality, nationally-ranked opponents. The Texas Longhorns were booked for the 1974 opener and Notre Dame for the first game of 1975. A nationally televised first meeting between the two Jesuit powers. "Bill Flynn can sure foul up your off season," joked Yukica.

It took a large guarantee to get the twelfth-ranked Longhorns to Alumni Stadium, but Flynn's belief that Boston College fans would turn out in significant numbers for the name schools was borne out; a record sellout of 32,227 grossed the Boston College athletic department an estimated $250,000.

On a warm Saturday night, Texas coach Darrell Royal unveiled the most highly-recruited Texas schoolboy running back in a decade, freshman Earl Campbell, and watched his Southwest Conference champs run up a 31–3 halftime lead and a 42–19 final. The score belied the fact that Boston College rolled up 422 yards in total offense, only two fewer yards than Texas.

The Sunday morning headlines were predictable: "Longhorns Toy With Eagles" (*Herald),*

"Texas Stampedes Boston College" (*Globe),* and the next week the criticism moved up a notch. After Temple shocked the thirteen-point favorite Eagles, Joe Giulotti of the *Herald,* wrote facetiously: "There was a rumor that Temple athletic director Ernest C. Casale was trying to line up a football game with Texas."

Yukica silenced the critics—temporarily, at least—by sticking with his "personnel," and seeing his 0–2 team turn it around. Next game, Navy went down 37–0 on hits from all the Boston College guns—Barnette scoring three touchdowns, Esposito carrying for 151 yards, Steinfort booting a fifty-yard field goal, and quarterback Mike Kruczek hitting Mike Godbolt with a thirty-three-yard pass. The only loss the rest of the season was to Pittsburgh, with Boston College hammering people (70–8 over UMass, 38–0 over Holy Cross, 45–0 over Syracuse) to such an embarrassing extent that Yukica was accused of running it up. "Not so," he claimed. "Those other kids [substitutes] worked too, and when you get a lead you like to play them. And when you teach a team to win, you teach the whole squad, not just part of it. So what do you tell your reserves when you find a spot for them—that they shouldn't try to score? That they should just run plays that will use up the clock? I can't operate that way."

The 1974 team was voted first in New England and third in the East. Esposito moved his all-time rushing record to 2,844, 5.7 yards-per-carry, much of it behind the blocking of All-America tackles Al Krevis and Tom Marinelli. He would have broken the 3,000–yard mark except for an out-of-bounds tackle against West Virginia in which he suffered a separated shoulder and missed the final four-and-a-half games of the season. The loss of Esposito put the pressure on Keith Barnette, who responded by becoming the nation's highest scorer with twenty-two touchdowns.

Graduation and the NFL claimed Esposito (Atlanta), Krevis (Cincinnati), and Marinelli (Oakland), but Yukica had returning what was generally thought to be his best team ever. He would need it for what still must rate as the most important Boston College football game since the days of the James Street scrums—Notre Dame vs. Boston College: the Fighting Irish against the Boston Irish in 61,000-seat Schaeffer Stadium, on a Monday night before a national television audience.

The game went beyond being a mere rivalry between two Catholic colleges and football powers. There was, for instance, the long shadow of Frank Leahy hovering overhead, and the longer memories of Boston College alumni who recalled that the great coach had brought bowl-calibre football to the Heights before jilting the team for Notre Dame. "There are old men at Boston College," wrote Mike Lupica, a young Boston College alumnus, in a special to the *Washington Star*, "who have never gotten over that . . . Monday night is seen by Boston College true believers as the first step in changing all that, a chance, finally, to shake down the thunder which the Notre Dame people sing about in their fight song . . . There is a ton of drama and emotion wrapped up in this football game."

Kruczek was the man Boston College was counting on. In the previous season's last six games he completed an awesome 68.9 percent of his passes and was already being talked about as the best quarterback in Boston College history. A win over Notre Dame would end the argument. Kruczek would eclipse O'Rourke.

"As a football player," he said, "nothing that's ever happened to me compares to Monday night. Everyone dreams of going to a major school with major exposure and playing major competition. We have all of that on Monday night. This is the peak, the top."

It looked like the right year for the Eagles to play the Irish. The oddsmakers made Boston College only a seven-point underdog, and, for the first time ever, *Sports Illustrated* genuflected in the direction of New England by ranking Boston College twentieth in the pre-season poll. "When we walk onto that field," said Kruczek, "we're going to be dead even with them and they know it."

"I don't think anything parallels all the talk and interest we've had about this game," said Yukica. "Not only on the team and among our alumni and in the Boston area, but beyond the confines of New England in all the areas where we recruit. It transcends what you usually associate with college football."

It also transcended the seating capacity of cavernous Schaeffer Stadium. "If the Pope wanted to get in, I couldn't find him a seat," said Boston College publicist Reid Oslin. "Nothing has ever generated this type of excitement at Boston College before. We've sold 6,000 season tickets to our student body of 8,000 because of this game."

Notre Dame won. They won just as they have won since the 1920s. Somehow.

A Steinfort field goal had Boston College even, 3–3, at the half. The Eagles were controlling the line of scrimmage and, while Notre Dame had stopped Barnette (fifty yards on seventeen carries for the game), seldom-used junior running back Glen Capriola introduced himself to the nation by running for a team high—107 yards on fifteen carries.

The game began to unravel for Boston College late in the third quarter. With the Eagles in Irish territory and driving toward what would have been the biggest upset in New England football history, Notre Dame defensive end Ross Browner recovered a fumble and brother Jim Browner concluded the ensuing drive with a nine-yard touchdown run early in the fourth quarter for a 10–3 Irish lead. At precisely this point, Joe Yukica's fortunes at Boston College turned irreversibly downhill. There was feeling among some observers that Yukica should have had Kruczek throw more, that the team was trying to keep it close rather than going all-out for the win.

Yukica's game plan called for possession football. Kruczek's top receiver, Dave Zumbach, the man who would set a Boston College career receiving record of 1,521 yards, was injured. Capriola was running well. The Boston College offensive line was outplaying Notre Dame. On the other hand, Kruczek—regardless of who he was throwing to—was the best percentage passer in the country, and with his club trailing, it was reasonable to expect him to go to the air. He didn't.

Typical was the commentary of the *Providence Journal:* "Boston College *surprisingly* (italics added) didn't pass more. Kruczek threw only thirteen

Unheralded halfback Glen Capriola made his mark in the 1975 Notre Dame game and went on to be BC's leading rusher the following year.

passes, completing nine." One of those incompleted passes was picked off by Notre Dame defensive back Al Hunter, who ran it back for a touchdown, the crusher in the 17–3 final.

Even Kruczek was puzzled by the play selection, which, he emphasized, was not his. "Yukica called all the plays. I thought we should have passed more but you never second-guess the coach," said the quarterback. A crestfallen Yukica said after the game, "We did what we set out to do. We wanted to control the line of scrimmage for three periods, but we made two mistakes and they took the game from us. It's so hard to lose when you do what you set out to do."

Boston College lost only three games the rest of the way—West Virginia, Tulane, and Syracuse. On the face of it, and for any other college in New England, 1975 was a marvelous season. Kruczek, who would go on to serve as Terry Bradshaw's back-up with the Pittsburgh Steelers, erased Roger Staubach's career college passing completion record of 63.1 percent, ending his career with 225 completions on 337 attempts for an NCAA record 66.7 percent. He also won the Bulger Lowe Trophy. Zumbach, in addition to

his record career yardage, set a team all-time career reception record with 113. Yukica's team recorded its seventh winning season in the coach's eight years. He was now at 54–29, the coach with the best record in Boston College history, but the shadow of the Notre Dame game—why didn't he go for it?—would not go away.

The *Herald* observed when Yukica's contract was renewed, "Many who have played for Yukica have gone on to play in the professional ranks . . . . This is one of the reasons Yukica has come under some attack by the alumni who wonder how he can have this kind of talent and not win the big games."

Fair or not, the question haunted the coach and his team until September 11, 1976 when Yukica and Boston College won a very big game.

There was a note of cavalier braggadocio in the wording of an invitation to a private party held the night before the 1976 season opener with Texas. "We've been waiting for this for two years," read the invitation, printed in formal script. "Last time the Texas Longhorns came to Chestnut Hill, there was a bit of a stampede, but now it's revenge time . . . Welcome to the Alamo,

BOSTON COLLEGE PLAYERS IN THE PROS

Boston College has produced more than its fair share of professional football talent. Following are among the more notable since 1946:

Mike Holovak, Chicago Bears
Charlie O'Rourke, Chicago Bears
Gil Bouley, Los Angeles Rams
Ed King, Baltimore Colts
Art Donovan, Baltimore Colts
Art Spinney, Baltimore Colts
Ernie Stautner, Pittsburgh Steelers
Ed "Butch" Songin, Boston/New England Patriots
Joe Johnson, Green Bay Packers
Frank Morze, San Francisco '49ers
John Miller, Washington Redskins
Alan Miller, Oakland Raiders
Don Allard, Washington Redskins
Jim Colclough, Boston/New England Patriots
Larry Eisenhauer, Boston/New England Patriots
Ross O'Hanley, Boston/New England Patriots
Dan Sullivan, Baltimore Colts
Lou Kirouac, New York Giants
Art Graham, Boston/New England Patriots
Dave O'Brien, St. Louis Cardinals
Jack Concannon, Philadelphia Eagles and Chicago Bears
Bobby Shann, Philadelphia Eagles
Jim Whalen, Boston/New England Patriots
Jim Chevillot, Green Bay Packers
Bob Hyland, Green Bay Packers and New York Giants

Mike Evans, Philadelphia Eagles
Brendan McCarthy, Atlanta Falcons
John Fitzgerald, Dallas Cowboys
Bob Bouley, Baltimore Colts
John Egan, Miami Dolphins
Fred Willis, Houston Oilers
Bill Thomas, Dallas/Kansas City Chiefs
Jeff Yeates, Atlanta Falcons
Gordie Browne, New York Jets
Tom Condon, Kansas City Chiefs
Al Krevis, Cincinnati Bengals and New York Jets
Gary Marangi, Buffalo Bills
Mike Esposito, Atlanta Falcons
Fred Steinfort, Oakland Raiders and Denver Broncos
Steve Corbett, New England Patriots
Mike Kruczek, Pittsburgh Steelers and Washington Redskins
Don Macek, San Diego Chargers
Joe Sullivan, Miami Dolphins
Dave Zumbach, New Orleans Saints
Peter Cronan, Seattle Seahawks and Washington Redskins
Steve Schindler, Denver Broncos
Tom Lynch, Seattle Seahawks and Buffalo Bills
John Schmeding, Buffalo Bills
Fred Smerlas, Buffalo Bills
Jim Rourke, Oakland Raiders and Kansas City Chiefs
Karl Swanke, Green Bay Packers
Tim Sherwin, Baltimore Colts
Bill Stephanos, Minnesota Vikings
Mark Roopenian, Buffalo Bills

Jack Concannon
Philadelphia Eagles

Art Graham
Boston Patriots—end

JIM COLCLOUGH
END
BOSTON PATRIOTS

*Jim Colclough
Boston Patriots—end*

*Arthur Donovan
Baltimore Colts—tackle*

Arthur Donovan
TACKLE   BALTIMORE COLTS

Art Spinney

GUARD-COLTS

*Art Spinney
Colts—guard*

Darrell." The reference was to Texas head coach Darrell Royal. The invitation, written by a group of Boston College alumni, had a more pointed and less humorous reference to Joe Yukica: "This is Yukica's last stand; if it doesn't change this time we don't invite Joe back—to the party or the game."

The invitation was signed "Santa Ana."

The odds on the defenders of the Alamo could not have been much worse than the thirteen and a half points that favored Texas, a team that was rated in the top ten of every major pre-season poll. The Longhorns came to town led by All-America fullback Earl Campbell, a pair of half-back burners in Johnny "Ham" Jones and Olympic sprinter Johnny "Lam" Jones, and one of the best kickers in college football, Russell Erxleben.

Then there was Boston College. Eagle quarterback Ken Smith who had yet to throw a pass in a varsity game. Starting tailback Anthony Brown was on the sidelines with a shoulder dislocation, his place taken by the inexperienced Neil Green. The outcome seemed inevitable, so much so that 1,500 seats went unsold at Alumni Field. But the 30,476 who were there saw the greatest home win in Boston College history.

The game was implausible from the start, with Green taking a pitchout from Smith on Boston College's twenty-six, getting a block from guard Tom Lynch, and racing seventy-four yards for a touchdown on the second play of the game. After Texas fumbled on Boston College's four-yard line, Smith engineered a twelve-play scoring drive that gave the Eagles a 14–0 lead. Texas came back to score before halftime on a thirty-five-yard Mike Cordaro-to-Alfred Jackson pass and it later looked as though the Longhorns would salvage the game when Johnny "Lam" Jones scored on an eighteen-yard sweep with 4:38 remaining.

Darrell Royal then did the courageously predictable: he went for the two-point conversion. "I don't play for ties," he would say later.

The call again went to "Lam" Jones. Boston College's Kelly Elias sniffed out the play and stopped Jones inches short of the goal line in what Boston College followers will refer to forever as "*The* tackle." "They were running counter

plays on the drive, and I learned something by the way their tight end was blocking," said Elias. "When I saw him block in on the extra points, I knew the play was coming outside, I moved up and stuck the guy. His specialty is speed, mine is hitting, so I hit him."

Even then the sweating wasn't over. A personal foul called as time ran out gave Erxleben a shot at a fifty-three-yard game-winning field goal. The previous season he had kicked a fifty-five-yarder with room to spare. The kick was long enough. "I held my breath," said Yukica, his ten-year career no doubt flashing before his eyes. "I thought it was good."

The kick was wide left, unleashing a flood of emotion seldom before seen on Boston College's home field. Fans ripped down the goal posts and the dressing room celebration was raging for two hours after the game.

"This is the greatest win the college has ever had," said college President Reverend J. Donald Monan, a man not generally given to overstatement.

"It's the biggest victory *I've* ever had," said Yukica.

"It's the best win in my time here," echoed Bill Flynn, whose "time" at Boston College had spanned five decades. Tackle-turned-linebacker Pete Cronan, who received the game ball for his fifteen tackles and would later be named ECAC Player of the Week, said, "It was the greatest thrill of my whole life."

These were no mere parochial ravings confined only to the locker room. Said the *New York Times*: "Not since Frank Leahy coached Boston College to an undefeated, untied season in 1940 have the Eagles spread their wings so wide."

But just as the Eagles are given to unexpected periodic soarings to great heights, so also are they prone to equally inexplicable plunges. After wins over Tulane and Navy had visions of bowl bids dancing in a few heads, there followed a loss to Florida State, and a few weeks later, back-to-back losses to Villanova and Miami of Florida. The season ended 8–3, with Yukica chosen to coach the East squad in the annual East-West Shrine game in Palo Alto.

For all of Yukica's accomplishments, however,

Second-string tailback Neil Green draws first blood against Texas with a 74–yard touchdown run on the second play of the game.

Quarterback Ken Smith ups the BC lead to 14–0, scoring on a keeper to conclude a twelve-play, 96–yard drive.

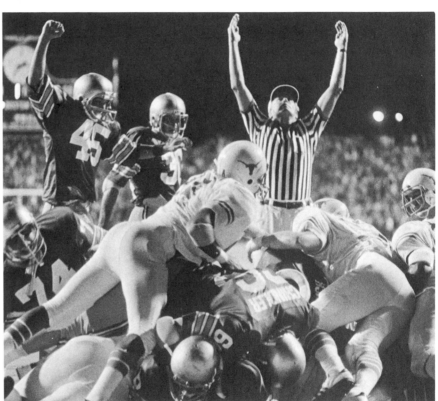

BC safety Kelly Elias makes "the tackle," stopping Texas' Johnny "Lam" Jones just short of the goal line in a two-point conversion attempt.

45

Boston fans and media never seemed to warm up to him the way they had to Cavanaugh, Leahy, and Holovak. Some felt that he was too conservative a coach, that the team should pass more. Perhaps more than any other successful Boston College coach, Yukica took a disproportionate amount of blame for losing and got little credit for winning.

But the underpinning of Yukica's football philosophy was that a good ground attack sets up and enhances a passing attack, and not the other way about. "No matter how many passes we throw, we can't win until we get our running attack established," he said on several occasions.

In 1976, Yukica found himself without the services of an outstanding back to establish a running game. Glen Capriola, 1976 rushing leader with 1,003 yards, had graduated, and there was no Fred Willis or Brendan McCarthy waiting to take up the slack. After a 44–0 opening day pounding by Texas (they remembered the Alamo, too), Yukica took the wraps off Ken Smith and went to the air as he never had before.

Smith had thrown an average of only twelve passes per game his junior year and now, though possessed of acknowledged talent, was also slow, overweight, and reportedly a discipline problem. By the opening game of the 1977 season, Smith was riding the bench behind Joe O'Brien and it wasn't until fifteen minutes before kickoff of the Tennessee game, the second of the season, that Yukica came to grips with his decision to emphasize the air attack. He told a surprised Smith that he was the starter and that he would be throwing. Smith responded to his reinstatement by completing twenty-five of forty-one passes for 343 yards, albeit in a 24–18 loss. The next week he justified Yukica's faith by hitting nineteen of thirty for 301 yards in a 49–28 win over Army.

With Boston College five and three and throwing the ball enough to appease critics and win games, Yukica and his new-look "wing and a prayer" Eagles seemed headed to a good if not great season. Until "Black Thursday."

Ken Smith showed up drunk at practice two days before the Syracuse game. After watching him bobbling snaps from center and stumbling through plays, Yukica ordered the quarterback

off the field and suspended him. It was a bad scene. "I was so gone I don't remember anything that happened," Smith would say later. "I don't remember the field, the locker room . . . nothing." His teammates remembered. Even after Boston College lost to Syracuse 20–3 behind the quarterbacking of a game but obviously nervous Jay Palazola, rumor was that his teammates did not want the errant Smith back in their midst.

Again it was Yukica, who in other years and through other hard times (though admittedly *on-field* hard times) had supported quarterbacks Harris, Marangi, and Kruczek, who stepped in to try to save Ken Smith. The Monday after the Syracuse loss Kelly Elias and co-captain Rich Scudellari had a meeting with Yukica where, said Elias, "Coach Yukica just reminded us of what Kenny had been through. I think we were too emotionally involved in this thing to see clearly. Kenny couldn't have gotten to be number-one quarterback without some pretty hard work. He certainly didn't get to be where he is by drinking every day."

Elias and Scudellari agreed to let Smith address a team meeting, preceding a vote to determine whether or not the quarterback would be allowed back on the team.

"I had to see the team face-to-face," said Smith later. "I had to let them know how I felt. I owed them an explanation."

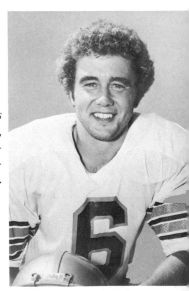

Ken Smith's cherubic looks masked a troubled personality, with impressive on-field performances intermixed with destructive off-field behavior.

Scudellari grilled Smith on his feelings for the team. Smith handled all but one question. "They asked me what I would do in their situation. I didn't know what to say."

The team vote came down overwhelmingly in Smith's favor.

"I'll tell you the feeling those guys gave me and the character they showed," Smith later told a *Globe* reporter. "I just can't say what I feel for them."

"We just have a bunch of real class guys," added Yukica. "They saw past the football player. They thought Kenny Smith the person was more important than Kenny Smith the quarterback."

The rest of the season was far from a Cinderella story for Smith or the team. The Eagles beat UMass 34–7 behind Smith's passing, but then went to Worcester and suffered a shocking 35–20 loss to Holy Cross.

It could have been the Smith incident, or it could have been that the strain of the 6–5 1977 season had taken a toll—whatever his reasons, Joe Yukica in early 1978 ended the longest reign of any Boston College varsity football coach—ten years and a 68–33 record. Specifically, he was hired to replace Jake Crouthamel as head coach at Dartmouth, the school where he had been an assistant thirteen years earlier.

"I drove up there for an interview and was still undecided on the way home," he recalls. "But the farther I got from Hanover the more I wanted to stay there."

At news of Yukica's impending departure, Bill Flynn's phone began ringing with calls from dozens of applicants, leading *Herald* columnist D. Leo Monahan to wonder, "If the Boston College coaching job is really the most thankless around, how come so many want it?" Indeed, Boston College would not go begging, but with Yukica's resignation coming after the first of the year, Flynn wanted a replacement by late January so the program would be disrupted as little as possible. For better and worse, he got Ed Chlebek.

Chlebek of Uniontown, Pennsylvania, had been a mediocre backup quarterback with the New York Jets until the team drafted Joe Namath, at which point Chlebek wisely departed to play five seasons with the Ottawa Rough Riders

in the Canadian League. Upon retirement, in 1970, he landed an assistant coaching job at his Alma Mater, Western Michigan, later moved on to Notre Dame as quarterback coach under Dan Devine, and in 1976 took over as head coach of Eastern Michigan. Here he gained national recognition when, after a 2–9 inaugural season, he turned the team around to 8–3 the next year.

"My method in seeking a coach," said Flynn, "is to talk to people all over the country. You hear names. One name that kept coming up was Ed Chlebek."

On a Wednesday, Chlebek met with members of the alumni screening committee and said the right things: that he was not a conservative coach; that he thought Boston College should pass more; that "this school is a lot like Notre Dame—I don't say we'd beat Notre Dame year after year, but I want to get our program up there." The next day the thirty-six-year-old Chlebek was named Boston College's twenty-eighth varsity football coach.

"We'll throw the football," the new coach promised the local media, "and if we don't play well I'm not going to alibi."

No alibi would have been adequate to explain 1978. It was the worst season in the history of Boston College football—no wins, no ties, eleven losses, most of them not even close. The only highlight of the season from a historical perspective was Boston College's 6,500–mile road trip to Japan to lose to Temple University 28–24 before 55,000 Japanese in the "Mirage Bowl." As one writer put it, recounting the shambles of the season, "He turned a Division I school into a Division II school in one season." Meanwhile, Dartmouth, under Joe Yukica, was winning the Ivy League championship.

"It was apparent to me that Ed, though he was popular with his players, just wasn't the answer to our prayers," said Flynn.

Boston College had never fired a coach after just one season, but on the Tuesday following the team's return from Japan, Flynn called Chlebek to his office. There Flynn disclosed that Boston College had given him permission to buy up Chlebek's contract and to begin the search for a new coach. Chlebek had time to meet with his

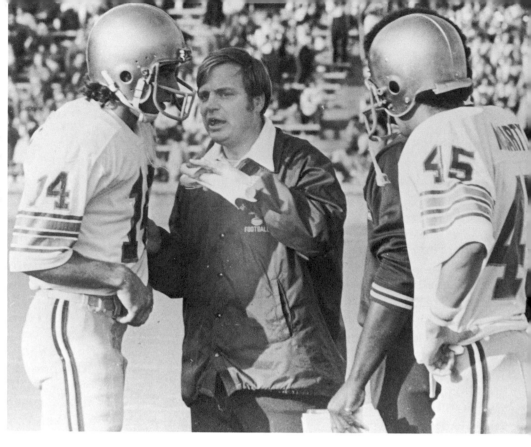

Ed Chlebek's three-year BC coaching career began with the worst season in school history, included a public non-firing, an epic win over Stanford, and ended with an abrupt departure.

team before a public announcement would be made at 6:00 p.m.

Chlebek said later that he was stunned. "Not in a million years did I think it would happen," he recalled. "Maybe after three years if you haven't reached your goal . . ." To which Flynn responded: *"Most* coaches would be fired after a zero and eleven season."

Chlebek reportedly had tears in his eyes when he assembled the team in the Roberts Center dressing room and told them of his dismissal. Team reaction was one of disbelief. "Some of the guys thought it was a joke," captain Fred Smerlas later told the *Boston Globe.*

Following Chlebek's hurried departure from the meeting, tri-captains Smerlas, John Schmeding, and Paul McCarty conducted an emotional meeting of their own with thirty-three other squad members. Concluding that the team backed Chlebek, the captains went upstairs to Flynn's office and told the athletic director that they hoped to see the coach re-hired. Smerlas told Flynn, "When you have a sincere person who loves his players you can't let a guy like that go."

"It wasn't a threat and they weren't belligerent," Flynn recalls. "I explained the reasons for my decision, then they explained why they believed in him."

By 5:00 P.M.—one hour before the firing was to have been announced,—Flynn called Chlebek. "The players want you," he said, "They stuck together on this. I told them, 'if this is the coach you want, fine . . . !' "

"I didn't even think about the players going to bat for me," said Chlebek, "But, as I said all season, they're a great bunch of young men. Responding [as] they did on my behalf was the greatest thing I've ever experienced."

Chlebek responded on his team's behalf by sticking with the pass-oriented veer offense, with Palazola of Gloucester as quarterback. After running the Boston College losing streak to twelve with an opening loss to Tennessee, the Eagles beat Villanova for Boston College's first win in almost two calendar years. After the game, a relieved Chlebek led his team in an "Our Father" in the locker room. Boston College had at last been delivered from evil, if not wholly redeemed.

By late October, however, the Eagles were 1–5 and rumors were flying again. "Chlebek Appears Doomed at Boston College," read a six-column headline in the *Herald.*

"Not so—yet," reacted Bill Flynn.

Again, Chlebek and his players pulled the by-now-well-charred chestnuts out of the fire, win-

48

ning five of the last six games to finish 5–6. Fresh-man running back Shelby Gamble and UCLA transfer Leo Smith ran well enough to lend credence to Chlebek's oft-repeated contention that he needed "one recruiting cycle" (i.e., four years) to attract the players who would turn the program around.

Still, with two games left in that 1979 season, Dr. Al Branca, then president of the Blue Chips, a private athletic booster organization, told the *Globe's* John Powers that he thought alumni sentiment was "roughly 55–45" against the coach. Meanwhile, Chlebek, a sad-eyed, puffy-faced person in the best of times, was beginning to look like the oldest thirty-seven-year-old on earth.

Chlebek did get his team turned around. In 1980, a defense led by future All-America linebacker Jim Budness of Chicopee, the Smith-Gamble running combination, and the arm of sophomore quarterback John Loughery of Gloucester, took the resurgent Eagles to a 7–4 season and wins in their last five games. The biggest win of all was a 30–13 victory over nationally-ranked Stanford, easily the team's biggest home victory since the 1976 Texas game.

The Stanford defeat seemed to vindicate Chlebek. Said senior tight end and co-captain Tim Sherwin after the game, "We really had faith in the man; we believed in his philosophy; we believed he's the kind of guy Boston College needed. He's a players' coach."

Seldom had a Boston College coach been as beloved by his players. It seemed natural after a 27–26 comeback win over Holy Cross, that Boston College would renew and extend Chlebek's contract, attaching what he (Flynn) called "a good raise."

Chlebek signed and it appeared that the once shaky relationship between the college and the coach was now resting on mutually stable ground. At a December 10 Gridiron Club banquet—during which Budness became one of only six juniors ever to receive the Bulger Lowe Award and the first Boston College man since Kruczek in 1975 to be named best in the East—Chlebek spoke optimistically of Boston College's football future. The team would be among the best of the eastern independents in 1981, he said.

Chlebek's public optimism was not unlike that voiced by Frank Leahy at another banquet thirty-nine years earlier. And, like Leahy, Chlebek was gone almost as soon as the echo of his words had died.

Before Christmas, Kent State offered Chlebek a five-year contract (he had two years remaining at Boston College) and more money than he had been making, and, though Boston College offered to extend the coach's contract, Chlebek was eager to get back into the Mid-America Conference where he had played and coached. He took the Kent State job.

Chlebek and Flynn parted amicably, the only irony being the obvious, if unspoken, fact that the coach was abruptly leaving many of the same players who, two seasons earlier, had saved his job. "Let's say it's not the happiest day of my life," said Flynn, once again faced with a hurry-up search for a new coach.

This time the athletic advisory board—a body composed of six alumni, three faculty members, the president and past president of the alumni association, and two student representatives—stuck out its collective neck and recommended forty-two-year-old Jack Bicknell, a former Boston College assistant under Yukica, and at the time of his selection, a losing (18–35–1) head coach at Maine. Where Yukica had been cool and aloof, and Chlebek warm and sympathetic, Bicknell was somewhere in between—a hot-tempered motivator.

"I don't like sloppiness or lack of intensity at practice," he said at his first news conference. "I hate to see someone going through the motions. The only honest way is to let them know how I feel. When I'm mad, I'm mad."

Bicknell grew up in Livingston, New Jersey, went to Rutgers, and later to Montclair State as a blue chip quarterback prospect. A neck injury ended his career and he turned to coaching. He was a high school coach before Yukica hired him in 1968. Bicknell describes himself as a coach with an eye for talent. "Some people look like Tarzan and play like Jane. I can tell the difference."

While he inherited a solid team featuring the Budness-anchored defense, Bicknell also inher-

The play of linebacker Jim Budness was instrumental in BC's 1980 upset of Stanford, and helped him win All-America honors and become one of six juniors ever to be named top player in the east.

Surprise choice to replace the suddenly-departed Ed Chlebek, ex-Maine coach (and BC assistant) Jack Bicknell led the 1981 Eagles through an ambitious schedule to a 5–6 conclusion.

ited a tough 1981 schedule that included Texas A&M, North Carolina, Penn State, Pittsburgh, and West Virginia.

Bicknell's trials began on the fifth day of practice when quarterback John Loughery injured the tendons in his passing hand, leaving the coach to choose between a pair of untested backups, Doug Guyer and Dennis Scala. It was Scala, replacing Guyer, who engineered Bicknell's debut win, a 15–14 upset of Texas A&M. But the key move was taking place at the lower reaches of the depth chart where a small 5' 10", 170-

pound, eighteen-year-old quarterback-safety and sometime punt returner was moved up from fifth to fourth string.

It would be four weeks after the A&M game before Doug Flutie of Natick would be named to the travelling team and sent in as cannon fodder in a lost cause at Penn State. Four weeks after that he would be generally regarded as Boston College's best freshman passer since Jimmy Fitzpatrick in 1916.

Flutie's most optimistic ambition coming into the 1981 season was "just to make third string quarterback." But a 56–14 loss to North Carolina—"We just got our butts kicked," said Bicknell—a 38–10 loss to West Virginia, and a 31–0 first-half debacle at Penn State left the Boston College coaching staff ready to disregard the depth charts and try anything. At halftime of the Penn State game, Boston College assistant coach Barry Gallup came up to Flutie: "Be ready to go in," he told the youngster, "and not just for a play or two."

Flutie was up for it if for no other reason, he said, than that there was a record crowd of 84,000 in the stands. "I thought I might never get to play in front of that many people again . . . I mean, last year at this time I was worrying about Dedham and Walpole high schools and here I am playing against Penn State!"

Flutie, to the surprise of everyone, including himself, engineered a scoring drive capped by a twenty-three-yard touchdown pass. In all, he completed seven of fourteen passes and had Boston College knocking on the door a second time before the drive was killed by an interception.

Bicknell stuck with Flutie through a loss to Navy and started him again at Army where Flutie, scrambling around the backfield so he could look between onrushing linemen, ("I'm too small to see over them") completed fifteen of twenty-one passes for 244 yards. "He gets better each week," was Bicknell's assessment when he announced the obvious decision to give Flutie the start against Pittsburgh, the number two team in the nation.

Flutie says he woke up that morning thinking of Pittsburgh quarterback Dan Marino, a 6'4"

Heisman candidate. "To me I'm still just the little freshman kid."

Nonetheless, against the number one defense in the major college ranks, Flutie completed twenty-three of forty-three passes for 347 yards (second highest ever for a Boston College quarterback) and revived memories of Fitzpatrick, O'Rourke, and Concannon, as he almost single-handedly stole a game the Eagles were expected to lose by something upwards of two touchdowns. They lost by less than one, 29–24.

"He was their whole team," raved Pittsburgh defensive coach Foge Fazio. "How he saw some of our guys coming and still got out of the way I'll never know."

In his first four games, Flutie passed for a freshman record 1,045 yards. In all, he finished

Natick phenom Doug Flutie smashed BC freshman passing records in 1981—105 completions, 1652 total yards—and raised fans' hopes for future successes.

the season having started the team's last seven games, winning four, losing three, and completing a freshman record of 105 passes in 192 attempts for 1,652 yards.

In the final game of the season he became the first freshman in thirty years, since Tommy Joe Sullivan in 1951, to win the O'Melia Trophy as the MVP of the Boston College-Holy Cross game, a 28–24 Boston College win in which Flutie was twelve for seventeen for 251 yards.

Bicknell said after the season that he wasn't really surprised. "The previous coaching staff was undecided whether or not to take Doug," the coach recalled. "They were afraid of his size, mostly. But we looked at the films (of Natick high school games), and he was always coming up with the big play, the pass, the interception, the tackle. Doug Flutie's been doing this Frank Merriwell stuff for years."

Doug Flutie of Cumford Avenue in Natick, potentially the best quarterback in the history of Boston College football, said after being told of Bicknell's remarks that he didn't know Frank Merriwell, nor Jimmy Fitzpatrick either.

3

Ice Hockey

THE GAME WAS called ice polo in the 1880s, and the only rule it shares with the more popular and sophisticated ice hockey of the 1980s is the oldest unwritten one: keep your head up. It was a wild, swirling game, played by men on long-bladed skates who used short, curved club-like sticks to try to knock a round ball into a goal. There were no offside rules—indeed, there were hardly any rules at all—and the game was usually played on a pond rather than in a rink.

Like football in its earliest days, ice polo was a game of anything goes. And, as football had once divided into the "hands off" soccer style game and the "hands-on" Rugby style or "Boston" game, so the ice game also divided between ice polo as played in the United States and the more structured ice *hockey* popular in Canada.

Boston College students are reported by Nat Hasenfus as playing pick-up games of ice polo in the 1880s, the same era in which informal games of football were popular. In one way the ice game made more sense at a college for the working class, because while urban real estate was expensive and football fields few, the frozen surfaces of ponds were free and open to the public. Bullough's Pond, Hammond Pond, Chan-

dler's Pond, and other ponds in or near Boston gave Boston College men ample opportunity to combine free ice with their free time.

In the winter of 1896–1897, as part of his scheme for using sports as a vehicle for promoting Boston College, college President Reverend Timothy Brosnahan officially sanctioned the first Boston College ice polo team. Concerned with publicity, Brosnahan named as team manager college publicist James E. O'Connell.

The same day ice polo received its administrative blessing, the team members walked to Boston's Wright and Ditson sports store to purchase, via the college's charge, the latest style in Canadian-made skates, sticks, shin guards, and goalie's chest protector. They are said to have run up a bill that dismayed Reverend A. J. Duarte, the college treasurer.

Members of that first Boston College ice polo team were Bill Lyons (a football and baseball star who would receive offers from three pro baseball teams), Joseph Loughery, James and Joseph O'Connell, John Kernan, Vincent Fitzpatrick, Frank Carney, Dick Teeling, and Jack McAllister.

The team practiced either on ponds or on a

The game was still called "ice polo" when BC sanctioned its first hockey team in the 1896–1897 season. Players included (standing) Joseph Loughry, Jim O'Connell, and Joe O'Connell; (seated) John Kiernan and Bill Lyons; and, (on floor) Vince Fitzpatrick.

flat stretch of ground behind Boston City Hospital and, as was the case with football, the first schedules were piecemeal affairs made up of club, amateur, and college teams. Two games were played on Wakefield's Lake Quannapowitt, one on Arlington's Spy Pond (where Boston College beat Harvard 1–0), and another on Franklin Field (where Boston College upset Brown 5–2), which the city used to flood in the winter. The team also defeated town teams from Wakefield and Lynn, and being more adept at ice polo than football, had no trouble in scheduling two games with Yale—though both were cancelled due to warm weather and the resultant bad ice.

Boston College's first-season win over Brown must go down as an upset, because whereas Boston College had played officially-sanctioned ice polo for one season, Brown had put a team on the ice as early as 1894. In fact, it was the influence of Brown University ice polo players that brought about the abrupt switch of American colleges from five-a-side freewheeling ice polo to the seven-a-side, more regulated Canadian game of ice hockey.

In the fall of 1894, a group of American collegiate ice polo players, most of them from Brown (none from Boston College), went to Canada to play four two-game series in Montreal, Ottawa, Toronto, and Kingston. In each case the series consisted of one game of ice polo and one of ice hockey. The Americans lost all four hockey games, and won two and tied two of the polo games. Nonetheless they returned to the States convinced that the Canadian game—with its flat puck, stiffer rules, and seven-man teams—was preferable. In the words of Alexander Meikeljohn, (Brown 1893) in the April, 1951, *Brown Alumni Bulletin:* "Their game was much more highly developed than ours . . . . First, they had flat-bladed speed skates as against our rockers. Moreover, our hitting a stroke with one hand would not move a flat puck along the ice. We were accustomed to playing with a ball, not a puck. A man was ruled offside if, at any point, he was ahead of the puck when a teammate was carrying it or shooting it. It was pretty well agreed among us that the Canadian game was better than ours."

By the winter of 1897–1898 (its second season of existence), the Boston College ice polo team had become an ice hockey team and had completely adopted the Canadian game—a transition that was mirrored at Harvard, Brown, and Yale. Thus, collegiate ice polo was history after only one season, but that had been a season in which Boston College had established parity with the more established Ivy League schools. It would take Boston College football two more decades to raise itself to the level of the Ivies.

Hockey proved a better game than polo. Besides making use of the more controllable puck (sometimes a wood disc wrapped in leather), which enhanced passing and stick-handling skills, hockey allowed for more men to play. A seven-man hockey team called for three attackers known as "rushes"; two defensemen, the forward of which was called the "point" and the other the "cover point;" one "rover," who, as the name implies, was free to go anywhere; and a goalkeeper, officially called the "goal tend." In six-man hockey, which came into vogue in 1922, the rover position was eliminated, and the point and cover point played side-by-side as "defensemen."

Harvard and Brown are credited with playing the first game of college hockey in the United States. At Boston's Franklin Field on January 19, 1898, Brown won 6–0 and the *Boston Herald* reported on a common fault of the reformed ice polo players: "The Harvard men seemed to forget that they were playing hockey, acting more like ice polo players. Instead of keeping their clubs close to the ice, they held them up in the air, and thereby missed quick opportunities for connecting with the puck."

Boston College, meanwhile, was playing most of its games on suburban ponds against club teams from Newton, Cambridge, Dorchester, and Boston. The Boston College team did not rate the newspaper coverage of Harvard or Brown, and its scores are lost to history, but thanks to the work of Boston College sports historian Nat Hasenfus, the names of some of the players survive. Of the original ice polo team, only Bill Lyons had graduated. New players (Boston College's first true *hockey* players) included John Kernan; Hugh Drum (later Chief of Staff for General Pershing in the First World War); Jerome Linehan (later a Cambridge contractor); and Timothy Ahern (later judge of the Roxbury District Court).

Boston schoolboys began turning out in large numbers to watch the Boston College and Harvard games at Franklin Field, and their youthful enthusiasm soon carried into the city and suburban school systems. Schoolboy hockey became so popular in and around Boston that it eventually presented a large player pool for Boston area colleges, especially Boston College. But that would be several years into a happier future.

In 1900, Boston College President Reverend W. J. Read Mullan discontinued all sports and though student pressure and fund-raising efforts restored football in 1901, hockey remained moribund for fifteen years. It took the arrival of a sports-minded president, Father Thomas Ignatius Gasson, and the move to a spacious campus in Chestnut Hill to revive hockey at Boston College.

In 1914, the first year that all Boston College classes were conducted at "the Heights," the administration approved formation of a four-team inter-class hockey league that would play a series of games on neighboring ponds. The sport proved so popular among students that the next year, the winter of 1915–1916, school officials agreed to the construction of a temporary rink on the tennis courts beside Saint Mary's Hall. By 1917–1918, access to even this little makeshift rink had done so much to improve the caliber of inter-class hockey that Boston College was once again prepared to sponsor a college team.

But the school had lost valuable ground, as the 1900s had been a decade of rapid progress in collegiate hockey. Harvard had built its first rink, also makeshift, in 1900; the original Boston Arena was built on Tremont Street in 1909; and college games, particularly Harvard's, were often scheduled at that new indoor facility. Equipment had also improved. Skates were no longer a flat blade clamped or riveted to a shoe but had progressed to the state of a curved or "radius" blade permanently mounted to a supportive boot. Sticks were longer and had flatter blades which allowed for greater puck control. Shorts and old football shirts had become the accepted hockey uniform and (breakthrough of breakthroughs!) full tights took the place of thigh-high stockings held up by ladies' garters.

As in most other facets of college sport, the Ivy League had virtually taken over ice hockey and attracted the best of the prep school stars (in part because the Ivies were the only colleges with the money, space, and inclination to build their own rinks). Typical was the Saint Paul's-to-Princeton linkage that combined to produce the greatest United States college hockey player of all time: "the wonder player of hockey," the *Boston Journal* called Hobey Baker when, as a junior, he captained Princeton in 1913.

However, Boston College soon developed its own unique and inexpensive answer to the Ivy League's preppy feeder system. "In the early days of hockey at Boston College," recalls John "Snooks" Kelley, a Boston College player in the 1920s and the team's coach through five decades, "we'd get the type of kid who grew up skating on the ponds or in what I call the pits—construction sites around the city that in winter would fill with water and freeze and be a kind of rink. Our kids came to us out of these pits and off the ponds. Later, we'd get the kind of kid who'd hang around the rink at all hours trying to get some free ice. Our players didn't come to us from schools with their own rinks. A lot of our players climbed out of those pits."

It wasn't Saint Paul's, but it got the job done.

The nation was at war when Boston College again resumed hockey, and the 1918 season was, perforce, an abbreviated one in which Boston College played two of its three games against service teams, beating Harvard Radio School and losing to Newport Naval Reserve. In its other game, Boston College's first intercollegiate hockey game of the twentieth century, the Eagles beat Boston University 3–1.

Faculty member Bob Fowler was assigned (and paid) to coach the 1918 team, and Boston College joined Boston University and Tufts to form the Boston Intercollegiate Hockey League. The tennis-court rink was improved, and the team's schedule called for afternoon practices on the campus rink with an occasional evening session at the Boston Arena. Stars of the Boston College hockey revival included rover Eddie Enright, who scored three goals in the 1918 Harvard Radio School game; center and captain Walter Falvey; cover point Frank Morrissey, (first of five sons this Medford family would send to Boston College); and Leo Hughes, a thick-necked, moon-faced Irishman who combined strength (not a common characteristic of hockey players) with skill and skating speed to become Boston College's first major hockey star. (Like most hockey teams of its day, the Boston College club used infrequent substitutions. There were only a few good skaters on each team and the prevailing belief was that a team should keep its best men on the ice for as long as possible. Exceptions occurred only in the talent-rich Ivy League, as when Boston College played Harvard in 1919 and the Crimson skated fifteen players to Boston College's eight, beating the Eagles 7–2.)

Hughes burst on the scene by scoring four goals in Boston College's 5–4 upset of Army in 1919, and went on to captain the 1922 team, undefeated in collegiate play. Following his graduation (the player whom Nat Hasenfus described in 1943 as "The cleverest player in all Boston College history"), skated with the Boston Athletic Association, the area's best amateur club. Hughes's hockey career ended tragically in 1925 when he lost an eye to a high stick in a game between the Boston Athletic Association, and Ft. Pitt. The injury prompted Boston College players to play a benefit game against the Boston Athletic Association, which Boston College won 2–0, and which, more to the point, raised $3,100 to pay for an artificial eye for Hughes.

That high sticking incident, while particularly gruesome, was not atypical of the hockey of these days. Like football, hockey was rough at its best, brutal at its worst. Such was hockey's reputation for mayhem that when Notre Dame students began lobbying for a team, the great football coach Knute Rockne (who was not keen on any sport competing with his football program) is rumored to have said, "If you think football is rough, try to imagine a bunch of Irishmen with knives on their feet and clubs in their hands."

In 1919, the Boston College administration voted hockey a major sport; in 1920, it awarded the first varsity letters to hockey players. A new, albeit still temporary, rink was constructed on the football field and Boston College expanded the schedule to seven games. The 1920–1921 schedule had originally included a game with Harvard, but athletic relations between the schools were broken following the football game of 1919, a 17–0 Harvard win in which some thought Boston College star Jimmy Fitzpatrick had been deliberately injured.

Hughes and Frank Morrissey, a rushing defenseman who captained the football and hockey teams, led Boston College to a 6–1 season in which it lost only to UMass. Victories for the resurgent team, coached by alumnus Walter Falvey, came against Army, Fordham, Boston University, Tufts, Massachusetts Institute of Technology, and one service team—the Yankee Division.

The season set the stage for 1921–1922, and

Boston College's first great hockey team, a club that won games and took the critical step across the threshold of public acceptance. When a 7,000 standing-room-only crowd packed the Boston Arena (newly rebuilt on St. Botolph Street, after a fire leveled the Tremont Street structure) for a Boston College-Dartmouth game, hockey had clearly established itself as a major sport. Boston College won the game 4–0, and now nothing would do but that Boston College (which had lost only two games, both to Canadian teams) must meet Harvard (which had lost one game, but tied two) in a game that would decide the unofficial New England championship, and arguably, the national championship.

No deal. Feeling between the schools' administrations was still running high, partly because of the 1919 football game and partly because the days of religious and social discrimination by Protestants against Catholics were not so far in the past as to be easily forgotten. There were not only legions of Boston College fans and Harvard fans in the proper sense of the term, there were also what Hasenfus referred to as "anti-Boston College and anti-Harvard rooters," and, as Father Maurice Dullea recalls, "There was always the fear of trouble in the stands."

Deprived of administrative sanction but backed by popular demand for a game, the Boston College and Harvard players agreed to meet each other at Boston Arena under the club names "Boston Eagles" and "Crimson Ramblers." Harvard played without its star and captain, George Owen Jr.—the absence of the captain thereby,

The ice Eagles of 1922–1923, well-stocked with talent from the Cambridge Latin School, defeated major contenders and lay controversial claim to the mythical national championship. Pictured: (standing, from left) Henry Groden, Len Morrissey, manager Bill Kelleher, coach Fred Rocque, manager Thomas Cannon, William Morrissey, and John Culhane; (seated, from left) Edmund Garrity, Daniel Murphy, John Fitzgerald, Leo Hughes, and James Foley.

somehow, making the game "unofficial"—but substituted for him with freshman star Clark Hodder. The Boston College team remained intact.

The unofficial but well-publicized game was sold out days before face off, and of the play Hasenfus wrote: . . . "a fast, hard, clean, slashing hockey game. Dashes up and down the ice by Hodder . . . were turned back by Jack Fitzgerald's excellent goaltending and hard checking by a desperate Boston College defense. Counter dashes by [John] Curry, Hughes, and [John] Culhane were repeatedly checked by burly Harvard defensemen."

Two goals by Hughes gave Boston College a 2–1 lead with less than a minute to play, when Harvard scored to send the game into overtime. The teams played two overtime periods rather than sudden death, during which Boston College got goals from Charles Donnellan and Ed Garrity for a 4–2 win. The victory gave Boston College the mythical national championship, because, so the argument went, the Eagles had defeated Harvard and Yale and those two schools had defeated all other major contenders. The next year Boston College would have an even more legitimate claim to the unofficial title.

By 1922, Boston College had tapped into what would be its main talent pool for the next forty years—Cambridge Latin School. "To this day," says retired hockey coach Kelley, "there have been more great Boston College players come out of Cambridge than any other school." Accordingly, the 1922–1923 team had six Cambridge alumni—John Curry, Sonny Foley, Henry Groden, John Culhane, Ed Garrity, and Jack Fitzgerald—who, combined with Medford's Morrissey brothers, Bill and Leonard, to give Boston College its best hockey team of the pre-World War II era.

Not even the great Canadian college teams could beat Boston College, and the team finished 13–1–1, the only loss to western amateur club champs, Duluth. Boston College sold out every home game at Boston Arena, and thousands were turned away for games with arch rivals Boston University and the Boston Athletic Association club.

But there was a negative side to Boston College's on-ice success; most other college teams knew they were no longer competitive with the Eagles. By 1923–1924, only one United States college—Army—was willing to schedule the Eagles, and the rest of Boston College's games had to be against Canadian colleges or American amateur clubs. "Few American colleges would risk certain defeat at the hands of Boston College," recalls Hasenfus.

Boston University, itself a beneficiary of the large number of "pit-'n'-pond" skaters in the greater Boston area, was the only United States college to play Boston College in 1924–1925. The Terriers won 1–0, their first victory over the Eagles in what would soon become the city's major college hockey rivalry. Otherwise, Boston College made history in an otherwise disappointing 6–8–0 season when the team beat Loyola of Montreal 3–1 in Canada, becoming the first United States college team to beat a Canadian college on its home ice.

The 1924–1925 season was also notable for propelling star center Jim "Sonny" Foley to national prominence. *Boston Transcript* sports writers, who had seen the best players the Ivy League could put on the ice, named the 5'6", 130-pound Foley the most exciting player in college hockey, commenting: "Whom would we rather watch play hockey than anyone else? Mr. Sonny Foley . . . because he never loafs, never quits, never stalls . . . because he is aggressive, talented, courageous—and all this despite the fact that he is a veritable midget in size."

The *Boston Post* said flatly, "[Foley is] the best player of the season, greatest center in collegiate ice hockey, and one of the best to have ever played at the Arena."

Such were Boston College's scheduling difficulties that the team may have gone on indefinitely playing Canadian college and amateur club teams had it not been for New York promoter Tex Rickard who, in 1925, was getting ready to open Madison Square Garden, the first of what he hoped would be a national chain of sports and entertainment palaces. Rickard was a former saloon owner, a hockey fan, and a man not averse to risk. As part of his dedication extravaganza for the opening of the new Garden, he held a four-team United States-Canada college hockey exhibition series. He invited Montreal and Royal Military Academy to represent Canada, while Princeton and Boston College were to be the United States teams.

The invitation brought new stature to the Boston College hockey team, prestige enhanced by the Eagles taking the tournament with a 4–2 win over Montreal and a 7–6 win over Royal Military. Boston College coach Fred Rocque had his team playing a disciplined short-pass game, in contrast to the hit-and-chase in vogue at the time, and the Rocque style made Boston College the darling of consecutive capacity Garden crowds.

Star of the 1925 team, as well as those of the two succeeding years, was Cornelius "Tubber" Cronin, a stocky right wing who, by dint of one of the hardest shots in college hockey, scored fifteen goals in fourteen games in 1925–1926. The next season, Cronin was elected team captain, making him the fifth consecutive Cambridge Latin alumnus to lead the Eagles. Cronin was also one of Boston College's few nationally recognized hockey stars, selected by New York sportswriters to the 1926 All-Intercollegiate team. The inscription on his trophy read, "The most deadly shot in college hockey."

But trouble was lurking around the corner for Boston College, in the form of the Boston Bruins Professional Hockey Club. The team was founded in 1924 and by 1927 it had built a large public following, some of it coming at the expense of area colleges. Even the big college games, such as Boston College-Boston University, were no longer guaranteed sellouts. Revenue was down, and with falling receipts came the inevitable cuts in travelling budget and schedule length. Between 1926 and 1927, Boston College dropped from a fourteen-game to a six-game schedule and made only one road trip, to Springfield, Massachusetts, where they beat the Springfield Outing Club 4–3.

In 1928, Sonny Foley, star of the mid-1920s, replaced Rocque as coach. Hockey had slipped in popularity among the student body since Foley's playing days, and the new coach found

he had to lure qualified Boston College students away from independent club teams. One of these was Boston College senior and former Cambridge star John "Snooks" Kelley. Foley wooed him away from the Boston Hockey Club. Kelley, a wavy-haired, square-jawed, pug-faced Irishman, noted as much for digging the puck out of the corners as for putting it into the net, scored the season's most spectacular goal—a rink-length solo against Holy Cross at Boston Arena in a game Boston College won 6–3. The victory was one of Boston College's few bright spots in an otherwise dismal 2–4–1 season.

But Kelly's modest playing role would one day be obliterated by his contribution as the single most important person in the history of hockey at Boston College. Four years after his graduation, Kelley would take over a hockey program that was in total disarray, and by force of his unrelenting Celtic will, would build Boston College into a national champion and direct its course for thirty-six successful seasons. No Boston College coach in any other sport—not Leahy or Cavanaugh or, later, Bob Cousy—would have as much impact for so long a time.

Kelley had left Boston College and begun a career as a teacher in Cambridge when Sonny Foley coached the 1928–1929 team to what would be the college's last hockey season in three years. The first tremors of economic hard times were already being felt in 1928, and the Great Depression was soon forcing cutbacks in unprofitable collegiate sports. Boston College hockey was no longer packing fans into the Arena, and, in 1928, the Boston College Athletic Association showed a $200 loss on a road trip to Yale. Clearly, a team that lost money at home and on the road placed a great strain on the limited resources of a tuition-supported college. Hockey had to go.

Ironically, Boston College's 1928–1929 team had one of its all-time greats in Lawrence Sanford, later a member of the United States National team, and good players in Nick Tedesco and Arthur Morrissey, along with a freshman team that was one of the best in the school's history. The hockey players besought the administration to retain the sport. The freshmen, realizing their pleas were in vain, entered their

SNOOKS KELLEY: MORE THAN 501

He is most apt to be remembered as the first and, so far, only college hockey coach to record 500 or more career coaching victories. In Snooks Kelley's case it was 501–243–15 over a thirty-six-year career, 1932 to 1972, with four seasons missed to Navy service.

That achievement is all the more remarkable in that Kelley spent his entire coaching career at the same college, and for thirty-four of those years, he also was a teacher in the Cambridge school system. Along with his records for victories and career longevity are other glittering, if less well remembered, achievements.

Kelley took Boston College teams to the NCAA finals nine times, the most championship appearances of any team in the East. In 1949, Kelley coached Boston College to the first NCAA tournament win by any eastern team, a 4–3 victory over Dartmouth at Colorado Springs. He also coached Boston College to eight New England championships, nine appearances in ECAC Division I post-season play, and the 1965 ECAC championship.

His natural persuasivness and an honest love of Boston College made Kelley one of the best recruiters in the country. "Snooks Kelley could talk a dog off a meat wagon," says former player Paul Schilling. Kelley also had an eye for talent. He recruited and coached a dozen players who earned All-America honors at Boston College: Ed "Butch" Songin (1947–1948, 1948–1949), Warren Lewis (1949–1950), Len Ceglarski (1950–1951), Bob Kiley, (1953–1954), Joe Jangro, (1958–1959), Tom "Red" Martin (1959–1960, 1960–1961), Billy Hogan (1961–1962), Jack Leetch (1962–1963), John Cunniff (1964–1965, 1965–1966), Jerry York (1966–1967), Paul Hurley (1968–1969), and Tim Sheehy (1968–1969, 1969–1970).

"But the thing I coached for and that I loved so much to see," says Kelley, "was a young player who would mature, make a contribution to his team and grow to love Boston College."

For ten years following his retirement, Kelley served as a special assistant to athletic director Bill Flynn, with special responsibility for administration

As a BC senior in 1927–1928, Snooks (first row, far right) was a standout scorer on an otherwise desultory Eagles squad.

College hockey's two winningest coaches ever are Kelley and Dartmouth's late Eddie Jeremiah. It was against Jeremiah-Dartmouth teams that BC won Kelley's 300th and 400th coaching victories.

Snooks oversees packing for BC's (successful) trip to the 1949 NCAA championship tournament. With Kelley are, from left, Giles Threadgold, captain Bernie Burke, and Len Ceglarski who, thirty-two years later, was to succeed Snooks as Eagles coach.

of the National Youth Sports Program at Boston College, a summer sports camp for inner city youths. Kelley ran the program from his small windowless office at the entrance to McHugh Forum, from whence thousands of Boston College students and passersby would hear his familiar booming greeting: "Hiya, son," or, for women, "How'r'ya, dear."

To the disbelief of many in the Boston College community—and to Kelley when he first heard of it—the professional National Hockey League came calling. In the summer of 1982, the seventy-five-year-old Kelley got an offer from the NHL's newly-relocated New Jersey Devils (formerly the Colorado Rockies) to join the team as a special assistant to the team's owners, with responsibility for evaluating hockey players in New England and the Midwest. Kelley says he will advise most would-be pros to get

their college education before trying their hands in the NHL.

"At first I couldn't believe a pro team would want a guy my age," said Kelley. But it was experience that the pros were buying. Kelley had built his college career around the development of the American hockey player, a group lately making a progressively bigger impact in the once entirely Canadian NHL. "The day is coming," observes Kelley, "when American players will be the equal of any in the world. Somewhere in this country there's going to be a Wayne Gretzky or a Bobby Orr."

Such young American superstars will soon be hearing the "Hiya, son," that will be so sorely missed by the first generation of Boston College students since the 1930s.

Kelley, surrounded by his players, celebrates his 500th victory, a 7–5 win over BU on February 23, 1972.

team, intact, in the Boston Arena Amateur League against the day of hockey's inevitable revival at Boston College. But they would graduate before Boston College would play another varsity hockey game.

By late 1932, the Depression was easing, and Boston College students, led by senior class President William Hogan, once again approached the administration to argue for reinstatement of varsity hockey. The administration still said no, contending that ice rental fees and a coaching salary combined to make hockey prohibitively expensive.

On hearing of this dilemma, Cambridge school teacher John Snooks Kelley, at Bill Hogan's urging, volunteered to spend his free hours coaching the team without pay. His offer was accepted, and on Friday, January 13 at 7:45 A.M., coach Kelley met with forty-five hockey candidates on the ice of Boston Arena.

"We didn't have any uniforms, just some old football shirts, and everybody had to supply his own equipment," Kelley remembers. "Most of our practice times were so early, sometimes three o'clock in the morning, that we got the nickname of the 'Milkmen.' But we still had the rink rats— the kids who would play any hour of the day or night. Any success Boston College has had in hockey, we owe to that type of kid: the rink rat."

The crusading and talented Hogan was elected captain, and fifteen days after holding his first practice, he led Boston College onto the Boston Arena for the school's first hockey game in four years. Boston College defeated Northeastern that night, 8–6, for what would turn out to be the first of Snooks Kelley's national-coaching-record 501 victories. Star of the game, with four goals, was Ray Funchion, a defenseman who rushed the puck in the fashion of the Bruins Eddie Shore.

Kelley's first team went on to turn in a respectable 3–2–1 season with both losses to Boston University. It was no doubt compensation of sorts that 4,000 turned out for the first Boston College-Boston University game since 1929, the Boston College exchequer being better able to absorb a loss on the ice than a loss at the gate.

By 1934, practice was still being held in the

early morning hours; Coach Kelley was still volunteering his services while working as a teacher, and the team was a dismal 2–7–1. Despite the hardships and losses, Boston College could put out a first team the equal of anyone's: Tim Ready was one of the best goaltenders in college hockey; Funchion, who teamed with John Ahern on defense, was an acknowledged star; and the entire first line of Fred Moore, Herb Crimlisk, and Frank Liddell were invited to play for University City Club in a post-season exhibition in Madison Square Garden. But hockey in the 1930s was becoming a game of frequent line changes and more tactically advanced coaching and increasing recruiting competition for the best schoolboy players.

Boston College hockey took a major step forward in 1935, when it was declared a major varsity sport, and players were once more entitled to earn letters. Kelley received some compensation, although not enough that he could leave his teaching post, and the schedule was strengthened to include three Ivy teams—Princeton, Dartmouth and Brown.

Northeastern and Brown fell in the first two games before Boston College went to Dartmouth for its first game in Hanover since the days of Leo Hughes. Dartmouth was the defending collegiate champion (though that was an unofficial title since there was not yet an NCAA championship playoff), and Boston College's 3–2 overtime win did as much as any single game since the hockey revival to help the Eagles regain stature as a national college hockey power. Defenseman Joe Walsh had two of the Boston College scores and Funchion added a third, but it was Tim Ready, another of the Cambridge Latin boys, who preserved the win with his goaltending. The season ended 7–3–0 and solidly reestablished hockey at the Heights.

The next hurdle confronting Boston College hockey was the same as that faced by several other city teams, notably Northeastern and Boston University—lack of an identifiable league. Their schedules were composed of a potpourri of Ivy League teams, eastern colleges, and local schools, but while a Boston College game against Boston University would sell out because of the obvious rivalry, games with MIT, Colgate, or St. Anselm's held little fan interest.

The problem of league affiliation was solved in 1937 when Boston College, Boston University, Northeastern, Colby, MIT, Middlebury, and the University of New Hampshire formed the New England Intercollegiate League. Standings were to be determined by winning percentage and an award, the Sands Trophy, was to be presented annually to the league champion.

Boston College won the first league title for the 1937–1938 season, with a record of 5–1–1 (8–4–1 overall) while being led by the smallest pair of forwards in the team's history—5′3″, 125–pound Peter Murphy and 5′5″, 125–pound Joe Hartigan. The latter led the team in scoring with fourteen goals, thirteen assists. More remarkable, Hartigan never had a penalty in his three-year varsity career. Supporting these small forwards was Bill "Lefty" Flynn, starting end on the football team and later Boston College's athletic director. In his senior year, 1938–1939, Flynn became the first Boston College player ever to score twenty goals and accumulate more than thirty points (goals plus assists) in one season. But Flynn's marks were soon to pale in the light of the achievements of hockey superstar, Ray Chaisson.

By the late 1930s, Boston College hockey had reached a plateau substantially above mediocrity but consistently and frustratingly below the national standard of excellence set by the Ivy League teams. For example, the 1938–1939 Boston College team went 9–7–0—but six of those losses (and none of the wins) were against Ivy competition. The Ivies, with their own rinks and traditional access to prep school stars (many prep schools also had their own rinks and therefore produced better players than the public or parochial schools) always seemed to be just out of reach. Ray Chaisson could reach them.

Chaisson was not a preppy star but yet another of the pit-'n'-pond players to come out of what was then the French-Canadian section of North Cambridge. As a schoolboy, he had caught the eye of and been beguiled by the considerably persuasive charms of Snooks Kelley.

"Ray Chaisson," insists Kelley to this day, "was the greatest Boston College hockey player of the pre-war era, and one of the three greatest of all time. And I'll tell you, there are people who saw him play that say he was the best ever."

Chaisson was the quintessential French-Canadian style player; his game was built on skating ability and a sixth sense for the net. In his freshman year, Kelley, who had a knack for the blending of lines, put Chaisson at center between Johnny Pryor and Al Dumond in a line that played together for three seasons and would become one of the best in college hockey.

In his first season, 1939–1940, Chaisson more than doubled Flynn's team scoring record with thirty-three goals and thirty-four assists for sixty-seven points—a single season mark that would stand for thirty years. However, while that team won the first of three consecutive New England League titles and finished 12–5–1, it recorded only one win over an Ivy League team, a 24–1 pounding of upstart Cornell. The Ivy League stranglehold wasn't broken until 1940–1941.

After an opening day loss to Yale, the 1940–1941 team finished the season with thirteen consecutive wins (and would run the streak to nineteen before losing to Dartmouth in 1942), including a victory over Princeton and two over Dartmouth. Chaisson had four goals in one of the Dartmouth games and picked up five points in Boston College's biggest win in fifteen years over Boston University, 12–3. "The greatest hockey team since the American championship clubs of 1923 and 1924," wrote Nat Hasenfus, who had seen all three teams play.

The players on the 1940–1941 team were good enough to attract the attention of the pros. The Boston Olympics, a Bruins farm team that played at the Arena, persuaded Chaisson, Dumond, and Bob Mee to play for the club at the end of the college season. The three players, unconcerned about college eligibility because they were virtually certain of being called up in the accelerating military draft, signed and played a few games for the Olympics. However, the wheels of conscription moved more slowly than anticipated, and, though the three were still enrolled at Boston College the next season, they were ineligible for hockey.

63

BC's 1940–1941 team was, at the time, adjudged to be the school's best since the 1923 "championship" club and included Ray Chaisson, whom coach Kelly calls "the greatest BC hockey player of the pre-war era." Pictured, from left: Chaisson, Al Dumond, captain John Pryor, Bob Mee, Hugh Sharkey, and Joe Maguire.

Adding to Coach Kelley's problems, Pryor had graduated and veteran Larry Houle had to leave hockey because of a head injury. Yet Kelley overcame all these difficulties to build another New England championship team, a club that also won the Amateur Athletic Union (AAU) national title and finished 12–2–0, the only losses to Dartmouth and Princeton. The stars of Kelley's hastily assembled aggregation were Wally Boudreau, a center who could also play defense; left wing Ralph Powers; and goalie Phil Carey, who accomplished a career high of fifty-two stops in a 5–3 win over Yale.

After clinching the New England college title in late February, Boston College decided to enter the largely club-dominated AAU championships to be held that year at Boston Arena. In an opening round game, the High Standard Hockey Club of New York found its standards not quite as high as Boston College's, the Eagles winning 3–2. Boston College went on to reach the championship final against the Messena (New York) Hockey Club where, after a 7–3 lead had slipped

to an 8–7 deficit, Boudreau scored with twenty seconds to play, forcing the game to overtime. Harry Crovo scored a goal to make it 9–8 Boston College, and the AAU national championship rested on the Heights.

Snooks Kelley did not know it at the time, but he would coach only one more game for the next four years. By the start of the 1942–1943 season, Kelley had joined the wartime Navy, his place as varsity coach taken by former freshman coach John Temple.

Boudreau and Carey remained on campus for the 1942–1943 season and they—with veteran James Edgeworth, whose fifteen goals led the team in scoring—took Boston College to a 9–2 season. A little-noted contribution of this team was its role in reestablishing athletic relations with Harvard; the Boston College hockey team met their Crimson peers in three unpublicized game-condition scrimmages. No scores or records were kept, but historian Hasenfus notes, "The gentlemanly type of play was a source of satisfaction to both college authorities and play-

64

ers. Had the war not made the sponsoring of hockey impossible, it is very likely that [Boston College and Harvard] would have scheduled contests in 1944."

Of course, the war did make it impossible. There was neither the time, money, nor manpower for hockey between 1943 and 1945, as America fought a war on two fronts, and the nation's colleges reduced their athletic programs and made their facilities available to the military.

Hockey enjoyed a limited revival in 1945–1946 when Father Joseph Glavin, as volunteer coach, and student John Buckley, as captain and organizer, put together a team that split a two-game series with Holy Cross and lost badly to Dartmouth, 11–0. But it would take the return to campus of Snooks Kelley to restore Boston College hockey to its pre-war stature.

It is a measure of Kelley's magnetism and reputation that candidates reported a record one hundred-strong to hockey tryouts at the Boston Skating Club in the fall of 1946. Among the hopefuls were several men, who, in three years, would take Boston College to its first *official* national collegiate championship. Defenseman Ed "Butch" Songin, center Warren Lewis, and goalie Bernie Burke were at the core of a team that would go 50–9–1 for the next three seasons.

Harvard appeared twice on the 1946–1947 schedule, with Boston College winning both games, 6–3 and 10–5 (there is no record of grandstand wars, holy or otherwise). Only Yale, Boston University, and the perenially strong Dartmouth could beat Boston College in the course of that 15–3–1 season.

By the late 1940s, the burgeoning NCAA was becoming increasingly involved in sponsorship of the official national collegiate championship tournaments. In 1947, the NCAA announced it would sponsor its first hockey championship to be held in March, 1948, at the Broadmoor Ice Palace in Colorado Springs. Here the two best teams from the West would meet the two best from the East in a two-game elimination playoff.

Boston College, by virtue of another New England League title, and Dartmouth, the Ivy League champion, represented the East against Canadian-dominated teams from Michigan and Colorado College. Underdog Boston College took Michigan into overtime before losing 6–4 in an opening round game (Michigan went on to win 8–4 over Dartmouth) in which Kelley's largely Boston-born team found itself skating against thirteen Canadian-born players. By the time he checked out of the Broadmoor, Snooks Kelley had reaffirmed in his own mind the principle that would be the cornerstone of his coaching philosophy:

> I decided early that one of the things I wanted to do at Boston College was to give the American boy the chance to compete with his brother from across the border. I never brought in a Canadian player. People have said I was anti-Canadian. I was never anti-Canadian. I was pro-American. Actually, I would have taken a Canadian player *if* I had found one willing to come here under the same terms and conditions that our other boys came here: no scholarships, early morning practices, all of the hardships. But most of them wanted a world with a fence around it. I was unprepared to give it to them. Most of the kids I had here were kids who came up the hard way. They had to work for everything they got. That's what I wanted. Now, there's nothing wrong, per se, with a Canadian boy going to school or playing hockey in the United States or even with an American coach going over the border to recruit him. What was wrong in a lot of these cases was that some of these boys were Canadian pros.

Kelley stood pat for 1948–1949, going basically with the same team he had had the year before, plus a few new faces such as sophomore star Lenny Ceglarski and the high-scoring Jack Mulhern. Songin, Lewis, and Burke were back, and the team rolled through its first nineteen games with only one loss—a 4–2 beating by Dartmouth that would prove to be the most fortunate defeat in the team's history.

"We went to the nationals again in 1949," Kelley remembers, "and we beat Colorado College 7–3 in the first game. Who should we meet for the national title but Dartmouth. I couldn't have picked a better team for us to play. I didn't even need a speech," he says, though let it be noted, he gave one anyway. "I reminded the boys that Dartmouth had put the only blemish on our

The 1948–1949 Eagles defeated Dartmouth in the NCAA championship game, for the most important victory in BC hockey history. Pictured: (standing, from left) manager Jack Connolly, assistant coach Jack Harvey, Ed Casey, Bill Walsh, Jack Talbot, Frank Shellanback, Red Ahearn, Ken Dooley, Norm Daily, trainer Larry Sullivan, and coach John Kelley; (seated, from left), Jack Mulhern, Walt Delorey, Len Ceglarski, Jack McIntire, Warren Lewis, captain Bernie Burke, Jim Fitzgerald, Giles Threadgold, Fran Harrington, Johnny Gallagher, and Butch Songin; and (kneeling) team mascot John Kelley, Jr.

record, and that now, by a strange twist of fate, we had a chance to get back at them."

Get back they did. Lewis gave Boston College a 1–0 lead and, though Dartmouth came back to take a 2–1 advantage into the second period, a Boston College power play goal by John McIntire tied the game, and the opportunistic Ceglarski jumped on a loose puck twelve feet out to send a backhander to the upper right hand corner for a 3–2 Boston College lead. Dartmouth tied the game in the third period only to have Lewis set up Jim Fitzgerald for the game winner, a three-foot stuff shot that went off the Dartmouth goalie's stick and dribbled into the net. The final thirteen minutes of the most important win in Boston College hockey history belonged to goalie Bernie Burke, who had a total of twenty-six saves in the game, and to Songin, who played almost the entire sixty-minute game on defense.

"Butch Songin, for his era, was the best defenseman Boston College ever had," says Kelley. "Even the people from Michigan and Colorado raved about him. Everyone said the same thing: 'There's a hockey player!'"

Songin, who was also a Boston College football standout, captained the 1949–1950 team that won nine games in a row before injuries to Lewis and Mulhern caused a three-losses-in-four-games tailspin that cost Boston College a third league championship. But 14–3–0 was good enough for second place in the East and another trip, along with New England champ Boston University, to the NCAAs—Boston College's third straight appearance in the championship playoffs.

Defenseman Walter Delorey picked up some of the slack left by an injured, but still playing, Songin, and scrappy forward Giles Threadgold emerged as one of the crowd pleasers of the tournament. However, in the end, neither Boston team proved a match for its western counterpart. Boston College lost both games, first to Colorado College, then to Michigan, and though Boston University, led by the immortal Jack Garrity, passed Michigan in the first round, the Terriers were hammered 13–4 by Colorado in the finals.

Boston College and Boston University, geographically separated by only three miles of Commonwealth Avenue asphalt, always had a

natural rivalry, a relationship that assumed classic proportions in 1950–1951. Despite the graduation of Lewis, Songin, and Burke, the Eagles still had a shot at the New England League title when they met Boston University at the Arena in the final game of the 1950–1951 regular season. Public attention centered on the matchup of Boston University's Garrity and Boston College scoring star Ceglarski (twenty-one goals, thirty-four points). The latter was the quintessential Kelley-style player, a boy possessed of such enormous desire that he once played several games with a broken nose and of whom Kelley says: "Lenny was one guy I never had to worry about. He'd do anything you asked him. He listened to every word I ever said, and he'd make any sacrifice just to play hockey."

Boston University won the game and with it the New England championship, 4–1. The star of the game was neither Garrity nor Ceglarski, but a journeyman Boston University defenseman named Jack Kelley (no relation to Snooks) who scored a goal and two assists. It was the same Jack Kelley who would return to Boston University twelve years later as head coach and whose rivalry with Boston College's Kelley would become one of the most intense and gentlemanly in eastern college hockey.

In the early 1950s, the college-hockey power

Ed "Butch" Songin, a triple-threat football-baseball-hockey star at Boston College in the late 1940s, was an outstanding hockey defenseman who often spent the full sixty-minute game on the ice.

centers of New England, Michigan, Minnesota, and Colorado, were joined by a bloc comprised of the formidable teams produced by three upper New York State colleges—Clarkson, St. Lawrence, and Rensselaer Polytechnic Institute (RPI). These schools formed their own league, the Tri-State League, and contended that the Tri-State champion deserved consideration for inclusion in the NCAA tournament. The eastern selection committee (they annually decided which teams would represent the East in the NCAA tournament) almost always selected the two teams with the best won-lost records. In 1951–1952, those teams were Boston University and Boston College, in that order. Boston College and Boston University players were practically packing their bags for Colorado Springs, when, in a surprise decision, the selection committee, chaired by Dartmouth coach Eddie Jeremiah, ordered a four-team playoff among Boston University (15–3–1), Boston College (15–3–0), Ivy League champion Yale (12–3–0), and Tri-State champion St. Lawrence (11–3–0), with the winners going West. The committee determined that it was too close a race to call.

Officials at Boston College and Boston University were outraged. Both schools refused to play again for the right they felt was theirs in the first place. Boston College's refusal read in part: "We believe this committee should name today the two eastern teams on the basis of their records . . . . the committee was appointed to select the eastern representatives to the NCAA tournament . . . Each member understood that he might be required to make a hard and difficult decision. The burden was on the committee [but] now it is being thrown back on the colleges."

Or, as one Boston University official put it, "How long do they want us to play? Until we lose?"

Nevertheless, the committee held firm. So did Boston College and Boston University. Yale and St. Lawrence went to Colorado Springs. Both lost in the first round.

The rise to All-America stardom of a gentlemanly senior center man with the unlikely name of Wellington "Wimpy" Burtnett and the steadily improving play of forward (later state representative) Sherman "Whip" Saltmarsh helped the 1952–1953 Eagles overcome graduation losses, two academic ineligibilities, and the loss of second-line center Joe Morgan to pro baseball and post an 11–4–1 record. But early season losses to Brown and Harvard put the team out of the NCAA tournament picture.

That loss to Harvard, which seemed like just another game at the time, took place in the first game of a little impromptu city tournament, a tournament that twenty-eight years later, *Sports Illustrated* would suggest outweighed in prestige the NCAA championship. The first annual Beanpot Hockey Tournament was an attempt by Boston Garden-Arena President Walter Brown to hype slumping college hockey attendance by booking a double-header in the Arena featuring the city's four major teams: Boston College, Boston University, Harvard, and Northeastern. If two teams could not fill the building, and in those days they could not, perhaps fans from four schools would.

On December 26, 1952, 5,105 (close, but not a capacity crowd) attended the first round of the Beanpot, where they saw Harvard beat Boston College 3–2 on Walt Greeley's goal (the Boston College goals were made by Saltmarsh and Frank O'Grady), and Boston University beat Northeastern 4–1. Boston College came back to beat Northeastern for third place honors, while Harvard won the tournament that would soon move into the 13,909–seat Boston Garden and become what Snooks Kelley would call "a tournament unique in all of hockey—the only place to be on the first two Mondays of February when these boys play for all the beans in Boston."

It was not always thus. In fact, a man of lesser faith in hockey than Walter Brown might have abandoned the Beanpot concept after a mere 711, barely detectable in cavernous Boston Garden, paid to see Boston College beat Northeastern 8–5 and Harvard nip Boston University 3–2 in the first round of the 1953 tournament. This set up the championship match with the best box office appeal, Boston College vs. Harvard. Even this rivalry drew poorly, attracting only 2,399. In that game Boston College center Bobby Babine scored an unassisted goal at 16:51 of the first period to give Boston College a 3–1 lead, and the Eagles held on to win 4–1 for the team's first Beanpot championship. Babine shared tourney MVP honors with teammate Jim Duffy, who scored the first and last Boston College goals.

The next season Boston College was 17–2, and secured its fourth trip to the championship playoffs in Colorado Springs, along with RPI. Boston College had lost only to Clarkson and St. Lawrence, and the team, led by Babine and defenseman Bob Kiley, was given a good chance of bringing a national title back to the East. However, in a first-round game against Canadian-laden Minnesota, Boston College gave up six first period goals and finally took 14–1 shellacking, falling before the superior skating and more physical game typical of the western college team. Ironically, eastern hockey's leading exponent of take-the-body physicality was RPI coach Ned Harkness, and his tough RPI team beat Minnesota in overtime that year to become the first eastern college since Boston College to annex the NCAA title.

The regular season schedule was expanded again in 1954–1955, this time to twenty–two games that included home-and-home series with each team in the Tri-State League. Best of the lot was a penalty-filled (twenty–one calls in all, eleven against Boston College), 5–3 win over defending national champion RPI that drew 4,500 to the Arena. Dick Michaud scored two of the Boston College goals, and goalie Chuck D'Entremont played one of the best games of his three-year varsity career. The rematch at RPI drew 7,500, Boston College winning again 5–3 in a less violent game.

In February, 1955, the future of the Beanpot went on the line, as another poor showing at the gate might have doomed the tournament. It was rescued by a Harvard-Boston College final that brought a record 5,664 to the Garden. The fans got what they came for. With the game tied 4–4 in overtime and Harvard killing a penalty, Crimson star Bill Cleary picked off a loose puck inside the Boston College blue line, beat the Boston College defense, and faked out D'Entremont for the game winner. Boston College also had its hero in captain Dick Dempsey, who had scored

only three goals all year but came up with two in the final 1:09 of regulation to force the overtime, the last goal coming with only six seconds left in the game.

Controversy again beset eastern college hockey in 1955–1956, with a brouhaha over the playing of freshmen on the already-powerful teams of the Tri-State League. Boston College, like all other eastern colleges except the New York schools, as a matter of college and NCAA policy, did not play freshmen on the varsity; instead they maintained separate freshman hockey programs. The combined use of freshmen and Canadian recruits was fast putting Clarkson and St. Lawrence into a class by themselves. For example, except for a late-season loss to Harvard, the Boston College team of 1955–1956 beat every team on its schedule, except Clarkson and St. Lawrence to whom the Eagles lost *both* ends of the home-and-home series. So wide was the gap that D'Entremont once faced sixty shots in a 5–3 loss to Clarkson.

In the 1956 Beanpot, Captain Ed Carroll (later Boston College associate athletic director), leading scorer Ed Quinn (thirteen goals), and centers Jim Tiernan and Joe Moylan took Boston College to another title and to the generally accepted status of "best team east of upper New York state." It appeared that Clarkson and St. Lawrence were automatic choices as the eastern teams in the NCAAs—until the NCAA itself stepped in and enforced its no-freshmen rule. The NCAA could suggest, but could not set, athletic policy for a member institution; however, the NCAA did control the rules pertaining to its sanctioned championships. The New York schools had a choice: drop the freshmen, or stay home. St. Lawrence took its freshmen off the roster, Clarkson refused to budge.

So Boston College, as the third best eastern team, was named to replace Clarkson and to join St. Lawrence in the 1956 NCAA tourney. Alas, neither team could abolish the supremacy of the western schools. Boston College lost 10–4 to Michigan Tech in the first round, while Michigan beat St. Lawrence 2–1. For the final indignity, St. Lawrence did not need its freshmen to beat Boston College 6–2 in the consolation.

The first two Mondays of February are sacrosanct on the calendar of any serious Boston area sports fan. These are the traditional dates of the Beanpot Tournament, the round-robin in which the area's four NCAA Division I hockey powers—Boston College, Boston University, Harvard, and Northeastern—vie for bragging rights to the city.

The Beanpot is widely and justifiably known as one of the toughest tickets in town. "In January I stop answering my phone," says former Boston College coach Snooks Kelley. "I know it's going to be someone asking 'Hey, Coach, can you do anything for me for the Beanpot?' " Adds another college official who is also deluged with requests for often non-existent tickets: "And they always tell you, 'I'll pay for them.' I feel like saying, 'You will? Gee, thanks.' "

Such is the fervor of Beanpot fans that 11,666 showed up February 6, 1978, during the famous blizzard of 1978. The storm closed roads, stopped trains, and immobilized trolleys. Yet thousands of fans stayed through the games and then happily sought shelter in downtown hotels or, in many cases, stayed overnight in Boston Garden for the privilege of seeing first-round Beanpot action. Such was the severity of the blizzard that the final round would not be played until March.

Nor was interest allayed by a 1979 ECAC rules change that meant tournament games no longer counted toward playoff eligibility. The Beanpot continued to sell out (sometimes save for a few obstructed view seats) and the competing teams continued to make victory in the Beanpot one of the season's three major goals. The other two were to gain the ECAC playoffs and the NCAA tournament. "And hockey aside," says Kelley, "the Beanpot has also become a *social* obligation for anyone connected with hockey."

The first Beanpot tournament was held in 1952 at the Boston Arena and was little more than an effort by Boston Garden-Arena president Walter Brown to hype slumping college hockey attendance by seeing if four teams would outdraw the standard two. After a rocky start—the first championship round drew 3,382, while the 1953 first-round drew a record low

711—the tournament grew steadily to its present prestigious status.

Competition is generally close and unpredictable. Although Northeastern had to wait until 1980 before winning its first Beanpot, the other three colleges are closely grouped in total victories. Boston University leads with twelve titles, Boston College is second with nine, and Harvard is a close third with eight. Boston College brought the silver Beanpot to Chestnut Hill in 1954, 1956, 1957, 1959, 1961, 1963, 1964, 1965 and 1976, and reached the finals on seven other occasions.

Francis O'Grady won a niche for himself in Boston College hockey history by scoring the Eagles' first Beanpot goal, December 26, 1952 (the first tournaments were not played on Mondays in February) in a 3–2 first-round loss to Harvard. Since then, several Boston College stars have put their names in the Beanpot record book: Boston College's Joe Mullen is the tournament's career goal scoring leader with ten through his four-year career, 1976–1979; Richie Smith (1973–1975) is tied with Harvard's Joe Cavanaugh as the tournament's career assist leader with twelve; Billy Daley holds the single-game assist record of six, picked up in a 15–1 bombing of Northeastern in 1961; Tim Sheehy is the tournament's second all-time high scorer, with sixteen points on nine goals, seven assists (three points behind leader Cavanaugh); goalie Jim Barton holds the record for most saves in one game with fifty-two in a 5–4 loss to Boston University in 1970; while Paul Skidmore holds the record for career saves with 235 recorded between 1976 and 1979.

Seven Boston College players have been chosen Beanpot MVP: Bobby Babine, 1955; James Tiernan, 1956; Joe Celeta, 1957; Jim Logue, 1959; Billy Hogan, 1961 and 1963; John Cunniff, 1964 and 1965; and Paul Skidmore, 1976.

But perhaps the most impressive record compiled over four decades of Beanpot play is not held by a player, coach, or team but by Boston's rabid college hockey fans—nearly 630,000 have turned out to watch their teams play for what Snooks Kelley calls "all the beans in Boston."

Coach Len Ceglarski holds the Beanpot Trophy during the ceremony following BC's triumph in the 1976 tournament. With Ceglarski are Mrs. Edward Powers, widow of former Garden president; and players Richie Smith (left) and Mark Albrecht.

By 1956 it was evident that Boston College needed more than the best of the Boston-area schoolboy hockey crop to bridge the gap between it and the feared Tri-State teams. Ice time was still a problem. It was expensive; there was never enough of it, and what there was came at strange hours in a rink halfway across Boston. Since the 1920s, Boston College had shared Boston Arena practice ice with rivals Boston University, Northeastern, Harvard, and various other tenants, including two Boston schoolboy leagues. By the mid-fifties, it was evident that Boston College needed a rink of its own.

Harvard opened its Watson Rink for the 1956–1957 season and immediately offered mute but compelling testimony to the value of unlimited prime-time practice ice. Harvard joined Clarkson and St. Lawrence as the only teams to beat Boston College twice in the 1956–1957 season (though not in the Beanpot, which Boston College won again with victories over Boston University and Northeastern).

At first, talks among Snooks Kelley, athletic director Bill Flynn, and the Boston College administration headed by Fr. Joseph N. Maxwell found Flynn and Kelley leaning toward a large, multi-use indoor auditorium while the administration seemed more inclined to put up a basic ice-and-boards outdoor facility. The rink Flynn wanted and Kelley needed would cost about $1.8 million; the rink Father Maxwell was willing to pay for would have cost $25,000. Flynn persisted, arguing that a 4,000–seat arena could be a revenue producer and that the scarcity of rinks in Boston would virtually guarantee ice rentals almost around the clock, while Kelley noted its appeal as a recruiting and training tool.

In the end, Father Maxwell accepted the argument that a first-class indoor rink was a better investment than a third-class outdoor rink. On the final day of his tenure as president, Father Maxwell signed the order authorizing the construction of a $1.8 million rink which already had a name—"Flynn's Folly."

Even as talks continued, the need for the finished rink was being dramatically and painfully underscored. The 1956–1957 team slipped to a sub-par, though still respectable 14–7–1—fourth in the East and out of the national playoff picture. Again the team came up two-time losers to Harvard, Clarkson, and St. Lawrence. The biggest win of the season was a 5–4 overtime victory over Boston University on a goal by Joe Celato that brought Boston College another Beanpot title.

The next season was worse. Boston College, still rinkless, slipped to 9–12–2, its first losing season since 1946 and Snooks Kelley's first losing season since 1934. Again the team dropped two games each to Harvard and Clarkson, and only the consistently excellent play of goalie Al Pitts saved Boston College from a double whammy by St. Lawrence. Pitts had forty-nine saves—seventeen of them in a frantic third period and five of those on breakaways—to shut out St. Lawrence 1–0 (the goal by Ron Walsh) at the Arena and then backstopped another Boston College win, 2–1, against the Larries in New York. Pitts, who in this season of frustration earned his place with Tim Ready and Bernie Burke as one of Boston College's best goalies of all-time, also established a personal high fifty-nine-save game in a 5–3 win over NCAA tournament-bound Boston University.

"I don't think most people would mention Al Pitts on a list of great goalies, but he belongs there," said Kelley. "He is an underrated hard worker. He'd be out there a half hour before practice getting anybody he could to shoot at him."

But personal accomplishment does not replace team achievement or overcome a losing bottom line. So, while Kelley suffered, he also sold. There was a rink going up on the Boston College campus, right down there behind the football stands, and Kelley made sure area schoolboys knew about it. One particular object of Kelley's salesmanship was Cambridge schoolboy sensation Tom "Red" Martin.

"I wanted him," says Kelley, "but I knew who else wanted him, too. Harvard wanted him. Badly. Red just about had the run of the rink over there. They'd let him skate any time the varsity wasn't using the ice. I think he had his own key. But I kept talking to him about Boston College and a Catholic education and the new

Three of coach Snooks Kelley's finest player/captains meet at a 1960 social affair (and not just to admire the then-newest style of goalie mask). From left: Tom "Red" Martin, standout defenseman on BC's fine teams of the early 1960s; Bill Hogan, the BC senior class president who singlehand-edly revived hockey in 1932 and talked Kelley into coaching the team; and Bernie Burke, captain and goalie for the 1948–1949 NCAA national championship squad.

rink, and when the time came, Red Martin en-rolled at Boston College."

Defenseman Martin enrolled with three other major local stars—center Bill Daley of Wellesley, goalie Jim Logue of Melrose, and forward Owen Hughes of Canton. And while the varsity was losing, the Martin-led freshmen were winning. "If Butch Songin was the best defenseman of the forties," says Kelley, "then Red Martin was the best of the fifties. He could shoot, stickhandle, pass, rush the puck, and play sixty minutes a game if you needed him."

On November 29, 1958, before a capacity crowd of 4,200—including Boston's Richard Cardinal Cushing, watching his first Boston Col-lege hockey game—Bill Daley scored in the first minute of play to spark a 3–1 win over Harvard in the dedication game for the new rink called McHugh Forum. "Flynn's Folly," which became one of the most modern and comfortable rinks in college hockey, was now officially named after Reverend Patrick McHugh, S.J., dean of the col-lege during the cash-short days of the 1920s.

Coincidentally, the 1958–1959 season also sup-plied Kelley with one of the best young teams of his thirty-six-year tenure. With Martin playing alongside veteran defenseman Joe Jangro of Melrose and leading the team with forty points

(3 goals, 37 assists), Daley scoring twenty-three goals, and Kelley supplying his team with two hours a day of practice ice, Boston College went 19–7–0. They won another Beanpot and earned another trip to the NCAA tournament.

For the first time, the playoffs came East. The tournament was played in RPI's home rink in Troy, New York, with Boston College and St. Lawrence representing the East, North Dakota and Michigan State the West. Boston College drew Michigan State in the first round. Trailing 4–1 in the third period, the Eagles seemed headed for another routine West-beats-East hu-miliation until goals by Daley and Bob Leonard made the score 4–3. With Martin playing hockey's equivalent of "point guard," Boston College dominated the closing minutes of play but couldn't manage to score again. North Dakota won the title, and Boston College took some measure of consolation in a 7–6 double overtime win over St. Lawrence on a goal by John Cusack.

Jangro was named to the All-Tournament team, and he, Martin, Daley, and Logue were selected All-New England. Snooks Kelley, archi-tect of one of the fastest and most successful turn-arounds in Boston College sports history, was voted "Coach of the Year" by the Amercian Hockey Coaches Association.

Full houses were the rule at McHugh Forum as Martin and Daley led the 1959–1960 Eagles to a winning (20–8–0) season and a place in a new ECAC-sanctioned post-season playoff held

Wellesley's Billy Daley became the Eagles' all-time leading scorer while playing defense on the crack teams of 1958–1961. Among other ca-reer highlights, Daley scored the first goal ever in McHugh Forum, in November, 1958.

to determine the two eastern representatives to the NCAAs. Boston College lost its first-round playoff game 4–3 to St. Lawrence at Canton, N.Y. before a crowd of 4,000 that included the Boston College band and hundreds of fans who had made the trip. College hockey was big-time again, and not just at Boston College. The largest crowd to see a college hockey game since before World War II—10,909—set a Beanpot attendance record for the semifinal round, wherein Boston College lost to a BU club headed by all-America Bob Marquis.

Hockey's popularity grew through the 1960s. A standing room crowd of 4600 turned out at McHugh Forum to watch Boston College play to a 1–1 tie with RPI and a similar mob jammed the rink for the team's 5–3 win over a Clarkson club coached by Len Ceglarski. Martin continued to control the tempo of games from his left point position while Daley set a team record 74 points (16 better than Ray Chaisson's 1941 mark) on 33 goals and 41 assists, to give him the team's all-time scoring leadership with 153 career points.

No matter how good the present, Snooks Kelley continued to plan for the future. Accordingly, he recruited another highly coveted Boston schoolboy star in Billy Hogan, Jr. of Belmont Hill, son of the man who, 29 years earlier, had talked then-schoolteacher Kelley into trying his hand at coaching. "Billy Hogan was probably the most intelligent player I ever coached," says Kelley. "He was always in the right place. He had a knack for the puck and for knowing where a play was going."

Seldom was Hogan Jr. in as many right places as the night of February 13, 1961, when he scored the first goal of the Beanpot final and then assisted on the next two (by Martin and Jack Leetch), as Boston College won the title 4–2 over Harvard before another record crowd—13,909, the Garden's first college hockey sellout in 30 years. The band played "For Boston" as Boston College fans littered the ice with streamers and Bruins president Walter Brown handed the Beanpot trophy to Kelley. As Kelley accepted the trophy a gravel-voiced fan in the balcony shouted, "The Bruins can't match this."

Another thing the Bruins could not match—

and very few teams could even dream about—was the Eagles rewarding their coach with his 300th career win, 10–2 over Dartmouth, on February 9, 1961. The day after the game, Dartmouth coach Eddie Jeremiah, Kelley's longtime friend and the coach who himself had 290 career wins, telegrammed Snooks:

"You bigamist. Wedded 25 years to Boston College hockey and 20 years to Marge. A triangle that bloomed beautifully for the mutual benefit and happiness of all three. Heartiest congratulations."

Logue, Martin and Daley graduated in 1961 and went on to play with the United States National team. Typically, Kelley replaced locals with more locals. The entire 1961–1962 team, save for Gloucester's Paul Lufkin, came from towns within the confines of Boston's circumferential highway, Route 128.

Paul Aiken (Arlington), Leetch (Braintree) and Hogan (Belmont) became one of the best Boston College lines since the Chaisson-Pryor-Dumond line. Malden's Charlie Driscoll took over for Logue in goal and, while it would be years before anyone could fully replace Red Martin on defense, East Boston's Jack Callahan and Charlestown's Rod O'Connor played well enough to help get the team back into the ECAC playoffs. Key to the 1961–1962 season was a February 24 game against an undefeated Colby team led by Ron Ryan, then the highest scorer in the history of college hockey. Boston College needed a win for a playoff spot. They got it when Billy Hogan scored four goals (including the equalizer and the winner) to go with goals by captain George Grant and Charlie McCarthy, to give Boston College a 6–5 win. The team finished the season 15–13–1, including a 9–4 playoff loss to old nemesis St. Lawrence. But, with only three seniors (Grant, McCarthy and Bucky Warren) it seemed reasonable that Boston College should apply for and be awarded the honor of hosting the 1963 NCAA championships. There was a good chance they would be dancing at their own party.

Aiken, Hogan, and Leetch were back. Sophomore Ralph Toran strengthened the defense, and Driscoll's place in goal was taken by Arlington's Tommy Aprille, another in the succession of outstanding Boston College goalies. Led by Leetch's twenty-seven goals and Hogan's forty assists, fifty-nine points, Boston College went 20–7–1 through the regular season. The biggest win being a 3–1 victory over Harvard for the team's sixth Beanpot championship in a game so exciting that visiting New York Rangers coach Red Sullivan said, "I didn't know that American [college] hockey could be so rough, so good, and so spirited. This was like the seventh game of a Stanley Cup final." The cheer from the Boston College band for most of the night was "Beat Holy Cross. Who ever heard of Harvard."

Boston College and Clarkson emerged as eastern representatives to face North Dakota and Denver as the NCAA tournament moved to McHugh Forum. However, the opening match might have been more accurately billed as "Tommy Aprille vs. North Dakota," as the Fighting Sioux, eventual tourney winners, took forty-seven shots on the Boston College net in a 4–2 win. The consolation game consoled no one at the Heights—Boston College lost to Clarkson 5–3.

"I never heard of John Cunniff until about 1960, when a fireman who lived in South Boston and had an interest in John brought him to see me and told me, 'This kid's a hockey player,'" says Snooks Kelley.

After a post-graduate year at Cambridge's New Prep, where he played for ex-Boston College star Owen Hughes, Cunniff, the hardnose kid from Southie, came to Chestnut Hill where he made the varsity in his sophomore year (1963–1964) and immediately established himself as one of the team's all-time great scorers.

As a sophomore wing he led the team in goals with twenty-seven, assists with twenty-five, and points with fifty-seven, including a four-goal game in a 6–5 Beanpot win over Boston University. Cunniff also netted both scores in a 3–2 ECAC playoff loss to RPI that closed out an 18–10–1 season.

Cunniff continued another year in 1964–1965, scoring thirty-one goals while teammate Phil Dyer of Melrose racked up a then-record forty-three assists. Together, they led the Eagles to a 20–6–0 regular season, a Beanpot championship, and another berth in the ECAC playoffs. Boston College roared through the playoffs, concluding with victories over Clarkson and Brown, to win another spot in the NCAA tournament held that year at Brown's new Meehan Auditorium.

After years of frustration, Boston College finally beat a western team, eliminating North Dakota 4–3 in the semifinals on two goals by Jerry York and singles by Cunniff and Dick Fuller. Most observers rated North Dakota a tougher foe than finalist Michigan Tech, but the Engineers had an All-America goalie in Tony Esposito (now with the Chicago Black Hawks and brother of ex-Black Hawk, Bruin, and Ranger Phil Esposito), who shut out the Eagles for two periods and backstopped his team to an 8–2 championship win.

Still, it was a good year for Boston College and a great one for Cunniff. The slick wingman was voted All-America, All-New England, All-East, and New England MVP as a *junior*.

Meanwhile, hockey in general was proliferating more rapidly than ever during the mid-1960s, spreading from the high schools down to

John Cunniff came out of South Boston, via Cambridge's New Prep, to become one of BC's all-time great scorers. Here, he receives the 1964 Beanpot MVP trophy from ex-Eagle star Billy Hogan, following Cunniff's four-goal effort in a 6–5 defeat of Boston University.

the younger set. Municipal and private rinks were being constructed throughout eastern Massachusetts, and community-sponsored youth hockey programs were expanding so rapidly that this era is popularly referred to as the "hockey boom." Bobby Orr's magnetic presence on the Bruins only helped fuel the popular fires.

One product of the youth hockey system was Melrose's Paul Hurley, a high scoring defenseman whose Melrose High School teams so dominated the tough Middlesex League that the town took to calling itself "Hockey Town, USA." Everyone wanted Hurley; Snooks Kelley, with his unfailing knack for recruiting Irish Catholics, got him.

"Paul the Shot," is what Kelley calls him to this day. "He had the hardest shot you've ever seen in a high school hockey player, and one of the hardest in college," says Kelley. In 1965, Hurley played his first Boston College varsity game, a match with RPI, and lived up to his nickname by blazing home a slapshot goal in a 9–0 Boston College win.

"I've seen the puck come to Hurley on his backhand side, and instead of taking a backhander or bringing the puck to his forehand, Paul would *switch hands* on the stick—shoot from his off side—and the puck would still go a hundred miles an hour," says Kelley. This feat is sufficiently rare as to have been done by only one professional player, Gordie Howe, and not very often even by him.

The 1966 season had the markings of a championship year until a shoulder separation cost Cunniff fourteen games. While Jerry York—a sleeper out of Boston College High who had not been heavily recruited—took up some of the scoring slack, tying Jim Mullen for the team scoring lead with twenty–one goals, Boston College dropped to a so-so 16–12 season, the fourteenth win of which was Kelley's four hundredth coaching victory. Again, the victim was Eddie Jeremiah's Dartmouth, the team Kelley's club had beaten for win number three hundred and for the 1949 NCAA title.

Boston College's record was good enough for a sixth-place finish in the ECAC regular season and a spot in the playoffs (top eight teams qualify). Here, the Eagles lost 9–0 to Cornell with, Cunniff, York, and "Paul the Shot" shut out by the Big Red's great goalie, Ken Dryden.

To help compensate for Cunniff's graduation, Kelley moved Hurley to wing for 1966–1967, teaming him on a line with York and David "Whitey" Allen of Winchester. Hurley responded by leading the team in goals with thirty-two, while York's forty-one assists and sixty-seven points led the team in those departments and helped York win All-America honors.

"Here was a kid, this Jerry York, who never got a scholarship. Who paid to come here. Who nobody else really wanted all that much. Who only asked me for a chance to play. Watching Jerry York work so hard that he made himself All-America was one of my greatest satisfaction's in coaching," says Kelley.

Less satisfying was another ECAC playoff loss, 12–2 to Dryden and Cornell. But Kelley, as usual, had planned two seasons ahead. In December 1967, Kelley unveiled the most highly recruited American-born hockey player up to this time, a boy from far beyond the asphalt border of Route 128 and the grounds that, heretofore, had been Kelley's prime recruiting area. Tim Sheehy of International Falls, Minnesota, was a "can't miss" kid who didn't.

"I was reading about him in some magazine," says Kelley in a story that might contain a touch of blarney, "and after reading that he was all-everything in Minnesota, there was one other thing that caught my eye—he was the head altar boy in his church. So I got on a plane and went to International Falls. Thirty degrees below zero. I thought I'd come to the end of the earth."

Sheehy, it turned out, was the nephew of football great Bronco Nagurski. It was Uncle Bronco himself who was calling the shots.

"The family picked me up at the airport," Kelley continues, "and we drove to this gas station called 'Bronco's.' I met Bronco—biggest man I ever saw in my life—and he asked me a few questions about Boston College. He said the family wanted a Catholic education for Tim. So I'm telling him about the school and all of sudden he stands up, grabs my hand and says, 'Kels, you got him!'"

In his first varsity year (1967–1968), Sheehy led the team in every scoring category: twenty-seven goals, thirty assists, and fifty-seven points. Along with Sheehy, Kelley had acquired West Point transfer right-wing Paul Schilling, left-wing Tom Snyder of New York City, and Arlington's Charlie Toczylowski, son of Henry Toczylowski of Boston College's Sugar Bowl football team.

It was one of Kelley's vintage teams, despite the absence of Paul Hurley, who took a year off to play with the United States Olympic team, and it was almost enough. In the ECAC playoffs, the Eagles downed St. Lawrence in overtime on Schilling's goal and beat Clarkson in double overtime on Sheehy's goal before meeting Dryden and Cornell again and losing 6–3. Second in the East was good enough for another trip to the NCAAs, held that year in Duluth, where Boston College lost 4–1 to the eventual national champion, Denver, a club skating just one American.

In 1968–1969, with Mike Flynn captain (his father, Bill, captained the 1938 football team), with Hurley back for his delayed senior year and with Sheehy now a bona fide All-America candidate, the Eagles had the talent to win every game. Except the ones that counted most.

After winning six in a row to start the season, the Eagles lost 6–3 to Cornell in the ECAC Christmas Tournament, 7–4 to Loyola in the Montreal Forum's Centennial Tournament, 4–2 to Boston University in the Beanpot finals, and 4–2 to Clarkson in the first round of the ECAC playoffs. All of which added up to an outstanding season record (19–7–0) but with little to show save Sheehy's selection as All-America.

The next season brought more of the same. Sheehy scored twenty-eight goals, forty assists for sixty-eight points to top Bill Daley by thirty-two points on the list of Boston College's all-time career scoring leaders. Yet, again, the team faltered in tournament games, losing to St. Lawrence in the first round of the Madison Square Garden Christmas Tournament, to Boston University in the first round of the Beanpot, and to Harvard in the first round of the ECACs. Sheehy repeated as All-America and sophomore defenseman Tom Mellor was named All-New England. These honors and a 19–7 record

Tim Sheehy was a two-time All-American who set a new career scoring at BC in the late 1960s. He was also exceptional in that, as a native of International Falls, Minnesota, he was one of the few non-Bostonians ever recruited by Snooks Kelley.

Woburn's Ed Kenty was the star of an inexperienced 1970–1971 BC team that suffered the Eagles' first losing hockey season in thirteen years. Kenty also scored a key goal in the most memorable victory of Snooks Kelley's coaching career.

momentarily belied the fact that the bottom was about to drop out.

In 1970–1971, an inexperienced team containing only three seniors—and without Sheehy and Schilling, both of whom had graduated—struggled through an 11–15 season, the first losing year since 1957–1958 and the first time in ten years Boston College finished out of post-season play. One of the few bright spots in the by now murky hockey picture was the play of 6′4″ 205-pound sophomore wing Ed Kenty of Woburn, Massachusetts and Malden Catholic high school who led the team with twenty–five goals, forty–eight points.

By now the question had to be asked (though not too loudly) when would John Kelley be stepping down? The most successful and widely beloved coach in college hockey was not a young man anymore. Kelley was in his 60s, forty years or more older than his players, all of whom were former high school stars, none of whom had ever had to pay the price of a 3:00 A.M. practice or

of solitary workouts in flooded and frozen construction site pits.

"Life is two sets of homes (jerseys) and two sets of aways," Kelley once said in sarcastic reference to the relatively cushy life of a modern-day hockey player. "Nowadays if you told a college team they had to practice at three in the morning, the players would think you were crazy. The only ones who'd come would be the guys on their way home from wherever they were the night before."

In 1971, Kelley was thirteen wins shy of his five hundredth, a plateau he was by no means certain of reaching in what projected to be an uncertain 1971–1972 season. No matter. Snooks called his own shot, and he chose not to make it easy on himself. He announced before the season that he would retire at the end of the year, five hundred wins or no five hundred wins.

Star defenseman Tom Mellor left Boston College to join the Olympic team, silver medalists in Sapporo, Japan, and Boston College struggled

78

through a win-one/lose-one type of year that by late February saw Kelley still two games shy of win number five hundred with just five games left to play. The Eagles beat Dartmouth 6–5 for number 499 and then came home for a February 23 Saturday night game against Jack Kelley's national champion (20–1–1) Boston University Terriers, the seemingly unbeatable Red Meanies of Commonwealth Avenue. No way, went the prognoses; Snooks would have to wait for the next home game against Army.

But for once the lamb killed the butcher. What the *Globe* referred to as an "overwhelmingly inspired" Boston College hockey team was actually leading Boston University 5–4 early in the third period, when Boston University defenseman Bob Brown beat Boston College's sophomore goalie, Ned Yetten, to tie the score—confirming Boston University's reputation as a great third-period team. But not on this night. Just 1:01 after Brown's goal, Kenty converted a Jim King pass for a 6–5 Boston College lead. With the band playing *For Boston* and the capacity crowd chanting "Snooks! Snooks! Snooks!" Boston College played bar-the-door defensive hockey. With less than a minute to play, Boston University turned up the heat, pulling goalie Tim Regan in favor of an extra attacker, only to have Kenty score

into the empty net for a 7–5 victory and Kelley's five hundredth win.

The band dropped *For Boston* and switched to *The Impossible Dream,* and the chants of "Snooks!" kept coming down from the stands. Boston University's Jack Kelley embraced his longtime rival at center ice and called his team's defeat "a tremendous victory for Boston College." Snooks Kelley, for once in his loquacious life, was virtually speechless, save for an occasional sniffle and some all-purpose remark about how "everybody had a part in it."

As writer Jim Sarni would say in a special edition of the *Boston College Sports Review* published to honor Kelley, "This was McHugh Forum, the House that Snooks built, and this was his night. And the stars would spell out his name above the towers on the Heights."

Having had a year to find Kelley's successor (one could hardly say "replacement"), Bill Flynn selected the man who very likely would have been Kelley's personal choice: Len Ceglarski, Boston College '51, who, in fourteen years as head coach at Clarkson, compiled a 255–97–10 record. Ceglarski returned to Boston College and immediately ushered in a season of revival.

Though he had recruited many Canadian players at Clarkson and had the freedom to do

Len Ceglarski was Bill Flynn's choice to succeed—not replace—Snooks Kelley in 1972. Ceglarski (shown here behind the Eagles' bench in Boston Garden) was a star on BC's 1948–1949 national championship team and had coached Clarkson to college hockey success.

so at Boston College, Ceglarski continued the Kelley policy of Americans-only and Bostonians-preferably. Also, a new NCAA rule made freshmen eligible, and Ceglarski quickly exploited this to play center Ed Reardon of Charlestown and Matignon High School, right wing Tom Songin (Butch's son) of Walpole, defenseman Paul O'Neill of Framingham, and the best of an outstanding lot, center Richie Smith of Natick. O'Neill would lead the team in scoring as a freshman (twenty-seven goals, fifty-eight points) and would become the team's all-time leading scorer over his four-year career.

In his first season on the Boston College bench, Ceglarski fashioned the third best record in Boston College hockey history, 22–7–1, went to the finals of the ECACs, losing 3–2 to Cornell, and took his team to the NCAAs where, as usual, West was best and Denver beat the Eagles 10–4. The Boston College resurgence was so impressive that the American Hockey Coaches Association voted Ceglarski "Coach of the Year."

The graduation loss of defenseman Tom Mellor left Ceglarski with a still powerful offense—led by Smith and Scituate's Bob Ferriter—but without much defense for the 1973–1974 season. This turned into a curious 16–12–0 year in which Boston College beat four playoff-bound teams (Boston University, Harvard, Dartmouth, and Providence), yet failed to make the playoffs itself. The slide continued and worsened the next season as Ceglarski came an 11–15–2 cropper and attendance began to drop off. After one stretch of eight games without a win, an all-time low of 1,200 showed up at McHugh Forum for a January 28, 1975, game against Yale.

It was obvious that Ceglarski had to do something and do it fast. Consistent with the "no-Canadians" policy but representing somewhat of a departure from Snooks Kelley's more parochial recruiting tradition, Ceglarski dipped into New York and Illinois to bring in three players who formed the foundation of another Boston College hockey renaissance. In an outstanding recruiting coup, Ceglarski attracted forward Joe Mullen of New York City's Power Memorial High School (heretofore best known for producing basketball star Kareem Abdul Jabbar nee Lew Alcindor), goalie Paul Skidmore of Smithtown, New York—a friend of Mullen's when the two played in the New York City Junior Hockey League—and 6'3", 210-pound defenseman Joe Augustine of Chicago, Illinois.

After losing its first three games in the

Key to the Eagles' third-best-ever 1972–1973 record and to rookie helmsman Ceglarski, winning collegiate coach-of-the-year honors, was center Richie Smith of Natick. By the time he graduated in 1976, Smith was BC's all-time leading scorer.

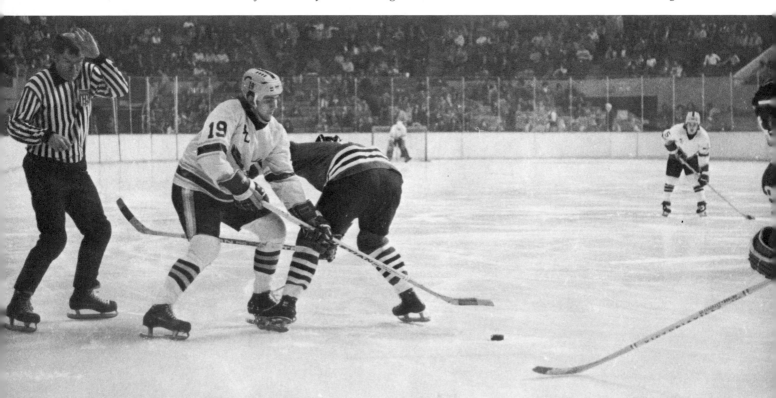

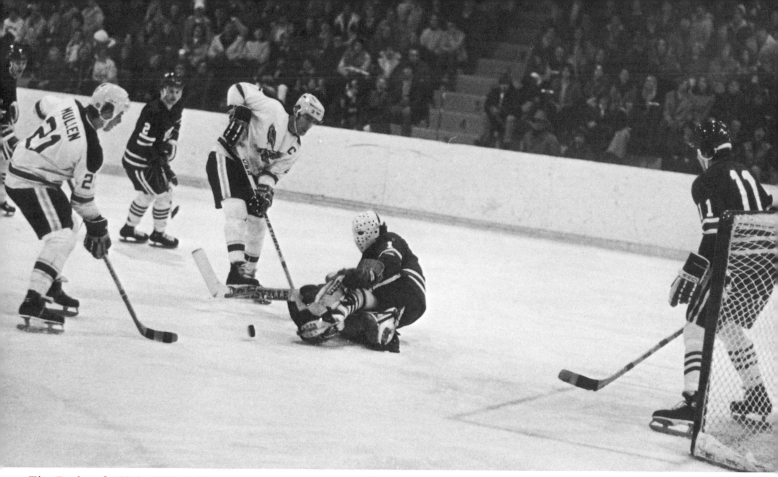

The Eagles of 1976–1979, led by New York forward Joe Mullen (shown here against Penn in '77), won 15 games, BC's first Beanpot in eleven years, an ECAC championship, and second-in-the-nation honors in 1978. Yet, they were overshadowed locally and nationally by a Boston University team featuring future Olympians Eruzione, Craig, O'Callahan, and Silk.

1975–1976 season, the Mullen-Skidmore-Augustine freshman triumvirate, aided and considerably abetted by Smith's forty-five point season, took Boston College to its first Beanpot win in eleven years (6–3 over a Boston University team lead by Mike Eruzione) and into the ECACs where Boston University took its 6–5 revenge. In all, the team fiished 15–13–1, attendance was up, and Boston College was a winner again.

Had it not been for a Boston University team that included the now immortal Olympic heroes Eruzione, Jim Craig, Jack O'Callahan, and David Silk, Mullen and his Boston College teammates might have owned the city in 1976–1977. As it was, Boston College held the mighty Terriers to a 6–6 tie in the teams' first meeting, then lost by a goal in the next two Boston University games, the last an 8–7 ECAC playoff shoot-'em-up in which Mullen scored four goals (two of them twenty–seven seconds apart), and Ferriter added two more—all the goals coming against Craig—before Rick Meagher scored the game winner with 2:33 to play.

Boston College and Boston University were always fierce rivals, but the head-butting seemed to reach its highest intensity in the 1977–1978 season. Although Joe Mullen tied Jack Mulhern's 1948–1949 record of thirty–four goals in one season and also tied Sheehy's record of sixty–eight points, and goalie Skidmore built himself a reputation as one of the best collegiate netminders since Dryden, it was still Boston University that won all three regular season confrontations between the teams by the overwhelming scores of 6–3, 12–5, and 10–5.

But when Boston University faltered momentarily, losing to Providence in the ECAC semifinals, Boston College was ready to exploit the opportunity—beating Providence for the ECAC championship and earning the right to go to the NCAAs. Boston University, by virtue of the selection committee's mandating a special playoff with Providence, joined Boston College as the other eastern team in the tourney, held at the Providence Civic Center.

The Eagles' shot at revenge became reality when Boston College beat Bowling Green and Boston University defeated Wisconsin in first-

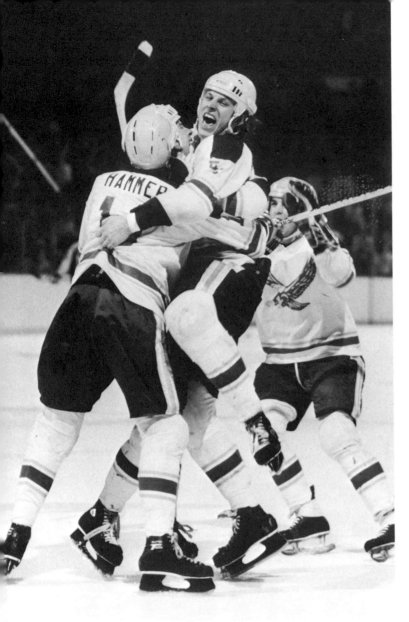

High point of recent Boston College hockey history came in 1978, when the Eagles topped Providence for the ECAC championship. Here, defenseman Joe Augustine exults after scoring the decisive goal in the 4–2 victory.

round games to set up the "Battle of Commonwealth Avenue," the first time in six years there had not been an All-West final for the national title (Boston University beat Cornell in 1972). The rivalry was further fueled by Jim Craig's pregame comment, "It will be a pleasure to shake their hands as losers again."

Whether motivated by Craig's taunt or merely playing with his normally exuberant style is a matter of conjecture, but it is a matter of record that Augustine's penalty at the nine-second mark and Mark Fidler's goal for Boston University twenty-seven seconds later gave Boston University a 1–0 lead. Mullen tied it with his thirty-fourth goal in thirty-four games and Bobby Hehir put Boston College ahead 2–1, but two goals by Tony Meagher, another by Fidler, and one by Silk gave Boston University a 5–2 lead in a game that never seemed to live up to its advance publicity. The Terriers won the national title 5–3 and only Skidmore's acrobatics—he stopped six Boston University breakaways—kept it that close.

Losers or not, Boston College was still the number- two team in the nation. Said vindicated senior forward Paul Barrett, "People were down on the coach and the program. They'll have to swallow their words. People wrote that Boston College would have to got out and get Canadians. But right now I couldn't be any happier for Coach Ceglarski."

What had been a healthy if intensifying rivalry with Boston University turned malignant in 1978–1979. The Eagles were all but out of the ECAC playoffs by February and had suffered two more losses to Boston University, one at the Walter Brown Arena—where Boston College had never won—and a 4–3 heartbreaker in the Beanpot finals. The kettle of frustration was set to boiling by another Jim Craig remark, along the lines of "Boston College gets most of the publicity, but what do they have to show for it?" Boston University, of course, was again headed for the NCAAs.

A February 27 game with Boston University at McHugh Forum would be the last home game for Mullen and Skidmore. Ceglarski, however, decided to sit his senior goalie, who had won only three of nine starts after coming back from early-season academic ineligibility, and to start freshman Doug Ellis of Burlington High School, the Eastern Massachusetts champs the year before. Ceglarski had also taken another freshman star, Massachusetts state schoolboy-scoring-champ Billy O'Dwyer of South Boston via Don Bosco High School, and put him at center on a production line that had Mullen at right wing and sophomore Mark Switaj of Ohio on left wing.

"The season was over for us," said Switaj. "The only thing left was to try to beat Boston University."

Jeff Cowles, a teammate of Ellis' in Burlington

and in their peewee days with the Boston Junior Braves, scored the first goal off a Mullen rebound. Boston University came back to take a 2–1 lead until, with 2:21 left in the second period, the freshman they were calling "Billy O" took a cross-ice pass from Mullen, deked Craig, and put in the tying goal. The Eagles took a 3–2 lead on George Amidon's goal and began to look like winners when Brian Burns, son of the Arlington High School coach Ed Burns (a Boston College player in the early 1940s), scored to make it 4–2. Still, it seemed Boston University's Tony Meagher was setting the stage for another heartbreaker when he closed the gap to 4–3 with half a period remaining.

Switaj said he knew what he was going to do as soon as he touched the puck on a breakaway in the last two minutes. "I dropped my shoulder and deked him [Craig]," said the wing, who, after faking Craig, scored on a little backhander. "He even complimented me on the goal," Switaj said of the Boston University goalie, adding, "Maybe that will shut them up."

Not quite. Craig was equal to the occasion: "I know they have talent, and they know we have talent. But nothing's different. They still don't like us and we still don't like them, [but] when it comes down to business we really respect each other."

Said goalie Ellis, "I just wish Craig was around a couple of more years so I could do it to him a few more times."

Joe Mullen was more reflective in his post-game comment: "Just the rivalry—our freshman year beating BU for the Beanpot, and then my sophomore year when I scored four goals against them . . . . It's going to be sad leaving here."

Ceglarski said nothing for a long time. "I had to gather myself. Gather my thoughts, alone," he finally said after the dressing room celebration had quieted. "Who ever expected us to do this? It's going to help in a lot of ways, especially in recruiting—that's the nice part."

Help it did, as during the next two years, Boston College attracted a trio of schoolboy stars in Ed Rauseo of Medford, heir to O'Dwyer's role as big gun at Don Bosco; George Boudreau, also of Medford but via state champ Matignon High;

and Stoneham's All-Scholastic Billy McDonough. But again, the star-studded Eagles went into another inexplicable period wherein an outstanding regular season was followed, seemingly inevitably, by a mouthful of ashes in the playoffs.

Boston College stood astride the hockey world for awhile in 1979–1980. "Billy O" and "Billy A" (North Providence's Bill Army) were on their way to twenty-goal seasons and Boston College was 8–1–1 when they got on the bus for another showdown at Boston University, for which, according to one Boston College official, "Tickets were as hard to come by as for any athletic event in five years" (a reference to Notre Dame football in 1976).

"Records mean nothing in a game like this," said Ceglarski before the game, and he was right. "You got to love it!" yelled Bill Army after Ewanouski's overtime goal gave Boston College a 7–6 win and first place in ECAC standings for the first time since 1965. "I told them before the season that I think we have the talent to go a hell of a long way," Ceglarski told the Globe's Joe Concannon. "If we don't, I'll be disappointed. If we don't, it'll be my fault."

Ceglarski ended up disappointed, although it is arguable as to whether it was his fault. The Eagles finished the season with twenty-five wins, more than any other varsity team in any sport in the school's history to this point, against only six losses. One of those losses was 5–4 in overtime to Northeastern in the Huskies' first Beanpot title ever. Far more disappointing was the seventh and final loss of the season to bottom-seeded Cornell, 5–1, at McHugh Forum in the first round of the ECAC playoffs.

Afterward, a desperate Ceglarski, whose team had been missing four players, including third leading scorer Lee Blossom, informally appealed to the mercies of the selection committee. "We're going to keep practicing. Maybe we can win an extra game or something like they gave Boston College [vs. Providence] a couple of years ago. It doesn't seem fair. We're too good a team and we've worked too hard to get knocked out so early," he said.

There was no second chance and the knock-outs would become more brutal. Another excel-

South Boston's Billy O'Dwyer (here, mixing it up with a Cornell foe) was a state schoolboy scoring leader at Don Bosco High before coming to the Heights to lead BC teams of the early 1980s.

lent regular season (20–7–1) in 1980–1981 had Boston College first in the ECAC in team defense, 4–0–3 in overtime games, and saw sophomore goalie Bob O'Connor of Billerica playing at a strong 2.99 average for twenty-four games. But, after ranking first in the nation in December, Boston College lost five of its last ten games to once more make the unanswerable "What's the matter with the Boston College hockey-team?" the city's winter equivalent of "what's the matter with the Red Sox?" This time it was seventh-seeded Providence beating second-seeded Boston College 5–2 in the ECAC's, again at McHugh Forum, eliminating the second best team in the East from the playoffs. "It's tough on the kids," said Ceglarski in a morgue-like Boston College dressing room. It was obvious that it was tough on the coach, too. The mineshaft became deeper still in 1981–1982.

"Boston College is a solid top-four club," predicted the *Globe* in its pre-season analysis. It was a conclusion most hockey experts agreed with.

And the experts were right. Boston College went on a tear, winning seven of its first nine games. To guard against mid-season slump, Ceglarski had reduced the team's pre-season workload of power skating and weight training. The move worked, as the Eagles accomplished eight wins in nine starts from early January through a first-round overtime Beanpot win over Northeastern.

The Beanpot championship game was where the season started to unravel again. Boston College lost 3–1 to a going-nowhere Boston University team. "I know what people are saying," said O'Dwyer a few days later. "They say we can't win the big ones. We'll just have to show them we can in the playoffs."

All season, O'Dwyer held up his end with a team-leading thirty-two points (eleven goals, twenty-one assists). Only Blossom had more goals—thirteen. Goalies O'Connor and Billy Switaj also played well, each stopping more than ninety percent of the shots they faced. Defensemen Boudreau, senior Mark Murphy of Watertown, Wakefield sophomore Jim Chisolm, and

Tom Wright of Ohio all played well. It is not possible to explain why Boston College lost its last four regular season games, dropping to 19–11, and in the process, losing home ice advantage for the first round of the ECAC playoffs. The Eagles had to bus the few miles to Harvard's three-year-old Alexander Bright Rink for their first playoff game, the one O'Dwyer said they would win.

But there are times in history when fate sticks out its hand—or in this case its foot—and says "No." Maybe it was luck. Maybe the ice gods were angered. Maybe there is no rational explanation how a once-in-the-history-of-hockey shot, a one-hundred-foot "dump in" intended to do nothing more than send the puck into the corner around behind the Boston College net, caromed off a referee's skate at the blue line and slid into the Boston College net behind a justifiably surprised O'Connor, who had left his cage to intercept the puck as it came out of the corner.

Harvard won the game 2–0.

A good Boston College team had not played badly, but for the third year in a row they were out of the playoffs in the first round.

The Boston College hockey team had won sixty-four games in three years, an extraordinary record, seemingly worth more than ashes. "Yeah. We can still hold our heads up," said an obviously disappointed O'Dwyer.

Indeed, keeping one's head up has been the name of the game since the days of ice polo.

4

Basketball

SOMEHOW THE MOMENT slipped away. At the turn of the century, basketball should have been the perfect sport for Boston College—a poor urban school, but one that had its own gymnasium. The new game required a minimum of equipment, little space, and only five or more players for a squad. More to the point, basketball was a new game, invented just twenty-eight years after the founding of Boston College. It was, therefore, a game not yet dominated by any one college or bloc of colleges, as had been the case with the Ivy League mastery in football and, to a lesser degree, hockey.

Instead of embracing the new sport, however, Boston College wavered, proceeding by false starts and half-steps that gave basketball the most tenuous existence of any major sport at the college. Three times Boston College officially abandoned the game—once for a span of twenty years—and on two other occasions the team had to be suspended due to world wars. Not until the mid-1940s was there serious administrative commitment to basketball, after giving so many competing teams the better part of a half-century head start. It was not until the late 1950s that

Boston College basketball teams began to attain the national stature reached decades earlier by the college's football and hockey teams. But, once in the national picture, the Boston College program established itself as an eastern regional power, and an occasional national force.

The history of basketball at Boston College has been alternately as frustrating and as rewarding as the game itself.

Basketball, unlike other sports, is less the product of haphazard evolution than the result of premeditated invention. It was created in 1891 with neccessity being very much its mother and Dr. James Naismith its universally acknowledged father. Naismith, a physical education instructor at the YMCA Training School in Springfield, Massachusetts (today Springfield College), needed an indoor winter sport to occupy a bored and increasingly hostile group of students in the stretch between fall football and spring baseball. Naismith's imaginative resort to versions of indoor soccer, lacrosse, and rugby took its toll in floor burns and broken windows; in desperation, he then nailed the now-famous peach baskets to the balcony, tossed out a soccer ball, drew up thirteen rules, and called his new game "basketball." (Though for a short time his grateful students tried to call it "Naismith ball.")

Basketball caught on so fast in academia that the first intercollegiate game was played just four years after the game's invention: On February 9, 1895, in Minneapolis, The Minnesota School of Agriculture beat Hamline College of St. Paul 9–3. The victors immediately laid claim to the "state championship of Minnesota" and thereby invented another popular college game—capitalizing on your wins.

Back East at Boston College, student enthusiasm for sports was at an all-time high as the nineteenth century drew to a close. The football team of 1899 was 9–1, having shut out all opponents except Brown. Baseball and track were well-established. The college had sponsored hockey for the preceding two seasons. Given that, the time seemed right for basketball. Additionally, as this note in a 1900 edition of *The Stylus* points out, everyone was doing it: "If we intend to live in Rome, we must do as the Romans do, and if we intend to maintain any place in athletics, we must do as other colleges do and be represented by a basketball team."

The thought was right, the timing wrong. The year 1900 was when the college administration, headed by president Mullan, decided that intercollegiate athletics were no longer an affordable luxury. The football schedule was cancelled and the other varsity sports discontinued. Basketball never got started, at least not as a varsity sport. Yet Boston College basketball enthusiasts fared somewhat better than their counterparts in the other sports. Since the school had a gym and the sport was cheap, the administration could hardly object if the boys wanted to play a few club teams and interclass games.

There are no records of Boston College basketball games played between 1901 and 1904. There is only an unpublished note by Nat Hasenfus stating that "some contests were undoubtedly played at the old gym, fostered by the students themselves as class games and games with local clubs and schools."

While Boston College hesitated, other colleges moved ahead. By 1901, Harvard, Yale, Columbia, Princeton, and Cornell had organized an intercollegiate basketball league, the Eastern League, while Holy Cross, Dartmouth, Amherst, and Williams had banded together to form the New England League. It is also interesting to note that in the vanguard of basketball enthusiasm were two women's colleges—Vassar and Smith—which added the infant sport to their athletic programs in 1892.

In 1903, Mullan was succeeded as Boston College president by Reverend William F. Gannon, S. J., a man more favorably disposed toward athletics than his predecessor. In 1904, Gannon granted administrative sanction for a varsity basketball team, and on December 26 of that year, in Lincoln Hall, Chelsea, Boston College played its first varsity basketball game. The Eagles lost in overtime 8–6 to a Navy team, Battery H.

Records are sparse and in some cases non-existent for the teams and games of this era. In fact, official Boston College basketball records did not even begin listing players' names until the 1945–1946 season. However, Hasenfus' research shows that among those playing· in 1904–1905 on the college's first basketball team were James Supple, Stephen Mulcahy, Henry McGuiness, David Fitzgerald, John Corcoran, Neil Bullman, and captain Joseph Lyons. And in all available records the coach is identified merely as "Higgins," an anonymity he doubtless would have wished to preserve during the early part of that first season. It was then that Boston College learned just how much ground it had lost to other teams. Dartmouth beat Boston College 60–13, Andover Academy hammered the new team 70–10, and a club team calling itself "East Boston Evening High School" ran it up to 77–4—this in an era of defensive basketball when typical scores were in the teens and twenties.

Like football and hockey, turn-of-the-century basketball was a rougher game than it is today. It was a defensively oriented game in which fouls were called only for the most flagrant abuses and the most violent physical contact. It would not be until 1908 that the Intercollegiate Basketball Rules Committee of the National Collegiate Athletic Association specified use of a second game official whose duty it was "to follow the players who have not the ball," and it was not until 1910 that charging would be made a foul. Naismith had conceived his game as a non-contact sport. It was seldom played that way.

Adding to the problem of general roughness was the fact that basketball was governed by three sets of rules—those of the YMCA, the AAU, and the college leagues. The rules of the latter allowed for the most physical contact. Therefore, a college team was at a disadvantage when it played against a YMCA or AAU club team, as was frequently the case with Boston College in the early days.

On the other hand, a trip to the James Street gym, located beneath the classroom building, posed problems for visiting teams. The old gym had six large floor-to-ceiling support beams standing on the court itself, each capable of being used to set a memorable pick on unwary Boston College foes.

Despite the clobberings by Dartmouth and others, Boston College did manage to win its first intercollegiate game ever that inaugural season, 23–17 over Tufts at Medford. The Eagles subsequently scored five other victories to close out the season at a losing, though respectable, 6–8.

New coach James Crowley (whose son would captain the Boston College baseball team thirty years later) took over the team in 1905–1906 and immediately sought to close ground on other colleges by organizing a freshman team to develop talent for the varsity—talent being one commodity that season's 7–18 varsity was clearly short on. Another thing it lacked was fan support. Ten spectators, including one reporter, appeared for Boston College's 16–13 loss to Tufts, and only games with Boston University and Holy Cross generated notable student interest.

The most important game of the second season saw Boston College take Holy Cross into overtime in Worcester, before losing 22–20 in a game that, according to Hasenfus, helped "make basketball very popular at Boston College and had the students clamoring for more." The game might well have ignited wider student interest—except that the flagship sport at Boston College, football, was about to make its comeback.

Boston College's first three basketball seasons fell within that six-year span (1902 to 1908), during which the college did not sponsor varsity football. Football had fallen into national disfavor because of its brutality and into local disfavor because of its expense. This would have been an ideal time for basketball to put down its roots at Boston College, and historians can only speculate as to why this never happened. The reasons could be several: losing seasons, hodge-podge schedules, no league affiliation, a barely adequate gym, the several-years' head start which other schools enjoyed in the building of their varsity programs.

By 1907, rules changes instituted by the fledgling National Collegiate Athletic Association returned football to popular favor, and Boston College made plans to field a team in 1908. Meanwhile, a basketball team captained by center Peter Sullivan and again coached by Crowley played only four games in 1906–1907, and only one of these was against another college—a 46–23 loss to MIT. The season ended 1–3, students stayed away in droves, and basketball was discontinued to the consternation of few, except the players.

It was not until 1910 that the initiative of students Matt Duggan and Johnny Churchward—the latter a starting end on the footbal team—achieved a brief, though ultimately abortive, basketball revival. Duggan captained a team that went 2–and –4 and continued to be handicapped by a gym now considered so outmoded that games and most practices had to be held at the nearby Vine Street gym. The situation was apparently too much for either the school or the players to cope with, and Boston College dropped the sport again after the 1910–1911 season. It was not to be revived until the college moved to Chestnut Hill.

Two years after its 1913 relocation, Boston College built a combination gridiron-diamond-track. It did not build a gymnasium and it had no plans to raise the funds to build one. Basketball would have to wait. And that it did, though impatiently.

After the move to the Heights, students continued to sponsor interclass games held at nearby gyms—and even at not-so-nearby gyms such as St. Mary's in Cambridge. Meanwhile, Boston College High, playing in the old six-poster James Street gym, began producing basketball teams that regularly contended for the New England championship. With so many good Boston College High players matriculating at Boston College, it was inevitable that there would be growing student pressure to re-establish basketball.

Late in 1916, the Boston College hierarchy was moved to revive basketball as a result of the interest of Paul Gately, a senior and former Boston College High basketball star, and of Paul McNally, S. J., a teacher and volunteer coach. Gately and McNally had no money, no gym, and no time to set up a representative schedule but they did have the administration's "go ahead."

The team commuted to the St. Mary's gym in Cambridge for games and practices. Among those joining Gately, who was elected captain of this first Chestnut Hill team, were James "Dutch" Holland, Joe Curry, Connie Manley, Frank Ramisch, and, on occasion, football standout Luke Urban, a former Fall River Tech schoolboy player who would become one of Boston College's first basketball stars.

Boston College's first varsity basketball game in almost six years was played in early 1917 at New Hampshire State College. The Eagles lost 35–20 with captain Gately scoring fourteen points. The revived team's first win came against St. Mary's of Cambridge 32–30, but the game that demonstrated the sport's potential impact on fan enthusiasm was the season finale, when, according to notes by Hasenfus, 3,000 watched Boston college beat Massachusetts College of Pharmacy 29–14. Despite its 2–3 record, the new team had succeeded in drawing fans and re-establishing basketball at Boston College. But again the timing was bad. In April 1917, the United States entered World War I, and sports at the Heights were disrupted, or in basketball's case, discontinued.

There was, however, no move to totally abandon the game, and when Boston College varsity athletics resumed in the fall of 1918, basketball was, briefly, an accepted part of the program. Two of the reasons for basketball's revival were

Luke Urban and his famous football sidekick, Jimmy Fitzpatrick.

Urban, a receiver in football and a forward in basketball, acted as player-coach; Fitzgerald, a passing halfback in football and a guard in basketball, kept his role as Urban's feeder. Joining them as the Eagles' center was former Boston College High star John Curtin. Together, the Urban-Fitzy-Curtin threesome in 1918–1919 led Boston College to a 4–1 season, the solitary loss coming to Connecticut, 45–27, at Storrs.

Prior to the opening of the 1919–1920 season, with Urban again on board as volunteer coach, the Student Athletic Association petitioned the administration to stop waffling and declare basketball a major sport. Their plea was granted, and for the first time maroon and gold varsity "B's" were awarded to basketball players.

Fitzy took over for Curtin at center; Urban resumed his forward spot; John Gannon moved in as the other forward; and Mahoney remained at guard, joined most of the time by Ike Kamp, another former Boston College High star and later a pitcher for the Boston Braves. The team went 5–3, generally winning by close scores (30–25 over Tufts, 19–14 over Rhode Island) and losing in blowouts (58–13 to Connecticut, 43–18 to Tufts.) Ironically, just as the administration began supporting basketball, the students began to let it down.

Boston College, again coached by Urban, won its first six games of the 1920–21 season and appeared to have one of the best teams in New England, a fact that had little effect on Boston College students who turned out in huge numbers for football and hockey but hardly at all for basketball. The Eagles drew better on the road than they did at home, as the team, and particularly Urban, was beginning to build a regional reputation. A headline in a Lewiston, Maine, paper—published before a Boston College-Bates game—read, "Luke Urban Here Tonight."

Meanwhile, home-game attendance grew so embarrassingly bad that, following a 36–27 Boston College win over Maine that gave the Eagles a 7–4 record, the administration cancelled the team's remaining games. Instead, Boston College resorted to the only guaranteed good draw in

William Coady coached BC—gratis—through three respectable seasons in the mid-1920s, before the sport was officially scrapped on the Heights for twenty years. Among his other achievements, Coady coached the Eagles to their first-ever victory over Holy Cross.

any of its athletic competitions and challenged Holy Cross to a best-two-out-of-three series. Boston College lost the challenge but won—or won back—its students and fans. One thousand Holy Cross fans and twice that many Boston College rooters filled St. Mary's gym to see Holy Cross win the first game 28–26. Another crowd of 3,000 went to the Worcester Casino to see Holy Cross wrap up the series 35–23, Urban's game-high sixteen points notwithstanding.

These victories underscore the fact that Holy Cross had been one of the first colleges to see the advantages of basketball as a small college sport. And, whereas the Purple had lost four of the five football games with Boston College from 1916 to 1922, dominance was reversed on the basketball court.

Among the problems Boston College confronted prior to the 1921–1922 season were that player-coach Urban had graduated, Roderick had transferred to Columbia, and there was still no solid indication that students wanted to see any basketball game not involving Holy Cross. Once more Boston College officials, according to Hasenfus, toyed with the idea of dropping the sport. The administration was dissuaded from such action only by the efforts of team manager John Toomey, who took the initiative in once again securing St. Mary's gym and who convinced his friend Bill Coady to coach the team without pay.

After losing their first three games of the season, Eagle players were successful in persuading Boston College student Jimmy Casell, former basketball and baseball star at Boston College High, to join the team. Casell reported just be-

fore a trip to Maine, where his eighteen points led Boston College to a 44–36 win—one of only three Eagles victories all season. Cassell's mid-season departure to sign with the Boston Red Sox left Boston College with only one first-class player, center Jim Hickey of Natick, hardly enough to ward off a 3–9 season in which the team again lost both games to Holy Cross.

The 1922–1923 Boston College team, captained by senior guard William Melley (later mayor of Chelsea) and paced by the shooting of junior forward Tommy Murphy (twenty points in the 28–24 opening win over Lowell Tech), met Holy Cross in the second game of the season and won 32–26, the first time the Eagles had won in the basketball division of this rivalry. The victory was one of the few bright spots in another losing season (4–5) that resulted in a 35–26 Holy Cross revenge. It also ended with Boston College basketball demonstrably in arrears of football and hockey in its development.

Greater Boston of the twenties was very much a hockey area, made so by climate, the abundance of ponds, the publicity given the ice game in the Boston papers, and perhaps to a lesser extent, by the large number of French Canadians and their descendants living in the towns north of Boston. While a Boston College-Boston University hockey game would sell out Boston Arena, a Boston College-anybody-except-Holy-Cross basketball game in Cambridge would go largely ignored.

The problem of lack of fan interest was circumvented, if not wholly solved, by scheduling all away games for the 1923–1924 team—except, of course, for the Holy Cross game. This road-show season saw senior forward Frank Mooney emerge as Boston College's new single-season scoring leader, his seventy-six points topping Urban's seventy-one of 1918–1919. But it was sophomore Andy Carroll who sank the most important basket of the respectable 8–3 season—arguably the most important points in the history of Boston College basketball to this time—when he hit a whistle-beater to defeat Holy Cross at Cambridge, 21–19. For creating enthusiasm, nothing beats winning your only home game against your arch rival before a full house.

The win over Holy Cross was not a fluke, as Boston College proved the next season by beating Holy Cross twice—the first time in Cambridge 23–19 and the second at Worcester, 26–25. Two victories over such a regional power should have been a giant step for Boston College basketball; instead, as had happened before when basketball seemed poised to come into its own, the sport was scuttled by the Boston College Athletic Association shortly before the 1925–1926 season was to begin.

In his notes on the decision, Hasenfus, five years out of Boston College, wrote: "To us on the outside this [decision] appears to have been a mistake, for granted that the sport . . . was difficult [to sustain], the seasons were successful in the brand of ball played and the Eagles won their share of games. That the students desired the court sport may be readily seen by the fact that they repeatedly requested the continuation of the game and formed independent teams from 1926 on."

But in dropping basketball Boston College was this time responding to the lead of the Boston public schools, which had abandoned the game following the accidental death of a schoolboy player the previous season. With a diminished local talent pool, no dormitories in which to house recruited players (the best of these being New York City boys), and still no gymnasium, Boston College's decision does not seem a wholly illogical one.

Without a formal, sanctioned program, Boston College basketball went underground. Several independent teams were wearing the school colors and slapping together schedules. The best of these teams was the appropriately named "Independents," generally made up of football players getting some off-season exercise. The team gradually made a local name for itself while keeping the hoop sport alive on the Heights.

In 1935–1936, Ted Galligan, a Boston College football player, organized a ten-game schedule for the Independents team made up of such football stars as Tilly Ferdenzi and Fella Gintoff. By 1937, the Independents had enough stature to secure a game with Holy Cross and enough ability to come close to winning it. After leading the Crusaders through three quarters (college basketball was played in quarters, not halves, in the 1930s), the Independents lost 29–26.

In the last part of that decade, after Galligan had graduated and joined the Boston College football coaching staff, he started another basketball team. Called "The Maroons," this team was composed mainly of freshmen football players who played in the Boston Park League.

There is no little irony in the fact that it was football players, more than any other group, who kept basketball alive at Boston College. The 1941 Sugar Bowl football team, for example, gave basketball one of its biggest boosts at the Heights. Under the leadership of 6′5″ center (in football and basketball) Chet Gladchuk, several of the football members comprised the core of an outstanding Independents team. In addition to Gladchuk, grid stars playing on the Independents included Charlie O'Rourke, Henry Woronicz, Joe and Ed Zabilski, and Mickey Connolly. Their biggest game of the 1941 season was a 35–21 loss to Holy Cross, where O'Rourke, as productive a guard as he was a quarterback, led all Boston College scorers with six points on three field goals.

The following season, 1941–1942, the Independents continued to fill the roster with football stars. Bob Jauron, Monk Maznicki, and John Kissell replaced the graduated O'Rourke, Gladchuk, and Joe Zabilski. There are no statistics on the season, but, according to Hasenfus, the team played several exhibitions in eastern Massachusetts—including matches against such established college teams as Providence and Holy Cross. The club was a popular sports attraction and might have helped bring basketball back to Boston College in 1943 had World War II not disrupted all sports and sent college enrollments plummeting.

There was no question as to whether or not Boston College would sponsor a varsity basketball team when men began returning to campus in 1945–1946. By this time, the sport was a raging success in high schools and colleges across the country, and plans were already afoot for the launching of a professional league to be called the "National Basketball Association." Boston

91

was due to have an NBA franchise by the 1946–1947 season. That team would be owned by the legendary sports entrepreneur, Walter Brown. In preparation, Brown (who was to dub his new pro team the "Celtics") had both of his buildings—the Boston Garden and Boston Arena—fitted with new hardwood basketball courts and made the facilities available to colleges and high schools for games and practices.

Boston College, still without a gym, took full advantage of Brown's offer. The team held most of its practices at the Boston Arena and opened Boston College's first official basketball season in twenty-one years at Boston Garden, December 13, 1945. The Eagles lost 50–44 in overtime to Manhattan College, a good showing against an established power that had won five straight before coming to Boston.

The team was led by Boston College's first paid (albeit meagerly) basketball coach, Al "The General" McLellan, nicknamed for the famous Civil War officer and for an approach to coaching that had a military cast. "He was what I'd call a real 1920s-style sports character," says Frank Power, coach of Mission High School at the time whose teams practiced at the Arena right after McLellan's Boston College team. "He was a huge man, maybe 6'5" or 6'6", and he must have weighed maybe three hundred pounds. Rumor was that he'd worked as a bouncer in a few places. But "the Gen"—that's what his players called him—had coached at Providence College and St. Anselm's; his teams had done well, and he had kind of a big local reputation."

A week after the Manhattan loss, the General took his troops to their first win, one of only three (against ten losses) they would have all season, a 53–50 victory over United States Merchant Marine at King's Point. Star of this game and of the Boston College season was Phil Kenney of Newport, Rhode Island, who would lead the team in scoring with 174 points.

Of greater importance to Boston College basketball, however, was the administration's announcement that it would begin raising money for a gym to be built on what was called the Freshmen Field near Beacon Street. Architects Maginnis and Walsh had already completed a

rendering of a four-story building, designed to house squash and tennis courts, administrative offices, and a 4,000–seat basketball arena. The alumni association vowed it would raise $400,000 as its contribution. At long last, basketball—heretofore the athletic stepchild—was to be welcomed into the Boston College sports family.

It never happened. A post-war recession and a stalled fundraising drive served to keep work from ever beginning.

Off campus, college basketball continued to grow in popularity, and games featuring teams from Boston College, Boston University, Providence, and others regularly packed Boston Garden. Obviously, some of basketball's appeal came from its now more wide-open, offense-oriented game compared to the push-and-shove basketball of the first quarter of the century.

As to the Eagles' offense, McLellan's team's average losing margin in the 1945–1946 season was almost fourteen points per game and Boston College was in desperate need of a big man who could score consistently and of a supporting cast who could get the ball in to him. To fill these needs, McLellan recruited 7'1" Texan Elmore Morganthaler and two ballhandling wizards from basketball-mad Brooklyn, Morton Stagoff and Danny Bricker, along with another New Yorker, Tom O'Brien. Boston College also upgraded its schedule for the 1946–1947 season, scheduling Georgetown, Georgia Tech, Michigan State, Bowling Green, and traditional rival Holy Cross.

Phil Kenney was back for another year and was the leading Boston College scorer in a season-opening 76–41 loss to LaSalle, in which Morganthaler was largely ineffective. But from that game on, McLellan had his way. Kenney adjusted to a new role as a feeder for Morganthaler and Boston College went on to win seven of its next ten games. One of those was a 66–49 crunching of always-powerful Providence in a game during which Morganthaler scored twenty-eight points. On December 21, 1946, Morganthaler set a new Garden college scoring record with thirty-seven points as Boston College vanquished previously undefeated Fordham, 72–50.

In the fifteen games he played before running afoul of mid-term exams and being declared ac-

92

First of BC's post-war basketball stars was 7'1" Elmore Morganthaler, whom coach Al McClellan recruited in Texas. Unfortunately, after scoring 271 points in his first fifteen games, Morganthaler was slam-dunked by grades and decided to leave school.

ademically ineligible, Morganthaler set Boston College career scoring records for field goals (100), free throws (71) and points (271). Without its giant center, Boston College lost four of its last seven games to finish 12–10. One of the final losses came, 90–48, to a soon-to-be national champion Holy Cross team led by Joe Mullaney, George Kaftan, and an unheralded freshman named Bob Cousy.

The Eagles received a seemingly bad break in the off season, when the academically struggling Morganthaler decided to leave school and return to Texas. One result of his departure was that the absence of a big man allowed New Yorkers Stagoff, Bricker, and O'Brien to assert themselves and Boston College improved its record to 13–10—including upset wins over Harvard, Providence, and Manhattan. There were no surprises against Holy Cross, however, as the increasingly well known Cousy helped to beat the Eagles twice.

Although thirteen of the 1947–1948 team's games were on the road and Boston College home games were still played at the Garden or the Arena, the college did build a temporary barracks-style practice gym on the southeast corner of the campus near the present site of Campion Hall. The makeshift structure allowed the Eagles to work out daily at home, even if it was not large enough to host a regularly scheduled varsity game.

"I remember it well," says Power, who as a Boston College assistant conducted several practices in the building in the mid-fifties. "The court was ninety by fifty-four feet, and I'll bet the building couldn't have been any bigger than maybe sixty by a hundred or so. You can figure out how cramped we were."

Cramped or not, Boston College did play its first home game since the James Street days, when, on March 3, 1948, the Eagles defeated Ft. Devens 46–43.

The advantage of a home practice court in 1947–1948 paid off in individual honors and the best team record since the 1920s. O'Brien was voted All-New England by the basketball writers, and Bricker received All-New England honorable mention. It was his shooting ability that allowed him to break Morganthaler's single-season scoring record by hitting 292 points.

Powerful Duquesne and DePaul were added to a murderous 1948–1949 schedule as Boston College appeared to be extending its football scheduling philosophy into basketball: ready or

Bob Cousy, one of the non-Boston College graduates who has figured most prominently in the college's athletic history, was born August 9, 1928, in a poor neighborhood in New York City's East Side. The family moved to Queens when Cousy was twelve. It was there that the scrawny youngster began to make his mark in basketball as an all-city selection at Andrew Jackson High School.

Cousy later said that it was on the courts and playgrounds of New York that he learned the two principles that guided his basketball life: "You give it back in spades to anyone who tries to give it to you

Cousy as a Celtic: six world championships, thirteen all-star games, four scoring titles, all-time NBA assist leader, and one league MVP.

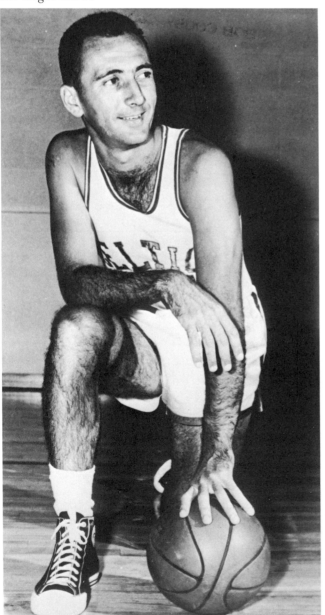

and every loose ball was mine." Later, in his years as coach at Boston College, Cousy said he tried to pass on those principles to his college players.

After his brilliant schoolboy career, Cousy was recruited by Holy Cross and, in his first year at Worcester, helped the Crusaders win the 1947 NCAA championship. Cousy was a small (6'1"), quick guard who supplemented his excellent shooting skills with a spectacular ballhandling and playmaking ability so advanced that he could make every move at top speed. By 1950, his senior year, he was chosen All-American and his college career totals stood at 1,775 points in 117 games, for a 15.1 per-game average.

The Tri-City Hawks picked Cousy in the 1950 NBA pro draft but almost immediately traded his rights to the Chicago Stags. The Stags folded before the season began, and in a move to redistribute three of the franchise's players—Andy Phillip, Max Zaslofsky and Cousy—NBA President Maurice Podoloff ordered the names placed into a hat. The hat passed among three of the league's weaker teams. One of them was the Celtics, and owner Walter Brown drew Cousy's name.

Still relying on tricky dribbling, superb playmaking, good shooting, and now playing trigger man for new coach Red Auerbach's fast break offense, Cousy became the dominant NBA player of the 1950s.

Until his retirement in 1963, the little guard played in thirteen all-star games. He was MVP in two, was named to the first all-star team ten times, was league MVP in 1957, and led the NBA in scoring for four consecutive seasons—1951 through 1955. He retired as the NBA's assist leader with 6,949 regular season assists, including twenty-eight in a game against Minneapolis in 1959. His 16,955 points in 917 games gave him an 18.5 career points-per-game average. More importantly, he led the Celtics to six world championships, in which flamboyant process he earned the nickname "Mr. Basketball." Walter Brown once praised him as "the most spectacular, inspiring, and greatest clutch performer I have ever seen in any sport."

Cousy continued his basketball magic as head coach at Boston College from 1963 to 1969. His teams won 118 games against 38 losses, for a .755 winning percentage. Cousy's percentage and total career victories remain Boston College basketball coaching records.

Cousy took Eagle teams to five post-season tour-

An emotional Cousy bids goodbye to Roberts Center fans in March, 1969, as wife Missie looks on. Cousy's six-year record as Eagles Coach: 188 wins, 38 losses, and five post-season tournament bids.

naments—the 1967 and 1968 NCAAs and the 1965, 1966, and 1969 NIT. His best Boston College teams included the 23–3 1967 squad that lost to North Carolina in the 1967 NCAA Eastern Regionals and his last team, the 24–4 1969 Eagles, that went to the finals of the NIT before losing to Temple. In the latter tournament, one of Cousy's all-time top players, Terry Driscoll, was chosen MVP.

After resigning from Boston College in 1969, Cousy was immediately hired as coach of the struggling Cincinnati Royals of the NBA, and he had his first brush with losing. His team (which relocated to become the Kansas City-Omaha Kings in 1972–1973) was 141–209 and never had a winning season during Cousy's five years at the helm. In his first year as coach, partly to hype lagging ticket sales, and partly to give himself a guard he thought he could count on, the forty-one-year-old Cousy came out of retirement to become the oldest man ever to play in the NBA. His comeback was short lived. Cousy played

thirty-four minutes in seven games in which he logged only one field goal, three free throws, and ten assists before retiring for good.

After leaving the NBA wars, Cousy returned to his home in Worcester where he lives with his wife, Missie, and pursues numerous business interests, including analysis and commentary on WBZ-TV Celtics telecasts.

In 1975, Cousy collaborated with author John Devaney on a book, *Killer Instinct*, largely devoted to the pressures and ethical questions of coaching, particularly college coaching. Of his years at Boston College, he writes: "Though Bill [Flynn] wanted to win every bit as badly as his coaches, he refused to compromise the rules. We would have disagreements, but I always respected Bill's position—and would even wonder in later years if Bill hadn't been right most of the time."

Cousy dedicated his book "To those who give a damn."

not, play the best teams you can. With Bricker, Stagoff, and O'Brien still on board, and having picked up sophomore scoring star Tony Deegan, the Eagles did well to finish an even 9–9. Yet once again, the team could not come close to beating Holy Cross or containing its now All-America star, Cousy.

"The irony is that Cousy might have come to Boston College," Power notes. "The Gen was recruiting him and Cousy came out to look at the school. When he found out he'd have to live off campus, that Boston College had no dorms, he decided on Holy Cross. The place he *really* wanted to go was Springfield College, but Springfield never recruited him."

If the great Cooz had harrassed Boston College in his freshman, sophomore, and junior years, he positively tortured the Eagles as a senior. On January 7, 1950, a winning Boston College team (they would finish 11–9) was embarrassed 93–46 by Holy Cross at Worcester as Cousy scored thirty-four points. This take-no-prisoners drubbing (Holy Cross coach Doggie Julian had his starters playing for the final five minutes) was commonly viewed as retaliation for the 76–0 football beating Boston College had given the Crusaders the previous November. In the return match before a standing room crowd of 7,045 at Boston Arena, Cousy tossed in a game-high twenty-two point goodbye present,

including an Arena record fourteen consecutive free throws as the Cross won 71–63—its twenty-third straight victory for that season.

Easily the most important year in Boston College's post-war basketball revival was a 1950–1951 season that saw the team win seven of its first eight games. Among the victories was the most shocking upset in the team's history, a 63–59 win over defending NCAA champion CCNY, in Boston College's first game ever at Madison Square Garden.

The Eagles were generally expected to be cannon fodder for the New Yorkers, and the game a breather for the powerful city college five. (Pre-game attention merited one paragraph in the *New York Times*.) A late surge by CCNY gave it a 59–58 lead with about a minute to play, when McLellan sent in Tom Deegan and Dick Fitzgerald. Fitzgerald came up with a steal, passed to Deegan who tossed to John Silk for an easy layup and what turned out to be the winning basket. The win, according to a front-page report in the next day's *Herald,* "took Boston College into basketball bigtime."

Yes and no. The win unquestionably drew national attention to a Boston College basketball team that would go 17–11 that season and win the post-season New England Tourney. However, in a sad foreshadowing of the troubles of seasons to come, it was proven after the season

The Eagles' first respectable team of the modern era was the 1950–1951 squad which achieved a 17–11 record, won the post-season New England Tourney, and scored an attention-getting upset of defending national champion CCNY. The starters, from left: Dick Fitzgerald, Tim O'Connell, Tom O'Toole, captain Tom Deegan, and Frank Duggan.

The basketball Eagles of 1951–1952 ran up an impressive record of 22–5, which would not be matched for fourteen years, and—even more important—defeated Holy Cross for the first time in 27 years. Stars of the team were forward John Silk (left), the team's scoring leader, and 6'7" center Tony Daukas (right), BC's first mobile big man.

that some CCNY players had been involved in a gambling ring and had conspired to shave points in certain games—including the Boston College game. In the latter case, the pre-game line had CCNY as thirteen-point favorites, and certain CCNY players were said to have been trying to keep their winning margin to less than that number. But if the victory over the national champions was tainted, wins over St. Francis, Harvard, and Providence proved that the Eagles could win over the better teams in the East.

Yet all the progress of the 1950–1951 season was little more than an overture to McLellan's finest team, a 1951–1952 squad that was also the first Boston College basketball team to win more than twenty games (22–5) in a season. Of far more interest to the Boston media and the team's

growing number of fans was the fact that the Eagles were mentioned as a possible invitee to the increasingly prestigious NCAA championships.

During the 1930s and 1940s, while Boston College administrators grappled with the question of whether to play basketball, colleges in the rest of the country were embracing the game and quickly making it the nation's favorite winter sports pastime. So great was basketball's popularity that in 1939 the NCAA decided to establish a national collegiate championship tournament. At first (1939–1950) eight teams were invited, then in 1951, the field was expanded to sixteen.

Boston College was undefeated through its first eight games in 1951–1952 and looked like a good bet as one of the eastern teams to be invited. Those happy expectations faded fast when the team dropped mid-season games to Seton Hall and Holy Cross, then followed another little (six game) win streak with losses to Canisius, Villanova, and—who else?—Holy Cross.

McLellan had a good team, if not a national contender. Captain Tommy O'Toole, a senior forward from Brookline, and John Silk, junior forward from Somerville, continued to play well. But the main reason Boston College beat all but its toughest opponents was the dominating presence of 6'7" sophomore center Tony Daukas from Maryland—the Eagles first ever mobile big man, a McLellan recruit.

Unlike the lead-footed Morganthaler, Daukas was agile and quick. He could take the shot or set up O'Toole or Silk. In no game was Daukas' versatility better illustrated than on March 3, 1952—an incredible twenty-seven years and thirteen consecutive defeats since Boston College had last beaten Holy Cross in basketball—when McLellan's team at last beat Holy Cross.

The Eagles did it with team basketball. Daukas scored only four points, spending most of his evening shutting down Holy Cross star Togo Palazzi. O'Toole's twenty-four points and Silk's twenty-three picked up the offensive slack. A delighted pro-Boston College Boston Garden crowd of 5,493 went home savoring a 64–61 victory over an opponent bound for a 21–3 record and an NIT bid.

Boston College, at 22–5, was not invited to the NCAAs or the NIT, and this would be the last chance a McLellan-coached Boston College team would have to play in a major post-season tournament. With graduation claiming O'Toole and Duggan, the 1952–1953 Eagles fell from the national picture and, at season's end, McLellan left to coach Belmont Abbey College in North Carolina.

The General's successor was Donald "Dino" Martin, a tennis pro and former guard with the Providence Steamrollers of the original NBA. At the time of his hiring by Boston College, Martin was spending six months a year as basketball coach at De La Salle Academy in Newport, Rhode Island, and six months a year as tennis pro at a country club in Willoughby, Ohio. The

latter job provided Martin with an outside income, a valuable commodity in view of Boston College's continued refusal to pay its basketball coach a full-time salary.

Martin's understanding with Boston College was that he would keep his tennis job and that most off-season work, including recruiting, would be handled by part-time assistant and freshman team coach Frank Power. Power, formerly varsity coach at Mission High and St. Sebastian's Country Day, remembers Martin as "a completely different type of coach than the General. He was more technical in his approach, and he taught me more about scouting an opponent, for example, than I ever thought there was to know."

Martin's tenure started well enough with Boston College, led by Daukas, going unbeaten through six games. However, the team still lacked the depth to be truly competitive, and it faltered when up against the likes of Villanova, Providence, or a Holy Cross team that now boasted a prolific scorer, Tommy Heinsohn. Low point of the 11–11 season was a 103–101 loss to Rhode Island in 1954 that set a Boston Garden college basketball record for total points scored.

With the fundraising drive faltering, construction costs rising, and plans for the new gym all but formally abandoned, Boston College continued to practice in its barracks-like gym and play most home games at the Garden or Arena. One scheduling innovation, an attempt to capitalize on college hockey's popularity, saw the inauguration of Boston College-Boston University basketball-hockey double headers at Boston Garden. It was not a success, however, as on February 9, 1954, only 1,862 appeared for the first double header. (For the record, Boston College won both ends, 6–5 in hockey, 70–58 in basketball.)

Martin's 8–18 second-year team continued its pattern, handily beating Merrimack, but turning around to lose to Holy Cross by scores of 95–42 and 102–63. Heinsohn scored twenty-eight points in thirty minutes playing time in the latter game. Boston College's few cage followers—by this time Garden crowds had fallen to the 2,500 range—could console themselves only with the brilliant play of another Somerville star, forward Dick Skeffington, who, in that grim 1954–1955 season, broke Daukas' one-season scoring record of 422 points by hitting for 464 (161 field goals, 142 free throws).

Boston College needed more Skeffingtons, and Martin made the effort to get them with such notable local talent as Attleboro's Dick Dunn, Wellesley's (by way of St. Sebastian's) Jimmy Brosnahan, and former Mission High stars Phil Powell and Paul McAdams. Massachusetts still lacked the strong high school basketball tradition that existed in other parts of the country, and Martin soon found himself reviving McLellan's New York City recruiting theme. "Dino's brother was also a religious brother assigned to St. Raymond's parish in the Bronx," says Power. "A parishoner, Jim Brody, was coach of one of the best amateur club teams in the area. Dino's brother would tell Brody, 'Hey, my brother the college coach needs players,' and Brody would steer some of his kids to us. Obviously, recruiting was much less sophisticated then."

Martin's locals had to suffer through another losing (6–18) season in 1955–1956. The season ended on one of the absolute low points of Boston College basketball history when NCAA tournament-bound Holy Cross beat the Eagles by a team scoring record 111–75. All-America Heinsohn scoring fifty-one points, also a team record. Help finally arrived the next season via New York and the Boston College freshman team in the form of George Giersch of the Bronx, a 6'4" sophomore forward who made his presence felt in the season's first game, scoring twenty-four points in a 76–58 win over Brown.

With the Bruins and Celtics consuming more Garden dates, the Arena reserved almost exclusively for college and high school hockey, and Boston College's practice gym declared structurally unsafe for spectators, the Eagles went through the entire 1955–1956 season playing every game on the road, including six "home" games at Brandeis. Still, the team managed to give Martin his first winning season, a 13–12 year in which Giersch led all scorers with 316 points.

Meanwhile, as part of the college's commitment to build a new football stadium and hockey rink there was a concurrent plan to incorporate a 3,200–seat gymnasium into the projected lower campus athletic center. This time the promise became brick and mortar, although for the 1957–1958 season, Martin once more had to coach a troop of basketball nomads that played seventeen of its twenty-two games on the road. Incredibly, one of these games was Boston College's first appearance in an NCAA tournament.

No one expected a team that barely broke .500 the previous year to play its way into the nation's most prestigious post-season playoff. But the team, led by Giersch and high-scoring John Magee, another Brooklyn boy, went undefeated through its first ten games (to this point the longest win streak in Boston College basketball history) before losing to UMass.

The streak did not include a game with Holy Cross, as the nomadic Eagles could schedule only one game with Holy Cross in 1957–1958, and that was to be February 23, 1958, at Worcester Auditorium. Boston College came into the game 15–2 with a win virtually assuring the Eagles of an NCAA bid. A win was also among the least likely eventualities of the evening.

Boston College had beaten the Crusaders only once in the twenty-two games that the teams had played since 1946, and that one win was six years before, in 1952. It looked like more of the same on this night, with Holy Cross leading 34–30 at the half and 53–50 with approximately twelve minutes to play. Then Giersch and Magee (a game high twenty-two points) paced Boston College through a six-minute 14–3 scoring run that landed the team a 73–68 win. It also landed the Eagles in Madison Square Garden.

The win over Holy Cross brought the hoped-for NCAA bid. Inexplicably, it also brought the end of Boston College's winning ways. The team dropped its last three regular season games—two to Boston University, one to Providence—before meeting Atlantic Coast Conference (ACC) champ Maryland in a first-round NCAA match that was also the first telecast game in the history of Boston College basketball. It was not much to look at. The outside shooting of Maryland's Paul Davis (twenty-two of his twenty-four points) sent the Terrapins to an easy 86–63 win.

Boston College's sudden prestige and limited but successful recruiting paid off in the late

1950s. In addition to such Brooklynites as Giersch and Magee, Martin was able to attract one of the better schoolboy players to come out of the Boston school system—Charlestown's Chuck Chevalier, a small, quick, Cousy-style guard.

Giersch was captain and Magee would be top scorer (340 points) on a 1958–1959 Boston College team that would finally have a roof over its head and a permanent court under its sneakers. The long-promised, long-awaited, long-needed gymnasium—Roberts Center, named after its prime benefactors, Mr. and Mrs. Vincent P. Roberts—was formally dedicated on December 8, 1958, with the awarding of an honorary doctorate to New York's Francis Cardinal Spellman. Four days earlier, the basketball team gave the gym its athletic baptism, beating Holy Cross 72–63 for the second time in a row and launching a successful 17–9 season.

With a modern gym and three consecutive winning years enhancing its recruiting allure, Boston College teams of the early 1960s were expected to take the step from regional power to national force and close the distance between itself and its bigger-name opponents. That did not happen until halfway through the decade. Two key academic failures, an ambitious schedule, and a rather limited recruiting network combined to keep Boston College basketball mired in mediocrity in 1959–1960.

Kevin Loughery, a New Yorker upon whom Martin was counting heavily, and Chevalier, who had led the freshmen to an 18–1 season in 1958–1959, were both declared academically ineligible before the 1959–1960 season began. Martin was left to rely on 6′5″ sophomore forward Jim Hooley of Roxbury, a former Boston College High star, and sophomore guard Billy Donovan of New York. The newcomers performed well—Hooley's 30 points versus Georgetown gave Boston College its first win ever over the Hoyas—but no one could stave off a dismal 11–13 season.

The result was a predictable attendance drop. Crowds were generally in the 2,000 range in the 1959–1960 season and only 1,900 appeared at Roberts Center for a December 3, 1960 game with Fairfield that opened the 1960–1961 season.

Forward George Giersch led the 1957–1958 Eagles through a 16–6 season that included a rare victory over Holy Cross and BC's first-ever appearance in a post-season NCAA tournament.

Nevertheless, that relative handful of true believers saw another upward turn in Boston College's ever-fluctuating basketball fortunes. Boston College, behind the thirty-four point scoring of Hooley, won 83–70 to begin a five-win rampage that had the Eagles positioned as the third-highest scoring team in the country, with an average of 88.8 points per game.

It looked as though another case of mid-season malaise might set in, when the win streak ended with a January 7, 1961, loss to Providence. Three days later, Boston College had to face Holy Cross and its latest scoring sensation, Jack "The Shot" Foley. Boston College was down 76–71 with two minutes to play when a Hooley one-hander from the side and a Billy Foley (a Worcester boy and

Jack Foley's best friend, though no relation) tap-in brought the Eagles to within one. Holy Cross resorted to playing stall-ball, but Hooley's deliberate foul of Crusader Dave Slattery saw the latter miss his free throw, only to have Boston College's 6'4" 200-pound sophomore forward Gerry Ward fouled on the rebound attempt. Ward sank both free throws to give Boston College a lead it never lost.

Boston College finished the season 14–9, and with Hooley, Donovan, Ward, and Chevalier (returned to academic good graces) all due back for the 1961–1962 season, it is little wonder that the team was rated third in New England, behind Providence and Holy Cross, in pre-season polls. Whispers of possible NIT or NCAA bids floated around Roberts Center. The Eagles did not disappoint, exploding into the 1961–1962 season with production basketball the likes of which

Doctor Naismith could not have imagined, Boston College won big—(109–96 over Yale, 104–92 over Maine, 108–94 over Pittsburgh, and 119–63 over Brandeis, a record Boston College point production and a game in which Hooley set a Boston College individual game record of forty-six points).

Hooley, whom Powers calls "a great pure shooter with an unstoppable hook shot," tossed them in from everywhere, every game. In the process he set a Boston College single-season scoring record of 533 points (sixty-nine better than Daukas' 1953–1954 record) and brought his career total to an all-time high 1,209 points, making him the second Boston College player (Daukas was the first) to pass the 1,000–point mark.

By late February the 15–4 Eagles were in contention for an NIT bid. So was Holy Cross. It was a foregone conclusion that the winner of the

Between them, Jack Hooley (with ball) and Gerry Ward dominated BC scoring for four years in the early 1960s, with Hooley's 533 points in 1961–1962 setting a new season record. Ward later played in the NBA, including a short stint with the Celtics.

101

THE BIG EAST

EAST IS NO LONGER LEAST OF THE NATION'S COLLEGE BASKETBALL HOTBEDS.

For decades the best teams in eastern college basketball were independent—St. John's, Providence, Boston College, Seton Hall, for example. They were good teams, but rarely good enough to beat the major conference powers from the likes of the Pac-Ten, ACC, SEC, Big Eight, or Big Ten.

Through the sixties and seventies, the domination of the great John Wooden-coached UCLA teams (ten championships from 1964 to 1975) seemed to further underscore the intercollegiate basketball pecking order: West was best, East was least, and rarely would the twain meet in the NCAA finals. Villanova managed to reach the 1971 finals but lost to UCLA and later had to forfeit its runner-up status because of the use of an ineligible player.

That imbalance of power began to change dramatically in 1979 when Providence athletic director and former basketball coach Dave Gavitt persuaded seven of the major eastern independents to come together in a new conference to be called, presumptuously some thought, the Big East. The original members were Boston College, Connecticut, Georgetown, Providence, St. John's, Seton Hall, and Syracuse. A year later, Villanova left the Eastern Eight to join the Big East.

In its first season, 1979–1980, the new conference had two of its members, Syracuse and St. John's, in the national top ten for most of the season. In postseason play, Georgetown emerged as the surprise of the NCAA playoffs, coming within a Sleepy Floyd missed-jump-shot of reaching the Final Four.

The Big East continued its success in 1980–1981 when six of its eight teams went to either the NCAAs or NIT. More importantly, the new conference also began to reverse the flow of eastern schoolboy talent to other regions of the country, an historical phenomenon that had seen the East lose the likes of Wilt Chamberlain (from Philadelphia to Kansas in 1955), Lew Alcindor (from New York City to UCLA in 1965), and Austin Carr (from Washington D.C. to Notre Dame in 1969). Players like Boston College's John Bagley of Connecticut, Seton Hall's Dan Callandrillo of New Jersey, and UConn's home-stater Corny Thompson all chose to play in the Big East. But the biggest coup was Georgetown's successful recruiting of Cambridge, Massachusetts schoolboy superstar Patrick Ewing, a player who had been recruited by UCLA and North Carolina and was widely regarded as the best prospect since Alcindor.

By 1981–1982, the Big East had also begun drawing heavy media coverage. Big East teams made a total of 168 television appearances, including five major national telecasts and a regular Wednesday night game carried on ESPN. For 1982–1983, the TV package expanded to include a 34-game series on USA-cable network. The effect of the intensive media coverage further helped the new league in its struggle to recruit players. Says Boston College's Martin Clark of Dorchester, Massachusetts, who as a schoolboy star received inquiries from 400 colleges, "The Big East had a lot to do with my choice of Boston College. Let's face it, it helps to have the media exposure."

Indeed, Gavitt claims the media and its positive effects on recruiting were part of the Big East master plan. "The Big East selected teams with great basketball traditions and large media markets, and we believe we have an opportunity to keep the best players home."

The conference lived up to its media ballyhoo in 1981–1982 when four of its teams—Boston College, Georgetown, St. John's, and Villanova—went to the NCAA's, as did Pittsburgh, which was to become the ninth Big East team in 1982–1983. Boston College, Georgetown, and Villanova gave the Big East three teams among the final eight, and the Ewing-led Georgetown team took North Carolina to the final minute of the championship game before bowing out.

How far off is the day when an eastern team wins the NCAA title? La Salle, 1954, was the last eastern team to win the championship.

"I can see it coming," says Gavitt.

Where the action is: BC bench erupts during late stages of the Eagles' stunning comeback victory over Syracuse in the 1982 Big East playoffs. From left: Coach Tom Davis, Burnett Adams, Marc Schmidt, Jay Murphy, Terrence Talley, and Stu Primus.

February 27 game at Roberts Center would go to Madison Square Garden. Boston College had already beaten the Cross at Worcester, despite Jack Foley's 34 points, and was expected to win again at home. But Foley, who now passed Cousy and Heinsohn as The Crusaders' all-time scorer, pumped in another 34, and this time the Eagle offense could not keep pace. Holy Cross won 87–76, and the next day accepted a bid to the NIT. Boston College had to be content with a 16–6 season and with seeing Hooley named UPI All-New England first team, and Chevalier named to the second team.

Donovan, Chevalier, and Hooley graduated in

1962 and, though big, tough Gerry Ward remained a player to build around, Dino Martin decided he had had enough of his double life. "He told me toward the end of the season," Power recalls, "that he didn't think it was fair to keep moving his family from Ohio to Massachusetts while he tried to work both the basketball and tennis jobs. He decided to stick with tennis, and I guess I have to say he made the right choice. A teaching pro has a lot more security than a college basketball coach."

Martin's departure left athletic director Flynn with a coaching vacancy that he wanted to fill in the spring of 1962. Flynn's usual method of

The BC-Holy Cross rivalry has been every bit as intense on the basketball floor as on the football field. Here, in a memorable 1962 matchup, Eagles guard Chuck Chevalier puts a move on the Crusaders' Jack Foley in a game which BC was expected to win. Instead, Foley—who had surpassed Bob Cousy and Tom Heinsohn to become Holy Cross' all-time leading scorer—shot for 34 points, the Crusaders won 85–76, and went on to the NIT.

searching for a coach is to listen closely to the grapevine. Whose name is most frequently mentioned? Who has the reputation as a comer? But this time he departed from his *modus operandi* and took a flyer.

"I'd heard Bob Cousy was planning to retire from the Celtics," says Flynn, "so one day I phoned Walter Brown and got Cousy's number. I knew we couldn't pay him much money, not anywhere near what he could make somewhere else, but I decided to call him just to see if he was interested."

Cousy was on the road with the Celtics when Flynn called his home, and his wife Marie—known to all as "Missie"—answered. Assistant coach Frank Power recalls the episode with relish: "Cousy told me this story many times," says Power. "Missie answers the phone, finds out what Flynn wants and says right away, 'Don't call anyone else. He'll take it!' A few days later, Cousy comes walking into Flynn's office and says, 'I'm your new basketball coach.'"

"The money wasn't that important to him," says Flynn.

"I thought it was a natural progression to go from playing to coaching," recalls Cousy. "I wanted to try college coaching and I didn't want to take my family out of the New England area. It seemed like the perfect opportunity."

But by the time Flynn and Cousy had struck a deal, Walter Brown had learned of Cousy's planned retirement, and the Celtic owner was not pleased that he was about to lose one of his biggest stars. The owner persuaded Cousy to play one more season, Cousy's thirteenth as a Celtic, before moving on to the Boston College job in 1963–1964.

"I knew I couldn't get anybody else of Cousy's stature," said Flynn, "so I agreed that, sure, he could take the job but not start for a year. Meanwhile, I hired our freshman coach, Frank Power, as interim head coach for 1962–1963."

Power was under no illusions. He knew he was keeping a seat warm for Cousy and did not object in the least. "I wanted Cooz more than anyone," he says. "I knew what he could do for Boston College."

With Ward (a future NBA player with St. Louis, Philadelphia, and for a few games, the Celtics) as his only returning starter, Power's team did well to record a 10–16 season. One of the few team achievements of that year was Boston College's win at the first basketball Beanpot Tournament, held at Roberts Center and featuring Boston College, Boston University, Northeastern, and Tufts. The hoop version of the hockey classic never was accepted by fans and the media, and was discontinued in 1976.

All that season, however, was so much preamble to the heralded arrival of the great Bob Cousy. His tears had hardly dried from one of the most emotional farewells in the history of Boston sports—a pre-game Garden ceremony at which a more or less continuous fifteen-minute standing ovation frustrated various attempts at superfluous speeches—before the new coach was sitting with Frank Power to plot his "New Deal" for Boston College basketball.

Power said, "Right from the start he wanted to put in Auerbach's system—the fast break, the pressure defense. He was right about a lot of things. But it took him a while to realize the Celtics had had two ingredients Boston College didn't have—Bill Russell and Bob Cousy."

Cousy's 1963–1964 team, his first, lacked height and experience (Ward had graduated), but it did have sophomore guard John Austin, a highly-recruited schoolboy from famed DeMatha High School in the Washington, D.C. area. Not coincidentally, Celtic coach Red Auerbach was, and still is, a Washington, D.C. resident during the off-season.

"No question Red Auerbach had a lot to do with us getting John Austin," recalls Power. "And shortly after Austin decided to come to Boston College, the NBA eliminated the territorial draft-rights rule that had given an NBA team priority on signing players within their geographical territory. The league was so afraid that Auerbach would stock up Boston College with future Celtics draft picks that they rescinded the rule."

In Cousy's first game as a college coach, the Eagles lost 69–63 to a Fairfield team they were favored to beat. Austin led all scorers with twenty points, but Cousy quickly discovered that Frank Power was right. The Celtics had no big Russell-style rebounder nor any Cousy-style ballhandlers to work a Celtic-style fast break. "But Cousy was a learner," said Power. "He'd go watch any college team any place to see if he could pick up something we could use."

Cousy did learn and adjust, although his team lost its second game and its third. His first win, 97–80 over a weak Colby team, was cause for celebration. But slowly, toward season's end, where other Boston College teams had staggered and some had fallen, Cousy's club hit stride. They won five of their last six to end the season at 10–11.

In his first year of coaching, Bob Cousy was a loser for one of the few times in his life. He handled it well, perhaps knowing he would not have to handle it long. "At first it appeared to be a dismal season," he said following the season-ending win over Boston University, "but we came out of it. We'll be better next year."

Boston College was *better* than better: The 1964–1965 team was one of the best ever to represent the college. "Cousy wasn't just a great coach," says Power. "He was also . . . well, he was Bob Cousy. The name still drew."

To complement John Austin—who in his first season broke Jim Hooley's single season scoring record with 614 points—Cousy the next year acquired the big man his team so desperately needed, 6'8" Willie Wolters of Brooklyn. Wolters was a devastating rebounder, a glass cleaner, who as a sophomore pulled down a team record 354 rebounds and averaged more than eleven points a game over twenty-nine games. Austin's fellow guard, junior Ed Hockenbury of Philadelphia, also came into his own, as the 1964–1965 Eagles became a running, rebounding, fast-breaking mirror image of the Boston Celtics.

"We turned Boston College around pretty much the same way any team gets turned around," says Cousy. "We recruited good players who were also good people. I don't say we were attracting the calibre of player they were getting at UCLA. But the kids we were getting developed well enough for us to play at a competitive level. And when I say we had good people—well, one thing I've always been proud of is that in my six seasons of coaching Boston College, every player

John Austin was a highly-coveted Washington, D.C. high school standout who (thanks to the intercession of Red Auerbach) became the first star of BC's Cousy era. Austin was the Eagles' leading scorer three years in succession, and directed the team's Celtics-like offense.

we recruited got his diploma."

In the second game of the season, Boston College went to Georgetown and beat the nationally-ranked Hoyas 89–71. Two wins and a loss later, Austin's half-court jumper at the buzzer beat Wisconsin 86–85, to send Boston College to the finals of the Milwaukee Classic against powerful UCLA. That one was a 115–93 loss, but the experience was testimony that the Cousy name was capable of getting Boston College invited to some of the nation's bigger holiday tournaments.

Halfway through the season, Cousy's team was 8–6 and poised for the longest winning streak in the team's history, fourteen victories that would send the Eagles to the post-season NIT at Madison Square Garden. There, in a tough first-round draw, three-time tournament champ St. John's gave its retiring coach Joe Lapchik a 114–92 going away present, and ended Boston College's season with a 22–7 record, the best since General McLellan's 22–5 1952 team.

In two seasons, Bob Cousy had given Boston College not just a winner but a basketball identity. The team was considered a good draw for the holiday tournaments, a contender for post-season play, a recruiter of top schoolboy talent, and an exciting team to watch. Once-infrequent sellouts at Roberts Center became commonplace, and the team was attracting students and alumni as well. "He put Boston College on the national basketball map," said then college sports publicist Eddie Miller.

There was more to come. Whereas other Boston College teams had reached the lower rungs of the ladder of national basketball prestige, only to slide back into the twilight zone, Cousy's team pushed on.

Most pre-season polls put the 1965–1966 Eagles in the national top twenty; a few had them in the top ten. Austin, Wolters, and Hockenbury were back, and up from the freshman team was local recruit Steve Adelman, a former Natick High star who literally shot his way into the starting lineup halfway through the season by averaging 25 points a game. Cousy took his team to a 21–4 season that saw Wolters set another rebounding record (431), and now All-America Austin become the team's all-time leading scorer (1,843 points)—a position he would hold for ten years. Once again Cousy's team went to the NIT, and this time they were able to win the team's first-ever post-season game. The Eagles topped Wes Unseld-led Louisville 96–90 in triple overtime and then lost to Villanova by a point, 86–85.

Another great season and still no backsliding. Cousy's coaching and recruiting compensated for the graduation of Austin, bringing along 6'7", 215-pound forward Terry Driscoll of Winthrop (via Boston College High) and 5'11", 165-pound guard Billy Evans of New Haven, Connecticut.

"Recruiting was a new game under Cousy," says Power. "He took a systemized, organized approach. For the first time we began subscribing to the scouting services that rank the best players in the East. We'd contact about a hundred of these boys by letter, then assistant coach Gerry Friel and I would follow up on the players who responded. Once we got it down to the players we really wanted, Cousy would move in with calls or personal visits."

With Wolters and Driscoll controlling the boards, Adelman on his way to becoming Boston College's fifth all-time top scorer, and Evans running the offense, Boston College won twenty-one regular season games and lost but twice—to Utah and Fordham. The biggest win of the season and one of the key victories in the history of BC basketball was an 83–82 victory over prestigious Providence College, a win that marked another turning point in Cousy's program. This time the post-season invitation came not from the NIT but for the ultimate playoff, the NCAAs.

Boston College beat Connecticut 48–42 in first-round NCAA play, overcoming the Huskies' stall-ball game, and then moved on to tackle St. John's before 13,043 at the University of Maryland's Cole Field House. Two Willie Wolters' free throws gave the Eagles a 61–60 lead with twenty-seven seconds to play, when St. John's coach Lou Carnesecca called time out to send in a play. But scrawny Billy Evans upset Carnesecca's designs, as he picked off an errant pass, drew a foul, sank his free throws, and just as surely sank St. John's.

North Carolina's legendary Tarheels, champions of the tough ACC, awaited Boston College the following night. The winner of that game would go to the final four. The winner was not an exhausted Boston College. North Carolina's Bob Lewis sank thirty-one points while Boston College's Adelman, hounded all night by North Carolina's All-America Larry Miller, scored only nine points. The Tarheels went to Louisville, and Boston College, 23–3, went home with the best record in the team's history and NCAA regional runnerup honors.

The impact of the NCAA victories and of Cousy's influence on the program was quickly reflected at the ticket counters. Boston College students bought a record 1,600 season tickets to see a 1967–1968 team that was ranked in the national top ten before the season began and one which would be rated an all-time-high sixth in the nation after opening wins over Dartmouth, Connecticut, and Fairfield. The team's first true test came January 27, 1968, when Boston College met UCLA, the defending national champion and a team led by its awesome 7'6" center, Lew Alcindor.

The game was played in Madison Square Garden and most of the 18,499 in attendance had come to see former New York City high school (Power Memorial) star Alcindor have his high-scoring way with Boston College's defense. After the giant had burned Boston College for twenty-two first-half points and a 46–36 Bruin lead, Cousy decided to have Terry Driscoll and substitute center 6'10" Tom Pacynski play Alcindor man-to-man. The strategy almost worked. Driscoll and Pacynski held Alcindor to six second-half points as Boston College returned from a

Cousy's BC brain trust included his assistant coach Gerry Friel (left) and freshman team coach Frank Power. Power has been associated with Eagle basketball since the early 1950s, as assistant coach (a rank he still holds), freshman coach, and head coach for the 1962–1963 season.

Cousy's 1967–1968 Eagles were pre-season top-ten picks and made it as high as sixth in the nation, before untimely losses resulted in a 17–8 season. Here, Bob Dukiet scores two fast-break points—as season scoring leader Terry Driscoll watches—in a Madison Square Garden loss to St. John's.

seventeen-point deficit to pull to within six, 79–73, with 1:30 to play before coach John Wooden's team restored college basketball's status quo with an 84–77 win.

Boston College won eight of its last ten regular season games to gain another bid to the NCAAs.

The team could hardly have drawn a tougher first-round opponent in the 1968 NCAAs than St. Bonaventure, undefeated (22–0) and ranked third in the nation, behind UCLA and Houston. When the teams met March 8 at University of Rhode Island's Keaney Gym, Cousy chose the

gutty course of shooting it out with the Bonnies. The surprising result was that Boston College scored more points on St. Bonaventure than had any other opponent that year. Still, the Eagles lost the game, 102–93, despite an 84–74 advantage in shooting from the floor. At the foul line, the Eagles shot a dismal nine-for-eighteen while the Bonnies went 28–for–39.

The 1968–1969 season saw Boston College reap the rewards of Cousy's variation of Red Auerbach's time-proven tradition of always planning several seasons ahead. In 1967, Cousy had

The 1968–1969 Eagles were BC's best basketball team ever, winning 24 (while losing four) and making it to the NIT finals (before bowing to Temple). It was also Cousy's last team. Kneeling, left to right: head coach Cousy, captain Don Crosby, Jim O'Brien, Mike Marks, Pete Sollenne, Greg Sees, Dennis Doble, Vin Costello, Frank Fitzgerald, Ray La Grace, Tom Veronneau, Bob Dukiet, Stafford Hilaire, Mike Dunn, Dave McAuliffe, Jim Downey, and senior manager Jim Gilroy.

recruited a Brooklyn-born ball-handling wizard, Jimmy O'Brien, who was the heir apparent to Billy Evans. (Not that O'Brien, of St. Francis Prep, had been a hard sell: his uncle, Tom O'Brien, had been Boston College basketball captain in 1949–1950.) O'Brien broke into the lineup as a sophomore in 1968–1969 and combined with Evans, Driscoll, Veronneau, Frank Fitzgerald, and a chorus of Boston College stars to produce a season that surprised everyone. (Anticipated star Bob Dukiet, a 6'5" forward who had averaged 13.6 points per game in 1967–1968, was sidelined for the season following pre-season knee surgery.)

Boston College opened with ritual defeats of LeMoyne, Connecticut, and Harvard, then dropped three of its next five. The Eagles looked like just another run-of-the-gym college basketball team following a 77–68 loss to Northwestern in the finals of the Gator Bowl Tournament on December 27. But Boston College was about to go almost three months before it lost another game; a streak, or, "The Streak," as it came to be known, that began with Fitzgerald's last-second jumper beating St. John's and continued with wins over California-Irvine (Cousy's one hundredth coaching win), Providence, and ulti-

mately sixteen other victims. In the midst of it all, came a most surprising announcement—Bob Cousy had decided to retire as basketball coach. "Cooz had been thinking about it since the summer," Frank Power recalls. "It was a lot of things. Of course, Cooz had a lot of outside interests [basketball camp, TV analysis work, PR assignments for various Boston companies], but mostly it was the recruiting. Cousy could see then the way college basketball recruiting was heading, with the cheating and the abuses we read about today."

"Recruiting was a big part of the decision," Cousy echoes now. "Every time I hear a coach say he enjoys recruiting I wonder if he's kidding himself or the public. It's a demeaning process for a coach to be sitting on a kid's doorstep to get him to go to a particular school and then to expect the player to have a lot of respect for the coach once he's enrolled. I mean, who needs who? Besides, there's something wrong with having to plead with someone to accept what was then a $6,000 or $8,000 free quality education. By now it's a $20,000 education."

Cousy announced during mid-term exam break that he would leave Boston College and college coaching at the end of the season. The decision did not spark any overt let's-win-it-for-Cooz sentimentality, but it did give his team something extra to shoot for, and the Streak continued.

Wins over Seton Hall, Canisius, Northeastern, Holy Cross, UMass, and a 105–70 humbling of Fordham brought The Streak to nine. It shot to twelve with victories over Penn State, Rhode Island, and with an overtime thriller at Georgetown. Wins over Detroit (Spencer Haywood notwithstanding), Boston University, and a second beating of Holy Cross ran The Streak to fifteen. By now, Boston College had been invited to the NIT.

NCAA-bound Dusquesne came into Roberts Center for the final regular season game. Goodbye ceremonies for Cousy before tapoff sidestepped the possibility of an anticlimax should Boston College lose. No danger. The ninth-in-the-nation Dukes fell 93–72, and Cooz left Roberts Center a winner.

The Streak carried over into Madison Square Garden. Jimmy O'Brien hit for seventeen as Kansas fell to Boston College 78–62 in the NIT opener. Next, O'Brien (24 points) and Driscoll (21) paced an 88–83 Eagles win over Missouri Valley Conference champ Louisville. Then came a highly-disciplined Army team that Cousy later confided he thought could beat Boston College. It couldn't. Boston College won 73–61 with Cousy calling the victory "the most satisfying win of the season for me."

The Eagles and the Temple Owls met March 22 for the NIT crown. It was a bad time for The Streak to end, but end it did, as Temple came from behind to take a 70–69 lead and then go into a semi-freeze with 6:33 to play. Boston College was forced to foul, the Temple players converted, and the final score soared to 89–76.

Terry Driscoll, who would soon be playing his basketball with the NBA Milwaukee Bucks, won the tournament's MVP trophy. "Whatever we are," said Driscoll after the game, "we owe to [Cousy], plus our own hard work. He inspired us and made us believers in ourselves."

"We developed a tradition," said Billy Evans. "We finally established a definite home court advantage. We knew we could beat anybody at home."

Tradition was exactly what Bob Cousy contributed most to Boston College. In six years he had turned a football-hockey school into a nationally-ranked basketball power which regularly appeared in post-season tournaments.

The tradition would soon disintegrate.

The search for Cousy's successor induced Bill Flynn to wade through the résumés of seventy-five candidates before he selected thirty-nine-year-old Duke assistant coach Chuck Daly, a big, wavy-haired, nattily-dressed young man with a slight Atlantic Coast Conference superiority complex. "Chuck Daly was a good basketball coach, a good role model, and good for the university image," recalls Frank Power, "but he was mesmerized by the reputation of the ACC. Daly gave me the impression that he thought Boston College was a notch below the ACC, that we couldn't compete at that level, and that we couldn't recruit at that level. As a result, I think we recruited a notch below where we could have."

At Boston College, Daly inherited Jim O'Brien, a Cousy recruit whose strong scoring (16.5 points per game) and All-East play combined with Tom Veronneau's under-the-boards muscle to keep the bottom from falling out in an 11–13 1969–1970 season. It was not an auspicious debut, considering that Cousy had not left the team bereft of talent.

Daly's team eked out a 15–11 season for 1970–1971, largely on the scoring of Cousy holdovers O'Brien (whose 492 points gave him 1,273 for his career, behind Austin, Driscoll, and Adelman on the all-time list) and Fitzgerald who had a career-high 376. O'Brien had twenty-two and Fitzgerald eleven in the season's biggest win, a 67–52 upset of eighth-ranked Dusquesne.

Later that spring, Daly leapt at an offer of the head coaching job at the University of Pennsylvania and left after just two seasons at the Heights. (He has since moved on to the pro ranks, as an assistant to Billy Cunningham at the Philadelphia 76ers, and a short-lived term in the top spot with the Cleveland Cavaliers.)

Daly's major achievement at Boston College may have been that of persuading the college to hire its first full-time assistant basketball coach in Bob Zuffelato, former freshman coach at Hofstra and Central Connecticut State. Now, it was Zuffelato who took over as the Eagles' head coach.

"Zuff was a good basketball man but I think he needed time to gain confidence in himself," says Power. Like many assistant coaches, Zuffelato was a mirror image of his mentor. "Sometimes he tried to be Chuck Daly," says Power. "He'd dress like Daly and talk like Daly."

Fortunately, he recruited like Bob Zuffelato—which is to say, he recruited well. While his 1971–1972 first team was going 13–13—a better season than might have been expected following the graduation of O'Brien and Fitzgerald—Zuffelato was recruiting three local players who would become known as "The Boston Connection." They would prove to be the temporary salvation of Boston College basketball: Bob "Smooth" Carrington, 6'6", 180-pound forward from Dorchester, widely considered the best schoolboy player in Massachusetts when he averaged 34 points per game for ex-Boston College great Chuck Chevalier at Archbishop Williams High School; Wil Morrison, 6'6", 190-pound forward from Dorchester who came to Boston College via Coach Joe Murphy's Boston Technical High School team; and Bill Collins, a 6'9", 195-pound forward, also from Dorchester, who arrived from Coach Kevin Mackey's Don Bosco High School club.

The Boston Connection didn't make much noise at first and neither did Boston College, with another losing season, 11–14, in 1972–1973. Collins played on the sub-varsity; Carrington, because of academic difficulties, played only four varsity games at season's end; and Morrison, the only one of the '72 freshmen trio to crack the starting lineup, averaged ten points and seven rebounds while playing twenty of the team's twenty-five games.

But Boston College's two-year basketball drought ended dramatically during 1973–1974, as the trio of Carrington-Morrison-Collins became a starburst. The three local players combined with New Yorkers Dan Kilcullen, Jere Nolan (1973 team MVP), and freshman Paul Berwanger. Along with Michigan's Mark Rater-

ink, they gave Boston College its best season since Cousy's departure: an 18–8 record and an NIT bid, the Eagles' sixth post-season tournament in ten years.

The opening match against Cincinnati was a cardiac case from the outset, with Nolan sinking a clutch free throw for a 63–62 Boston College lead with twenty-six seconds to play. Nolan then narrowly dodged goat horns, as he failed to inbounds a pass, and with nine seconds left, affording the Bearcats three shots at a game-winner, all of which missed.

Boston College cut it even thinner in its second-round game with Connecticut, which had defeated the Eagles a month earlier in the regular season. UConn was up 75–74 with five seconds to play and Boston College struggling to

Leader of the "Boston Connection" recruited by coach Bob Zuffelato in 1972 was Dorchester product Bob "Smooth" Carrington. In three seasons, Carrington would net a total 1,849 points—an all-time BC career mark that still stands.

come back from a deficit that once saw them behind 13 points with 13 minutes to play. Nolan had the ball. (Nolan would reveal after the season that he was playing with a broken right wrist.) Nolan passed to Raterink. Raterink, double teamed, gave it back to Nolan. With two seconds to play, Nolan passed to freshman Paul Berwanger. Berwanger shot a five-footer off the glass and into the hole. Buzzer, Boston College won 76–75.

"I just wanted to get it away," Berwanger said later. "I've never taken a shot like that in my life [but] everyone has to take one like that sometime."

The win sent the Eagles to the semifinals against high-scoring Utah State—in this case, *too* high-scoring Utah State. An emotionally drained Boston College lost 117–93 and the following night had to settle for third place tournament honors with an 87–77 win over Jacksonville, a game in which Nolan's fourteen assists set an NIT record.

The next season, 1974–1975, Nolan's role as playmaker fell to captain Mel Weldon of New Jersey, a 1973 transfer from Mercer Junior College and a member of the 1972 United States National team. Collins, Carrington, and Morrison were back for their junior years and 6' 11" center Berwanger was already a veteran, though only a sophomore.

Pre-season polls had Boston College in the nation's top twenty, a reasonable assessment of a potentially great team but, in reality, a slight overrating of a good team. Boston College had returned to the lower rungs of the ladder of basketball prestige, but it still got its fingers stepped on by St. John's (75–62), Georgetown (90–82), and Holy Cross (77–70) in the course of an 18–8 regular season. This was, nevertheless, good enough to take the Eagles to the ECAC regional playoffs, gateway to the NCAAs, and here the team's overwhelming individual talents began to coalesce.

Relatively unknown freshman Jeff Bailey of Illinois came off the bench to score eleven second-half points and that output, plus Carrington's team-high nineteen, gave the Eagles a 68–58 first-round win over Connecticut at the Springfield Civic Center. In the same round, Holy Cross beat Providence to establish a Boston College-Holy Cross final. Collins (21) and Carrington (17) were the heroes here, taking Boston College to a 69–55 win and an automatic passage to the first round of the NCAAs at Charlotte, North Carolina.

Once the Eagles were on the national stage, Wil Morrison took his turn in the spotlight with twenty points, leading the way to an 82–76 Boston College win over Furman. The victory guaranteed the Eagles' safe passage back to New England for the NCAA East Regional Semifinals at the Providence Civic Center, where the team promptly had its fingers stomped on again. Kansas State's jump-shooting Chuckie Williams personally destroyed Boston College with a game-high 34 points, as his team scored a 74–65 victory. Two nights later, Boston College lost the consolation game to North Carolina, 110–90, to finish 21–9 for 1974–1975.

Two consecutive 21–9 seasons, two consecutive post-season tournament appearances, the return of the Boston Connection, and a great recruiting year (among the newcomers: Ernie Cobb, Cornwall, New York; Mike Bowie, San Francisco; and Tom Meggers, Chicago, Illinois) had Boston College basketball fans caught in a pre-season whirlwind of superlatives. "What a year it should be!" raved the 1975–1976 basketball program.

What a year indeed. After tune-up wins over Bentley, LeMoyne, and Harvard, Boston College absorbed a 105–82 home-court thrashing from Rutgers in which team play was virtually non-existent. To quote the partisan campus newspaper, *The Heights:* the team "showed that [its] five separate units could not compete successfully against opponents that recognized the benefit of an unselfish, team-oriented approach."

Part of the problem could be attributed to a rift that had developed between Zuffelato and his players, particularly the moody Carrington, who showed an increasing tendency to freelance. Beginning with the Rutgers loss, Boston College dropped five in a row to effectively eliminate itself from the national picture by New Year's Day. The team finished the season losing twelve of its last sixteen, for a 9–17 disaster of a year. The showing did little to help recruiting, and Zuffelato found he was able to attract only one top-quality ball player that spring, New Jersey's Jim Sweeney.

Recruiting problems and the graduation of Morrison, Carrington, and Collins—virtually the whole offense—left Zuffelato with little to work with in 1976–1977. After a fistful of early-season losses, the coach faced growing fan and alumni displeasure. A bad beating by Clemson in the consolation game of the Milwaukee Classic, 126–76, was sufficient inducement for Zuffelato to announce his intention to resign at season's end. Boston College limped to an 8–18 season under its lame-duck coach, and another recruiting year slid by.

Bill Flynn searched for a new coach in his usual manner, paying little attention to unsolicited résumés and much attention to the NCAA grapevine. "Bill came to me late that season," recalls Power, "and asked me, 'What do you know about a Tom Davis at Lafayette?' I told Bill I didn't know Tom personally, but everything I'd ever heard about him indicated he was one hell of a coach, a brilliant young man. Everyone spoke well of him."

Well they might. In six seasons at Pennsylvania's Lafayette College, Davis' teams were 116–44 for a .725 winning percentage, and had secured a reputation for exceptional hustle, tenacity, and intelligent play. The coach was noted for his "cerebral" approach to the game, the reputation abetted somewhat by the fact that, in the course of his apprenticeship at the University of Maryland, Coach Davis had become Doctor Davis by earning his Ph.D. in sports history.

All of which was good enough for Flynn.

Davis, 38, arrived at Boston College in the spring of 1977. It was too late in the school year to do any major recruiting, so Davis concentrated not on superstars, but on what he described as "intelligent, good people; guys who want to go to school and excel on and off the court." Among his first recruits were Chris Foy of Philadelphia and Vin Caraher of East Meadow, New York, neither a first-magnitude star but both destined for key roles in Boston College's basketball resurgence.

Davis won his Boston College debut 99–70 over Le Moyne and had his team, predicted to do no better than .500, at 14–7 by mid-February with upsets over Georgetown and Fordham. "Unlike years before, players were hustling on defense, they were diving for loose balls and there was passing to open teammates," noted *The Heights*. "There was discipline and there was pride."

Dr. Tom Davis—a legitimate Ph.D. in sports history—came to the Heights from Lafayette College and immediately restored the Eagles to winning ways. Before departing for Stanford University in 1982, Davis' hustling teams achieved a 100–47 five-year record, won a Big East championship, received four post-season tournament bids, and weathered a sensational point-shaving scandal.

There was ultimately a 15–11 season in which Davis received Coach of the Year honors from *Eastern Basketball* magazine, and Ernie Cobb's 22.8 points per game earned him All-East honors. Boston College was headed up the ladder again.

A great recruiting year in 1978—aided by Davis assistant Kevin Mackey, formerly a coach at Boston's Don Bosco High—brought in much-publicized Don Bosco star guard Dwan Chandler and little-known Nashua, New Hampshire, forward Rich Shrigley, a banger, hustler, and diver-after-loose-balls. "When people think of Boston College's style of basketball, they should think of Rich Shrigley," said Davis.

Davis, using waves of substitutes, full-pressure defense, and a no-stars system brought Boston College home 21–8 and in the process returned fans to Roberts Center. Most of those fans were students.

"There was not a great tradition of basketball in New England or at Boston College," Davis observes. "The Boston schools played hockey through the thirties and into the forties, and let's face it, Boston College was a hockey school. But what we saw happening here was that our first support came from students and then that started to broaden to include alumni. We felt we were starting to build a tradition."

Rebuild, really. Davis' 1978–1979 Eagles went to the ECAC New England regionals, the first step toward the NCAAs. Even though the team lost to Connecticut, it was Boston College's first post-season appearance since 1975. "We've been able to regain the respect of our opponents," said Davis after that season. "The next thing we want is for them to fear us."

After leading the team in scoring for the third straight year, his 1,760 career points placing him third behind Carrington and Austin on the all-time list, point guard Ernie Cobb had played his last season. His departure left Davis with a huge hole to fill. He did so with another player not many Division I schools wanted, six-foot John Bagley of Warren Harding High School, Bridgeport, Connecticut, a player that Davis saw as "an outstanding fundamental basketball player in all areas of the game."

While Davis continued to strenghten his team, athletic director Flynn was weighing a proposal that might make or break Boston College basketball: to join or not to join a new league that was to call itself "the Big East." It consisted of Providence, Georgetown, St. John's, Seton Hall, Syracuse, and Connecticut (Villanova would join in 1980, Pitt in 1982). To join such a powerhouse league would greatly increase the difficulty of Boston College's schedule. But, says Flynn, "not to join would be to leave yourself on the outside looking in. Maybe we couldn't even schedule these teams anymore." Flynn didn't hestitate. Boston College was in.

"Thanks to a quick, firm step and the foresight of Bill Flynn, we got into the Big East Conference and that has made an enormous difference in our program," Davis would say later. "It added immeasurably to our success." At the time, however, Boston College was chosen to finish last in the new league's first season, 1979–1980.

No team with John Bagley was likely to finish last in anything. The freshman took over Cobb's role as point guard, and playing at both ends of the court, he led the team in scoring (343) and was named to the Big East all-rookie team. The Eagles beat Georgetown in a dramatic overtime game at the ECAC Holiday Festival, Caraher tossing in the winner—a clutch last-second jumper. And later, for the second season in a row, Boston College went on to post-season play. Despite losing to Connecticut in the first Big East championship, Boston College received an invitation to the NIT. There the Eagles beat Commonwealth Avenue rival Boston University in the first round, before losing to a Ralph Sampson-led Virginia.

The Dr. Davis prescription—astute scouting, recruiting, and cohesive team basketball—continued into 1980–1981. That season, with the help of assistants Power and Mackey, Davis brought in 6'8" Martin Clark of Don Bosco, a native of England; rail-thin 6'9" center Jay Murphy of Meriden, Connecticut; and sharp-shooting guard Tim O'Shea of Wayland, Massachusetts.

With underclassmen holding down four of the five starting positions and senior Chris Foy "the glue that holds us together," according to Davis, the Eagles' crew of clutching, scrambling, floor-

"When people think of BC's style of basketball," said architect Tom Davis, "they should think of Rich Shrigley." The aggressive forward (here rebounding against UConn) was a board-banger and floor-scraper who keyed the Eagles for three seasons.

One of the most electric BC players of all time, John Bagley (here driving against Providence) was a skilled playmaker and devastating one-on-one scorer. In 1980–1981 he was the Big East player of the year and in 1981–1982 he led the Eagles to the Midwest regional finals of the NCAA championships before turning pro.

BC center Jay Murphy goes to the hole against Georgetown counterpart Patrick Ewing, in the Eagles' biggest regular season win of 1981–1982. The 80–71 drubbing of the top-ten Hoyas inspired BC on the way to its own post-season heroics.

dusters laid to rest pre-season predictions that Boston College would finish sixth in the eight-team conference. A sweep of the holiday Music City Tournament in Nashville coalesced the team's play, and a 58–57 win over 18th-ranked Connecticut on January 14, 1981, put the Eagles at 9–2 at the halfway mark.

The morning after the UConn win, Boston College players awoke to read less about their disturbing upset than about a more shocking

federal investigation. The United States organized crime strike force, the press reported, was looking into allegations that Boston College players (the first names mentioned were Rick Kuhn, Jim Sweeney, and Ernie Cobb—the investigation would eventually focus on Kuhn) conspired with gamblers to shave points in as many as eleven games during the 1978–1979 season, Davis' second at Boston College.

The first reactions were ones of disbelief. "Not as hard as we worked, as much effort as we put out," lamented Dwan Chandler.

As the investigation and attendant publicity continued, Tom Davis was left facing the toughest challenge of his heretofore stable career—keep the 1980–1981 train on the tracks. None of the three players implicated was a Davis recruit, nor were any active players implicated; "Still," said Power, "something like that touches all of us."

Boston College's official posture was to cooperate with the Justice Department and to say nothing publicly. Team practices were closed to the public and media. "I told the players I wanted the rest of the season to be as normal as possible," said Davis. "I told them that they shouldn't dwell on it because it was none of their doing. It was history as far as they were concerned."

Later, Davis would reveal that he was not able to follow his own advice: "When you hear horror stories about the children of your friends—how they're hooked on drugs or have been arrested or whatever—you say to yourself 'I can't believe that happened to that parent. I thought they were raising their kids perfectly.' But it happens. And now, that's how I feel."

Flynn took it harder. "I know the actions of one or a few people are not the actions of a university," he later recalled, "but I also know that Tom Davis and I probably overreacted to this. We took the news very hard. But, on the whole, the Boston College family was not critical of the team, the coach, or the athletic program. On the road it was a different story. We heard a lot of stuff."

Opponent fans in one gym serenaded the Boston College team with the Gillette shaving song ("Don't even look up," assistant coach Mackey advised the players). And more than one banner carried messages similar to the one at Holy Cross: "Want a close shave? Try Boston College."

Elsewhere there was sympathy for Flynn and Davis. Catholic University coach and former Boston College player Jack Kvancz told the *Washington Post*: "Bill Flynn and Tom Davis—Heck, their whole lives have been an open book, proof that you could put your values first and still get enough victories. It's a tragedy to have these pages written in their book. It's worse than that. It's disgusting because it makes no sense. So many louses, if it happened to them you'd want to cheer. I just want to scream, 'These are the wrong guys.'"

Through it all, the team kept winning. Bagley, by all observations the only truly exceptional player on the team, would lead Boston College in all scoring departments while the supporting cast of Foy, Shrigley, Chandler, O'Shea, Clark,

One of BC's greatest athletic triumphs occurred on Sunday afternoon, March 14, 1982, when the Eagles met DePaul in second round NCAA playoff action—and defeated the number-two ranked Blue Devils, 82–75. Here John Bagley shoots over DePaul all-American Terry Cummings.

Murphy, and Burnett Adams continued to do what Davis wanted them to do—play unselfish, poised, intelligent, and relentlessly aggressive basketball.

The point-shaving investigation and subsequent trial would continue for another year, concluding with the conviction and sentencing of Rick Kuhn (ten years) and of four racketeers on various counts, for their roles in attempting to shave points in six Boston College games.

Yet, through the catcalls and derisive cheers, what Davis called his "fragile" team, "a typical college team which has suddenly developed a [winning] attitude that is not typical at all," won the Big East regular season championship, while Bagley (20.2 points per game) was the Big East Player of the Year.

Providence upset Boston College, 67–65, in the first round of the Big East playoffs, a setback that proved to be only momentary when the NCAA tournament selection committee invited Boston College to play for the national title. Boston College beat Ball State 93–90 in the opening round game at Tuscaloosa, Alabama and followed that with a 67–64 win over nationally-ranked Wake Forest. In the latter game, Bagley scored a season-high thirty-five points, twenty-two of them in the second half.

Those wins put Boston College in the final sixteen and sent the team to the NCAA Midwest Regional Playoffs in Bloomington, Indiana. There, poor shooting (.389 from the floor, ten points for Bagley) was the principal culprit, giving St. Joseph's a 42–41 win, ending the Eagles' season. Said the ever-candid Davis of his young team, "It was the pressure of being here that did it to us."

Boston College would have to become accustomed to the pressure—there was more to come. Rangy John Garris, a 6'8" center and transfer from Michigan who had to sit out a year before playing at Boston College, and lightning-quick guard Michael Adams of Hartford, Connecticut, were the major additions to Davis' 1981–1982 collection of ordinary people. The team began playing like critics had said they would play the two previous seasons—poorly— and eleven games into the schedule, Boston College was 5–6. One

of the losses was a 22-point shellacking by Villanova, the worst loss in Davis' career.

Road wins over Syracuse and Providence and a 102–81 hosing of Holy Cross in which Bagley scored thirty points provided the first hints that better things were in store. Increased playing time for Garris and Michael Adams was creating new spark in the offense; Shrigley was improving with every game, and Bagley was more confident than ever. But still ahead lay Georgetown and freshman star Patrick Ewing, intent on restoring status quo to the Big East.

The February 17 Georgetown game at Boston College was the toughest ticket in town, probably the most challenging Boston College ticket since the 1975 Notre Dame football game. The Hoyas were ranked thirteenth in the nation at the time (they would, of course, go on to play in the NCAA championship game), and Ewing was ranked somewhere between Kareem Abdul-Jabbar and Bill Russell in his potential as a basketball star, having led nearby Cambridge Rindge and Latin to three straight Massachusetts high school titles. The game, then, was expected to be a little hometown recital for Ewing's family and friends and for the local college that had tried so hard, yet failed, to recruit him.

The show, however, was Boston College's and Bagley's.

Ewing played well, jamming in 23 points and a game-high six rebounds. But Bagley hit for 26, Shrigley shot four-for-four, Garris grabbed five key rebounds, and Boston College won 80–71. The Eagles would not lose a game for the rest of the season and would take an 18–8 record into the Big East playoffs at Hartford.

History threatened to repeat itself for the Eagles in The Big East's playoff opener, as the team fell behind to lightly-regarded Syracuse, 92–84, with 1:58 to play. The loss would eliminate Boston College from the tournament, and very likely, from NCAA playoff consideration. All the Orangemen had to do was slow the game, kill the clock, and shake hands. Instead, they threw the ball away, failed to inbound passes, and missed obvious shots. Meanwhile, clutch shooting by the Eagles tied the game. With three seconds to play, Dwan Chandler had the ball sixteen feet from the basket. He wanted to pass to John Bagley, who at the time had several Syracuse players trying to get inside his shirt. So Chandler, whose college career never quite attained the glory of his high school years, went for the shot that beat Syracuse 94–92.

The delirium that swept the Boston College bench was short-lived. The win over Syracuse had earned Boston College the questionable distinction of facing 21–6 Villanova in the semifinals. The Big East regular-season champion had already defeated the Eagles twice in 1981–1982. Despite a furious second-half Boston College comeback attempt, Villanova breezed to a 74–71 triumph. The Eagles returned to Chestnut Hill to practice and await the decision of the NCAA selection committee.

"There's more to come," predicted Martin Clark, and he was right. The selection committee, in a controversial decision, declared that a 19–9 Big East team was good enough for the forty-eight-team NCAA tournament, a decision which Boston College supported with a 70–66 first-round win over San Francisco at Dallas. The victory sent Boston College into a match with the number-two team in the nation, 26–1, DePaul (twenty-one wins in a row) on Sunday, March 14.

Davis, matching wits with the Blue Demon coaching legend Ray Meyer, decided to attack DePaul with high-pressure defense and an offense designed to draw fouls. By halftime, five DePaul players had three fouls each, all were exhausted, and Boston College trailed by only two points, 30–28. The pressure continued into the second half with dogged work by Shrigley, Bagley, and Michael Adams, the little guard who was quickly becoming the crowd's adopted hero. Boston College tied the game at 49–49, with Shrigley crashing for his own rebound, and then went ahead on a pair of Adams' free throws.

"We just kept attacking," said Davis later. And DePaul folded. Three consecutive Blue Demon turnovers led to a 57–49 Boston College lead that more or less ended competition for the afternoon, as Boston College rolled to an 82–75 win over the most highly-ranked opponent in its history.

Meyer credited the press and Bagley. "I didn't think their press would bother us that much . . . Bagley controlled the game almost single-handedly."

Back at Chestnut Hill the win set off a spontaneous student celebration resulting in an athletic non-sequitur—the tearing down of the football goalposts. The win also sent Boston College to the St. Louis Checkerdome and the Midwest Regionals, beginning with a game against eighteenth-ranked Kansas State.

With Bagley unable to penetrate the KSU zone, it was left to Michael Adams to pick up the slack. He did, with 21 points and a game-saving steal. With ninety seconds left and Boston College clinging to a 61–59 lead, KSU got a two-on-one break that would have likely tied the game, except that Adams swiped the ball from the Wildcats' Ed Galvao. With Boston College killing the clock and KSU forced to foul, Bagley and Martin Clark hit free throws for a 69–65 win that made the Eagles one of three Big East teams to reach the final eight (Villanova edged Northeastern, and Georgetown drubbed Fresno State).

Only the run-and-gun University of Houston Cougars stood between Boston College and the Eagles' first trip to the fabled Final Four in New Orleans. But the impossible string of upsets ended. Houston handled Boston College's full-court press with ease, as All-America Rob Williams and guard Reid Gettys helped the Cougars to a 99–92 win.

"I know that Houston beat our press early and that they are tremendously talented," conceded Jay Murphy. "But, damn, we didn't set up well and we rebounded horribly."

It was a hard loss, but not as hard as that which surfaced as soon as the season ended. It was rumored that Boston College was losing Tom Davis to Wisconsin or Stanford. The rumors proved true. In late March, Davis told Flynn he would be leaving Boston College to accept the head coaching position at Stanford with a reported salary-benefits package totaling $150,000 a year.

It was a friendly parting. Flynn credited Davis with giving Boston College a basketball identity, and Davis said, "When I first came here, I'd heard that Bill Flynn was not that interested in basketball. I think that has been disproved. His

To succeed Tom Davis, BC athletic director Bill Flynn named American University coach Gary Williams. A former Davis assistant at both Lafayette and BC, Williams was chosen in part because he favored the Eagles' aggressive, pressing, disciplined style of play.

direction and his getting us into the Big East were the things that have made basketball a major sport at Boston College."

In seeking to replace Davis, Flynn listened to the advice of Boston College's players, who were eager for a coach who would continue the Davis style. Davis' legacy—besides a 100–47 Boston College record and four post-season tournament appearances—provided the Eagles with a reputation as a pressing, fast-breaking, aggressive, disciplined bunch of over-achievers. The players wanted that legacy maintained. So did Flynn.

To do the job, Flynn chose 37-year-old Gary Williams, who had worked as Davis' assistant for seven years at Lafayette and one year (1977–1978) at Boston College before accepting the head coaching job at Washington's American University. There he took a team that had to practice

in an armory ten miles from campus to a 72–42 record over four seasons and 47–18 during his last two years.

Williams had no problem following in Davis' footsteps. "I like the pressure defense and the running game. Basically, I do run the same system Tom does," he said the day it was announced he had accepted the job. Williams also said that he was "looking forward to meeting Bagley, one of the top guards in the country."

The remark had an ironic edge, as five weeks later Bagley, one of sixteen children in a financially-strapped family, decided to forgo his senior year in college, declare "hardship," and enter the NBA draft.

Williams handled the news of his departing superstar gracefully. According to Williams, he had known of the possibility of losing Bagley.

"You have to think what John gave Boston College in three years. He did a tremendous job."

But competing in the Big East without John Bagley could be a new coach's undoing. Departure of the star point guard raised the spectre of Boston College again slipping into basketball oblivion and repeating once more the climb-and-slip pattern that characterized most of its ninety-year basketball history.

"But Tom Davis' contribution to Boston College basketball has been to put the sport on a solid and permanent basis here," countered Bill Flynn. "In the past we could have some good seasons and then a bad season or two, and we could wonder if basketball was really that important to us.

"But our achievements and our successful competition in a conference like the Big East have made basketball a very important part of our athletic program. So the days when we might question what basketball meant to us—well, those days are gone forever."

Gone with the peach baskets and the James Street gym with six posts in the floor.

5

Baseball, and Track and Field

BASEBALL

A GAME BELONGS to the people who play it more than it will ever belong to those who follow it from the safety of the grandstand or press box. While college football, basketball, and, in the north, hockey, attract vast media coverage and a following of millions, there exists on most American campuses another, less visible level of sport. These games draw less widespread interest, athletic scholarships are fewer, and yet athletes compete with all the effort and enthusiasm of those in the so-called "major"—or revenue-producing—sports.

At Boston College, some of these less noted sports, particularly baseball, and track and field, have as long and distinguished a history as do the three major sports.

"It's *not* a minor sport. Don't ever call baseball a minor sport. Baseball is the greatest game there

is. It's just not a *money-making* sport." So says Eddie Pellagrini, former Red Sox star and Boston College baseball coach since 1958. Pellagrini has three times taken a team for which there are no scholarships to the College World Series to compete with the likes of USC, where baseball is a well-supported (i.e., a "major") sport.

Pellagrini has his own explanation for college baseball's general failure to attract a large following outside of the sunbelt. "Take the kids who've been cooped up in the classroom and the library since September," he says. They've been studying all winter, and now comes spring and those students are thinking of final exams and summer and going out to the beach. They're not thinking of going to a weekday afternoon baseball game. It's different on a cold winter night when the students say, 'hey, let's go down to the gym for a basketball game,' I mean, what else is there to do?"

"I think what hurts college baseball," Boston College Athletic director Bill Flynn elaborates, "is the shortening of the academic calendar. We used to draw big crowds for baseball in the twenties and thirties when we played from mid-April to mid-June or so. Now the academic year ends about May first and the students are off campus and working before we play Holy Cross. And we can't start any earlier than we do because of New England weather."

Flynn and Pellagrini are speaking to the heart of baseball's curious lack of stature in most northern intercollegiate sports programs. Football, basketball, and, at some colleges, hockey, are a college's athletic flagships, the sports by which an institution is judged by alumni and the general public and is assigned its niche in the national athletic pecking order. Still, at Boston College and elsewhere, baseball remains somehow a basic sport, and teams are fielded even though they cost more money than they will ever raise.

Such was not always the case. In 1923, a three-game series between Boston College and Holy Cross drew an estimated 80,000, including a one-game Braves Field crowd of more than 30,000. Boston College baseball has a history that is older than football's and hockey's, and in the historical perspective, more successful and stable than that of basketball.

The first record of baseball at Boston College comes from historian Nat Hasenfus, who reports that Boston College students were staging inter-class games at Miller's Field, Roxbury, in the early 1870s. As noted in Chapter One, the star of these games was catcher Dennis J. Sullivan, who went on to a professional career with the Boston Nationals.

The first recorded lineup of any Boston College team comes, undated, from the Sullivan era: pitchers—John F. Malloy, P. H. Callahan; catchers—Dennis J. Sullivan, Michael Glennon; first base—Joseph Keyes; second base—John F. Quirk; third base—Nicholas R. Walsh; shortstop—Edward J. Haynes; left field—John F. Broderick; center field—John Gallagher; right field—Charles Curtis.

In the mid 1870s, these Boston College class teams came together to form an intramural league that existed well into the next century.

In the spring of 1883, about the same time Boston College students were agitating for the formation of a Boston College athletic club and for administrative support of intercollegiate athletics, a Boston College baseball team referred to in the *Stylus,* the campus literary magazine, simply as "the College Nine" lost a game to Holy Cross at Worcester. No score, lineup, or account of the game has been preserved.

Because of a lack of record-keeping that unhappily is common through most of Boston College's baseball history and in the history of most non-revenue sports, decades of Boston College baseball lore have been lost. Games were played

Baseball's long and erratic history at Boston College hit a peak in 1923 when a crowd of 30,000–plus filled Braves Field (now the site of BU's Nickerson Field) to watch BC beat Holy Cross.

125

but box scores were not saved, players were mentioned by their last names only (in the journalistic fashion of the time), and college publications responsible for reporting games inevitably finished their publishing year long before baseball concluded its schedule. The college game, perhaps in perfect keeping with its tradition of being a player's game, seems rarely to have inspired the obsession with statistics or records that existed in college football—or even in professional baseball, for that matter. It seems to have been very much a game played for its own sake. We do know that, even before the formation of the Boston College Athletic Club in 1885, Boston College avenged its 1893 loss to Holy Cross with a 5-1 win on November 21, 1884.

Two years later, an unsigned letter in the *Stylus* refers to the formation of the Boston College Baseball Association and to student attempts to raise money so that "grounds may be obtained into which the players will be permitted to enter at all times." This view that for want of a field, baseball games were being lost is the dominant theme of the first three decades of Boston College baseball. Pitchers and catchers could, and did, work out in the gym, but the team seems never to have secured a proper home field (unless we wish to count the Mass. Avenue grounds even the players called "The Dump") and played most of its games at various public fields or at the home field of its opponent.

There were other problems in those early years. A *Stylus* note in 1895 upbraids players for their indifferent attitude: "More interest must be shown in baseball practice if the team is going to fulfill the bright hopes entertained for it, not to speak of the obligation under which the members lie of worthily representing the College." The next year, the campus publication shifted its attention to fans, complaining in May 1896 that neither students nor alumni have supported the team: "It seems to us an unpardonable shame that the efforts to place athletics on a firm basis have not met with more generous cooperation from the alumni and the greater part of the student [body]."

The same issue of the *Stylus* carries news that the Boston College team opened its 1896 season

with a split of four games, beating Tufts 14–13 and Exeter Academy 8–7, but losing to Andover 12–7 and Bowdoin 14–5. While there are no complete year-end records such as exist in other sports, it is apparent from the few scores which do exist that Boston College was not a dominant team and was often below .500. The addition of a season-opening April "southern trip" in 1899—though the team never went south of New Jersey—produced three straight Boston College losses: 12–5 to Manhattan, 17–10 to Seton Hall, and 12–2 to Fordham.

(Ironically, at the same time college baseball was struggling to gain a foothold in Boston, *professional* baseball was booming. The National League had had a team—the Beaneaters—in Boston since the league's inception in 1876, and the new American League appeared on the local scene in 1901, with an entrant that went by several names—mostly, the Pilgrims—before becoming the Red Sox in 1907. Just two years after its birth, in 1903, the popular upstart Boston American League club played in and won the very first World Series before overflow crowds in the 16,000–20,000 range.)

In 1902, the college tried to solve one of its baseball problems by purchasing a nine-acre tract on Mass. Avenue (see box, Chapter 2, page 12) for use as a combination football-baseball field. While the football team began practicing on these grounds in spring, 1902 (just before football was discontinued at Boston College for five years), the baseball team used the much-maligned facility for practices and a few home games throughout the early 1900s. In 1911, the college, then committed to the move to Chestnut Hill, sold the property to the Edison Company.

The schedules of the 1890s and 1900s generally found Boston College playing college baseball powers Fordham, Seton Hall, and Holy Cross, along with such major New England teams as Brown, Rhode Island State, Massachusetts Agricultural College, and Boston University. Results and fan support were apparently so lackluster that the college administration considered dropping baseball in 1907. A story in the April 1907 *Stylus* tells of a March communion breakfast that turned into an impromptu rally for baseball as, one after another, the four class presidents arose to speak out in favor of Boston College fielding a team. The decisive speech apparently came when one "Reverend Father Lyons, S.J. . . . earned the applause of the students by the unmistakable manner in which he pronounced himself in favor of all branches of athletics."

Baseball seems to have regained firm ground by 1908, when Boston College appointed a part-time coach, James W. Driscoll of Lynn, and the team received some financial support from the sale of season tickets to the alumni and student body. Batting star of the 1908 and 1909 teams was leftfielder Bernie O'Kane (later Monsignor O'Kane), whose election to baseball captaincy in 1909 made him one of the college's few three-sport captains (he also captained basketball and track).

It is an interesting measure of baseball's stature, and of the student body's predisposition to academics, that interest in baseball in this era lags behind interest in the Boston College debating society, which in 1910 defeated Georgetown and Fordham. An unsigned note in the May 1911 *Stylus* put baseball and Boston College athletics in general in its then popular perspective: "What Holy Cross is on the diamond, what Fordham is on the gridiron, what Georgetown is on the track, Boston College is in the forum."

By 1913, with its field sold and the college in the process of relocating to the suburbs, Boston College baseball played its last season in Boston, scheduling six home games on the Eustis Street grounds, two (Seton Hall and Mass. Agricultural) at Fenway Park, and the Holy Cross game at Braves Field (then generally known as "the National League grounds"). There is no complete final-season record, outside of Eagle victories over Colby, St. Michael's, and Dean Junior College, and losses to Exeter, Middlebury, and Seton Hall. Following the season, coach Tom Scanlon, a former Fordham star, left Boston College and was replaced by Joe Monahan, former catcher with the Boston Nationals.

An examination of the record, albeit an incomplete record, suggests that Monahan turned the team around in 1914. After opening with four straight losses (Maine, Manhattan, Exeter,

and Rhode Island State), Boston College won five of its next six, defeating Colby, St. Anselm's (twice), New Hampshire, Mass. Agricultural, and Connecticut. Ace of Monahan's pitching staff was Leo Halloran, who pitched a no-hitter in an 11–0 win over Connecticut at Storrs, May 31, 1914. By April, 1915, after forty-five years of playing at what often seemed like any available vacant lot in the city of Boston (including Cleveland Circle field near the new campus), Boston College obtained its own home baseball diamond—the soon-to-be-called Alumni Field. On April 29, 1915, Boston College and Halloran defeated mighty Georgetown 5–4 in ten innings for its first real "home" win ever. Alas, the previous day Boston College had lost its first home game on Alumni Field, outscored by Bates, 14–6.

Despite the new facility and coach Monahan's winning ways, Boston College baseball in general failed to fire the imagination of the student body. Only ninety-one students turned out for the 1915 game against Holy Cross, causing *Stylus* sports editor Francis W. Milward to write: ". . . too harsh a censure cannot be given. We will say nothing more of it here. We will try to keep such a disgraceful thing a secret."

Less secret and more successful was the Boston College coup of scheduling its 1916 season opener with the then World Champion Boston Red Sox. Boston College lost 9–1 in its first meeting with a professional club, though Halloran, who came on to relieve Bob Gill in the sixth, gave up only four hits in the three innings he pitched. The real winner of the game was the Boston College Athletic Association treasury, which received $500 in gate receipts. This was also the year Boston College added a legitimate southern road trip (as opposed to the earlier three-game New York swing), travelling to the Baltimore area in mid-April to play (and lose to) Fordham, 3–2; Catholic University, 4–0; Mt. St. Joseph's, 7–4; and Georgetown, 12–11 before beating Maryland 3–0.

By spring of 1917, pitcher Halloran, several of his teammates, and a good part of the student body had entered military service. In Halloran's place came a lefthander whose pitches heretofore were made with footballs—Jimmy Fitzpatrick. Predictably, the man catching most of Fitzpatrick's pitches was fellow four-sport phenomenon Louis J. Urban.

With Fitzpatrick on the mound, Urban behind the plate, and the team now under the tutelage of player-manager Tom Gildea, a second baseman, Boston College beat Holy Cross for the first time in seventeen years, 4–1 on a Fitzpatrick five-hitter. The 1917 team finished its season at 12–3, probably the most successful year for baseball to this time.

Following a war-shortened 1918 schedule, Boston College fielded a 1919 team—led by Fitzpatrick, Urban, and left fielder Phil Corrigan, and coached by the now-graduated Gildea—that would take the school into the 1920s as one of the strongest college nines in New England. Fitzpatrick beat powerful Fordham on a five-hitter

in his first 1919 start, followed that performance with a no-hitter over Maine, and went on to help Boston College post a 14–4 record. Urban's average hovered around the .400 mark throughout 1919 and broke .400 in 1920. The yearbook report fails to give the precise average, but it says of the catcher and sometime shortstop: "Luke could come through in the pinch like a pair of tweezers. Many's the run old Luke drove in when the rally counted for a win."

In 1922, former Red Sox player Olaf Henriksen was made head coach of a Boston College nine whose stars were hard-hitting outfielder Chuck Darling and freshman pitcher Frank "Cheese" McCrehan, a product of Cambridge Latin. A year later, in 1923, McCrehan's pitching, plus the hitting of Darling and left fielder Frank Wilson, who hit safely in twenty-seven

1919 saw BC field the first of several excellent baseball teams of the post-World War I era, a contingent that numbered two multi-sport athletes as its stars: slugging catcher Luke Urban (middle row, center) and pitcher Jimmy Fitzpatrick (middle row, far right). Others shown (only last names survive): (back row, from left) O'Regan, Morrissey, Mahoney, Burke (manager), Tom Gildea (coach), Boyce, Dooley, McLaughlin; (middle row, from left) Mulcahy, Halligan, Urban, O'Dougherty, Fitzpatrick; (seated, left) Dempsey; (right) Bond.

Typical of college athletes of his time, Chuck Darling shone on the gridiron in the fall and on the diamond in the spring (when spring football drills were unheard of). In 1924, outfielder Darling was the hitting star of the Eagle nine.

Henriksen's team turned in a 20–5 season in 1924, but by 1925, the coach had resigned and his place had been taken by another former Red Sox player, Jack Slattery. Boston-native Slattery had played college baseball at Fordham, logged professional time with the Red Sox, White Sox, Indians, Cardinals, and Senators, and had been a Harvard coach for five years before coming to the Heights. Later, in 1928, he would put in a brief stint as Braves manager.

Slattery developed winning teams that could often take the measure of Holy Cross. Boston College split its two-game series with the Crusaders in 1926 and then came back in 1927 to sweep a three-game series, mainly on the pitching of Hugh McNulty, who won two of the games, and the .400-plus hitting of football star Al Weston.

Slattery was succeeded in 1928 by Hugh Duffy, who, if not Boston College's best baseball coach ever, was the best former major leaguer to hold the·job. In his seventeen-year, six-team (including the Braves) major-league career, Duffy accumulated a .330 lifetime batting average that helped land him in baseball's Hall of Fame in 1945. The easygoing Duffy, who also managed four major league teams, inherited a power-hitting Boston College team led by the two top hitters in eastern college baseball, 1928 batting champ Al Weston (.465) and third baseman Hank O'Day.

Duffy had a reputation as a great batting instructor, a role he would later fill with the Red Sox, and he proved his worth in that capacity in 1929 when every player in the Boston College starting lineup, except for pitchers, hit better than .300. The maroon and gold Murderer's Row consisted of: first base, Weston; second base, Paddy Creedon; third base, O'Day; shortstop, Andy Spognardi (a future Boston College captain and Red Sox shortstop); catcher, George Colbert; and an outfield of Weston Shea, Frank Reegan, and Johnny Temple. Power notwithstanding, Duffy's 1929 team lost two out of three to Holy Cross and one to Georgetown to finish 12–3 for the year, a good record and one prompting the yearbook to claim that Boston College baseball "now stands in its rightful place

games for a .450 average, took Boston College to its best baseball season ever, a 30–3 effort that featured twenty-one wins in a row and a split with Holy Cross.

So successful was the team, and so keen was the Boston College-Holy Cross baseball rivalry, that 30,000-plus (one estimate said 40,000), then a record crowd for college baseball, filled Braves Field on June 18, 1923, to watch McCrehan "slow ball Holy Cross to death" (the yearbook quote), 4–1. Holy Cross came back to win the Worcester half of the series, 2–0, but the college yearbook sports editor considered Boston College's record strong enough that the school could lay claim to the mythical intercollegiate baseball title.

Early-season southern road trips were a must for the Eagles if they were to hone their skills before meeting more traditional foes in the late spring. Accordingly, the 1926 team paid an April visit to the U.S. Marine base at Quantico, Virginia.

as a real major sport . . . second only to the manly art of football." It should be noted that this statement was made at a time when there was no varsity basketball at Boston College and hockey games were played in a rink halfway across the city.

In 1931, Frank McCrehan, star pitcher of the early twenties, was made head coach, moving up from the Boston College freshmen team he had coached since 1926. His arrival could not have been more ill-timed. After a 13–7 debut season, Boston College baseball, like other sports on most campuses, was hard-hit by the Depression and the 1932 baseball schedule was reduced by about half. As the *Sub Turri* noted, "Many of the teams who were scheduled have cancelled games because of the Depression [and] a trip for us [is] impossible."

Undaunted—or possessed of a farsightedness greater than that of any of the nation's economists—McCrehan in 1932 established Boston College's first junior varsity baseball team, coached by former Boston College shortstop and freshmen coach Fred Moncewicz. Former catcher George Colbert took over the freshmen. Thus, with three levels of play in action, McCrehan had created a small farm system, a baseball program to go with his baseball team.

The hitting of second baseman Dave Concannon of Dorchester and the pitching of Waltham's Bob Duffy, both sophomores, helped Boston

College to a 10–7 record in 1933. Boston College once again opened the season with a game against the Boston Red Sox at Fenway Park and once again lost 7–2. The team fared better against its more traditional rival, however. After dropping the first of a three-game series 15–1 to Holy Cross, the Eagles came back to beat the Cross 6–5 on Concannon's tenth inning triple, and then crushed the Crusaders 17–8 in the rubber game.

Former star pitcher Frank "Cheese" McCrehan took over as BC baseball coach in 1931, and guided the program through a period of expansion and success in the 1930s. McCrehan is shown here with catcher George Colbert, later to be freshman coach.

130

Boston College's diamond improvement continued into 1934 when the addition of pitcher Charlie Marso, outfielder Jerry Pagliuca, and third baseman (and hockey goalie) Tim Ready helped the team to an 11–3 season in which it lost only two games to college teams, both to Holy Cross. The other loss was to the Alumni, with coach McCrehan taking the mound to shut out his charges 3–0.

Holy Cross, Georgetown, Fordham, and Seton Hall were among the baseball powers of this era, but Boston College had gained sufficient recognition that, in 1939, the Eagles were chosen to play Fordham in a May 13 game at Cooperstown, New York. The game was billed as the "Centennial Game," marking 100 years of baseball, though college baseball had only been played since 1859, the first game having been played between Williams and Amherst.

1939 was the same year Fred Maguire, a former Holy Cross star and Boston Braves second baseman, took over the reins of Boston College baseball. Roxbury native Maguire built his teams around strong pitching, particularly around righthander Fred Leahy of Somerville. On April 19, 1940, Leahy pitched Boston College to an upset of defending Eastern Collegiate Champion Fordham, 3–1, on a three-hit, one-run performance. The tradition of good pitching continued into 1941 on the arms of George "Lefty" Bent of Roslindale and Dick Ferriter of Allston. In one stretch early in 1941, Bent beat Fordham and St. John's, then two-hit powerful Seton Hall before losing 2–1 in eleven innings.

These were the days of Sugar Bowl football mania at Boston College, and though the baseball and hockey teams might win more than their share of games, King Football was securely on his throne, lord of the grandstands and ticket windows. Not for long. War loomed again, threatening football and all intercollegiate sports.

In the first three weeks of the 1943 season, Maguire's team lost three players to the military draft, and, by 1944, military call-ups left Boston College without a baseball team. It was a situation that would persist for two more seasons.

When peace—and, with it, players—returned in 1946, Boston College baseball, still under the tutelage of Maguire, entered its best years since the twenties. It began with the first formal ath-

In May, 1940, as the German Wermacht was sweeping across Europe, BC athletic director, the Reverend Patrick H. Collins, S. J., interrupted baseball practice to heed Pope Pius' XII call for world prayer. Four years later, the baseball program would be suspended for three seasons, due to military callups.

During the ten-year coaching tenure of former Braves infielder Frank Maguire, BC appeared in its first NCAA baseball championship tournament—and played its first night game. Maguire, who was later a Red Sox scout, is shown here with 1940 team pitcher Fred Leahy (left) and catcher Jim Byrne.

letic contest between Boston College and Harvard in twenty-five years (the hockey teams had met in unofficial games). The Eagles upset the Crimson 5–1 at Cambridge. That first post-war Boston College team would go on to sweep Holy Cross, finish the season 17–2, and lay claim to the Eastern Collegiate Championship. Biggest win of the season was a 6–1 defeat of Holy Cross at Worcester in which the Eagles handed Crusader pitcher Harper Gerry the only loss of his varsity career. Boston College mainstays were first baseman (and hockey captain) John Buckley and Eastern College all-star second baseman Jerry Daunt.

Baseball continued to grow as a players' sport in the years after the war, and by 1947 a record 100 candidates reported for baseball tryouts. One of them future Massachusetts governor Ed King, who would make the team as back-up catcher and frequent pinch hitter. The top pitcher on the team was sophomore Bob Quirk, a Manchester, New Hampshire, native whose team-leading four-wins, no-losses performance sent him on the way to a three-year varsity record of 12–1.

Quirk was supported by pitchers Steve Stuka of Clinton and Don O'Brien of Cambridge, who in 1948 combined for six of Boston College's wins in a 16–4 season. Boston College's success was such that the Eagles were considered as pos-

sible NCAA District I representatives to the one-year-old NCAA-sponsored National Collegiate Baseball Championship, more generally known as the College World Series. Instead, Yale, runnerup to California in the first World Series at Kalamazoo in 1947, received its second invitation.

There was no such frustration for Boston College the next year, as the team opened the 1949 season with ten straight wins and went into the Holy Cross series at 15–2, compared with the 12–1 Crusaders. It was generally understood that the NCAA selection committee would make its selection of the District I entrant after the first two games of the scheduled three-game series.

Maguire sent sophomore Gerry Levinson of Gray Gables to the mound, and the youngster justified the decision by pitching a six-hitter against the Cross while Boston College bats hammered Crusader starter Matty Formon for twelve hits in a 3–1 win. It was Levinson vs. Formon again in the second game at Boston College, and this time Levinson had to last into extra innings until Newton's Billy Ryan hit a home run in the bottom of the twelfth for a 3–2 Boston College victory. After the game, the Eagles were invited to take a trip to New York as District I NCAA representative in the first-round playoffs.

Boston College met St. John's in the best-of-three series, with the first two games scheduled

The home-grown infield that led Boston College into its first-ever NCAA baseball championship playoff in 1949 included, from left: first baseman Eddie Collins of Newton, second baseman Johnny Brosnahan of Dorchester, shortstop Johnny Yurewicz of Brighton, and third baseman Ed Clasby of Natick.

as a day-night double header. Boston College and Levinson lost the opener, and in the night game (the first time a Boston College baseball team had played under the lights) seven Eagle errors paved the way to a second St. John's win.

Maguire's success in taking Boston College to a national championship playoff brought him the offer of a full-time position on the Red Sox scouting staff. To replace Maguire, Boston College hired Johnny Temple, a Boston College varsity player from 1929 to 1931, who later spent several years in the Class B Northeastern League before returning to his native Cambridge to work in the city's school system and recreation department.

Temple's first team made a run at the NCAA championships, but a pair of late-season losses to Tufts eliminated the Eagles from consideration and won a nod for the Medford school instead. Levinson turned in another good season

(6–2), as the youngster from the Cape pitched his way to a pro contract with the Boston Braves.

The steady hitting of catcher Mike Roarke and first baseman Joe Morgan, and the pitching of fastballer Bob McKinnon helped produce two successive winning years—12–8 in 1951, 12–7 in 1952—but each season was marred by a pair of June losses to Holy Cross. Catcher Roarke later had a four-year stint with the Detroit Tigers, while infielder Morgan, though he played briefly for four major league teams, has gained stature in organized baseball as the long-time, successful manager of the Pawtucket Red Sox.

The 1951 and 1952 teams did little to suggest the success that would come to the 1953 team, champions of the newly-formed Greater Boston League (GBL) and Boston College's best nine to this time. Behind a raft of stars, notably first baseman Jim Cisternelli, second baseman Bob Flanagan, and outfielders John Ruggiero and

Catcher Mike Roarke was a standout baseball (and football) performer at BC in the early 1950s. Roarke, who would later play professionally for the Detroit Tigers, now assists former Eagle teammate Joe Morgan (see box) as a coach of the Pawtucket Red Sox.

133

JOE MORGAN: MAJORING IN THE MINORS

Boston College was the defending national ice hockey champion in 1949–1950, the year Walpole High's Joe Morgan came to the Heights. Morgan was another schoolboy hockey star following the irresistible recruiting call of Snooks Kelley. "I went to Boston College mainly as a hockey player," recalls Morgan, "but I had played baseball most of my life, and it was always in my mind to play in college."

While Morgan's hockey skills won him a varsity berth as a center in his sophomore and junior years, his baseball talents as a good hitting shortstop soon brought him to the attention of the pros. In 1951, the 5'10", 155-pound lefty led coach Johnny Temple's team in RBIs, and the next season Morgan, along with Boston College catcher Mike Roarke, signed a contract with the Boston Braves.

Morgan was elected baseball captain at the end of the 1952 season, but he had to decline the honor (and also relinquish his last season of hockey eligibility) to turn pro. "I was playing summer ball in the old Blackstone Valley League, an excellent league," says Morgan, "but they folded in my junior year so I thought I should take advantage of the opportunity to play professional ball in the summer."

Morgan spent the summer of 1952 with Hartford in the Eastern League. He returned to Boston College to earn his degree in 1953 and then launched a fifteen-season odyssey in minor league baseball—"Let's say I've ridden a few busses,"—with call-ups to major league teams in 1959 (Milwaukee, Kansas City), 1960 (Philadelphia, Cleveland), 1961 (Cleveland), and 1964 (St. Louis). His longest major league stay was a mere twenty-six games with the 1960 Phillies.

Morgan's was neither a starry nor a big-money career. Nevertheless, "I learned a lot about the game," he says. Like many players who must struggle to master their sport, Morgan developed a deep technical knowledge of the game along with the ability to pass on that knowledge to other players, a combination that would eventually make him a better coach than he was a player.

Morgan made the jump to a managerial career in the Pittsburgh Pirates organization in 1966 when he was player-manager with Raleigh in the Carolina League. There he was voted the league's all-star manager while taking his team to a 71–66 third-place finish. He then retired as a player. In his first season as full-time manager, Morgan led Raleigh to a first place finish and a playoff berth.

After eight seasons with various Pittsburgh farm clubs, Morgan joined the Red Sox organization in 1974 and has managed Pawtucket in the Triple-A International League ever since, taking the PawSox to the 1977 and 1978 league playoffs.

While admitting that he "would like to manage in the majors," Morgan also takes justifiable pride in his player development work. "In the minors you get to do a lot of real coaching in addition to the managing," he says. Some of the major leaguers emerging from Morgan's Pawtucket clubs include Jim Rice, Fred Lynn, Rick Burleson, Wade Boggs, Gary Allenson, Rich Gedman, Bobby Ojeda, Dave Stapleton, Glenn Hoffman, and Reid Nichols.

In 1981, Morgan gave the Red Sox organization another maroon and gold tinge when he hired his former Boston College teammate, Mike Roarke, as pitching-catching coach. Like Morgan, Roarke, of West Warwick, Rhode Island, had gone to Boston College to play a sport other than baseball. In Roarke's case, it was football. He was 1951 football captain and 1952 baseball captain. After a thirteen-year pro baseball career, including four years (1961–1964) in the majors with Detroit, Roarke retired to go into coaching, first with the Tigers and then with several minor league teams until joining Morgan at Pawtucket.

"We were teammates at Boston College and also in the minors," says Morgan who played with Roarke in Jacksonville, Wichita and Louisville. "Mike knows the game and he works well with young players, which is one of the things this league is all about."

A BC baseball standout in the early 1950s, Walpole native Joe Morgan has been manager of the Red Sox' top minor league farm team since 1974. At Pawtucket, Morgan has been responsible for helping to launch the careers of Jim Rice, Fred Lynn, Wade Boggs, Rich Gedman, and many others.

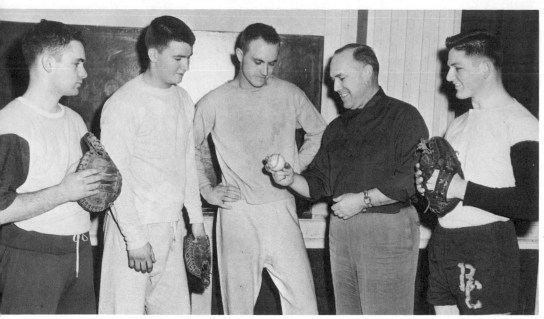

Coach Johnny Temple demonstrates his curve to 1952 team members (from left) George Ciovacco, Ray Manning, Bill Scholz, and Chet Hanewich. Cambridge native Temple was to take BC to its best baseball season ever and its first visit to the College World Series, in Omaha, during his eight years as Eagles coach in the mid-1950s.

Jack McGrath, Boston College won eight of its first ten 1953 games and gained entry to a regional playoff to determine the District I representative to the NCAAs. First-round tournament wins over Trinity (10–6) and Springfield (9–2) wrote Boston College's first ticket to Omaha, Neb., now the permanent site of the College World Series.

The NCAA championship format called for an eight-team double-elimination playoff. In the opener, McKinnon fireballed the Eagles to a 6–2 win over Houston; that was followed by a 6–2 loss to free-swinging Michigan. McKinnon again played the hero in the third-round game against Duke, coming in as a reliever to choke off a Duke threat in the ninth and singling to right in the eleventh to score Ruggiero with the winning run in a 7–6 game. Boston College was eliminated by Lafayette in the next round, however, when pitcher Eddie DiLorenzo of East Boston lost a 2–1, three-hit heartbreaker on a Boston College error in the twelfth.

After soaring to the upper levels of national baseball prestige, Boston College slipped back several notches in the mid-fifties to become just another good New England college baseball team. The Eagles went 9–6 in 1954 and 12–6 the following year, a stretch during which Boston College lost five straight games to Holy Cross before righthander Ed Buckley broke the streak with a five-hit, 4–0 win in 1955. Bursitis took Buckley out of the 1956 lineup and, with his departure, Boston College slipped to a 9–6 record that included 16–3 and 12–0 thumpings from Holy Cross. The slide continued into 1957,

with Boston College falling to 5–10–1 and Coach Temple resigning at the end of the season. Temple's departure sent new athletic director Bill Flynn in search of a baseball coach and, as had happened so often with Boston College baseball in the past, the best prospects appeared to be former major leaguers. Flynn's choice was Eddie Pellagrini, a schoolboy star at Roxbury's Catholic Memorial in the late 1930s who had gone directly from high school to minor league ball. Pellagrini came up with the Red Sox as a shortstop in 1946, hit a home run in his first major league at bat, and concluded his playing career with the Pittsburgh Pirates in 1954.

Pellagrini first heard of the Boston College job from Red Sox farm club director Neil Mahoney, and his initial reaction was that he wasn't interested. "I was starting up a real estate business on the South Shore," he remembers, "and I had always turned down coaching and managing jobs that had come my way."

Eddie Pellagrini had starred at Roxbury's Catholic Memorial, and played nine years in the major leagues (the first two for the Red Sox) before becoming baseball coach in 1958—a position he still holds. Here, the rookie skipper is measured for a uniform by long-time BC trainer Frank Jones.

Mahoney convinced Pellagrini that a part-time, four-month baseball job would not interfere with his business, and Pellagrini decided to give it a try. "When he made up his mind he was very aggressive about it," Flynn recalls. "He came in one day and told me he was the best candidate for the job, the only guy who should get it."

Pellagrini got the job and has held it ever since. He began to reconstruct his team by firing a verbal warning shot in his first team meeting. "I don't care who made the ball club last year," he told the players. "No one's automatically on the team. He'd better show us something before he plays for our club."

Pellagrini showed Boston College something. After a 7–10 first season, the wiry little straight-talking, street-wise ex-big leaguer produced a 12–7 winner in 1959 to begin a string of eleven consecutive winning seasons in which Boston College would make three appearances in the NCAAs.

Much of Pellagrini's 1959 success could be attributed to the arms of Bill Robinson of Brookline and to knuckleball artist Bob Niemiec of Chicopee. A 2–1 win over a UConn team, then ranked first in New England, and a 5–4 victory over Holy Cross, sent the Eagles packing for their second trip (Pellagrini's first) to Omaha. Robinson drew the first start in the College World Series and beat Colorado State 8–3 on a four-hitter, but the Eagles were then eliminated on successive losses, 5–2 to USC and 1–0 to Oklahoma State.

"We were the fans' delight, though," recalls Pellagrini. "Those people knew we don't have baseball scholarships, yet here we were, up against the mighty Trojans who probably have twenty-five players on scholarship."

Scholarships or not, Pellagrini had enough talent to field one of the best-hitting teams in Boston College history in 1961. Robinson and Niemiec were back, along with sophomore lefthander Charlie Bunker and a hard-hitting outfield made up of Bob "Beaver" Martin (center), Bill Cunis (left) and Gerry Hamel (right), a Long Islander who, in high school, battled Carl Yastrzemski for schoolboy batting titles. The team also featured football star Art Graham at second and basketball guard Chuck Chevalier at short.

1961 was also the season the team got a new field, one built exclusively for baseball. Called Commander John J. Shea Field and erected on filled land adjacent to Alumni Field (see box), the facility was dedicated on May 21, 1961, with a 3–2 win over Fordham. Later that season Boston College won its first Greater Boston League title since 1953 and its second consecutive trip to the College World Series, on the strength of its District I playoff wins over Springfield and Connecticut.

In Omaha, Niemiec went all the way for a 3–2 win over Western Michigan in the opener, but once again Boston College came up against USC in the second round and once again lost, 10–3. Robinson's 4–3 win over Duke kept Boston College hopes alive and set up another game with USC, this one with Niemiec on the mound.

The Trojans had trouble getting a bat on Niemiec's knuckleball and Boston College was looking good with a 3–0 lead after six when Niemiec had to leave the game with a pulled back muscle—probably the most costly injury in a century of Boston College baseball. USC went on to win the game in the tenth and, ultimately, to win the national championship. Boston College came home as the third-ranked team in the tournament and with a coach who kept saying, "If Niemiec doesn't get hurt, we win the game."

Niemiec and Robinson graduated in 1961, signing pro contracts with Houston and the Mets, which left lefty Charlie Bunker as the ace of the staff. The loss of two top pitchers was too much to overcome, and though Boston College reached the District I playoffs in 1962, they were eliminated on successive one-run losses to Vermont (3–2) and Bridgeport (4–3).

The 1963 season was a bit of a throwback to the 1920s, as football passing star Jack Concannon established himself as an outstanding pitcher while his favorite football receiver, Art Graham, found a home in the outfield and batter's box. Shades of Fitzpatrick and Urban. "Concannon was just a great natural athlete," says Pellagrini. "I think he had pro potential, but face it, it's easy to make a choice between pro baseball and pro football. In pro football you sign and the year after college you're in the NFL. In baseball, you

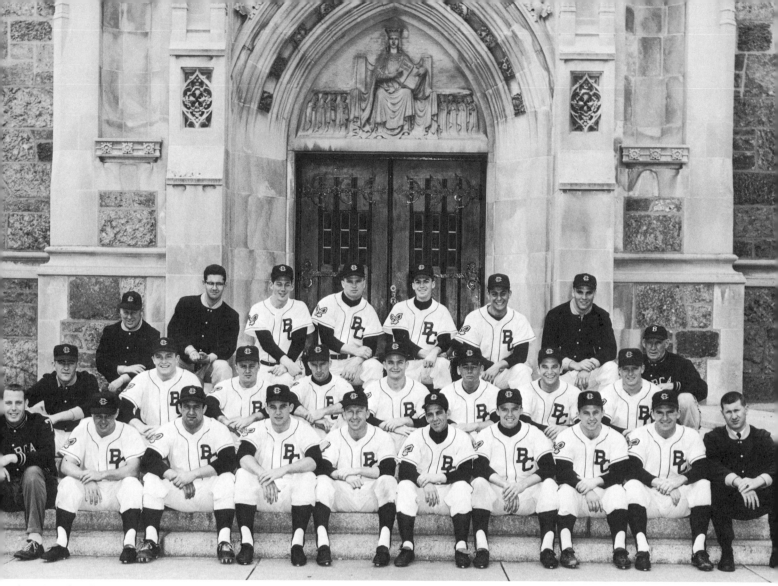

The 1961 baseball Eagles led BC to its second consecutive College World Series, where the team won two games before a costly injury brought defeat. First row, from left: Ed Harrison (assistant manager), Gerry Hamel, Frank Robotti, Bill Robinson, Bob Martin, Ed Pellagrini (coach), Bob Graham, Bob Niemiec, Charlie Bunker, John Nugent (manager); second row, from left: Paul Comeau, Gerry Greeley, Jack Coyle, Chuck Chevalier, Bernie Kilroy, Bill Nagle, Frank Faggiano, Bill Cunis; third row, from left: Frank O'Keefe (equipment manager), Bill Noveline (junior manager), Bob Ciero, Jack McGrahan, Tom McGahan, Bob DeFelice, Art Graham, Frank Jones (trainer).

Centerfielder Bob "Beaver" Martin captained the hard-hitting Eagle team that achieved national ranking and respect in the early 1960s. Here, Martin slides into third base in a Greater Boston League match against North-eastern, in 1961.

137

COMMANDER JOHN J. SHEA, '18

Commander John J. Shea Field, the first major Boston College athletic facility to be named after a former athlete, was opened May 21, 1961, and formally dedicated to the memory of one of Boston College's most distinguished alumni, a man who made his mark as scholar, athlete and war hero.

Shea was born in Cambridge in 1899, the son of parents whose emphasis on education was successful enough that young Shea was only eleven when he entered Boston College High. There, his superb grades and prowess in Latin soon earned him the nickname "Virgil."

In 1914, Shea took the highly competitive Boston College scholarship exam in which he won one of only two full, four-year scholarships. Coming to the new Chestnut Hill campus in September, 1914, his athletic activities were at first confined to class baseball.

It was not until his sophomore year that Shea went out for football and not until his junior and senior years, the 1916 and 1917 football seasons, that he was able to earn a letter as a scrappy 160-lb. center on Coach Charles Brickley's teams. But sports was still only a small part of Shea's life at Boston College. By his senior year he had risen to vice president of the Fulton Debating Society, was on the yearbook staff, and occasionally contributed poetry to the literary magazine, *The Stylus*. The final verse of his 1917 poem, "Youth," foreshadowed events of Shea's adult life:

"My strength shall measure the might of the ocean;
The fiercest elements will I dare:
I'll pluck the wings from the swift flying eagle
And glide, ever glide through the depths of the air."

After graduation, Shea enlisted in the Naval Reserve, earned his wings, and was commissioned an ensign.

In 1930, the Navy recalled Shea to active duty as executive officer of Squantum Naval Air Station, and in 1941 Shea, now risen to the rank of Commander, was assigned to the aircraft carrier USS Wasp for action in the Guadalcanal campaign.

In June, 1942, from his cabin on the ship, Shea wrote a letter to his then five-year-old son Jackie. The message, which would later be reprinted in hundreds of newspapers and magazines, stressed the values of religious faith, leadership, and loyalty to family and country. Four decades later, Boston College still receives requests for copies of Shea's letter.

Shortly after noon, on September 15, 1942, after fifteen of the Wasp's planes had shot down a four-engine Japanese bomber, three Japanese torpedoes struck forward on the ship in the vicinity of the magazines and gasoline tanks. Bombs, gasoline, oil and ammunition caught fire and explosions rocked the ship. Shea was at his post on the bridge when the ship was hit. Wasp Captain Forrest P. Sherman of Melrose later recalled the aftermath: "Shea personally took charge of fighting the fire on the flight deck, displaying great courage (and) disregarding exploding ammunition and debris."

Twice Shea rushed into the flames to rescue shipmates. A third time he went in and did not return. The Official Naval Report listed him as one of 193 Wasp officers and crewmen "missing in action."

Eleven years later, Shea's son, John R., the "Jackie" to whom Shea had written shortly before his death, enrolled at Boston College and began following in his father's impressive academic footsteps. The younger Shea majored in Classics, graduated in 1958, and went on to earn a Ph.D. from Harvard. In 1961, he returned to Boston College to unveil the plaque dedicating the 10-acre varsity baseball and general athletic field to the memory of his father.

Ironically, Jack Shea never played varsity baseball at Boston College but, as then President John F. Kennedy said in a telegram to Boston College President the Very Reverend Michael P. Walsh, S.J., on the occasion of the field's dedication: "Jack Shea's life is a splendid inspiration for all young men, and it is most fitting that he is given this recognition. . ."

Among those present at the 1961 dedication ceremonies for the new Commander John J. Shea baseball field at Boston College were, from left, the Very Reverend Michael P. Walsh, S.J., BC president; Shea's son, John R., a 1958 BC graduate; Rear Admiral Bartholomew W. Hogan, USN (retired); and the Archbishop of Boston, Richard Cardinal Cushing.

Shea Field in Chestnut Hill borders on MDC park, whose rocky elevations provide casual spectators with a natural grandstand.

Like their Red Sox neighbors down Commonwealth Avenue, the Eagles had an "impossible dream" season of their own in 1967, leading all the way to another College World Series appearance in Omaha. Pitching stars were Bill O'Brien (left), whose heart condition had once prompted doctors to forbid him to play baseball; and John "The Sheik" Brazillian, a little-used relief man who stole the show in the NCAA playoffs.

go to the minors and you might never see the big leagues."

In 1963, for the fourth year in a row, Boston College reached the 1963 District I playoffs, but for the second year in a row, they were eliminated in two straight. This time the losses came in a double header with Holy Cross, 4–0 and 7–4.

The Pellagrini-Boston College string of post-season play came to an end in 1964, with a team that struggled to an 11–8 record and sorely missed the services of Concannon, whose new pro football contract forbade him to play baseball. The following year, Boston College went 10–9 and returned to District I playoffs, largely on the pitching talent of Bill O'Brien.

"O'Brien had a heart problem and doctors wouldn't let him play," recalls Pellagrini. "So on his own he went to Doctor Paul Dudley White, the great heart specialist. White gave him absolute clearance to play and sent me a letter saying he thought it would be good for him if he did play."

In O'Brien's first year, the Eagles reached the playoffs, where they beat UMass but were denied a trip to Omaha in a 10–2 loss to Northeastern. It was a different story the next year.

The 1967 Boston College baseball season seemed something of a local collegiate prelude to the Red Sox famed Impossible Dream experience of the same year, with impossible comeback following impossible comeback all the way to Omaha.

"Collectively, the 1967 team was my best hitting team ever," says Pellagrini, citing Mike Robertson, John Salmon, Mickey Amick, and captain Bill Kitley as the crunchers who, along with O'Brien's pitching, took the Eagles to a three-game District I playoff against Dartmouth. Dartmouth won the opener 9–8 and had Boston College down 13–3 in the sixth inning of the second and apparently final game, when the Eagles began the most incredible comeback in their baseball history. Boston College sent fifteen men to the plate in the bottom of the sixth, produced ten runs to tie the game, and then won it in the eighth on Robertson's home run.

The game's unlikely hero was John "the Shiek" Brazilian, a little-used relief pitcher who entered the game in the fourth inning with an 0–2 record on only five innings pitched. Brazilian proceeded to pitch five-and-one-third innings of two-hit, nine-strikeout, shutout ball in what Pellagrini still calls "the greatest comeback I've seen in forty years of baseball." Brazilian helped his own cause with two hits and four runs batted in.

There followed another best-of-three series with UMass for the honor of going to Omaha, Boston College splitting the first two games (a 4–1 win by O'Brien and a 6–5 extra-inning loss) and then producing another spectacular comeback in the rubber game. After trailing 6–2, the Eagles came back to a 6–6 tie on the bats of Dan Zailskas, Tom Sarkisian, Ed O'Neil, and Harvey Doneski; then, in the twelfth inning of this four-hour-and-twenty-minute game, Doneski doubled home Robertson for a Boston College win and the Eagles flew on to Omaha as the nineteenth-ranked team in the nation.

"We don't have the best talent in the world, but we have more clutch players than you can shake a stick at," said Pellagrini on his arrival in Omaha.

Pellagrini was right. In the opener against fifth-in-the-nation (30–6) Rider College of New Jersey, Boston College trailed 1–0 in the ninth when Salmon singled in the tying run and Bill Plunket delivered a bases-loaded double for a 3–1 Boston College win. O'Brien went all the way on the mound, scattering seven hits and striking out ten.

Arizona State—a team whose 48–10 record took in more games than Boston College would play in more than two years—beat the Eagles in the second round, 8–1. A third-round win over Houston would have kept the Eagles alive, and, for a while, it looked as though Boston College might pull it out of the fire again. The game was tied 2–2 in the twelfth inning and O'Brien, pitching on only one day's rest, looked strong. In the thirteenth, the Eagles loaded the bases with one out, but uncharacteristically, they failed to score. A leadoff Houston home run in the

Coach Pellagrini's 24-plus years at the BC baseball helm have included three College World Series invitations, an eleven-year winning streak, and a bout with tuberculosis. "Nobody makes a lot of money out here," goes a favorite Pellagrini observation of BC baseball, "but we sure can do a lot of praying."

bottom of the inning settled the issue, eliminating Boston College from the tournament.

The graduation loss of O'Brien did not prevent Boston College from winning eleven straight to open the 1968 season, but a loss to Providence launched a 3–9 losing streak that took the Eagles out of the playoff picture.

However, the playoffs were the least of Pellagrini's worries in 1969, as the coach contracted a case of tuberculosis that necessitated a year's rest. No work, no baseball, "just sleep and eat," Pellagrini recalls.

Bill Cunis, freshman coach the previous five years and a player on Boston College's World Series teams of 1960 and 1961, took over the varsity while Pellagrini spent a spring and summer worrying about whether or not a portion of his lung might have to be removed. By late September he got word that his medication and rest had worked, that no operation was needed, and that he could return to work and to baseball.

Pellagrini came back to take the 1970 Eagles to a 13–8 record, just missing qualification for the District I playoffs. This was to be the end of Boston College's eleven-year winning streak, as the next season saw the start of a particularly trying three-year (1971–1973) losing skein in which Boston College teams went 11–12, 9–14–1, and 8–14–1.

Pellagrini's reaction at the time suggests how far the ex-pro had removed himself from the professional ethic. "It's tough to go through a stretch of losing seasons," he said, "but if the players are putting out and not quitting and digging—and our players are—then they're gaining by the experience."

Among Pellagrini's better players of this era was righthand pitcher Bill Ruane, who broke into the lineup as a freshman in 1972 and went 3–1 with a 2.04 ERA. Ruane and power-hitting first baseman (and hockey goalie) Ned Yetten brought Boston College back to a 15–9 record in 1974, only to miss the playoffs by percentage points.

It is a truism of Boston College baseball that late starts due to the vagaries of New England weather ("Sometimes we don't get outside until two or three days before the opener," says Pellagrini), a policy of not granting baseball schol-

arships, and the loss of a few players each year to spring football practice, make it a major coaching achievement for Pellagrini to keep his teams near the .500 mark. Nevertheless, he did this in 1975 (13–12–0) and 1976 (10–13–0), a time in which Pellagrini frequently repeated one of his favorite one-liners about coaching at Boston College: "Nobody makes a lot of money out here but we sure can do a lot of praying."

The mid-seventies was also the time that Pellagrini would refine the pitching skills of GBL all-star Rod Luongo and George Ravanis, working them in a two-man rotation (with occasional appearances by Bob Meara) that helped Boston College fight its way back into the District I playoffs with a 16–9 regular season record in 1977. The Eagles' first playoff opponent was a 22–8 Maine team already well along in its program to become the top college nine in New England; Boston College upset Maine 4–1, only to lose 2–0 to Connecticut in the finals.

In 1978, a highly-touted pitching staff of Ravanis, Meara, and newcomer Mike Gallagher was not enough to offset a lack of hitting. It was a Jekyll-Hyde season, in which the Eagles plummeted from a 12–2 record to 14–10–1 and saw a seemingly sure playoff bid slip away.

1978 proved to be Pellagrini's last winning season for several years. Catcher Tim Dachos and designated hitter Greg Stewart added power to the 1979 lineup, but now the club lacked pitching and limped in at 6–18–0. It was Pellagrini's worst season in twenty-one years as Boston College coach. The addition of a pre-season conditioning trip to Florida in 1980 marked a major step forward in Boston College's commitment to baseball; still, it failed to produce immediate results, as Boston College went 8–15 in 1980 and 11–12 in 1981.

"This is tough on the kids," says Pellagrini, a man who once thought he didn't want to get involved with college coaching and now says he would never want to leave it. "I know we have some fine athletes. I'll tell you, despite the hardships, these guys have been great to work with. You hear a lot of things about the spoiled athlete, but in all my years at Boston College, I never had a player I didn't like as a person. I know we don't

142

have the big stadium, or the fifty-game schedule, or the scholarship money, or even the sunny weather, but we have kids who put out and know they have to hustle for everything they get.

They've all shown me something."

That they show him something is all Eddie Pellagrini has ever asked for. It has become a rite of spring at Boston College.

TRACK AND FIELD

The story of Boston College track and field is essentially the story of two coaches. This does not diminish the achievements of generations of Boston College runners, jumpers, and weight men; rather, it underscores what these athletes themselves have so often said.

Jack Ryder, head coach from 1919 to 1952, and Bill Gilligan, head coach from 1953 to 1978 and field events coach until 1981, are to Boston College track-and-field history what Frank Cavanaugh, Frank Leahy, Joe McKenney, Snooks Kelley, Bob Cousy, Tom Davis, and Eddie Pellagrini are to their sports, dominant and decisive historical figures who personally determined the fortunes of their teams. Ryder and Gilligan were good and gentle and strong-willed men, but there is time enough to let their athletes speak of that.

We know, largely through the research of Nat Hasenfus, that track—that is to say foot racing—was a popular ingredient of the Miller's Field picnics of the 1870s. So was tug o'war. Unlike tug o'war, track quickly developed into one of the major sports at Boston College before the turn of the century. And why not? Track was an inexpensive sport, requiring little in the way of equipment, and the college already had its own gym.

The fledgling Boston College Athletic Association of 1885 gave its support to a track program by sponsoring the college's first intramural meet on October 17, 1885, at a nearby field referred to simply as "the baseball grounds." The winning times, heights, and distances look exceedingly modest a century later: 100-yard dash–J. E. Kelly ('87), 11.25 seconds; shotput (12½ pounds.)–A. F. Judge ('88) 38 feet, 5 inches; run-

ning high-jump–J. E. Kelly ('88), E. C. Callahan ('88) tie, 4 feet, 11 inches. Other major events of the meet included a three-legged race and a baseball throw, the latter providing one of the most impressive statistics of the day, a winning throw of 343 feet by A. F. Judge.

College and class meets continued into the 1890s, when Boston College at last ventured to give official support to a varsity track and field team. The first published report of an intercollegiate meet appears in the November, 1893, *Stylus* and recounts a dual meet between Boston College and Holy Cross held October 19, 1893: "Boston College won but the victory was by no means a walkover. The result of the contest could not be foreseen until almost all the events were finished. First one college would forge ahead then the other would lead by a few points. But when the running broad jump and the mile were won in succession by Boston College, her friends, who were out in full numbers, were wild with delight knowing that victory was assured."

The undisputed star of Boston College's fledgling team—indeed, one of the most outstanding athletes the college has produced—was sprinter Bernie Wefers, the 1893 football captain, who in 1895 would be America's number one sprinter at the Manhattan Games. At one time, Wefers held the world's record in the 100-yard dash (9.8 seconds) and the 220 (21.6).

A Boston College track team entered a meet sponsored by the prestigious Boston Athletic Association (BAA), on February 11, 1894, and defeated Boston University in a relay race in which team captain Wefers ran the anchor leg to win by three-quarters of a lap. The next month, at an indoor meet at MIT, Wefers set a college record of 7.8 seconds for the 75-yard dash.

By 1895, the BCAA took the bold step of holding an "open" meet of its own, despite reported opposition to such an ambitious proposal and some doubt as to whether Boston College had the prestige and ability to pull off the project. On April 7, 1896, Boston College sponsored a meet at the West Newton Armory. The event attracted several club and military teams, along with varsity teams from Georgetown and Holy Cross.

Flushed with its modest success, the BCAA hosted a far more ambitious meet the next year at Boston's old Mechanics Hall. The *Stylus* notes of the meet, "It is the intention of the Association to make the occasion a memorable one and to initiate a set of contests under the auspices of Boston College which will be regarded as permanent."

The meet was staged on Thursday, March 11, 1897, at a cost to Boston College of $1400, $200 over budget and a huge outlay for an athletic venture in those days. But the so-called "Boston College Open" was an unqualified success, attracting local clubs and a large college contingent, including teams from Harvard, Amherst, Tufts, MIT, Boston University, Holy Cross, Georgetown, and Williams. With one report noting that "Mechanics (Hall) was crowded from cellar to garret," the BCAA netted $500 on its undertaking and stuck by its resolve to make the meet an annual event. By 1900, crowds of 4,500 were attending what Hasenfus calls "the greatest track meet in early Boston College history."

However, Boston College was entering an era when sports were falling into administrative disfavor; the football team was disbanded in 1902, while the previous year the BCAA had voted to discontinue the popular open track meets. The college did not abandon track completely, however, and, in 1901, a three-man team consisting of Arthur Curry, Charles McCarthy, and James Brennan represented Boston College in the annual meet of the Intercollegiate Association of Amateur Athletes of America (IC4A). Boston College also continued to enter teams and runners in major local meets such as those sponsored

by the BAA, and to hold the college's traditional intramural meet.

By 1908, the year football was resumed, intercollegiate athletics were creeping back into administrative good graces, and Boston College track, under the captaincy of star sprinter Bernie O'Kane, might have seized the moment and recaptured past glories—except that now the sport had lost its student support. A *Stylus* editorial of the period railed that "the recent scarcity in the number of aspirants for the track team again provokes our editorial wrath . . . The first call for candidates brought out about twenty-five . . . . but, whether through stage fright or lack of self confidence, that number has dwindled down to a mere handful."

Given the college's overall athletic situation, it was unfortunate that Boston College students chose to turn their backs on track. As a 1909 *Stylus* article points out: "If there is one branch of sports in which we can gain prominence it is in track athletics. In baseball and football we are greatly handicapped by lack of facilities; the field is poor and at great distance from the college. But in track work all is different—down in our gym we have one of the best indoor tracks in the city and we have to go down but a few steps to reach it."

The BCAA must have grasped the truth of the statement, as in 1909 it attempted to revive the old Mechanics Hall meets, only to be frustrated by finding the available dates fell during Holy Week. Boston College was finally able to resume sponsorship of its open meet in February 1913 at the James Street gym during the college's last days in the South End.

Two years later, track was probably the only Boston College sports activity that suffered, at least temporarily, from the move from Boston to Chestnut Hill. "Lack of a board track at University Heights has made it necessary for the men to use the Columbus Avenue Oval," complained a note in a 1916 issue of the *Stylus*, "Members of the squad must journey a distance of five or six miles for their daily practice."

Few athletes were willing to add that time and distance to their daily commute. The result, as noted in the same edition of the *Stylus*, was that "the college which produced Bernie Wefers . . . must resort to [the practice] of begging men to come out for the team."

Cross-country did not require a track, however, and that sport was added to the sports program in the fall of 1917, though with little competitive success. The team lost its first three dual meets: Tufts, Holy Cross, and Harvard.

After its encouraging beginnings in the 1890s, Boston College track in the early days at Chestnut Hill had become a rudderless ship. It was a program with few top caliber athletes, a small following of fans, no board track of its own, and a succession of volunteer coaches who each lasted less than two seasons. That situation changed abruptly in 1919.

The same year that Boston College hired the Iron Major, Frank Cavanaugh, to lead its football team to national prominence, the college also obtained the services of a locally well-known coach to do the same with track and field. The man was Jack Ryder, former track coach with the South Boston A. C. and the Boston Athletic As-

sociation, the group that sponsored the prestigious Boston Marathon. Nine head football coaches would come and go before Ryder retired as coach and founding father of one of New England's best college track programs.

Ryder was a low-key but intensely dedicated track evangelist, who would build his program through coaching and motivation more than through recruiting. He did enjoy one bit of luck in that his first two stars were already enrolled at Boston College when he took over the team. These two were 1920 team captain and New England Intercollegiate Athletic Association broad jump champion Bill Dempsey, and middle distance runner James W. "Jake" Driscoll, anchor man on a relay team that would defeat Colgate and Ohio Wesleyan at the Penn Relays and later set a world record for the indoor quarter mile.

But Ryder, a trim, bespectacled man, did not want to coach only champions; he wanted to proselytize among the unconverted. Typical was the language of his first call for track candidates:

"Indulgence in competitive athletics is a matter

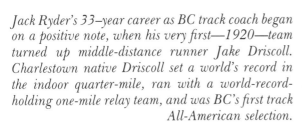

Jack Ryder's 33–year career as BC track coach began on a positive note, when his very first—1920—team turned up middle-distance runner Jake Driscoll. Charlestown native Driscoll set a world's record in the indoor quarter-mile, ran with a world-record-holding one-mile relay team, and was BC's first track All-American selection.

for individual determination. This is not a call for athletes. Athletes will report anyway. This is an invitation to all the students to enjoy the physical benefits that may be obtained for the asking."

The response was a record turnout. True to his word, the new coach did not simply select the best and discard the rest; instead, he chose his top candidates in each event, and below them added what he called his "health squad."

In his first year at Boston College, Ryder solved the problem of lack of a track by locating an old BAA board track that had been rotting under the stands at Harvard. He salvaged it for Boston College and the ten-laps-to-a-mile track was set up on Alumni Field after the football season and used by the track team during the winter.

Ryder's success—he would prefer to have it reported as the success of his runners—was instantaneous. Driscoll set his quarter-mile record in 1920; Boston College finished first in the 1920 Eastern Intercollegiate Meet, a competition in which Boston College's Walter Downey also won the 100-yard dash; and in 1921, Boston College won its first relay victory over Holy Cross in twenty-five years.

Driscoll, a Charlestown native, was Ryder's first All-America selection in 1920 and a member of the United States Olympic team in 1922, the year he also won the IC4A and AAU 440s. Another early Ryder star was hurdler John "Joe" Sullivan of Somerville, who won the 1921 Eastern and New England Intercollegiate 120-yard high hurdle championships, the New England AAU high hurdles, and who set Boston College records in the 120-yard high hurdles and the 120 and 220-yard low hurdles.

Ryder had been at Boston College less than a year when a student wrote of him, "In the short time that he has been here he has worked wonders, mainly by reason of his winning personality and his sincere desire to help others."

Great relay teams were the centerpiece of Ryder's track squads. His 1921 mile relay team, made up of Sullivan, Driscoll, Jim Caffrey, and Walter Nolan, set a world's record at the Penn Relays, beating the likes of Notre Dame, Ohio State, and Columbia in 3:24:4. Ryder's greatest

relay team was the 1924 two-mile squad of William McKillop, Patrick Mahoney, Thomas Cavanaugh, and Louis Welch, which defeated Georgetown and favored Penn State before 40,000 at the thirtieth annual Penn Relays Carnival. Boston College's time of 7:47:6 shaved 1.2 seconds off the then world record, held by Penn State. "We were all local runners on the team then," Louis Welch later recalled in an unpublished memoir of the Ryder years. "There wasn't any money for track scholarships, but Jack Ryder was so highly thought of that I think a lot of high school coaches directed some of their best athletes to Boston College."

Later in that 1924 season, Ryder's team handed Holy Cross one of the Crusaders' worst beatings in the dual meet series, 86½ to 39½. In the competition, Cavanaugh set a Boston College dual meet one-mile record of 4:17:8; Bob Merrick set a dual meet record for the 120-yard high hurdles, 15.6 seconds; and Clarence Flahive, who also won the IC4A indoor and outdoor high jump championships that year, won the high jump.

Not surprisingly, the Eagles were the 1924 New England Intercollegiate champions. In five years, Jack Ryder had brought Boston College track to regional domination and national prominence, to levels of achievement arguably higher than those of the beloved football team. Whether that fact annoyed football coach Cavanaugh or if football coaches of that era naturally regarded track as a second-rate sport is unknown, but Louis Welch clearly remembers that trackmen did not have the best of it:

I entered Boston College way back in the fall of 1921 and the first thing I remember learning was to hate football players, particularly Boston College football players. At the time there was a rigid rule: NO HOT WATER IN THE SHOWERS FOR TRACK MEN UNTIL FOOTBALL PRACTICE IS OVER! The [shower and locker room] was presided over by a wizened little gnome (a custodian) named Billy Frazier. Billy could be an arrogant, irritating, autocratic little tyrant, until he got to know you. He'd sit in his little closet, off the shower room, holding his pushbroom like an emperor's sceptre and chant-

146

The first of many great Ryder-coached relay teams was the 1924 two-mile squad which defeated Georgetown and Penn in the celebrated Penn Relays, setting a new world record (7:47:6) in the process. Pictured, from left: William T. McKillop, Patrick J. Mahoney, Louis R. Welch, Thomas F. Cavanaugh, and Coach Ryder.

ing his battle cry all afternoon—"What do you mean you want a clean towel? I gave you one last Monday . . . only one clean towel a week for track men." Then, whenever he saw a cloud of steam coming out of the showers, he was really in his element. In he'd clomp, banging his broom handle on the wall and shouting, "Turn off that hot water! Major Cavanaugh says no hot water for track men until football practice is over."

As a part-time taxi driver, I had learned some of the seamy facts of life. Like what kind of cigars Billy smoked. Then, whenever I was luxuriating in a nice hot shower, and he'd come in with his war cry, "Turn off that hot water! The major says . . . Oh, it's you, Louis . . . er, would you like a clean towel?"

For his part, Ryder cared nothing for the pecking order of the locker room. He did his work on the track.

"I think if I can describe a typical afternoon of track practice," Welch continues, "preferably a cold winter's afternoon, you will understand

how lucky I was to have the kind of . . . coach I had. At that time we had only the old outdoor wooden track of ten laps to a mile to practice on in the winter. Every time it snowed, that track had to be shoveled off by hand. The first one down on the track, shovel in hand, would be the coach, and as classes started to let out, he would be quickly joined by members of the track squad."

A narrow and sometimes icy track was too dangerous for the running of group races so Ryder used to work his men, one at a time, in daily time trials. "Everything was determined by the times on the coach's stop watch," says Welch. "He would stand out there in the cold for hours, bundled up in his big overcoat, his overshoes, and his earmuffs, holding his stop watch in one bare hand and on the dark late afternoons, a flashlight in the other hand so that he could watch the sweep of the second hand as he called out the times for each lap to each runner."

Though a runner's place on the team hinged

on his daily time trials, Ryder was able to maintain an exceptionally strong *espirit de corps* during what could have been a divisive practice.

"We always had six to eight middle distance runners whose times never varied by more than a few seconds or fifths of a second," says Welch. "The competition was constant and fierce. Yet all the candidates for those [relay] teams, whether they had finished their time trials or not, would stand around the coach on that cold track urging each runner on, even though they knew that if his time was fast enough some one of them would not make the next trip . . . . You could hear their shouts echoing from College Road to the Reservoir: 'Come on. Come on. Get out there.' Then, as the runner staggered around the last lap, the cries changed to 'Come on, all you've got now. All you've got!' "

Throughout the 1920s, Ryder produced a seemingly endless succession of track and field stars, including George Lermond, 1925 New England two-mile champ; dash man Frank Hussey, a member of the 1924 United States Olympic team; 1927 captain Henry F. (Luke) McCloskey, who got out of a sickbed to help Boston College to the two-mile relay title at the 1927 Penn Relays; 1926 New England AAU 600 champ Joe Ingoldsby; and middle distance star Frank Daley.

In 1928, Ryder received recognition for his achievements, when he was chosen to coach the United States Olympic squad.

Though he was a part-time coach at Boston College, Ryder was also the coach of the private BAA, and so was able to make a full-time living out of two part-time jobs. He received several offers to coach at other colleges, including one from Harvard, but he routinely turned these down. Ryder loved his Boston College position, and the feeling was fully mutual. In 1930, the yearbook wrote of him: "Alumni Field wouldn't be the same if Jack wasn't down there with a little rope cigar in his mouth, giving fatherly advice, chinning and chatting and smiling at everyone. Jack Ryders don't happen every day in the week. He's one in a million."

While Ryder's teams of the 1930s failed to produce headlines like those of the teams of the early and mid-twenties, Boston College contin-

ued to turn out individual stars and outstanding relay teams. Among the latter was the 1930 team that won the Millrose Games at Madison Square Garden on the strength of James O'Leary's anchor leg.

It was about this time that Ryder experienced what he considered to be one of his greatest coaching achievements; typically for him, it was not the development of a superstar, but a reclamation project, the making of a non-runner into a winner. Ed Kickham came to Boston College in 1932. He had never run competitively, and, on a whim, decided to go out for track and to specialize in the hurdles. After spending a year learning proper form, Kickham made such dramatic progress that he won the New England AAU high hurdles title in the summer of 1935, took third in the 1936 Boston Knights of Columbus meet, and was elected captain of the 1936 Boston College track team.

Though he liked to develop his own stars, Ryder, like other Boston College coaches, also benefited from the multi-sport abilities of Boston College athletes. Among the multi-talented who competed under Ryder were javelin specialist Al Ricci '32, also a football and baseball player; and football guard Dimitri Zaitz '37, who set a Boston College shotput record of 53 feet, 4 inches and was a member of the 1936 United States Olympic team, Boston College's first Olympian since Frank Hussey.

Ryder's biggest star of the 1930s was Richard Gill of East Boston, a middle distance runner and relay anchor. Before his graduation in 1938, Gill would set Boston College records in the 440 (48 flat) and 880 (1:54.3), and place second in the 880 at the 1937 IC4As and fifth in the 1937 NCAAs at Berkeley, California. Another star of the era was broad jumper Frank Zeimetz, a converted sprinter whom Ryder coached to second place in the 1939 national AAU meet.

The performances of the field men began to catch up with those of the track stars in the 1940s. Football player Joe Zabilski set a Boston College record for the sixteen-pound hammer with a throw of 171 feet, 4 inches; football teammate Al Morro set a Boston College discus record and won the New England championships with a throw of 165 feet, 4 inches; and javelin thrower Justin McGowan set a school record of 193 feet, 3 inches.

Among the runners, the period 1942 to 1944 belonged to a Ryder coaching masterpiece, Herbert H. McKenley. The son of a country doctor in Jamaica, British West Indies, McKenley arrived on campus with a fair reputation as a sprinter. In his freshman year, he finished second to Princeton great Harvey Kelsey in the IC4A 220 and came back two weeks later to win the National Junior 220 crown in 47.7 seconds, the fastest clocking for an American at that distance all year. McKenley won the 220 in the 1943 New England Intercollegiate meet at MIT and finished second in the NCAAs at Milwaukee. Alas, McKenley did not burn up the academic track. His scholastic failure at Boston College led to his transfer to Illinois, from whence he would become one of the greatest sprinters of the decade.

While Boston College's track program survived the war years, it did so with a great re-

Cambridge's Ralph King was a standout sprinter on BC track teams of the late 1940s, and, in 1949, the first black man elected to captain a BC varsity sports team.

duction in dual meets (there was only one such meet—a win over New Hampshire—in the spring of 1945) and a corresponding reduction in the number of student athletes.

After the war, Ryder persuaded the BCAA to allow him to hire an assistant coach who would specialize in working with the field-events men. The BCAA approved, and in 1948, Ryder hired Bill Gilligan, a hammer thrower and sometime sprinter who had captained Boston College's 1940 track and field team.

The year 1948 also marked an historic development in Boston College athletic history, though one that passed with scarcely a ripple of publicity at the time. That year the track team elected Ralph King of Cambridge, a black sprinter, to the team captaincy, making King the first black to captain a varsity sport at Boston College.

By the 1949–1950 season, Ryder and Gilligan had rebuilt Boston College track to the point where it was once again producing pre-war caliber runners, among them New England 440 champ Irv Howe and half miler Jim Taylor. But by 1950, Ryder was seventy-four and celebrating his thirty-first year coaching at the Heights, and while, as the yearbook said, "all Boston College men hope he goes on forever," it was apparent that he soon must contemplate retirement.

"I honestly don't expect too much this year," Ryder said at the start of the 1950–1951 season. Then, as if to prove that the magic was still there, he proceeded to build one of his strongest relay teams ever, a one-mile team anchored by captain Irv Howe. The relay unit's biggest win occurred in the dual meet with Holy Cross, a meet in which Bill Gilligan's work began to manifest itself. Among the field men, Joseph "Red" Sweeney won the hammer, Jim Low won the discus, and an unknown Hal Connolly, who would become the greatest Boston College weight man ever, took the shot put.

Ryder retired following the 1952 spring season, and he died the following winter. His remarkable 33-year Boston College career had concluded with an upset win over a highly-regarded Bowdoin team, a meet held on Ryder's seventy-sixth birthday.

Ryder was succeeded by his one-time captain

From birth, Harold Connolly had been burdened with a defective arm that left the athletic Brighton boy to spend much of his adolescence searching for a niche in sports. Early efforts at wrestling and football resulted in his breaking the weak left arm four or five times.

Connolly finally turned to field events and specialized in the shot-put, where all of the work was done by his right arm. In his first three seasons at Boston College, 1949–1950 to 1951–1952, under head coach Jack Ryder and assistant Bill Gilligan, Connolly performed well in the event. But one afternoon at practice, as an exercise that he thought would help him strengthen his bad arm, Connolly began tossing the hammer back to the team's regular hammer throwers. He discovered that "I could throw it back farther than they could throw it out." When Gilligan, himself a former hammer thrower, took over as Boston College's head track coach in 1952, he quickly grasped Connolly's potential and, in one year, was able to develop the former shot-putter into one of the best hammer throwers in the East.

After graduating in 1953, Connolly taught in the Boston school system and began to train seriously for the 1956 Olympics. To motivate himself, Connolly pasted a photograph of world champion Russian hammer thrower, Mikhail Krivonosov, to the visor of his car where it would stay, Connolly told himself, until he beat the Russian.

Connolly made the United States Olympic team for the games to be held in November in Melbourne, Australia. Still, though now a world-class hammer thrower, Connolly was given little chance against the experienced Krivonosov. However, in an informal and friendly practice before the Olympic competition, Connolly and Krivonosov worked out together, and the American gained a psychological advantage by outthrowing the Russian. No matter. The real competition went as expected—at least at first. Krivonosov took the early lead with an Olympic-record throw of 206 feet, 8 inches. With three of his six throws remaining and a record in hand, Krivonosov appeared to have the gold all but won. But on his final throws, the uncharacteristically nervous Krivonosov fouled each time, actually lurching out of the ring on his last attempt.

Connolly also fouled on his first throw and then failed to equal the Russian's record on throws two, three, and four. With two chances left, Connolly recalled that "my hands were sweating so badly I could hardly hold onto the handle." On his fifth attempt, Connolly took a three-whirl windup (he had been using four) and sent the iron ball sailing 207 feet, 3 inches for a new world record and the Olympic gold medal. Krivonosov was the first to congratulate the American. The two later shared a victory cake Krivonosov had ordered for himself, and Connolly promised the Russian that he would remove his photo from the car visor.

The gold medal was not Connolly's only Olympic victory. In the Melbourne Olympic Village he had met and begun courting Czechoslovakian discus thrower Olga Fikotova, who, like Connolly, would also win a gold medal and set an Olympic record with a throw of 176 feet, 1¾ inches.

After leaving Melbourne, Connolly and Fikotova continued their courtship through letters. In 1957, Connolly went to Czechoslovakia on a ten-day visa and asked Czechoslovakian President Antonin Zapotocky for permission to marry Olga and take her back to the United States. Zapotocky, not anxious to see a Communist country lose a gold medal winner to the United States, replied negatively. Said Connolly, "No force in the world will be able to separate me forever from the girl I love."

Connolly was right. The United States State Department stepped in and helped cut through the red tape. Fikotova and Connolly were married in Prague, March 27, 1957. There were three ceremonies: one civil, to satisfy the government; another Catholic, in compliance with Connolly's faith; and one Protestant, consistent with Fikotova's religion.

The couple lived in Boston for a year before moving to California, where Connolly taught school and both trained for future Olympics. Though neither repeated their 1956 championships, the Connollys represented the United States in the 1960 Olympics in Rome.

In a non-Olympic 1962 dual meet with the Soviet Union, Harold Connolly shattered the then world's record with a throw of 231 feet.

Olympic gold medalist Harold Connolly was right when he said, "No force in the world will be able to separate me forever from the girl I love." Harold and Czechoslovakian discus thrower Olga Fikotova were married in 1957. This photo was taken in 1968.

and assistant of five years, Bill Gilligan. A West Roxbury native and a guidance counselor in the Boston school system, Gilligan spent most of his Boston College coaching career working at his school job during the day and reporting to Boston College for track practice in late afternoon.

Among Gilligan's first stars were sprinter Bob McAllister; hurdler and 1955 national hop-step-and-jump champion Pat Lochiatto; and, by far the brightest star, weight man Connolly. It was to their mutual good fortune that the careers of the two men overlapped at Boston College, as Gilligan had specialized in the hammer and was able to coach Connolly to the status of college champion, Olympic gold medal winner, and the greatest hammer thrower of his time (see box).

Connolly was a shot put specialist until he took up the hammer his last year at Boston College. His initial workouts were not impressive, largely because Connolly demanded much of himself. All Gilligan demanded was effort. "I feel that any part I had in Harold's success," the coach later said, "was to keep him going . . . . Like a lot of young people, he got frustrated and on occasion wanted to give it all up."

But in one of his first competitions, a dual meet against Maine in 1953, Connolly sent the hammer sailing ten feet beyond Joe Zabilski's previous record mark for a new Boston College record of 177 feet, 9 inches. Connolly would finish his collegiate career with All-New England, All-East, and All-America honors before putting the glittering crown on his amateur career with a first-place finish in the 1956 Olympics.

Despite Connolly's achievements and Gilligan's dedication, Boston College track slipped into a decline in the mid 1950s. A 1954 sports note in *The Heights* observes that the track team "gets about as much support as the Camera Club." That same year Gilligan was forced to seek team recruits through a notice in the campus newspaper; the item extended invitations to any Boston College student who could run, jump, or throw, and added, in the time-honored spirit of Jack Ryder, "No experience necessary."

Like Ryder, Gilligan was able to get the most out of the material at hand. His 1956 one-mile relay team of Joe McDonald, John Kryzovic, Ed Allard, and John Joyce took first place in that year's Knights of Columbus games and second place in the BAA meet.

With the dedication of Alumni Stadium in 1957, Boston College track had the promise, though not yet the reality, of a new artificial-

Assistant coach Bill Gilligan succeeded Jack Ryder in 1952, and inherited a budding superstar in field-event specialist Hal Connolly. Gilligan was himself a former BC hammer thrower, and was able to help Connolly convert from the shot put and send him on his way to winning the 1956 Olympic gold medal in the hammer throw (see box).

surface track around the football field. The fact that the hockey and basketball teams now had permanent on-campus homes, while the track team had no indoor facility and only the old temporary board track outdoors, led the 1958 yearbook to comment:

"We have often wondered what makes the track team trudge through the snow with shovels to clear off an ancient board track, run their workouts in freezing temperatures, and then compete with teams which, because of facilities and numbers of participants, are superior in strength. . . . The inspiration rests in their coach, Bill Gilligan . . . . We believe he is living the legend of Jack Ryder."

The opening of Roberts Center for the 1958–1959 academic year provided the track team with some indoor practice space, and a new temporary board track was set up on the north end of the football field. These improvements helped produce a track revival at Boston College in 1960, with Boston College going 10–1 in dual- and tri-meet competition. The team also won the Greater Boston Intercollegiate meet over Tufts, Northeastern, and Boston University on the strength of first-place finishes in the one- and two-mile events by Bob O'Leary, in the 1,000 yard by Jim Duff, the 600 by captain Ed Quinn, and the dash by Bill Falla. Later that year, O'Leary established a new school mile record of 4:10.5 while placing fifth in the IC4As. Coach Gilligan called this triumph over the best local collegiate competition, "Boston College's most important meet victory in ten or twelve years."

The track resurgence continued into 1961, when, at the prestigious BAA meet, Boston College relay teams defeated national powers Villanova, Manhattan, and Holy Cross. The team of Duff, Mike Scully, Jim McMahon, and Larry Rawson took the two-mile event, while Larry Flynn, Jim Rinella, Jack McNamara, and Duff won the one-mile.

Campus logistical problems impeded the progress of the 1962–1963 team. The first phase of the $40–million McElroy Commons campus expansion partly supplanted the old cinder track on the upper campus; thus, with the Alumni Stadium track not yet completed, the Boston College team had to commute to tracks at MIT and Brandeis for daily workouts. Nevertheless, despite the obstacles, Gilligan was able to develop a team that won another Greater Boston Intercollegiate meet, a club led by All-America hammer thrower George "Dizzy" Desnoyers, miler and relay anchor Larry Rawson, and triple jump specialist Vincent Samir of Iraq, who, in 1963, set a Boston College triple jump record of 50 feet, 3½ inches.

In 1963, a Boston College two-mile relay team of Jim Owens, Tom Meagher, John Carroll, and Chris Law won the BAA championship.

By 1964, Boston College had its new outdoor, quarter-mile facility, appropriately named the Jack Ryder Track. It was an artificial surface Tartan track, one of the outstanding running surfaces in the world.

It is one measure of Boston College's transition from a commuter to a residence college that among the track stars of the 1960s are four out-of-staters: Chuck Zailkowski of Rhode Island, a hurdler and quarter miler; Bob Gilvey of New Jersey, a quarter miler undefeated in dual meet competition in 1965; Lucien Tessier of New Hampshire, a sprinter, hurdler, and pole vaulter; and John Fiore, another Rhode Islander, a 1966 All-America hammer thrower (Gilligan's third) and holder of the current Boston College record of 202 feet, 10 inches, while Massachusetts resident Bill Norris of Beverly won the New England Intercollegiate and IC4A steeplechase titles and set a then school record of 9:04.1. In 1967, the tradition of great Gilligan-coached hammer throwers was continued by Boston College's Jim Kavanaugh, who placed third in the 1967 NCAA hammer throw and later won the AAU decathlon.

Ironically, Gilligan's great love for the hammer nearly cost the coach his life six years later. During a Boston College–Northeastern meet in February 1973, Gilligan stood watching a hammer thrower when the thirty-five-pound weight slipped out of the thrower's hand, hurling into Gilligan's chest. The force of the blow might have killed the coach except that he was wearing an alpaca-lined overcoat with a large notebook stuffed in-

Coach Gilligan's prowess at developing world-class weight men continued into the 1960s with the emergence of George "Dizzy" Desnoyers (left) and John Fiore. Both men gained all-American status in the hammer throw, while also participating in other field events.

One of BC's greatest all-around athletes, Jim Kavanaugh was a nationally-ranked hammer thrower, an AAU decathlon champion, and a football end who was the Eagles' leading pass receiver in 1966. Here, track-team captain Kavanaugh confers with Coach Gilligan at the start of the '68 season.

side it. The handle of the hammer swung up into the coach's jaw, breaking some teeth, but the coat and notebook absorbed the blow to his chest. Gilligan spent two days in intensive care and eight days in the hospital recovering.

The early 1970s were a period of substantial progress for Boston College track. On St. Patrick's Day, 1972, Boston College got its long-awaited indoor track, a one-eighth-mile, Tartan-surface unbanked facility located in the newly-opened William J. Flynn Recreation Complex. The same year, Boston College successfully recruited New Bedford schoolboy track star Keith Francis, the Massachusetts and New England 880 champion who would become the dominant Boston College track star of the 1970s.

Francis set five Boston College records on his blistering way to All-America honors. He set indoor marks in the 600, 880, 1,000 and indoor mile, and in his sophomore year set perhaps his most impressive mark, the current record 4:00.8 for the outdoor mile. In his junior year, Francis won the 1,000–yard run at Madison Square Garden's Millrose Games and ran anchor on an outstanding 1976 relay team that also included Phil Hazard, Bob Scales, and Dave Nelson.

As Jack Ryder had added a field events specialist to his staff when he hired Bob Gilligan in the late 1940s, so Gilligan in the 1970s added a track specialist, former Boston College middle distance star Tom Meagher. It was Meagher who was principally responsible for honing Francis' vast natural talents.

Other Boston College stars of the first half of the 1970s included John Bykowsky, the best high hurdler in New England in 1970; Dave Nelson, who took the 1976 indoor long jump title with a leap of 23 feet, 8¾ inches; discus thrower Mike Woicik, who won the 1976 New England discus championship with a throw of 180 feet, 5 inches; Mark Murray, 1970 New England 440 champ; and sprinter Mike Johnson, who ran a Boston College record 9.7 100-yard dash in 1970, only to have Don Schneider break that record with a 9.6 in 1973. Though the record only lasted until Keith Francis inevitably got around to breaking it in 1975, Jack McDonald set a Boston College indoor mile record of 4:07.0 in 1972.

New Bedford product Keith Francis dominated the BC track scene in the mid-1970s, setting four indoor and one outdoor mark in middle-distance races. The runner on the right, here representing the Greater Boston Track Club, is BC grad and current track coach, Jack McDonald.

Brightest track star of the mid-seventies was dash man Phil Hazard, who won the 1977 and 1978 New England Intercollegiate 100-yard dash title and the 1977 IC4A title. In 1977, Hazard tied Schneider's school record of 9.6.

McDonald was one of Gilligan's best recruits. The coach first noticed the schoolboy runner at Braintree's Archbishop Williams High School in 1969. "I was the oldest of eleven children" McDonald recalls. "My father had died and I was all set to focus my career on pumping gas." Instead, Gilligan persuaded McDonald to come to Boston College. Here, in addition to his athletic endeavors, McDonald began to acquire the coaching skills that later in the decade would make him Gilligan's successor—Boston College's third track coach and the first to hold the job full-time.

In 1978, after twenty-five years of coaching track at Boston College—or, as he put it, "of getting home at seven and seven-thirty every night"—Gilligan stepped down as head coach, electing to concentrate on being coach of field events until his full retirement in 1981. Like Ryder three decades earlier, Gilligan saw to it that the head coaching job passed into the hands of his former assistant coach, Jack McDonald.

At first, McDonald wasn't sure he was up to the challenge. "I have a very empty feeling about his retirement," McDonald said of Gilligan. "In the spirit of Bill Gilligan is the spirit of Jack Ryder, and to think of filling those shoes. . . ."

Free to concentrate on field events, Gilligan quickly produced another outstanding weight man in Karl Swanke of Connecticut. Swanke was a shot-put specialist who in 1980 set a Boston College record of 57 feet, 4¾ inches. He was complemented on the 1980 team by high jumper Rob Lanney of Saugus, who, at the Dartmouth Relays, became the first Boston College man ever to break seven feet, and by middle distance runner Tom Horton of New York, who set a Boston College indoor mile record of 4:04.6 in 1980.

The early 1980s also ushered in a new era of distance running. In 1982, Boston College sophomore Fernando Braz of Peabody won the New England 10 kilometer championship and set a school record 29:35.5 in that event and a school record 14:18.1 for the five kilometers.

One of the major advances in the history of Boston College track occurred at this time and took place far from any gym. In fact, it was considered basketball news when it happened: the formation of the Big East Conference in 1979–1980, which was to include track competition as well as the more publicized basketball matchups. At the inaugural Big East meet in 1980, Boston College finished second to host St. John's.

"No question the formation of the Big East Conference, the joining of many of the prestigious eastern college track powers in one conference, will help raise the profile and publicity opportunities for Boston College track," says McDonald. "The Big East is very important to us."

"We have some scholarship money now, two excellent tracks and, I think, a fairly good rep-

In 1980, Rob Lanney of Saugus set a BC high-jump record of 7'1", and in the process became the first BC athlete to clear the seven-foot mark.

utation for fielding quality track teams," remarked the coach, speaking from behind his desk in a ground-floor office in Roberts Center, the walls of which are adorned with photos, memorabilia, and track bric-a-brac.

Two oversized, framed black-and-white photographs dominate McDonald's office, One, behind his desk, shows Ryder and 1920s track star Jake Driscoll; the other, on another wall, shows Bill Gilligan and Hal Connolly. "Someday I'm going to take those two pictures and hang them together behind my desk. There have only been three of us, you know."

6

Women's Sports

THE PREVAILING, IF patronizing, attitude of male students toward women's sports in the early part of the century seems captured by this poem that appeared in a 1929 edition of *The Stylus*:

Feather-footed one,
Do you know
That when you run
You do not show
A trace
Of grace?
And that, my dear, is not mere chance;
Yours is not the rhythm of the race,
Yours is the rhythm of the dance.

Whatever a woman's place on the campus of the 1920s, that place apparently was not on the field, track, or court.

Though Boston College was an all-male school for almost ninety years, there were occasional women graduate students. The first to earn a degree from Boston College was Margaret Ursula Magrath, a Mt. Holyoke graduate who received her Master of Arts from Boston College in 1926. But women did not attend Boston Col-

lege in appreciable numbers until the early fifties when the School of Education was founded and began accepting women. The School of Nursing opened in 1947 but that school did not move to the Chestnut Hill campus until 1960.

Because there were no varsity or intramural sports programs for women as there were for men, and because standard educational practice was for Education majors to take at least one physical education course, Boston College instituted in 1952–1953 a mandatory (but non-credit) women's physical education course. Absence of women's varsity sports notwithstanding, the college occasionally attracted an outstanding female athlete such as Belmont's Pat Sullivan, one of New England's top ranked amateur tennis players of the mid-fifties.

Boston College women's first big step out of the shadow of male athletic dominance came in 1964 when Doctor Theresa Powell, a faculty member in the School of Education, was named Boston College's first full-time Director of Women's Physical Education. Chief among her duties was development of the then new Boston College Women's Recreation Association (WRA), a dues-supported organization charged with sponsoring all women's athletic programs. Between the required physical education courses and the recreational and instructional programs offered by the WRA, Boston College women could choose from a variety of popular if low-profile sports, including tennis, volleyball, tumbling, square dancing, sailing, swimming, skating, basketball, golf, horseback riding, modern dance, and riflery. Like the BCAA of the 1900s, the WRA seemed to be permanently on the financial ropes in its early years until student-run fund raising projects and a small influx of university funds supplemented the regular dues and allowed the WRA to expand its programs.

The idea of women's intercollegiate competition—as opposed to purely recreational sport—began to catch on in the mid- and late sixties. Between 1964 and 1971, there was limited intercollegiate women's competition in tennis, basketball, fencing, sailing, swimming, and volleyball.

Boston College took a small step in the direction of coeducational athletics in 1969 when the college eliminated the Physical Education requirement for women Education majors and replaced it with a Physical Education minor open to both men and women. About the same time, the WRA was renamed the Boston College Recreation Association and many of its programs were open to both men and women. In 1971 the BCRA was taken out of the jurisdiction of the School of Education and placed under the aegis of the Boston College Athletic Department as part of an expanded, campus-wide coeducational athletic program.

But the most dramatic progress for women's sports at Boston College came in the early seventies in the architectually futuristic form of a new student recreation complex and in the legalistic form of federal legislation.

By the late sixties, it was obvious that Boston College's limited and varsity-oriented fields, courts, and rink were not adequate to support the general recreational needs of the student body. In 1970, Athletic Director Flynn proposed that Boston College build a recreation center on filled land behind the football stadium. He took his proposal to the board of trustees. Since, at the

time, the trustees were faced with the iron necessity of a tuition increase to forestall an operating deficit, they turned down Flynn's proposal. Undaunted—perhaps not even surprised—Flynn took his case to the students. Would the Boston College students, he asked, be willing to stand a surcharge of $25.00 per year to fund a recreation complex? At first it seemed a case of extraordinarily bad timing and uncommonly poor judgment for Flynn to ask that question at a time when students across the nation were expressing more interest in burning campuses than in building them; Boston College students were holding demonstrations and otherwise protesting the latest tuition increase. Nevertheless, the student government agreed to put the question to a campus-wide student referendum in 1971. To Flynn's delight and to a lot of people's surprise, students approved the idea by an overwhelming 75 percent majority. The $25 charge to students, plus user fees for neighbors and other non-students, would about cover the costs of the proposed $1.6–million building.

The trustees voted their enthusiastic approval and agreed to mortgage virtually the entire athletic ranch—Alumni Stadium, McHugh Forum, Roberts Center, and Shea Field—to enable Flynn to give the go-ahead to Daniel Tully's Creative Building Company of Melrose. What Tully created was a contemporary structure he called a "hyperbolic parabaloid," a building constructed in such a fashion that it had no space-stealing support posts to consume usable recreation space.

The new recreation complex—or "RecPlex," as it was called—opened its doors on St. Patrick's Day, 1972. The new building contained six tennis courts, some of which could be converted to serve for volleyball, badminton, and basketball; an eight-laps-to-the-mile unbanked track, golf cages, batting cage, swimming pool and separate diving well; handball, squash, and racquetball courts; saunas; men's and, for the first time, women's lockers; and, adjacent to the building, six new outdoor tennis courts.

"More than Title Nine or the national movement toward women's sports—more than anything else—the Recreation Complex was the key

Women swimmers hit the water in BC's new William J. Flynn Recreation Complex, or "Recplex." More than any other single factor, says assistant athletic director Bobbi Carson, "The Recreation Complex was the key to the growth of women's sports at BC."

to the growth of women's sports at Boston College," says Mary Miller (Bobbi) Carson, who has been the assistant athletic director at Boston College since 1973.

Sara Groden, a swimmer and one of Boston College's first major woman sports stars, agrees: "The RecPlex gave the biggest boost to women's sports. It helped the men's teams and the student body, too."

In 1979 the so-called "RecPlex" was formally named the William J. Flynn student recreation complex, the first Boston College building ever to be named for a living employee.

But there was more to the rise of women's sports than the construction of a new building. In the early seventies, federal legislation was having its impact on almost every college athletic program in the country. In 1972, Congress passed the Education Amendments Acts, the famous Title IX of which is devoted to non-dis-

crimination on the basis of sex in any education programs or *activities* (italics added) receiving federal financial assistance. The activities referred to covered intercollegiate sports. Passage of the act meant that all colleges had the legal responsibility to offer equal opportunities to men and women to participate in intercollegiate athletics. One of the immediate results was that the early and mid-seventies saw a national explosion in women's intercollegiate varsity sports.

Boston College was somewhat ahead of the national movement in 1971–1972 when the college raised women's basketball to varsity status, making it the first women's varsity sport. Tennis, and volleyball had to await completion of the Recreation Complex and were added in 1972–1973, field hockey in 1973–1974, and varsity swimming in 1974–1975.

Unlike the situation in men's sports, the NCAA did not sponsor women's intercollegiate championships in the seventies (and would not do so until 1981), nor did it extend its jurisdiction over women's college sports. The major championship-sanctioning bodies for women's sports were the Eastern Association of Intercollegiate Athletics for Women (EAIAW), which Boston College joined in 1971 and the national Association of Intercollegiate Athletics for Women (AIAW), which the college joined in 1973.

While Boston College women's teams and athletes have earned regional and national recognition in several sports, it was the swimming and diving team, coached by former Boston College letterman Tom Groden, that in its first season began to establish itself as one of the flagships of Boston College women's athletics. The team also produced several outstanding women athletes, among them the aforementioned Sara Gro-

den, a Minnesota native who did not have visions of swimming pools dancing in her head when she first enrolled at Boston College. "I had swum competitively a little bit when I was a kid but that was all. I came entirely for the academics," she says. But before she concluded a four-year varsity career, Groden had made a name for herself as a three-time team MVP, a 200-yard freestyle pool record holder, two-time team captain, and an almost unbeatable force in dual meet competition where she had a career-winning percentage of .897.

Groden was by no means the only star of a team that between 1975–1976 and 1977–1978 won thirty-five consecutive dual meets. That team also had Mary Ellen Sullivan, '78, the 1977–1978 MVP, a three-year All-New England selection and the first woman to win the Nat

BC's first successful women's sports teams was also one of its best ever, the 1976–1977 swim team which was undefeated in sixteen meets. Members of the team (back row, from left): Tom Groden (coach), Cathy Cuthbert, Janille Blackburn, Donna Gerstner, Katie Miles, Mary Judge, Mary O'Keefe, Siobhan Campbell, Arlene Snow, Sara Groden; (middle row, from left): Kim Morahan, Marti Long, Barb Weaver, Sue Weyrauch, Kathy Derr, Patty McGuire; (front row, from left): Bea Grause, Rose Reidy, Anne McDermott, Mary Ellen Sullivan (co-captain), Laurie O'Reilly (co-captain), Winnie McCarthy.

Sara Groden (left) and Mary Kay Finnerty were two of BC's first top women's swimmers and among its best women athletes ever. Groden was a three-time swim team MVP, while Finnerty was the first woman inducted into the BC Hall of Fame. In this photo, the pair prepare to cut the cake celebrating their team's undefeated 1976–1977 season.

Captain Tamie Thompson led the BC women's lacrosse team to an impressive 10–3 season in 1979–1980, and a second-place finish in the New England Women's Lacrosse Association Division II championships.

Hasenfus Eagle of the Year Award (1978); Mary Kay Finnerty, '76, who recorded a career dual meet record of 148–5 and in 1981 became the first woman inducted into the Boston College Hall of Fame; and Siobhan (a Gaelic name pronounced Shavaun) Campbell, who in 1976 became the first Boston College female athlete to qualify for national intercollegiate competition when she went to the AIAW meet in Miami. Campbell, whose father Elmore played tennis for Boston College, qualified for national competition in three of her four years (1976, 1977, and 1978) and in 1978 set Boston College and New England pool records off the one- and three-meter boards. Campbell was All-New England as a diver, and also enjoyed a three-year varsity lacrosse career in which she was team MVP in 1977 and co-captain in 1978–1979.

Like so many Boston College athletes before them, Groden and Campbell became part-time coaches at Boston College following their graduation. In 1981 Campbell became coach of both men's and women's varsity divers. Despite the graduation of Campbell, Groden, and several other stars, Boston College swimmers and divers were the first-ranked team in the New England Women's Intercollegiate Swimming and Diving Association for 1981–1982 and were ranked thirteenth nationally in AIAW Division II.

It would have been inconceivable to most of the boys at James Street at the turn of the century, but by 1975–1976 women's undergrate enrollment at Boston College for the first time accounted for more than half (51 percent) of the student body. Rising female enrollment inevitably led to greater demand for more women's varsity sports. Golf achieved varsity status in 1973–1974, lacrosse in 1977–1978, indoor and outdoor track and cross-country in 1978–1979, and soccer in 1980–1981.

Women's varsity sport was not the only area of athletic expansion. Following the 1972 opening of the Recreation Complex, general student use increased from 5,000 to about 7,500 per week. By 1974, the Boston College student government asked for more recreation space, and once again the students were willing to pay for it. This time the recreation fee jumped from $25

to $32 with the additional revenue used to finance a 42,000–square-foot addition to the complex. Opening in 1976, it included a new lobby, four additional tennis courts, more handball, squash, and racquetball courts, and a multi-purpose area that could be used for basketball, judo, karate, dance, and wrestling.

In an interview with the *Boston Herald's* Tim Horgan, Flynn explained that the impact of the new 117,000-square-foot complex went well beyond men's and women's varsity sports: "Our Admissions Office loves it because it helps sell prospective students. It's brought the whole college community together—students, staff, and faculty. It's created jobs for many of our work-study students. And it ties in with our varsity sports. For instance, our tennis teams have improved since we built our own courts, and it wasn't until we got our own pool that our swimming team beat Holy Cross for the first time in history."

While female swimmers, divers, runners, tennis, volleyball, and basketball players joined the rest of the student body in making ample use of the Flynn Complex, (often at a rate of 2,000 or more per day) women's field sports, heretofore confined mainly to field hockey, grew to include a successful lacrosse program in 1977. After the fashion of the swimming team—and also benefiting from the considerable athletic talents of Campbell—the women's lacrosse team went to a good if not spectacular 10–6 over its first two seasons before turning in a 10–3 1979–1980 year in which it entered post-season play for the first time, finishing second (beating Middlebury and Smith, losing to Plymouth State) in the New England College Women's Lacrosse Association Division II championships at Dartmouth and finishing seventh in the AIAW National Championships in Baltimore. The team's strength was one of the East's best defenses, led by 1981 Division II All-America Mary Beth Ripp and cover point Carolyn Megan.

Women's lacrosse had long been a popular sport at most prep schools and some public high schools, but as women's sports became increasingly more competitive it appeared that the image of women's lacrosse as an easy-going game to be played on a shaded prep school sward on a lazy spring afternoon had become largely, if not violently, dated, as witnessed Siobhan Campbell: "We're not as rough as the men but I got whacked on the head, back, arms, and legs enough times to feel it. Thank God I had the mouthpiece. I would have lost half my teeth without it."

Less violent than lacrosse but as intensely competitive and demanding as any sport is varsity tennis, another of the building blocks of Boston College women's sports. The women's tennis team was among the first varsities to establish itself as a winner and a regional power.

Ann Marie Lynch, daughter of two teaching pros, became the youngest coach ever hired at Boston College, when in 1973, at age 18, she was named head coach of women's varsity tennis. By the 1975–1976 season, Lynch had built a team that would string together seasons of 9–1, 9–2, and 7–2. In her eight seasons as head coach (1972–1981) Lynch's teams compiled a 46–25 record. But more historically significant as another measure of interest in women's sports is that the number of candidates for the tennis team doubled from thirty in 1972 to sixty by 1976. In 1981–1982, Lynch was succeeded by coach Howard Singer, who in his first season saw his team's top player, sophomore Bernadette Diaz, reach the quarter-finals of the New Englands. Diaz was the EAIAW Division II singles champion while the team won the AIAW Eastern Regional championship and qualified for the national tournament in Colorado.

Like lacrosse and tennis, field hockey is among the most traditional of women's sports and, as such, got its start as a varsity sport relatively early, in the fall of 1973. The sport enjoyed some of its best years during the four-year (1975–1979) coaching tenure of Maureen Enos, whose teams compiled a 26–11–5 record. The 7–3–2 1977–1978 season saw the team advance to post-season competition for the first time in the 1977 New England College Field Hockey Association Division A tournament at Amherst, where it beat Central Connecticut, tied Lyndon State, and lost to Middlebury. The field hockey team is among the leading producers of all-star female athletes;

players chosen for post-season all-star play include Mary Beth Hollingworth '81, Meg Hurley '79, Carol Flaherty '79, Meg Fahey '78, Debbie Ruel '80, Janet Davidson '79, and Patty Gallacher '81.

"It used to be in the early seventies," says former assistant swimming coach Sara Groden, also Boston College's women's sports publicity director, "that the schools with women's physical education majors, colleges like Springfield or Central Connecticut, could dominate women's sports. They had all the athletes. Now women can play varsity sports at a high level at more colleges and competition is beginning to even out."

There is ample recent evidence of that "evening out" in the currently popular sports of women's cross-country and soccer.

In the mid-seventies, then men's head track and cross-country coach Bill Gilligan used to let a few women run with the men's cross-country team. By 1978, women's cross-country had evolved into a full-fledged varsity sport in its own right under the coaching of Gilligan's successor, Jack McDonald, and by 1980, men's and women's assistant track coach Fred Treseler was coaching the women's cross-country team to an undefeated (10–0) season (20–1 over two seasons) and first place in the EAIAW Eastern Regionals.

Women's varsity track and field also got its start in 1978–1979, and by 1980–1981, the team had followed in the sixty-year-old Boston College tradition of producing extraordinary middle distance runners, including Clare Connelly, who holds the Boston College women's track record in the 800-meters (2:13.6). Coaches McDonald and Treseler have also produced several long-distance running stars such as three-year team captain Cheryl Panzarella, Nancy Small, and Mary Cobb, all of whom also star for the cross-country team.

Few women's teams got off to a faster start than soccer. In 1979, while it was still a club sport, Boston College was ranked ninth in the East. Soccer moved up to varsity status in 1980–1981 and, like women's swimming and track, first came under the direction of men's head coach and former NASL pro Ben Brewster, with daily coaching by part-time assistants Michael Lavigne

BC's women's varsity track and field team was launched in 1978–1979 and yet, under the direction of coach Jack McDonald, has produced a number of middle-distance stars. Kathleen Daley (left) was an all-American in the 3,000–meter event, while Patricia McGovern holds the team's 10,000–meter record.

and his assistant Peter Counsell. The team went 10–4 in its first season, was generally ranked between ninth and tenth in the East, and narrowly missed selection to the eight-team EAIAW post-season tournament.

Soccer is one of eight women's varsity sports for which there is some financial aid for athletes. The others are swimming, field hockey, lacrosse, tennis, track, and cross-country; and perhaps the most competitive sport of all from a recruiting standpoint, women's basketball. Boston College also sponsors women's varsity golf, fencing, sailing, skiing, and volleyball though, as yet, participants in these sports are not eligible for athletic grants-in-aid.

It is perhaps ironic that basketball, the first of the ten women's varsity sports and the women's sport with the highest level of fan interest across the country, has struggled to establish itself as a consistent winner. The most successful era for women's basketball was from 1973–1976, when then head coach Maureen Enos put together teams with a combined three-season record of 25–14 and a championship in the 1975 Bentley College Invitational in which sophomore Maureen McAuliffe was tournament MVP.

The latter part of the seventies saw a skein of losing seasons that was halted with a 12–11-year in 1980–1981, Margo Plotzke's first season as head coach. But the most encouraging development for Boston College women's basketball was the decision of the newly formed Big East Conference to begin regular-season round-robin competition in women's basketball in 1982–1983 (each college to play every other conference college once) with a post-season championship play-off. While the Big East will also sponsor post-season women's tournaments in cross-country, tennis, swimming, volleyball, and indoor and outdoor track, only basketball will feature regular season competition, a fact which Flynn and Carson believe will help attract some of the better players to Boston College and will increase the general popularity of the sport.

Beyond the fact that women's sports exist and are growing at a pace the earliest Boston College graduates could not have imagined—the college spent $100,000 in 1981 to build women's train-

The Big East Conference sponsors women's basketball competition among member colleges, but the BC entry has yet to fare as well as its male counterpart. New head coach Margo Plotzke (here conferring with a player during a break in the action) made a start in the right direction by halting a string of losing seasons during her first year, 1980–1981.

ing, equipment, and locker rooms—there are also changes in women athletes that are just as profound as the changes in athletics. "Even in the relatively short time of ten years," says Carson, "I can see a change in the dedication women are beginning to bring to their sports. Some women work out almost year-round. They make a very serious commitment to their sport, as much as some of the men do."

"They're among the most dedicated athletes we have," says track and cross-country coach Jack McDonald, whose athletes' dedication to their sports is legendary and, in McDonald's case, includes a pair of Division II 1982 All-Americans in 3,000-meter runner Kathleen Daly and 10,000-meter runner Nancy Small, and the 1982 New England Heptathlon champion, Jane Haubrich.

It has been more than a half century now since the poet—doing no more than innocently reflecting the opinions of his time—told women that theirs "is not the rhythmn of the race." Indeed, theirs has since become not only the rhythmn of the race, but many of its victories.

7

Soccer, Golf, and Tennis

SOCCER

THE SIXTIES MARKED a transition decade for United States soccer, a time when American football's poor cousin experienced a major growth in popularity manifested by the founding of the professional North American Soccer League (NASL) in 1968 and the rapid growth of community youth soccer programs. It is understandable and appropriate that Boston College soccer got its start in the mid sixties, beginning as a club sport in 1964 and moving up to varsity status in 1967.

Hungarian Gyorgy Lang, a librarian at the Boston College law school, was the first varsity coach. He took a team of foreign students and Americans—some of the Americans never played organized soccer until college—to a surprising 7–5–1 season in 1967. Stars of the early era included Alfred "Skip" Gostyla of Bloomfield,

Connecticut, and Frank Mwaura of Kiambu, Kenya, both of whom scored a team-leading nine goals in 1968.

Lang once recalled his earliest teams as not particularly sophisticated soccer talents but as hustlers and scrappers: "Even back when the disparity [in talent] was very great, the fighting spirit was always there." But it would take more than fighting spirit to win in the fast-improving New England college soccer scene of the early seventies. After an encouraging start, Lang's teams dipped to below .500 for the next three seasons.

In addition to inconsistencies in talent, the team had to face problems in its campus field, the area now occupied by the Flynn Recreation Complex, formerly a filled space that became a quagmire after the slightest rain. A heavy rain

Ben Brewster (right, with 1980 assistant Mike Doran) resigned as BC soccer coach in 1972 to pursue a pro career and returned in 1976 determined to lead the Eagles to national soccer eminence. By 1980 they had won an ECAC championship and were one of the country's top teams.

could force the relocation of the game to Shea Field, site of the 1971 5–4 triple-overtime win over Holy Cross.

After the 1971 season, the demands of Lang's law school position prompted his resignation from the soccer post. His place was taken by a young former Brown All-American and 1971 Yale freshman coach, Ben Brewster. Brewster, a product of Concord's Middlesex school, was one of the rarest of soccer phenomena in these days—an American-born college star. Brewster was an advocate of defensive-style soccer and tried to install this system at Boston College. But, while his team was able to cut its goals-allowed from 39 to 23, an anemic offense left the club with a dismal 3–9–2 record. At the end of the season, Brewster, still a player at heart, left Boston College to turn pro with the Connecticut Wildcats of the American Soccer league and later with the Boston Minutemen of the NASL. "The chance to play was there," he says, "and it was too much to try to practice, play pro ball, and still devote time to Boston College."

Brewster's departure cleared the way for the entry of Hans Westerkamp, a sociology professor who took over as part-time coach. Westerkamp inherited most of Brewster's improving young players but none of the former coach's defensive predisposition. "I wanted to put more fun, more excitement into the game," he once told the *Heights*, "so I shifted to a completely offensive game."

It worked. Westerkamp's first team, led by high scorers John Lojek and Bill Fraser, goalie Ryder D'Elia, and Greater Boston League (GBL) all-star fullback John Pfeiffer, took the 1973 Eagles to a 7–6–3 record. True to his word, Westerkamp inspired his charges to more than double the team's offensive output—from 17 to 37 goals.

The next year, Boston College slumped to a still respectable 6–8–2 in a season that included a 2–1 upset of always powerful Boston University. But then in 1975, as Westerkamp once recalled it, "The roof fell in." Graduation, injuries (at one point fourteen of twenty players were hurt), and six one-goal losses combined to drop the team's record to 4–10–2. It was a painful record, softened only by the fact that one of the wins was a 1–0 shutout of Notre Dame.

The next season brought some improvement, as the still offense-minded Eagles rebounded to 6–7–1. That year saw the arrival of two former Boston College High schoolboy stars: Marty Lusk and Tom McElroy, and the player who over the next four years would become Boston College's brightest soccer star, Bermudian midfielder Emerson Davis.

In spite of the influx of talent and the obvious promise of a winning future, Westerkamp resigned for personal reasons after the 1976 season. The way was then open for Brewster's return. He came back to the Heights with four seasons of pro play to his credit, a new and deeper commitment to coaching, and as he would be quick to point out, a dedication to the promotion of the game. In his first season back, Brewster fared little better than had his predecessor, bringing the Eagles to a 6–9–1 record. But the next year, 1978, saw the dramatic turnaround of Boston College soccer.

The spectacular Davis was switched from midfield to sweeper, where he anchored a defense that recorded eight shutouts. Davis and midfielder Lou Papadellis earned All-New England honors and goalkeeper Tom McElroy, a midfielder in his scholastic days at Boston College High, began to show the form that would eventually make him a GBL all-star. The team roared through a 13–5 season, won its first GBL title, and finished the year ranked eighth in New England among NCAA Division I teams.

By now, Brewster was looking beyond regional respectability toward the western horizon of national recognition. Accordingly, in 1979 Boston College played the toughest schedule in its soccer history when the Eagles took on St. Louis and 1978 defending national champion, San Francisco. After losing to the Billikens 2–0, Brewster's team came within a shot of pulling off one of the upsets of the college soccer year when—thanks largely to the play of goalie McElroy—they held San Francisco to a scoreless tie at Alumni Stadium, the first time in three years any team had kept the Dons off the scoreboard.

Tragically, several months after the conclusion of the 1979 season, McElroy learned from doctors that he was seriously ill with a virulent form of cancer. He told coach Brewster of his condition, but witheld the information from his teammates. Because he had sat out the 1976 season, McElroy had one year of eligibility remaining. Despite his worsening physical condition he played seven games that final season and ended his career by setting several Boston College goalkeeping records: most shutouts one season (10), most shutouts career (20), most games played career (43), and lowest career goals against average (1.05). "Tom's development as a goalie was truly remarkable," Brewster recalls. "As a sophomore, he could hardly fall over and catch a ball at the same time. He used to get furious with himself in practice. However, by his senior year he was a top college keeper and a definite pro prospect."

In 1980, McElroy, with midfielder Papadellis and team MVP Steve LeBlanc, paced 15–3–3 Boston College to its second GBL title and its first ECAC playoff championship, a 3–1 victory over Bridgeport. On July 17, 1981, McElroy, credited accurately by Brewster as a man with "courage rarely seen in college athletics," died in Massachusetts General Hospital.

In addition to his obviously successful job of building Boston College soccer into a winner, Brewster also made good on his vow to raise the stature of the sport on campus. Gradually, through the late seventies and into the eighties, Brewster added those small but significant touches that can elevate a team from the shadows to the spotlight: games were played under the lights of Alumni Field, the team had its own slick thirty-two-page program, there was an admission charge

for games, refreshment stands were opened, and the national anthem was played for all home games. Minute details to be sure, they were nonetheless the recognizable trappings of a sport that would like to be regarded as "major." "When you're a soccer coach, promotion goes with the territory," says Brewster.

By 1981, winning was a given. In its third game of the season, Boston College shocked nationally-ranked UCLA 2–1 and went on to a 13–6–1 regular season mark that included a third GBL title and a fourth-in-New England ranking, accomplishments all the more remarkable since they were compiled by a team with no seniors. Only a 2–1 overtime loss to Boston University prevented the Eagles from successfully defending their ECAC championship.

For Brewster, the most significant statistic of the 1981 season was probably not the won-lost record or Peter Dorfman's team-leading sixteen points. It was not Jon Farrow's three game-win-

The late Tom McElroy was a converted midfielder who went on to set a number of BC goalie records. Cancer-victim McElroy, said coach Brewster, showed a "courage rarely seen in college athletics."

ning goals or all-GBL goalie Gordie Farkouh's moving to within one shutout of McElroy's career record. It was the 115 letters the coach received from schoolboy stars hoping to play at Boston College. "That, and the fact we are able to sched-ule the caliber of teams we play—the UCLAs and San Franciscos—says that Boston College soccer had come to a point where we were recognized as among the top thirty or so teams in the country."

GOLF

It is not surprising that sixty-five years passed before students at Boston College would field a golf team. Golf was a rich man's sport. It was a game for those wealthy enough to belong to country clubs and to have the leisure to polish their games, requirements that disqualified many Catholics during the late nineteenth and early twentieth centuries.

Golf was an established sport on many eastern college campuses. This, and gradually growing affluence of those attending Boston College after World War I, inspired the pursuit of golf. Students Vin Roberts and Charley Dooley organized an informal college team at Boston College in 1928. After playing five intra-squad matches (most at nearby Commonwealth Country Club), Dooley, Roberts, Joe Farrington, and Bill Tobin were selected to meet the Holy Cross team in the season's only intercollegiate match. Boston College won, and the impetus of that victory led the 1929 team to play a six-match intercollegiate schedule. In its second year the still non-varsity team went undefeated; two of its wins came against established golfing powers Wesleyan and Brown. In 1930, the Boston College Athletic Association recognized golf as a varsity sport, and in 1931, as evidence of its ambition if not of its stature, golf team members financed a southern trip. Boston College lost to powerful North Carolina and Georgetown, while managing ties against William and Mary and George Washington.

These first golf teams made do without a head coach. The schedule was arranged by a student manager while an elected captain was the team's nominal leader. Otherwise, players were left to work on their own games. That changed in 1936 when Fred J. Corcoran of Cambridge became the first varsity golf coach. One of his first acts was to persuade his friend, pro Gene Sarazen, to come to Chestnut Hill and give the team a clinic.

World War II worked its disruptive effect on Boston College golf, as it did on most Boston College sports of the forties. The team regrouped in 1947 under the charge of hockey coach John "Snooks" Kelley, who had an equally great—if less well publicized—success in golf as he had in hockey.

Boston College won the New England Intercollegiate championship in 1947 and 1948, thanks to the talents of Harry Ernst, Dick Kinchla, and Bob Crowley—three of the best golfers in the team's history. Kelley's first two teams also went to the NCAA championships, playing Michigan in 1947 and California in 1948. In the Michigan tournament, Kinchla was the only player, other than eventual tournament champion Bob Harris, to turn in a sub-par round. In 1949, his senior year, Kinchla led the Eagles to a third consecutive New England title and later won the New England Intercollegiate Singles championship.

The 1950s continued the golden era of Boston College golf as former Boston College High star and Massachusetts State Amateur finalist Dick Grace helped the team to the 1952 and 1953 New England Intercollegiate crown, giving Kelley's teams five titles in seven seasons.

In 1955, Kelley resigned as golf coach to concentrate exclusively on hockey, leaving golf to pass into the hands of another hockey man, Bernie Burke, the assistant varsity hockey coach and goalkeeper on the 1949 NCAA championship hockey team. Burke's successful teams of the mid-fifties were built on the talents of two of Boston College's all-time golfers, Fordie Pitts and Charlie Volpone.

Volpone, who would make a name for himself as a pro golfer following his graduation in 1958, won the 1957 Massachusetts State Amateur title.

Pitts was a former caddy who gained fame while in the Air Force as an outstanding golfer in service tournaments. He refused several pro offers and golf scholarships to attend Boston College. Pitts captained the 1955 and 1956 teams, was runner-up in the 1956 New England Intercollegiates, and was champion of the prestigious (if not intercollegiate) 1956 Massachusetts Golf Association Tournament. While he had a reputation as nerveless with a golf club in his hands, Pitts evidently presented a good sense of humor when off the golf course. A writer once asked him what was the toughest course he ever faced, to which Pitts replied, "Father Shortell's Ethics course." Fordie Pitts took over as golf coach in 1959, the same year talented freshman golfer Larry Sanford arrived on campus. Sanford starred for Eagle golf teams from 1960 to 1962.

After Pitts had coached the team for two years, former hockey star Eddie Carroll, Associate Athletic Director at Boston College, became golf coach for the 1961 season. Carroll has remained with the team ever since, the longest tenure of any Boston College golf coach.

Carroll's teams continued to use Charles River Country Club as a home course, but the expansion of golf to a two-season sport—fall and spring—in the early seventies necessitated the adoption of a second "home" course. Carroll and Boston College were fortunate enough to reach agreement with New Seabury Country Club near Falmouth, an oceanside course and one of the most picturesque and demanding layouts in New England.

Among the major stars of the Carroll-coached golf teams of the sixties, seventies, and eighties are 1965 captain Jimmy Sullivan; 1976 captain Doug DeBettancourt, later head pro at Farm Neck Country Club on Martha's Vineyard; 1977 captain Dave Magdalenski, and 1981 captain Richard "R.D." Haskell.

"We generally find that, unlike some of the southern schools with scratch handicap players that don't even make the team, Boston College and most New England teams generally have one outstanding player and several very good ones," says Carroll.

Carroll also noted another historical change in the makeup of Boston College golf teams: "I think in the Snooks Kelley era and even later, maybe ninety percent of the players were former caddies, kids who learned the game by working around golf courses, and ten percent of the players were what you might call the country club set. Now I think the proportions are almost reversed. A lot of our players developed their games because their families belonged to country clubs."

TENNIS

Tennis, like golf, a rich man's game, did not get its start at Boston College until after World War I when students began organizing an annual fall intramural tournament. Students Edward J. O'Neil and Raymond McLaughlin organized a tennis team during 1924–1925, and though the team played some intercollegiate matches, tennis was not recognized as a varsity sport by the Boston College Athletic Association.

By 1928, the yearbook was bemoaning the peculiar status of tennis as being "in the twilight zone that marks the distinction between a full-fledged and an unrecognized Boston College sport." Further, it noted that all the team's ten matches for 1927–1928 were played on the road because of delays in the construction of eight new tennis courts at Boston College. The courts, located on the middle campus near the site of

172

what would later become McGuinn Hall, were opened in the fall of 1928. Such was the impact of the new facilities and the generally increasing popularity of tennis that the Boston College AA recognized tennis as a varsity sport by the spring of 1929. The members of that first team were Vin Roberts, George O'Connell, Frank Broughton, senior class president Bill Flynn (not the current athletic director), and team captain Frank Haggerty. As in the case of golf, tennis operated without a coach through its early years. A captain and student manager combined to run the team, and a fall tournament determined which players won places on the varsity.

By the early thirties, the tennis team was working around the vagaries of New England spring weather by opening its season with a southern trip. The 1931 team defeated George Washington, Loyola, and Maryland on the squad's historic first swing through the Washington-Baltimore area.

World War II proved more disruptive to tennis than to most other varsity sports, with Boston College left without a team from 1942 to 1948. But, during 1948–1949, tennis was revived as both a varsity and freshman team sport, and former player John Brennan, '42, a College of Business Administration faculty member, was named varsity coach.

Brennan rebuilt the program quickly. In 1951 and 1952 Boston College teams reached the quarter finals of the New England Intercollegiates. But by the mid-fifties, tennis reverted to a club sport, as construction on the middle campus claimed most of the courts.

It was not until the 1967–1968 season that tennis was restored to varsity status under coach Dick Ashworth.

The opening of new outdoor tennis courts on the now athletically-oriented lower campus and the arrival in the early seventies of head coach Mike MacDonald ushered in a new era of success for Boston College tennis. The 1973 Boston College team, led by Ted Basset, John Correa, and Nick Florescu, was among the better teams in New England and the first Boston College club to defeat Holy Cross, taking all singles and doubles matches to win by a 13–0 shutout. Through the mid-seventies, Boston College teams went, in the words of the *Heights*, "from a motley, enthusiastic crew of tennis troubadors to the status of a New England powerhouse."

By 1980, MacDonald and his team took a step up to eastern regional status with the formation of the Big East Conference. While the conference made news for its work in uniting major eastern basketball powers, conference athletic directors also agreed to sponsor a Big East Fall Tennis Tournament to be held at the new indoor courts in Boston College's Flynn Recreation Complex. In October 1981, MacDonald's freshman-dominated team won the third annual Big East Tournament, with Boston College captain John O'Conner becoming the tournament's first two-time champion in doubles.

MacDonald's philosophy called for carrying as many players as possible and for working those players into matches as frequently as he could: "Everyone gets a chance to play," he says, " and more importantly, everyone feels like they were key ingredients to our success." A more important statistic than match appearances is academics, says MacDonald. The coach justifiably boasts that his team "plays well without sacrificing academic commitments. No one on the team has ever missed the Dean's List."

Year-by-Year Major Sports Team Records

FOOTBALL

KEY: — = loss, T = tie, (H) = home game, (A) = away game, (N) = neutral site

1893 Coach: Joseph Drum
Captain: Bernie Wefers

St. John's Institute	4	0
M.I.T.	0	6—
Newton Ind.	0	10—
Somerville High	10	6
West Roxbury High	0	6—
Boston University	10	6

WON 3, LOST 3, TIED 0

1894 Coach: William Nagle
Captain: Maurice Flynn

St. Anselm's	0	22—
Andover Academy	0	32—
St. Anselm's	0	10—
Marlboro A.C.	16	0
Whitman A.C.	0	6—
Brockton Y.M.C.A.	4	12—
Boston University	0	28—

WON 1, LOST 6, TIED 0

1895 Coach: Joseph Lawless
Captain: John Brewin

Andover Academy	0	22—
Campello	10	28—
Tufts	0	28—
Hyde Park	6	6T
Whitman A.C.	0	0T
Fitchburg	6	0
Marlboro A.C.	14	0
Boston University	0	22—

WON 2, LOST 4, TIED 2

1896 Coach: Frank Carney
Captain: Joe Walsh

Campello	0	24—
Andover Academy	14	6
Exeter Academy	8	0
Tufts	8	22—
Holy Cross	6	2
Holy Cross	8	6
Boston University	10	0

WON 5, LOST 2, TIED 0

1897 Coach: John Dunlop
Captain: Arthur White

Campello	14	4
Whitman High	14	4
Holy Cross	4	10—
Harvard Law	6	0
Tufts	0	12—
Exeter Academy	4	10—
Holy Cross	12	0

WON 4, LOST 3, TIED 0

1898 Coach: John Dunlop
Captain: Bill Koen

Exeter Academy	0	18—
Newton Ind.	0	5—
Brown University	0	6—
Tufts	5	6—
Campello	6	0
Holy Cross	0	0T
M.I.T.	0	6—
Holy Cross	11	0

WON 2, LOST 5, TIED 1

1899 Coach: John Dunlop
Captain: Charlie Kiley

Exeter Academy	2	0
Bates	0	0T
M.I.T.	24	0
Newton	6	0
Andover Academy	6	0
New Hampshire A.A.	6	0
Massachusetts	18	0
All-College	6	0
Brown	0	18—
Holy Cross	17	0

WON 8, LOST 1, TIED 1

1900 TEAM DISBANDED

1901 Coach: John Dunlop
Captain: Joe Kenney

Brown	0	12—
Dartmouth	0	45—
Bates	0	6—
Exeter Academy	11	0
New Hampshire	17	0
Andover Academy	0	11—
Holy Cross	0	11—
Tufts	0	12—
Massachusetts	0	11—

WON 2, LOST 7, TIED 0

1902   Coach: Arthur White
Captain: Pat Sullivan

Massachusetts	0	30—
Bates	5	17—
Andover Academy	0	24—
New Hampshire	6	10—
Exeter Academy	0	29—
Tufts	0	6—
Holy Cross	0	22—
Tufts	0	26—

WON 0, LOST 8, TIED 0

1903–1907   TEAM DISBANDED

1908   Coach: Joe Reilly & Joe Kenney
Captain: George Pearce

Bridgewater State	10	12—
St. Anselm's	0	0T
Dean Academy	0	18—
New Hampshire	0	18—
Connecticut	0	0T
Col. of Osteopathy	9	0
St. Anselm's	11	0
Alumni	0	6—

WON 2, LOST 4, TIED 2

1909   Coach: Charles McCarthy
Captain: George Pearce

St. Alphonsus	0	6—
Andover Academy	0	10—
Rhode Island	0	9—
New Hampshire	6	11—
Col. of Osteopathy	35	0
St. Anselm's	6	6T
Connecticut	17	0
St. Anselm's	7	0

WON 3, LOST 4, TIED 1

1910   Coach: Jim Hart
Captain: Ed Hartigan

New Hampshire	0	11—
Andover Academy	0	11—
Cushing Academy	5	5T
Holy Cross	3	34—
Dean Academy	8	12—
Connecticut	0	0T

WON 0, LOST 4, TIED 2

1911   Coach: Joseph Courtney
Captains: John Hartigan
& Dan Hurld

Holy Cross	5	13—
Colby	0	18—
New Hampshire	0	12—
Cushing College	0	17—
Dean Academy	0	6—
Rhode Island	0	25—
St. Anselm's	3	6—

WON 0, LOST 7, TIED 0

1912   Coach: William Joy
Captain: John Hartigan

Fordham	0	14—
Massachusetts	0	42—
Colby	0	55—
Cushing College	6	6T
Dean Academy	7	40—
Connecticut	13	0
St. Anselm's	7	0

WON 2, LOST 4, TIED 1

1913   Coach: William Joy
Captain: Leo Daley

Maine	0	6—
Springfield	6	27—
Holy Cross	0	13—
St. Anselm's	19	0
Worcester Tech	40	0
Fordham	27	27T
Rhode Island	27	0
Connecticut	47	0

WON 4, LOST 3, TIED 1

1914   Coach: Stephen Mahoney
Captains: Harry Kiley &
Jim Linnehan

Maine	6	27—
Rhode Island	21	0
Bowdoin	0	20—
New Hampshire	20	3
Norwich	28	6
St. Anselm's	27	0
Holy Cross	0	10—
Fordham	3	14—
Catholic University	14	0

WON 5, LOST 4, TIED 0

1915   Coach: Stephen Mahoney
Captain: James Duffy

O	9 (A) Bowdoin	0	14—
O	16 (A) Maine	0	14—
O	23 (A) Tufts	0	26—
O	30 (H) Holy Cross	0	9—
N	6 (H) Fordham	3	0
N	13 (A) Connecticut	7	6
N	26 (H) Norwich	35	0

WON 3, LOST 4, TIED 0

1916   Coach: Charles Brickley
Captain: Maurice Dullea

S	23 (H) Neponset Wanderers	16	0
S	30 (A) Dartmouth	6	32—
O	12 (H) New Hampshire	19	0
O	21 (A) Tufts	0	13—
O	28 (A) Trinity (CT)	21	7
N	4 (H) Rhode Island	39	0
N	18 (H) Worcester Tech	49	0
D	2 (H) Holy Cross	17	14

WON 6, LOST 2, TIED 0

1917   Coach: Charles Brickley
Captain: Charles Fitzgerald

S	29 (H) Norwich	26	0
O	6 (H) Naval Reserves	40	0
O	12 (H) Tufts	20	0
O	20 (A) Brown	2	7
N	3 (H) Rhode Island	48	0
N	10 (H) Holy Cross	34	6
N	17 (H) Middlebury	31	6
N	24 (A) Army	7	14—

WON 6, LOST 2, TIED 0

1918   Coach: Frank Morrissey
Captain: Frank Morrissey

O	26 (H) Camp Devens	13	0
N	2 (H) Norwich	6	0
N	9 (H) Camp Bumpkin	38	7
N	16 (H) Fordham	0	14—
N	23 (A) Harvard	6	14—
N	30 (H) Tufts	54	0
D	7 (H) Mineola Aviators	25	0

WON 5, LOST 2, TIED 0

1919   Coach: Frank Cavanaugh
Captain: James Fitzpatrick

S	27 (H) U.S.S. Utah	22	0
O	4 (H) Harvard	0	17—
O	11 (H) Middlebury	25	0
O	18 (A) Yale	5	3
O	25 (A) Army	0	13—
N	8 (H) Rutgers	7	13—
N	15 (H) Holy Cross	9	7
N	29 (H) Georgetown	10	9

WON 5, LOST 3, TIED 0

1920   Coach: Frank Cavanaugh
Captain: Luke Urban

O	9 (H) Fordham	20	0
O	16 (A) Yale	21	13
O	30 (A) Springfield	12	0
N	6 (H) Boston University	34	0
N	13 (H) Tufts	17	0
N	20 (H) Marietta	13	3
N	27 (H) Georgetown	30	0
D	4 (H) Holy Cross	14	0

WON 8, LOST 0, TIED 0

1921   Coach: Frank Cavanaugh
Captain: Tony Comerford

O	1 (H) Boston University	13	0
O	8 (H) Providence	25	0
O	15 (A) Baylor	23	7
O	22 (H) Detroit	0	28—
O	29 (A) Fordham	0	0T
N	5 (H) Marietta	14	0
N	19 (H) Georgetown	10	14—
N	26 (H) Holy Cross	0	41—

WON 4, LOST 3, TIED 1

1922   Coach: Frank Cavanaugh
Captain: Bill Kelleher

O	7 (H) Boston University	20	6
O	12 (H) Fordham	27	0
O	21 (A) Detroit	8	10—
O	28 (H) Lafayette	0	19—
N	4 (H) Villanova	15	3
N	11 (H) Baylor	33	0
N	18 (H) Canisius	13	7
N	25 (H) Georgetown	0	0T
D	2 (H) Holy Cross	17	13

WON 6, LOST 2, TIED 1

1923		Coach: Frank Cavanaugh		
		Captain: Chuck Darling		
S	29 (H)	Providence	28	0
O	12 (H)	Fordham	20	0
O	20 (H)	Canisius	21	0
O	27 (H)	Marquette	6	7—
N	3 (H)	Georgetown	21	0
N	10 (H)	Centenary	14	0
N	17 (H)	Villanova	41	0
N	24 (H)	Vermont	0	0T
D	1 (H)	Holy Cross	16	7
WON 7, LOST 1, TIED 1				

1924		Coach: Frank Cavanaugh		
		Captain: Joe Kozlowski		
S	27 (H)	Providence	47	0
O	13 (H)	Fordham	28	0
O	18 (A)	Syracuse	0	10—
O	25 (H)	Allegheny	13	0
N	1 (H)	Haskell Indians	34	7
N	8 (H)	Marquette	34	7
N	15 (H)	Centenary	9	10—
N	22 (H)	Vermont	33	7
N	29 (H)	Holy Cross	0	33—
WON 6, LOST 3, TIED 0				

1925		Coach: Frank Cavanaugh		
		Captain: John Donoghue		
O	3 (H)	Catholic University	6	0
O	12 (H)	Haskell Indians	7	6
O	17 (H)	Boston University	54	7
O	24 (H)	Allegheny	14	7
O	31 (H)	Providence	51	0
N	7 (H)	West Virginia	0	20—
N	14 (H)	West Virginia Wesleyan	6	7—
N	28 (H)	Holy Cross	17	6
WON 6, LOST 2, TIED 0				

1926		Coach: Frank Cavanaugh		
		Captain: Joe McKenney		
O	2 (H)	Catholic University	28	0
O	12 (H)	Fordham	27	0
O	23 (A)	St. Louis University	61	0
O	30 (H)	West Virginia Wesleyan	27	6
N	6 (H)	Villanova	19	7
N	13 (H)	Haskell Indians	21	21T
N	20 (H)	Gettysburg	39	0
N	27 (H)	Holy Cross	0	0T
WON 6, LOST 0, TIED 2				

1927		Coach: Leo Daley		
		Captain: Tom O'Brien		
O	1 (H)	Duke	9	25—
O	12 (H)	Geneva	0	13—
O	22 (H)	West Virginia Wesleyan	33	0
O	29 (A)	Fordham	27	7
N	5 (H)	Villanova	7	13—
N	12 (H)	Georgetown	0	47—
N	19 (A)	Connecticut Aggies	19	0
N	29 (H)	Holy Cross	6	0
WON 4, LOST 4, TIED 0				

1928		Coach: Joe McKenney		
		Captain: Warren McGuirk		
S	29 (H)	Catholic University	38	6
O	7 (A)	Navy	6	0
O	12 (H)	Duke	19	0
O	27 (H)	Boston University	27	7
N	3 (H)	Manhattan	60	6
N	12 (H)	Fordham	19	7
N	17 (A)	Canisius	24	0
N	24 (H)	Connecticut Aggies	51	13
D	1 (H)	Holy Cross	19	0
WON 9, LOST 0, TIED 0				

1929		Coach: Joe McKenney		
		Captain: Paddy Creedon		
S	28 (H)	Catholic University	13	6
O	5 (H)	Maine	42	0
O	12 (H)	Villanova	7	7T
O	19 (A)	Dayton	23	7
O	26 (H)	Canisius	40	6
N	2 (H)	Duke	20	12
N	9 (H)	Fordham	6	7—
N	16 (A)	Marquette	6	20—
N	23 (H)	Boston University	33	0
N	30 (H)	Holy Cross	12	0
WON 7, LOST 2, TIED 1				

1930		Coach: Joe McKenney		
		Captain: John Dixon		
S	27 (H)	Catholic University	54	7
O	6 (H)	Quantico Marines	13	7
O	13 (H)	Fordham	0	3—
O	18 (A)	Villanova	0	7—
O	25 (H)	Dayton	15	6
N	1 (H)	Marquette	0	6—
N	8 (H)	Georgetown	19	20—
N	14 (A)	Loyola (IL)	19	0
N	22 (H)	Boston University	47	0
N	29 (H)	Holy Cross	0	7—
WON 5, LOST 5, TIED 0				

1931		Coach: Joe McKenney		
		Captain: Joe Kelley		
S	26 (H)	Catholic University	26	7
O	3 (H)	Dayton	13	0
O	12 (H)	Fordham	0	20—
O	17 (H)	Villanova	6	12—
O	24 (H)	Marquette	0	7—
O	31 (H)	Georgetown	20	2
N	7 (A)	Western Maryland	19	13
N	11 (H)	Centre College	7	0
N	21 (H)	Boston University	18	6
N	26 (H)	Holy Cross	6	7—
WON 6, LOST 4, TIED 0				

1932		Coach: Joe McKenney		
		Captain: Philip Couhig		
O	1 (H)	Loyola (MD)	14	0
O	12 (H)	Centre College	6	0
O	22 (A)	Marquette	0	13—
O	29 (H)	Fordham	3	0
N	5 (H)	Villanova	9	20—
N	11 (H)	Western Maryland	20	20T
N	19 (H)	Boston University	21	6
N	26 (A)	Holy Cross	0	0T
WON 4, LOST 2, TIED 2				

1933		Coach: Joe McKenney		
		Captain: Frank Maloney		
S	30 (H)	St. Anselm's	22	0
O	7 (H)	Loyola (MD)	37	0
O	12 (H)	Centre College	6	0
O	21 (A)	Fordham	6	32—
O	28 (H)	Boston University	25	0
N	4 (H)	Georgetown	39	0
N	11 (H)	Villanova	9	0
N	18 (H)	Western Maryland	12	9
D	2 (H)	Holy Cross	13	9
WON 8, LOST 1, TIED 0				

1934		Coach: Joe McKenney		
		Captain: Dave Couhig		
S	29 (H)	St. Anselm's	18	6
O	6 (A)	Springfield	14	0
O	12 (H)	Fordham	0	6—
O	20 (A)	Western Maryland	0	40—
O	27 (H)	Providence	7	13—
N	3 (H)	Villanova	6	0
N	12 (H)	Centre College	7	0
N	17 (H)	Boston University	10	0
D	1 (H)	Holy Cross	2	7—
WON 5, LOST 4, TIED 0				

1935		Coach: Dinny McNamara (3–1)		
		Harry Downes (3–2)		
		Captain: Joe O'Brien		
S	28 (H)	St. Anselm's	13	2
O	5 (A)	Fordham	0	19—
O	19 (H)	Michigan State	18	6
O	26 (H)	New Hampshire	19	6
N	2 (H)	Providence	20	6
N	9 (H)	Western Maryland	6	12—
N	16 (H)	Springfield	39	0
N	23 (H)	Boston University	25	6
N	30 (H)	Holy Cross	6	20—
WON 6, LOST 3, TIED 0				

1936		Coach: Gil Dobie		
		Captain: Alex Pszenny		
O	3 (H)	Northeastern	26	6
O	12 (H)	Temple	0	14—
O	17 (H)	New Hampshire	12	0
O	24 (H)	Providence	26	0
O	31 (H)	Michigan State	13	13T
N	7 (H)	North Carolina State	7	3
N	14 (H)	Western Maryland	12	7
N	21 (H)	Boston University	0	0T
N	28 (H)	Holy Cross	13	12
WON 6, LOST 1, TIED 2				

1937   Coach: Gil Dobie
Captain: Tony DiNatale

S	25	(H)	Northeastern	35	2
O	2	(H)	Kansas State	21	7
O	12	(H)	Temple	0	0T
O	23	(H)	Detroit	0	14—
O	30	(H)	North Carolina State	7	12—
N	6	(A)	Western Maryland	27	0
N	13	(H)	Kentucky	13	0
N	20	(H)	Boston University	6	13—
N	27	(H)	Holy Cross	0	20—

WON 4, LOST 4, TIED 1

1938   Coach: Gil Dobie
Captain: Bill Flynn

S	24	(H)	Canisius	63	12
S	30	(H)	Northeastern	13	0
O	12	(H)	Detroit	9	6
O	21	(A)	Temple	26	26T
O	29	(H)	Florida	33	0
N	5	(H)	Indiana	14	0
N	11	(H)	Boston University	21	14
N	19	(H)	St. Anselm's	0	0T
N	26	(H)	Holy Cross	7	29—

WON 6, LOST 1, TIED 2

1939   Coach: Frank Leahy
Captain: Ernie Schwatzer

S	30	(H)	Lebanon Valley	45	0
O	6	(H)	St. Joseph's	20	6
O	12	(H)	Florida	0	7—
O	21	(H)	Temple	19	0
O	28	(H)	St. Anselm's	28	0
N	4	(H)	Auburn	13	7
N	11	(A)	Detroit	20	13
N	18	(H)	Boston University	19	0
N	25	(H)	Kansas State	38	7
D	2	(H)	Holy Cross	14	0
			Cotton Bowl, Dallas, Texas		
J	1	(N)	Clemson	3	6—

WON 9, LOST 2, TIED 0

1940   Coach: Frank Leahy
Captain: Hank Toczylowski

S	21	(H)	Centre College	40	0
S	28	(A)	Tulane	27	7
O	12	(H)	Temple	33	20
O	19	(H)	Idaho University	60	0
O	26	(H)	St. Anselm's	55	0
N	2	(H)	Manhattan	25	0
N	9	(H)	Boston University	21	0
N	16	(H)	Georgetown	19	18
N	23	(H)	Auburn	33	7
N	30	(H)	Holy Cross	7	0
			Sugar Bowl, New Orleans, LA		
J	1	(N)	Tennessee	19	13

WON 11, LOST 0, TIED 0

1941   Coach: Denny Myers
Captain: Al Morro

S	20	(H)	St. Anselm's	78	0
S	27	(A)	Tulane	7	21—
O	11	(H)	Clemson	13	26—
O	18	(H)	Manhattan	26	13
O	25	(H)	Georgetown	14	6
N	1	(H)	Temple	31	0
N	8	(H)	Wake Forest	26	6
N	15	(H)	Tennessee	7	14—
N	22	(H)	Boston University	19	7
N	29	(H)	Holy Cross	14	13

WON 7, LOST 3, TIED 0

1942   Coach: Denny Myers
Captains: Mike Holovak & Fred Naumetz

O	3	(H)	West Virginia	33	0
O	10	(H)	Clemson	14	7
O	17	(H)	North Carolina Naval Flyers	7	6
O	25	(H)	Wake Forest	27	0
O	31	(H)	Georgetown	47	0
N	7	(H)	Temple	28	0
N	14	(H)	Fordham	56	6
N	21	(H)	Boston University	37	0
N	28	(H)	Holy Cross	12	55—
			Orange Bowl, Miami, Florida		
J	1	(N)	Alabama	21	37—

WON 8, LOST 2, TIED 0

1943   Coach: Moody Sarno
Captain: Ed Doherty

O	17	(H)	B.C. Army Training	7	0
O	24	(H)	Camp Hingham	42	6
O	31	(H)	Brooklyn College	37	6
N	7	(H)	Rome Air Force	64	0
N	14	(A)	Harvard	6	6T

WON 4, LOST 0, TIED 1

1944   Coach: Moody Sarno
Captains: Pete Baleyko & George Donelan

O	7	(H)	Harvard	0	13—
O	13	(H)	C.C.N.Y.	33	0
O	20	(H)	New York University	42	13
O	28	(H)	Syracuse	19	12
N	4	(H)	Melville P.T.	0	45—
N	12	(H)	Brooklyn College	24	21
N	26	(H)	Holy Cross	14	30—

WON 4, LOST 3, TIED 0

1945   Coach: Moody Sarno
Captain: George Donelan

S	29	(H)	Squantum N.A.S.	13	0
O	6	(A)	Brown	6	51—
O	12	(H)	New York University	28	0
O	27	(A)	U.S. Merchant Marine	20	33—
N	10	(A)	Villanova	0	41—
N	17	(H)	Scranton	12	0
N	25	(H)	Holy Cross	0	46—

WON 3, LOST 4, TIED 0

1946   Coach: Denny Myers
Captains: Game Captains

S	27	(H)	Wake Forest	6	12—
O	5	(A)	Michigan State	34	20
O	11	(H)	U.S. Merchant Marine	56	7
O	25	(H)	Villanova	14	12
N	2	(A)	New York University	72	6
N	9	(H)	Georgetown	20	13
N	16	(H)	Tennessee	13	33—
N	23	(H)	Alabama	13	7
N	30	(H)	Holy Cross	6	13—

WON 6, LOST 3, TIED 0

1947   Coach: Denny Myers
Captain: Angie Nicketakis

S	26	(H)	Clemson	32	22
O	10	(H)	Kansas State	49	13
O	17	(H)	L.S.U.	13	14—
O	24	(H)	Villanova	6	0
N	1	(H)	Georgetown	27	6
N	8	(H)	Wake Forest	13	14—
N	15	(H)	Tennessee	13	38—
N	22	(H)	St. Mary's	25	7
N	29	(H)	Holy Cross	6	20—

WON 5, LOST 4, TIED 0

1948   Coach: Denny Myers
Captain: John Furey

S	24	(H)	Wake Forest	26	9
O	1	(A)	Georgetown	13	6
O	9	(H)	St. Bonaventure	7	7T
O	15	(H)	Villanova	20	13
O	23	(A)	Mississippi	13	32—
O	29	(H)	Clemson	19	26—
N	13	(H)	William & Mary	14	14T
N	20	(H)	St. Mary's	19	7
N	27	(H)	Holy Cross	21	20

WON 5, LOST 2, TIED 2

1949   Coach: Denny Myers
Captain: Art Spinney

S	23	(H)	Oklahoma	0	46—
S	30	(H)	Wake Forest	13	7
O	8	(A)	Penn State	14	32—
O	14	(H)	Mississippi	25	25T
O	21	(H)	Georgetown	7	10—
O	28	(H)	Villanova	14	28—
N	5	(A)	Clemson	40	27
N	12	(H)	Fordham	20	12
N	26	(H)	Holy Cross	76	0

WON 4, LOST 4, TIED 1

1950   Coach: Denny Myers
Captain: Phil Coen

S	22	(H)	Wake Forest	7	7T
S	30	(A)	Oklahoma	0	28—
O	7	(A)	Mississippi	0	54—
O	13	(H)	Fordham	6	26—
O	20	(H)	Georgetown	10	20—
O	27	(H)	Georgia	7	19—
N	4	(H)	Penn State	13	20—
N	11	(H)	Clemson	14	35—
N	18	(H)	Villanova	7	29—
D	2	(H)	Holy Cross	14	32—

WON 0, LOST 9, TIED 1

1951 Coach: Mike Holovak
Captain: Mike Roarke

S	21	(H)	Wake Forest	6	20—
O	5	(A)	Mississippi	7	34—
O	12	(H)	Fordham	19	35—
O	19	(H)	Detroit	13	19—
O	27	(A)	Georgia	28	35—
N	2	(H)	Richmond	21	7
N	10	(A)	Clemson	2	21—
N	17	(H)	Villanova	20	13
D	1	(H)	Holy Cross	19	14

WON 3, LOST 6, TIED 0

1952 Coach: Mike Holovak
Captain: John Toppa

S	26	(H)	Richmond	14	7
O	4	(A)	Wake Forest	7	7T
O	10	(H)	Drake	20	14
O	17	(H)	Villanova	7	28—
O	24	(H)	Fordham	14	13
O	31	(H)	Clemson	0	13—
N	7	(A)	Detroit	23	20
N	15	(H)	Xavier	0	6—
N	28	(H)	Holy Cross	7	21—

WON 4, LOST 4, TIED 1

1953 Coach: Mike Holovak
Captain: Joe Johnson

S	26	(H)	Clemson	14	14T
O	3	(A)	L.S.U.	6	42—
O	11	(H)	Villanova	7	15—
O	16	(A)	Fordham	20	13
O	25	(A)	Xavier	31	14
O	31	(H)	Richmond	0	14—
N	7	(H)	Wake Forest	20	7
N	15	(H)	Detroit	33	20
N	28	(H)	Holy Cross	6	0

WON 5, LOST 3, TIED 1

1954 Coach: Mike Holovak
Captain: Joe Mattaliano

S	25	(A)	Detroit	12	7
O	2	(A)	Temple	12	9
O	9	(H)	V.M.I.	44	0
O	16	(A)	Fordham	21	7
O	23	(H)	Springfield	42	6
O	31	(H)	Xavier	14	19—
N	5	(A)	Marquette	13	7
N	13	(H)	Boston University	7	6
N	27	(H)	Holy Cross	31	13

WON 8, LOST 1, TIED 0

1955 Coach: Mike Holovak
Captain: John Miller

S	24	(H)	Brandeis	27	0
O	8	(H)	Villanova	28	14
O	15	(H)	Detroit	23	0
O	21	(H)	Marquette	13	13T
O	29	(A)	Xavier	12	19—
N	4	(A)	Miami (FL)	7	14—
N	12	(A)	Boston University	40	12
N	26	(H)	Holy Cross	26	7

WON 5, LOST 2, TIED 1

1956 Coach: Mike Holovak
Captain: Henry Sullivan

O	5	(A)	Miami (FL)	6	27—
O	13	(A)	Marquette	26	19
O	20	(A)	Rutgers	32	0
O	28	(A)	Detroit	7	12—
N	2	(H)	Villanova	7	6
N	10	(H)	Quantico Marines	6	20—
N	18	(H)	Boston University	13	0
N	24	(H)	Brandeis	52	0
D	1	(H)	Holy Cross	0	7—

WON 5, LOST 4, TIED 0

1957 Coach: Mike Holovak
Captain: Tom Joe Sullivan

S	21	(H)	Navy	6	46—
S	28	(H)	Florida State	20	7
O	5	(H)	Quantico Marines	13	7
O	12	(H)	Dayton	41	14
O	19	(H)	Villanova	12	9
O	26	(A)	Detroit	20	16
N	9	(A)	Boston University	27	2
N	16	(H)	Marquette	19	14
N	20	(A)	Holy Cross	0	14—

WON 7, LOST 2, TIED 0

1958 Coach: Mike Holovak
Captain: George Larkin

S	20	(H)	Scranton	48	0
S	27	(A)	Syracuse	14	24—
O	4	(H)	Villanova	19	21—
O	18	(A)	Marquette	21	13
O	25	(H)	Miami (FL)	6	2
N	1	(H)	College of Pacific	25	12
N	8	(H)	Detroit	40	0
N	15	(H)	Boston University	18	13
N	22	(A)	Clemson	12	34—
D	6	(H)	Holy Cross	26	8

WON 7, LOST 3, TIED 0

1959 Coach: Mike Holovak
Captain: Frank Casey

S	19	(H)	Navy	8	24—
S	26	(A)	Army	8	44—
O	10	(H)	Villanova	39	6
O	17	(H)	Dartmouth	35	12
O	25	(H)	Marquette	16	0
O	30	(A)	Detroit	21	9
N	7	(H)	Pittsburgh	14	22—
N	14	(A)	Boston University	7	26—
N	29	(A)	Holy Cross	14	0

WON 5, LOST 4, TIED 0

1960 Coach: Ernie Hefferle
Captain: Terry Glynn

S	17	(H)	Navy	7	22—
S	24	(A)	Army	7	20—
O	8	(A)	Marquette	12	13—
O	15	(H)	Detroit	17	19—
O	22	(H)	V.M.I.	14	14T
O	28	(A)	Miami (FL)	7	10—
N	5	(A)	Villanova	20	6
N	12	(H)	Boston University	23	14
N	19	(H)	Clemson	25	14
N	26	(H)	Holy Cross	12	16—

WON 3, LOST 6, TIED 1

1961 Coach: Ernie Hefferle
Captain: Joe Sikorski

S	23	(H)	Cincinnati	23	0
S	30	(A)	Northwestern	0	45—
O	7	(A)	Houston	0	21—
O	13	(A)	Detroit	3	20—
O	21	(H)	Villanova	22	6
N	4	(H)	Iowa State	14	10
N	11	(A)	Texas Tech	6	14—
N	18	(A)	Boston University	10	7
N	25	(H)	Syracuse	13	28—
D	2	(A)	Holy Cross	26	38—

WON 4, LOST 6, TIED 0

1962 Coach: Jim Miller
Captain: Art Graham

S	22	(H)	Detroit	27	0
S	29	(A)	Villanova	28	13
O	6	(H)	V.M.I.	18	0
O	13	(A)	Syracuse	0	12—
O	20	(H)	Navy	6	26—
O	27	(H)	Houston	14	0
N	3	(A)	Vanderbilt	27	22
N	10	(H)	Texas Tech	42	13
N	17	(H)	Boston University	41	25
D	1	(H)	Holy Cross	48	12

WON 8, LOST 2, TIED 0

1963 Coach: Jim Miller
Captain: Joe Lukis

S	21	(A)	Syracuse	21	32—
S	28	(H)	Wichita	22	16
O	4	(A)	Detroit	20	12
O	12	(H)	Villanova	34	0
O	26	(A)	Air Force	7	34—
N	2	(H)	Vanderbilt	19	6
N	9	(H)	Buffalo	15	0
N	16	(H)	Virginia	30	21
N	30	(A)	Holy Cross	0	9—

WON 6, LOST 3, TIED 0

1964 Coach: Jim Miller
Captain: Bill Cronin

S	19	(H)	Syracuse	21	14
S	26	(A)	Army	13	19—
O	10	(A)	Tennessee	14	16—
O	17	(H)	Cincinnati	10	0
O	24	(H)	Air Force	13	7
N	7	(A)	Villanova	8	7
N	13	(A)	Miami (FL)	6	30—
N	21	(H)	Detroit	17	9
N	28	(H)	Holy Cross	10	8

WON 6, LOST 3, TIED 0

1965 Coach: Jim Miller
Captain: Charlie Smith

S	18	(H)	Buffalo	18	6
S	25	(H)	Villanova	28	0
O	2	(A)	Army	0	10—
O	9	(H)	Penn State	0	17—
O	23	(H)	Richmond	38	7
O	30	(H)	V.M.I.	41	12
N	5	(A)	Miami (FL)	6	27—
N	13	(H)	William & Mary	30	17
N	20	(A)	Syracuse	13	21—
N	27	(A)	Holy Cross	35	0

WON 6, LOST 4, TIED 0

1966 Coach: Jim Miller
Captain: Ed Lipson

S	17	(A)	Navy	7	27—
S	24	(H)	Ohio University	14	23—
O	1	(H)	V.M.I.	14	0
O	8	(A)	Penn State	21	30—
O	15	(H)	Syracuse	0	30—
O	22	(H)	Buffalo	22	21
N	5	(H)	William & Mary	15	13
N	12	(A)	Villanova	0	19—
N	19	(A)	Massachusetts	14	7
N	26	(H)	Holy Cross	26	32—

WON 4, LOST 6, TIED 0

1967 Coach: Jim Miller
Captain: Joe DiVito

S	23	(A)	Villanova	27	24
S	30	(H)	Army	10	21—
O	14	(H)	Penn State	28	50—
O	21	(H)	Buffalo	14	26—
O	28	(H)	Maine	56	0
N	4	(A)	Cincinnati	21	27—
N	11	(H)	V.M.I.	13	26—
N	18	(H)	Syracuse	20	32—
N	25	(H)	Massachusetts	25	0
D	2	(A)	Holy Cross	13	6

WON 4, LOST 6, TIED 0

1968 Coach: Joe Yukica
Captain: Gary Andrachik

S	28	(A)	Navy	49	15
O	5	(H)	Buffalo	31	12
O	12	(H)	Villanova	28	15
O	19	(A)	Tulane	14	28—
O	26	(H)	Penn State	0	29—
N	9	(A)	Army	25	58—
N	16	(H)	V.M.I.	45	13
N	23	(A)	Massachusetts	21	6
N	30	(H)	Holy Cross	40	20

WON 6, LOST 3, TIED 0

1969 Coach: Joe Yukica
Captain: Jim McCool

S	27	(H)	Navy	21	14
O	4	(H)	Tulane	28	24
O	18	(H)	Villanova	6	24—
O	25	(A)	Army	7	38—
N	1	(A)	Penn State	16	38—
N	8	(H)	Buffalo	21	35—
N	15	(H)	V.M.I.	49	32
N	22	(H)	Massachusetts	35	30
N	29	(A)	Syracuse	35	10

WON 5, LOST 4, TIED 0

1970 Coach: Joe Yukica
Captains: Joe Coppola,
Frank Harris &
Fred Willis

S	19	(A)	Villanova	28	21
S	26	(A)	Navy	28	14
O	3	(H)	VMI	56	3
O	10	(H)	Penn State	3	28—
O	24	(A)	Air Force	10	35—
O	31	(H)	Army	21	13
N	7	(H)	Buffalo	65	12
N	14	(A)	Pittsburgh	21	6
N	21	(A)	Massachusetts	21	10
N	28	(H)	Holy Cross	54	0

WON 8, LOST 2, TIED 0

1971 Coach: Joe Yukica
Captains: Kevin Clemente &
Ray Rippman

S	11	(A)	West Virginia	14	45—
S	18	(A)	Temple	17	3
S	25	(A)	Navy	49	6
O	2	(A)	Richmond	24	0
O	9	(H)	Villanova	23	7
O	16	(A)	Texas Tech	6	14—
O	23	(H)	Pittsburgh	40	22
N	6	(A)	Syracuse	10	3
N	13	(H)	Northern Illinois	20	10
N	20	(H)	Massachusetts	35	0
N	27	(A)	Holy Cross	21	7

WON 9, LOST 2, TIED 0

1972 Coach: Joe Yukica
Captains: Dave Bucci &
Dave Ellison

S	15	(H)	Tulane	0	10—
S	23	(H)	Temple	49	27
S	30	(A)	Navy	20	27—
O	7	(A)	Villanova	21	20
O	14	(H)	Air Force	9	13—
O	21	(A)	Pittsburgh	20	35—
N	4	(H)	Syracuse	37	0
N	11	(A)	Georgia Tech	10	42—
N	18	(H)	Penn State	26	45—
N	25	(A)	Massachusetts	7	28—
D	2	(H)	Holy Cross	41	11

WON 7, LOST 4, TIED 0

1973 Coach: Joe Yukica
Captains: Jim Combs, Tom
Condon & Gary
Marangi

S	15	(H)	Temple	45	0
S	22	(A)	Tulane	16	21—
S	29	(A)	Texas A&M	32	24
O	6	(H)	Navy	44	7
O	12	(A)	Miami (FL)	10	15—
O	20	(H)	Pittsburgh	14	28—
O	27	(H)	Villanova	11	7
N	10	(A)	West Virginia	25	13
N	17	(A)	Syracuse	13	24—
N	24	(H)	Massachusetts	59	14
D	1	(A)	Holy Cross	42	21

WON 7, LOST 4, TIED 0

1974 Coach: Joe Yukica
Captains: Brian Clemente, Mike
Esposito, Ken Ladd &
Alex MacLellan

S	14	(H)	Texas	19	42—
S	28	(A)	Temple	7	34—
O	5	(A)	Navy	37	0
O	12	(H)	William & Mary	31	16
O	19	(A)	Pittsburgh	11	35—
O	26	(A)	Villanova	55	7
N	2	(H)	West Virginia	35	3
N	9	(H)	Tulane	27	3
N	16	(H)	Syracuse	45	0
N	23	(A)	Massachusetts	70	8
N	30	(H)	Holy Cross	38	6

WON 8, LOST 3, TIED 0

1975 Coach: Joe Yukica
Captain: Mike Kruczek

S	15	(N)	Notre Dame	3	17—
S	20	(A)	Temple	27	9
S	27	(A)	West Virginia	18	35
O	4	(H)	Villanova	41	12
O	11	(H)	Tulane	7	17
O	18	(H)	Navy	17	3
O	25	(A)	Syracuse	14	22
N	1	(H)	Miami (FL)	21	7
N	8	(A)	Army	31	0
N	22	(H)	Massachusetts	24	14
N	29	(H)	Holy Cross	24	10

WON 7, LOST 4, TIED 0

1976 Coach: Joe Yukica
Captain: Peter Cronan

S	11	(H)	Texas	14	13
S	25	(A)	Tulane	27	3
O	2	(A)	Navy	17	13
O	9	(H)	Florida State	9	28—
O	16	(H)	West Virginia	14	3
O	23	(A)	Army	27	10
O	30	(A)	Villanova	3	22—
N	6	(A)	Miami (FL)	6	13—
N	13	(H)	Syracuse	28	14
N	20	(A)	Massachusetts	35	0
N	27	(H)	Holy Cross	59	6

WON 8, LOST 3, TIED 0

1977 Coach: Joe Yukica
Captains: Kelly Elias, Bob
Moore & Rich Scudellari

S	11	(A)	Texas	0	44—
S	17	(A)	Tennessee	18	24—
S	24	(H)	Army	49	28
O	1	(H)	Pittsburgh	7	45—
O	8	(H)	Tulane	30	28
O	15	(A)	West Virginia	28	24
O	22	(H)	Villanova	17	0
O	29	(A)	Air Force	36	14
N	12	(A)	Syracuse	3	20—
N	19	(H)	Massachusetts	34	7
N	26	(A)	Holy Cross	20	35—

WON 6, LOST 5, TIED 0

1978 Coach: Ed Chiebek
Captains: Paul McCarty, John
Schmeding & Fred Smerlas

S	16	(H)	Air Force	7	18—
S	23	(H)	Texas A&M	2	37—
S	30	(H)	Navy	8	19—
O	7	(H)	Pittsburgh	15	32—
O	14	(A)	Tulane	3	9—
N	4	(A)	Villanova	16	28—
N	11	(A)	Army	26	29—
N	18	(H)	Syracuse	23	37—
N	25	(A)	Massachusetts	0	27—
D	2	(H)	Holy Cross	29	30—
D	10	(T)	Temple	24	28—

WON 0, LOST 11, TIED 0

180

1979   Coach: Ed Chlebek
Captains: Jeff Dziama, Jack
Kent & John Schmeding

S	15	(H)	Tennessee	16	28—
S	22	(H)	Villanova	34	7
S	29	(A)	Stanford	14	33—
O	6	(A)	Pittsburgh	7	28—
O	13	(H)	West Virginia	18	20—
O	20	(A)	Miami	8	19—
O	27	(A)	Army	29	16
N	3	(H)	Tulane	8	41—
N	17	(N)	Syracuse	27	10
N	24	(H)	Massachusetts	41	3
D	1	(A)	Holy Cross	13	10

WON 5, LOST 6, TIED 0

1980   Coach: Ed Chlebek
Captains: Mike Mayock
& Tim Sherwin

S	13	(A)	Pittsburgh	6	14—
S	20	(H)	Stanford	30	13
S	27	(A)	Villanova	9	20—
O	4	(A)	Navy	0	21—
O	11	(H)	Yale	27	9
O	18	(A)	Florida State	7	41—
O	25	(H)	Army	30	14
N	1	(A)	Air Force	23	0
N	15	(H)	Syracuse	27	16
N	22	(A)	Massachusetts	13	12
N	29	(H)	Holy Cross	27	26

WON 7, LOST 4, TIED 0

1981   Coach: Jack Bicknell
Captains: Budness & Dyer

S	19	(H)	Texas A&M	13	12
S	26	(A)	North Carolina	14	56—
O	3	(H)	West Virginia	10	38—
O	10	(A)	Penn State	7	38—
O	17	(H)	Navy	10	25—
O	24	(A)	Army	41	6
O	31	(H)	Pittsburgh	24	29—
N	7	(H)	Massachusetts	52	22
N	14	(A)	Syracuse	17	27—
N	21	(H)	Rutgers	27	21
N	28	(A)	Holy Cross	28	24

WON 5, LOST 6, TIED 0

FOOTBALL COACHING RECORDS

Name	Seasons	GP	W	L	T	PCT	Years
Joseph DRUM	1	6	3	3	0	.500	1893
William NAGLE	1	7	1	6	0	.143	1894
Joseph LAWLESS	1	8	2	4	2	.375	1895
Frank CARNEY	1	7	5	2	0	.714	1896
John DUNLOP	4	34	16	16	2	.500	1897–1899, 1901
Arthur WHITE	1	8	0	8	0	.000	1902
Joe REILLY & Joe KENNEY	1	8	2	4	2	.388	1908
Charles McCARTHY	1	8	3	4	1	.438	1909
Jim HART	1	6	0	4	2	.167	1910
Joseph COURTNEY	1	7	0	7	0	.000	1911
William JOY	2	15	6	7	2	.467	1912–13
Stephen MAHONEY	2	16	8	8	0	.500	1914–15
Charles BRICKLEY	2	16	12	4	0	.750	1916–17
Frank MORRISSEY	1	7	5	2	0	.714	1918
Frank CAVANAUGH	8	67	48	14	5	.754	1919–26
D. Leo DALEY	1	8	4	4	0	.500	1927
Joe McKENNEY	7	65	44	18	3	.700	1928–34
John McNAMARA	½	4	3	1	0	.750	1935
Harry DOWNES	½	5	3	2	0	.600	1935
Gil DOBIE	3	27	16	6	5	.685	1936–38
Frank LEAHY	2	22	20	2	0	.909	1939–40
Dennis MYERS	7	66	35	27	4	.561	1941–42, 46–50
Amerino SARNO	3	19	11	7	1	.605	1943–45
Mike HOLOVAK	9	81	49	29	3	.623	1951–59
Ernie HEFFERLE	2	20	7	12	1	.375	1960–61
Jim MILLER	6	58	34	24	0	.586	1962–67
Joe YUKICA	10	105	68	37	0	.648	1968–77
Ed CHLEBEK	3	33	12	21	0	.364	1978–80
Jack BICKNELL	1	11	5	6	0	.455	1981–

HOCKEY

(A) — Boston Arena
(G) — Garden
(H) — Home Game (McHugh Forum)
(L) — North Shore Sports Center, Lynn
(R) — Road game
(S) — Boston Skating Club, Brighton

1917–1918   Coach: Robert Fowler
Captain: Walter Falvey

Harvard Radio School	7	1
Newport Naval Reserve	2	4—
Boston U.	3	1

WON 2, LOST 1, TIED 0

1918–1919   Coach: Robert Fowler
Captain: Walter Falvey

Commonwealth Pier	3	0
Harvard	2	7—
Army	5	4

WON 2, LOST 1, TIED 0

1919–1920 Coach: Walter Falvey
Captain: Frank Morrissey

Yankee Division	4	2
U. Mass.	4	5—
Army	5	0
Fordham	0	0T
Boston U.	9	0
M.I.T.	5	4
Tufts	5	2

WON 5, LOST 1, TIED 1

1920–1921 Coach: Fred Rocque
Captain: Leo Hughes

Bates	5	0
M.I.T.	4	3
Amherst	4	2
Dartmouth	4	0
M.I.T.	3	4—
U. Mass.	2	1
Shoe Trades	1	7—
M.I.T.	5	1

WON 6, LOST 2, TIED 0

1921–1922 Coach: Fred Rocque
Captain: Leo Hughes

St. Paul's School	2	0
McGill	0	3—
Pere Marquette	2	5—
M.I.T.	3	2
Melrose H.C.	1	1T
Yale	7	0
B.A.A.	2	4—
M.I.T.	6	1
Harvard	4	2

WON 5, LOST 3, TIED 1

1922–1923 Coach: Fred Rocque
Captain: Edmund Garrity

Boston H.C.	3	3T
McGill	3	1
M.I.T.	4	0
Victoria	3	1
Boston U.	3	2
Boston U.	7	2
Queen's College	2	1
Army	9	1
Hamilton	7	1
Nichols Club	3	2
Nichols Club	3	0
B.A.A.	2	0
Duluth	1	2—
New Haven	3	2

WON 12, LOST 1, TIED 1

1923–1924 Coach: Charles Foote
Captain: John Fitzgerald

Toronto	1	3—
Toronto	0	3—
B.A.A.	1	3—
Berlin H. C.	1	3—
Maple A. A.	1	2—
Boston H. C.	4	3
Maple A. A.	1	0
Abegweits	3	0
Army	6	3
Montreal Nationals	3	1
Nashua Nationals	7	3
Ottawa Shamrocks	0	3—
B.A.A.	1	3—
Montreal Victoria	1	6—

WON 6, LOST 8, TIED 0

1924–1925 Coach: Charles Foote
Captain: John Culhane

McGill	1	2—
Boston U.	0	1—
Toronto	2	4—
Queen's College	7	1
Boston All-Stars	1	1T
Boston U.	3	0
McGill	2	2T
McGill	1	2—
Montreal U.	3	0
Montreal U.	4	2
B.A.A.	4	5—
Loyola (Montreal)	3	1
B.A.A.	2	0
B.A.A.	2	2T

WON 6, LOST 5, TIED 3

1925–1926 Coach: Fred Rocque
Captain: Henry Groden

M.I.T.	7	1
Pere Marquette	2	3—
Montreal	4	2
Royal Military Academy	7	6
Toronto	1	6—
Toronto	1	5—
Truro	3	6—
Pere Marquette	3	4—
Boston U.	2	1
Loyola	5	3
Sherbrooke	3	4—
Pere Marquette	5	5T
Boston U.	0	3—
Ottawa Burgs	2	1

WON 6, LOST 7, TIED 1

1926–1927 Coach: Fred Rocque
Captain: Cornelius Cronin

Toronto	1	4—
University Club	0	2—
M.I.T.	1	0
Boston U.	1	3—
Springfield O. C.	4	3
Loyola (Montreal)	8	6

WON 3, LOST 3, TIED 0

1927–1928 Coach: James Foley
Captain: Joseph Fitzgerald

Yale	2	5—
Boston U.	3	3T
Saint Francis	1	2—
Holy Cross	5	4
Holy Cross	6	3
Boston U.	2	3—
Boston U.	0	5—

WON 2, LOST 4, TIED 1

1928–1929 Coach: James Foley
Captains: Nicholas Tedesco &
Arthur Morrissey

Loyola U.	0	6—
Dartmouth	2	5—
Boston U.	1	4—
Pennsylvania	6	1
Boston U.	1	4—
Yale	0	5—
Holy Cross	4	0
B.A.A.	2	1
Loyola	3	5—
Sherbrook Pacific	2	3—
Holy Cross	6	1

WON 4, LOST 7, TIED 0

1932–1933 Coach: John "Snooks" Kelley
Captain: William Hogan

Northeastern	8	6
M.I.T.	2	1
Boston U.	1	5—
Brown	3	3T
B.C. Alumni	7	4
Boston U.	2	7—

WON 3, LOST 2, TIED 1

1933–1934 Coach: John "Snooks" Kelley
Captain: Raymond Funchion

Union Boat Club	3	6—
Berry H. C.	2	3—
Brown	2	3—
Saint Anselm	7	4
Northeastern	5	5T
Saint Dominique's	3	4—
Boston U.	2	3—
Boston U.	3	6—
Nichols Jr. College	3	1

WON 2, LOST 6, TIED 1

1934–1935 Coach: John "Snooks" Kelley
Captain: Frank Liddell

Northeastern	5	4
Brown	4	2
Dartmouth	3	2
Northeastern	3	2
Boston U.	2	1
Princeton	1	6—
Boston U.	1	5—
Saint Anselm	7	5
Brown	4	5—
Colgate	4	2

WON 7, LOST 3, TIED 0

1935–1936 Coach: John "Snooks" Kelley
Captain: Fred Moore

Dartmouth	0	3—
Fitchburg	19	0
Boston U.	3	4—
Northeastern	6	3
Clarkson	1	5—
Northeastern	8	2
M.I.T.	5	4
Boston U.	3	2
Princeton	1	1T
Saint Anselm	6	4
Brown	2	3—
Colgate	7	3

WON 7, LOST 4, TIED 1

1936–1937 Coach: John "Snooks" Kelley
Captain: John Burgess

M.I.T.	5	2
Northeastern	1	1T
Boston U.	6	5
Dartmouth	3	5—
Williams	6	4
Saint Anselm	11	6
Colby	3	2
New Hampshire	7	1
Boston U.	1	2—
Princeton	3	5—
Brown	3	7—
Northeastern	6	2
Colgate	15	0

WON 8, LOST 4, TIED 1

1937–1938 Coach: John "Snooks" Kelley
Captain: Joe Hartigan

D	4	(R)	Princeton	2	6—
D	17	(R)	Brown	4	5—
D	20	(G)	Dartmouth	*4	5—
J	10	(A)	Northeastern	7	9—
J	13	(R)	New Hampshire	3	4—
J	20	(R)	U. Mass.	6	3
J	22	(R)	Middlebury	11	2
F	3	(A)	St. Anselm's	6	0
F	8	(A)	Boston U.	2	7—
F	10	(A)	Colby	6	3
F	12	(R)	Williams	5	4
F	17	(A)	Brown	5	2
F	25	(A)	Boston U.	3	2
M	1	(A)	M.I.T.	*4	3
M	4	(A)	Northeastern	7	1

*—overtime
WON 9, LOST 6, TIED 0

1938–1939 Coach: John "Snooks" Kelley
Captain: Paul Moore

D	7	(R)	Princeton	2	13—
D	13	(A)	Northeastern	8	3
D	27	(1)	Colgate	3	1
D	29	(1)	Dartmouth	4	11—
J	3	(R)	Brown	1	3—
J	7	(A)	Colby	7	0
J	19	(R)	U. Mass.	5	2
J	20	(G)	Brown	3	4—
J	31	(A)	New Hampshire	6	3
F	4	(A)	Boston U.	*5	7—
F	8	(R)	Dartmouth	1	9—
F	14	(A)	Northeastern	7	6
F	18	(A)	Boston U.	4	5—
F	21	(A)	M.I.T.	8	3
F	22	(R)	Williams	4	3
M	1	(A)	Jr. Olympics	8	7

*—overtime
WON 9, LOST 7, TIED 0
1—Playland Ice Casino, Rye, N.Y.

1939–1940 Coach: John "Snooks" Kelley
Captain: Ralph Dougherty

D	12	(R)	Princeton	5	9—
D	20	(G)	M.I.T.	6	3
D	27	(1)	Cornell	24	1
D	29	(1)	Dartmouth	3	4—
J	4	(G)	McGill	3	9—
J	9	(A)	Northeastern	11	3
J	16	(A)	Boston U.	12	3
J	20	(R)	Army	*5	5T
J	30	(A)	Northeastern	5	2
F	2	(R)	New Hampshire	6	1
F	10	(R)	Colby	4	2
F	11	(R)	St. Dom's	5	6—
F	13	(A)	New Hampshire	10	2
F	17	(R)	Williams	5	1
F	19	(R)	Dartmouth	0	7—
F	23	(A)	Colby	*6	5
F	24	(A)	Boston U.	7	4
F	27	(A)	M.I.T.	4	3

*—overtime
WON 12, LOST 5, TIED 1
1—Playland Ice Casino, Rye, N.Y.

1940–1941 Coach: John "Snooks" Kelley
Captain: John Pryor

D	14	(R)	Yale	3	4—
D	17	(A)	M.I.T.	15	1
D	20	(R)	Princeton	9	6
J	1	(1)	Colgate	11	4
J	3	(1)	Dartmouth	4	3
J	7	(A)	Northeastern	9	5
J	14	(A)	Boston U.	10	3
J	15	(R)	New Hampshire	11	1
J	17	(A)	Dartmouth	8	3
J	21	(R)	New Hampshire	13	2
J	25	(R)	Army	6	2
F	11	(A)	Boston U.	6	3
F	18	(A)	M.I.T.	14	6
F	25	(A)	Northeastern	11	5

WON 13, LOST 1, TIED 0
1—Playland Ice Casino, Rye, N.Y.

1941–1942 Coach: John "Snooks" Kelley
Captain: Ralph Powers

D	13	(R)	Yale	4	3
D	16	(A)	Northeastern	5	3
J	6	(A)	M.I.T.	6	3
J	8	(R)	New Hampshire	7	5
J	13	(A)	Boston U.	8	2
J	17	(R)	Colby	*5	4
F	2	(G)	Dartmouth	2	7—
F	3	(R)	Northeastern	9	5
F	10	(A)	Boston U.	5	2
F	12	(R)	Princeton	2	5—
F	28	(A)	Colby	7	5

National A.A.U. Tourney

M	7	(A)	High Standard H.C.	3	2
M	7	(A)	Massena (N.Y.) H. C.	*9	8
M	8	(A)	St. Nick's H. C.	6	4

*—overtime
WON 12, LOST 2, TIED 0

1942–1943 Coach: John Temple
Captain: Wally Boudreau

D	14	(A)	Northeastern	11	5
D	18	(A)	Princeton	8	2
J	12	(A)	Dartmouth	2	14—
J	13	(R)	Yale	4	2
J	19	(A)	Northeastern	*6	5
J	25	(R)	Dartmouth	*5	6—
F	4	(A)	Boston U.	8	3
F	6	(R)	Princeton	7	2
F	23	(A)	Boston U.	11	0

*—overtime
WON 7, LOST 2, TIED 0

1945–1946 Coach: Joseph Glavin, S.J.
Captain: John Buckley

J	19	(R)	Holy Cross	0	4—
F	2	(S)	Holy Cross	3	2
F	11	(R)	Dartmouth	0	11—

WON 1, LOST 2, TIED 0

1946–1947 Coach: John "Snooks" Kelley
Captain: John Murphy

D	10	(A)	Boston U.	5	9—
D	16	(A)	Holy Cross	8	4
D	20	(R)	Dartmouth	0	4—
D	23	(A)	Northeastern	10	1
D	30	(A)	Harvard	6	3
J	9	(R)	Ft. Devens St.	4	1
J	14	(A)	M.I.T.	12	1
J	15	(A)	Tufts	12	3
J	21	(A)	Tufts	11	3
J	25	(R)	Yale	2	9—
J	26	(A)	Colby	13	2
J	28	(A)	Boston A.A.	*4	3
F	1	(R)	Colby	7	2
F	4	(A)	Northeastern	11	2
F	5	(A)	Boston U.	*5	5T
F	17	(A)	Harvard	10	5
F	24	(S)	Holy Cross	5	1
F	28	(1)	St. Nick's H. C.	6	1
M	4	(A)	M.I.T.	8	4

*—overtime
WON 15, LOST 3, TIED 1
1—Crystal Ice Palace, Norwalk, Ct.

1947–1948 Coach: John "Snooks" Kelley
Captains: John Corcoran &
Bob Mason

D	3	(A)	Harvard	3	4—
D	15	(A)	Ft. Devens St.	4	2
D	22	(A)	M.I.T.	6	4
J	5	(A)	Northeastern	7	6
J	12	(A)	Dartmouth	4	3
J	27	(A)	Northeastern	8	5
J	29	(R)	Dartmouth	4	6—
F	3	(A)	Boston U.	3	5—
F	10	(R)	Princeton	4	5—
F	16	(A)	New Hampshire	9	2
F	20	(1)	Georgetown	8	1
F	23	(S)	Ft. Devens St.	7	0
F	25	(A)	Harvard	6	1
F	27	(A)	M.I.T.	9	2
M	1	(A)	Middlebury	15	1
M	3	(A)	Boston U.	9	2

New England Tourney

M	8	(A)	Bowdoin	10	1
M	9	(A)	Northeastern	6	4

NCAA Tourney, Colorado Springs

M	19	(N)	Michigan	*4	6—

*—overtime
WON 14, LOST 5, TIED 0

1948–1949 Coach: John "Snooks" Kelley
Captain: Bernie Burke

D	1	(A)	M.I.T.	13	5
D	6	(S)	Brown	5	1
D	11	(R)	Yale	3	1
D	13	(S)	Ft. Devens St.	22	1
D	15	(A)	Harvard	9	4
D	21	(A)	Boston U.	5	1
J	2	(A)	Colorado Col.	6	5
J	10	(S)	M.I.T.	11	5
J	12	(A)	Harvard	8	5
J	27	(R)	Dartmouth	2	4—
F	1	(A)	Northeastern	7	4
F	7	(S)	Princeton	5	2
F	2	(A)	A.I.C.	10	2
F	9	(A)	Northeastern	9	1
F	18	(1)	St. Nick's	8	2
F	22	(A)	Dartmouth	7	4
F	25	(R)	A.I.C.	6	3
M	1	(A)	Boston U.	6	2

New England Tourney

M	8	(A)	Northeastern	5	4
M	9	(A)	Boston U.	6	5

NCAA Tourney, Colorado Springs

M	18	(N)	Colorado Col.	7	3
M	19	(N)	Dartmouth	4	3

WON 21, LOST 1, TIED 0
1–Norwalk Ice Palace. Ct.

1949–1950 Coach: John "Snooks" Kelley
Captain Ed "Butch" Songin

D	7	(R)	Brown	7	1
D	13	(A)	Boston U.	4	3
D	20	(A)	Harvard	8	5
D	28	(A)	McGill	8	2
J	2	(A)	Northeastern	9	4
J	7	(R)	Princeton	9	3
J	31	(A)	Tufts	6	4
F	2	(R)	Dartmouth	4	2
F	4	(R)	Yale	6	4
F	7	(A)	Northeastern	7	3
F	13	(A)	Boston U.	1	8—
F	25	(A)	Montreal U.	2	6—
F	27	(A)	M.I.T.	7	2
F	28	(A)	Harvard	8	9—
M	2	(A)	Dartmouth	10	3

New England Tourney

M	6	(A)	Bowdoin	15	3
M	7	(A)	Boston U.	2	1

NCAA Tourney, Colorado Springs

M	16	(N)	Colorado College	3	10—
M	18	(N)	Michigan	6	10—

WON 14, LOST 5, TIED 0

1950–1951 Coach: John "Snooks" Kelley
Captain: Len Ceglarski

D	11	(A)	Brown	4	1
D	16	(L)	McGill	3	6—
D	18	(A)	Tufts	11	2
D	20	(A)	Harvard	3	5—
D	27	(A)	Michigan	2	11—
D	29	(A)	Colorado College	3	1
J	2	(A)	Northeastern	4	2
J	8	(A)	Boston U.	4	2
J	26	(R)	Dartmouth	5	4
J	30	(A)	Northeastern	2	0
F	5	(A)	Harvard	10	9
F	6	(A)	A.I.C.	9	6
F	15	(L)	Dartmouth	*4	5—
F	17	(R)	Yale	4	5—
F	21	(R)	Brown	2	11—
F	22	(L)	Toronto U.	4	3
F	26	(A)	Boston U.	4	7—
M	3	(A)	M.I.T.	12	4

New England Tourney

M	5	(A)	Tufts	14	1
M	7	(A)	Boston U.	1	4—

*—overtime
WON 12, LOST 8, TIED 0

1951–1952 Coach: John "Snooks" Kelley
Captain: Pete Maggio

D	6	(R)	Brown	5	2
D	10	(A)	Tufts	20	0
D	12	(A)	M.I.T.	14	1
D	15	(R)	Yale	2	1
D	17	(A)	Northeastern	3	2
D	19	(A)	Harvard	5	0
D	21	(L)	Princeton	4	6—
J	1	(A)	U.S. Olympics	5	4
J	9	(A)	Harvard	*6	5
J	28	(A)	Northeastern	*2	3—
J	30	(A)	A.I.C.	4	0
F	1	(R)	Clarkson	5	3
F	2	(R)	St. Lawrence	3	2
F	4	(A)	Boston U.	6	4
F	7	(R)	Dartmouth	3	2
F	13	(A)	Boston U.	1	7—
F	20	(A)	Brown	5	2
F	22	(R)	Laval	4	3
F	25	(A)	M.I.T.	15	1
M	6	(L)	Dartmouth	5	1

*—overtime
WON 17, LOST 3, TIED 0

1952–1953 Coach: John "Snooks" Kelley
Captain: "Wimpy" Burtnett

D	9	(L)	Yale	6	4
D	13	(A)	Brown	4	6—

Beanpot Tourney (3rd)

D	26	(A)	Harvard	2	3—
D	27	(A)	Northeastern	2	0
J	3	(A)	Northeastern	5	0
J	8	(R)	Brown	5	4
J	14	(G)	Boston U.	7	3
J	17	(R)	Princeton	4	2
J	31	(A)	Boston U.	2	5—
F	5	(R)	Dartmouth	7	1
F	7	(A)	Northeastern	2	0
F	11	(G)	Harvard	6	2
F	13	(A)	Boston U.	0	3—
F	17	(L)	Dartmouth	4	2
F	27	(A)	Northeastern	*2	2T
M	6	(A)	Tufts	13	4

*—overtime
WON 11, LOST 4, TIED 1

1953–1954 Coach: John "Snooks" Kelley
Captain: Bob Babine

D	1	(R) Providence	8	5
D	8	(G) Northeastern	6	0
D	14	(G) Harvard	5	3
D	15	(R) Brown	3	2
D	17	(A) Dartmouth	5	4
D	19	(L) Princeton	4	3
D	22	(G) Boston U.	10	2

Boston Arena Tourney

D	29	(A) St. Lawrence	1	4—
D	30	(A) Middlebury	5	2

Beanpot Tourney (1st)

J	11	(G) Northeastern	8	5
J	12	(G) Harvard	4	1
J	15	(R) Clarkson	2	3—
J	16	(R) St. Lawrence	5	1
J	30	(R) Yale	5	3
F	4	(R) Dartmouth	4	2
F	9	(G) Boston U.	6	5
F	15	(G) Harvard	4	1
F	24	(A) Northeastern	6	2
M	1	(G) Brown	4	1

NCAA Tourney Colorado Springs

M	11	(N) Minnesota	1	14—
M	13	(N) Michigan State	2	7

WON 17, LOST 4, TIED 0

1954–1955 Coach John "Snooks" Kelley
Captain Dick Dempsey

D	7	(G) Providence	4	2
D	10	(G) Harvard	4	3
D	14	(G) Northeastern	9	0
D	18	(A) R.P.I.	5	3
D	20	(G) Clarkson	1	5—
D	22	(G) St. Lawrence	1	6—

Boston Arena Tourney

D	27	(A) McGill	3	6—
D	29	(A) Harvard	2	8—
J	4	(R) Brown	7	4
J	8	(R) R.P.I.	5	3
J	12	(A) Yale	2	3—
J	31	(G) Northeastern	11	2
F	3	(R) Dartmouth	3	4—

Beanpot Tourney (2nd)

F	7	(G) Boston U.	9	5
F	8	(G) Harvard	*4	5—
F	11	(R) Clarkson	3	2
F	12	(R) St. Lawrence	1	4—
F	14	(G) Boston U.	11	1
F	16	(A) Dartmouth	5	3
F	26	(R) Princeton	8	0
M	1	(G) Brown	6	5

*—overtime
WON 13, LOST 8, TIED 0

1955–1956 Coach John "Snooks" Kelley
Captain: Eddie Carroll

D	6	(G) Tufts	13	5
D	13	(G) Northeastern	3	2
D	14	(R) Brown	4	1
D	16	(G) Harvard	5	3
D	17	(G) Princeton	3	1

Boston Arena Tourney

D	26	(A) Brown	5	3
D	28	(A) St. Lawrence	2	6—
D	30	(A) Clarkson	6	7—
J	10	(A) Boston U.	7	5
J	15	(A) U.S. Olympics	0	8—
J	17	(G) Dartmouth	11	3
F	2	(R) Dartmouth	4	3
F	4	(R) Yale	4	1

Beanpot Tourney (1st)

F	6	(G) Northeastern	7	1
F	8	(G) Harvard	4	2
F	10	(L) St. Francis Xav.	7	4
F	17	(R) Clarkson	2	5—
F	18	(R) St. Lawrence	2	6—
F	25	(A) Harvard	3	5—
F	28	(A) Boston U.	7	3

NCAA Tourney, Colorado Springs

M	15	(N) Michigan Tech	4	10—
M	17	(N) St. Lawrence	2	6—

WON 14, LOST 8, TIED 0

1956–1957 Coach: John "Snooks" Kelley
Captain: Joe Moylan

D	4	(G) Tufts	6	3
D	7	(A) Brown	3	6—
D	11	(G) Yale	11	2
D	15	(A) Clarkson	2	3—
D	17	(A) St. Lawrence	2	6—
D	18	(R) Brown	5	0

Boston Arena Tourney

D	27	(A) Providence	6	2
D	28	(A) Brown	6	2
D	29	(A) Harvard	2	4—
J	4	(R) Princeton	8	2
J	7	(A) Northeastern	12	3
J	28	(A) R.P.I.	2	1

Beanpot Tourney (1st)

F	1	(G) Northeastern	2	0
F	5	(G) Boston U.	*5	4
F	7	(R) Dartmouth	6	3
F	11	(G) Boston U.	2	1
F	13	(A) Harvard	3	5—
F	15	(R) Clarkson	0	5—
F	16	(R) St. Lawrence	1	9—
F	18	(A) Dartmouth	8	7
F	23	(R) Army	8	4
F	25	(A) Boston U.	*4	4T

*—overtime
WON 14, LOST 7, TIED 1

1957–1958 Coach: John "Snooks" Kelley
Captain: Jack Cadagan

D	4	(A) Northeastern	7	1
D	7	(R) Brown	*1	1T
D	11	(A) Harvard	1	6—
D	16	(A) Clarkson	3	7—
D	17	(A) St. Lawrence	1	0

Boston Arena Tourney

D	26	(A) Dartmouth	7	5
D	27	(A) Brown	*4	3
D	28	(A) Providence	5	2
J	4	(L) Princeton	2	8—
J	18	(L) Providence	2	4—
J	20	(G) Boston U.	4	7—
J	30	(1) Dartmouth	3	6—

Beanpot Tourney

F	3	(G) Boston U.	4	5—
F	5	(R) Yale	8	6
F	8	(R) Army	4	5—

Beanpot Tourney Finals

F	10	(G) Harvard	3	7—
F	12	(R) Providence	3	2
F	14	(R) Clarkson	1	3—
F	15	(R) St. Lawrence	2	1
F	19	(A) Harvard	1	8—
F	26	(A) Boston U.	5	3
M	3	(A) Brown	4	10—
M	5	(A) Northeastern	*4	4T

*—overtime
WON 9, LOST 12, TIED 2
1–New Haven, Ct.

1958–1959 Coach: John "Snooks" Kelley
Captain: Joe Jangro

N	29	(H) Harvard	3	1
D	3	(H) Brown	3	2
D	10	(H) Yale	7	3
D	12	(R) Princeton	6	3
D	16	(H) St. Lawrence	*6	5
D	19	(H) Clarkson	2	6—
D	20	(H) R.P.I.	10	5

Boston Arena Tourney

D	27	(A) Mich. St.	0	6—
D	29	(A) Providence	7	2
J	3	(H) Northeastern	8	2
J	6	(H) Brown	7	5
J	9	(H) Harvard	*3	2
J	14	(A) Boston U.	1	5—
J	17	(R) Colby	6	3

Beanpot Tourney

F	2	(G) Harvard	6	4
F	5	(R) Dartmouth	3	4—
F	7	(R) Army	8	4

Beanpot Tourney (1st)

F	9	(G) Boston U.	7	4
F	10	(R) Providence	6	4
F	14	(R) Clarkson	2	7—
F	15	(R) St. Lawrence	4	6—
F	18	(R) Harvard	5	3
F	21	(H) R.P.I.	1	4—
F	25	(H) Boston U.	3	1
F	28	(H) Providence	5	3
M	3	(H) Dartmouth	5	1

NCAA Tourney, R.P.I.

M	13	(N) Mich. St.	3	4—
M	14	(N) St. Lawrence	**7	6

*—overtime
**—Double overtime
WON 20, LOST 8, TIED 0

1959–1960 Coach: John "Snooks" Kelley
Captain: Ed Smith

D	5	(H)	Harvard	4	2
D	8	(R)	Brown	5	1
D	12	(R)	R.P.I.	4	5—
D	18	(H)	Princeton	8	2
D	19	(H)	St. Lawrence	5	5T
D	22	(H)	Laval	5	4
D	27	(H)	Toronto	4	5—
D	29	(H)	North Dakota	3	5—
J	4	(A)	Northeastern	6	2
J	7	(H)	Dartmouth	4	3
J	9	(H)	Clarkson	6	3
J	13	(R)	Yale	7	0
J	16	(H)	R.P.I.	6	1
J	29	(H)	Colby	4	3
F	4	(R)	Providence	1	5—

Beanpot Tourney

F	8	(G)	Boston U.	2	5—
F	10	(H)	Brown	2	1
F	12	(R)	Clarkson	7	2
F	13	(R)	St. Lawrence	5	6—

Beanpot Finals (4th)

F	15	(G)	Northeastern	5	6—
F	20	(H)	Army	6	3
F	24	(H)	Boston U.	5	0
F	27	(H)	Providence	5	4
M	8	(H)	Boston U.	2	4—

ECAC Playoffs

M	11	(R)	St. Lawrence	3	4—

WON 15, LOST 9, TIED 1

1960–1961 Coach: John "Snooks" Kelley
Captain: Tom Martin

D	3	(H)	Brown	12	1
D	7	(H)	Yale	6	1
D	10	(H)	R.P.I.	*1	1T
D	17	(H)	Clarkson	5	3
D	27	(H)	Laval	2	1
D	30	(H)	Toronto	6	2
J	2	(H)	Harvard	*1	2—
J	4	(R)	Brown	7	2
J	7	(H)	St. Lawrence	6	4
J	11	(R)	Harvard	1	4—
J	14	(R)	R.P.I.	4	7—
J	28	(R)	Princeton	12	2
J	30	(R)	Providence	4	1
F	3	(H)	Colby	8	2

Beanpot Tourney

F	6	(G)	Northeastern	15	1
F	9	(R)	Dartmouth	10	2
F	11	(H)	Providence	7	2

Beanpot Finals (1st)

F	13	(G)	Harvard	4	2
F	16	(H)	Colby	6	3
F	18	(R)	Army	3	2
F	22	(H)	Boston U.	7	2
F	24	(R)	St. Lawrence	0	3—
F	25	(R)	Clarkson	2	3—
M	4	(H)	Northeastern	10	0
M	7	(H)	Boston U.	4	2

*—overtime
WON 19, LOST 5, TIED 1

1961–1962 Coach: John "Snooks" Kelley
Captain: George Grant

D	6	(R)	Brown	9	2
D	9	(H)	St. Lawrence	*4	5—
D	12	(H)	Providence	4	3
D	16	(R)	R.P.I.	3	4—
D	19	(A)	Northeastern	10	2

ECAC Holiday Festival

D	21	(N)	St. Lawrence	1	8—
D	22	(N)	Boston U.	2	2T
D	27	(H)	Laval	3	0
D	29	(H)	Queen's	5	2
J	3	(H)	Dartmouth	6	3
J	5	(R)	St. Lawrence	0	4—
J	6	(R)	Clarkson	2	1
J	10	(H)	Harvard	2	3—
J	13	(R)	Colby	1	2—
J	25	(R)	Providence	2	0
J	27	(R)	Princeton	3	2
J	30	(H)	Boston U.	3	2
F	3	(H)	Northeastern	4	1

Beanpot Tourney

F	5	(G)	Harvard	1	6—
F	7	(R)	Yale	6	3
F	9	(H)	Clarkson	*2	3—

Beanpot Finals (3rd)

F	12	(G)	Northeastern	4	0
F	17	(H)	Army	2	5—
F	20	(A)	Boston U.	1	4—
F	24	(H)	Colby	6	5
F	26	(G)	West Germny	2	6—
F	28	(H)	R.P.I.	0	4—
M	3	(H)	Brown	6	1

ECAC Playoffs

M	6	(R)	St. Lawrence	4	9—

*—overtime
WON 15, LOST 13, TIED 1

1962–1963 Coach: John "Snooks" Kelley
Captain: Paul Aiken

D	5	(H)	Yale	6	3
D	8	(R)	Princeton	12	1
D	12	(H)	Brown	6	0
D	14	(A)	Northeastern	13	2
D	15	(A)	Clarkson	0	3—

ECAC Tourney, Mad. Sq. Gard.

D	20	(N)	St. Lawrence	5	1
D	21	(N)	Clarkson	3	1
D	27	(H)	Laval	10	2
D	29	(H)	Colorado Col.	4	8—
J	5	(R)	Colby	10	1
J	9	(A)	Boston U.	4	1
J	12	(H)	Providence	3	4—
J	26	(H)	St. Lawrence	3	2
J	29	(R)	Dartmouth	*3	2
J	31	(H)	Providence	3	2
F	2	(H)	Northeastern	7	3

Beanpot Tourney (1st)

F	4	(G)	Boston U.	2	1
F	6	(R)	Brown	5	3
F	9	(H)	Colby	6	0

Beanpot Finals

F	11	(G)	Harvard	3	1

F	16	(H)	Army	4	2
F	19	(R)	Harvard	1	3—
F	22	(R)	Clarkson	2	4—
F	23	(R)	St. Lawrence	1	5—
F	27	(H)	Boston U.	3	1
M	1	(H)	Norwich	8	3

ECAC Playoffs (2nd)

M	5	(H)	Army	3	1
M	8	(A)	St. Lawrence	6	2
M	9	(A)	Harvard	*3	4—

NCAA Tourney, Chestnut Hill

M	14	(H)	North Dakota	2	8—
M	16	(H)	Clarkson	3	5—

*—overtime
WON 22, LOST 9, TIED 0

1963–1964 Coach: John "Snooks" Kelley
Captain: Tom Aprille

D	4	(R)	Brown	4	1
D	7	(H)	Providence	4	1
D	10	(A)	Northeastern	4	2
D	14	(H)	St. Lawrence	4	2
D	17	(H)	Princeton	7	0

ECAC Holiday Festival, New York (2nd)

D	19	(N)	Army	10	2
D	20	(N)	Clarkson	3	9—
D	23	(G)	Toronto	1	9—
D	27	(A)	U.S. Olympics	2	3—
D	28	(H)	McGill	6	2
D	30	(H)	Loyola	9	2
J	3	(R)	St. Lawrence	6	5
J	4	(R)	Clarkson	3	4
J	8	(H)	Harvard	2	4—
J	11	(A)	Boston U.	*5	6—
J	24	(H)	Dartmouth	4	2
J	28	(R)	Providence	8	9—
J	30	(H)	Clarkson	5	1

Beanpot Tourney

F	3	(G)	Northeastern	7	4
F	5	(R)	Yale	5	1
F	7	(H)	Colgate	6	1

Beanpot Finals (1st)

F	10	(G)	Boston U.	6	5
F	15	(R)	Colby	13	1
F	19	(H)	Brown	*4	4T
F	22	(R)	Army	1	5—
F	26	(H)	Boston U.	0	1—
F	29	(H)	Northeastern	5	4
M	7	(H)	Colby	10	0

ECAC Playoffs

M	10	(H)	R.P.I.	2	3—

*—overtime
WON 18, LOST 10, TIED 1

1964–1965 Coach: John "Snooks" Kelley
Captain: Eddie Downes

D	2	(H) Yale	6	2
D	5	(R) Providence	6	1
D	8	(R) Brown	2	7—
D	11	(H) Colby	6	5
D	14	(H) St. Lawrence	5	3
D	18	(G) R.P.I.	5	1
D	19	(G) Royal Military	4	2
D	26	(H) McGill	13	6
D	29	(H) Colorado Col.	7	9—
J	2	(H) Loyola	8	3
J	5	(A) Northeastern	*4	5—
J	8	(H) Boston U.	*5	4
J	13	(R) Harvard	3	2
J	16	(H) Brown	5	3
J	28	(R) Princeton	11	4
J	29	(R) Colgate	7	2
F	3	(H) Northeastern	9	1
F	6	(R) Dartmouth	*9	8

Beanpot Tourney

F	8	(G) Harvard	*5	4
F	13	(R) Army	6	2

Beanpot Tourney (1st)

F	15	(G) Boston U.	5	4
F	19	(H) Providence	8	4
F	23	(A) Boston U.	4	5—
F	26	(H) Clarkson	3	5—
M	2	(H) Cornell	5	6—
M	4	(R) Colby	12	1

ECAC Playoffs

M	9	(H) Dartmouth	5	3
M	12	(A) Clarkson	*3	2
M	13	(A) Brown	6	2

NCAA Tourney, Providence

M	18	(N) North Dakota	4	3
M	20	(N) Michigan Tech.	2	8—

*—overtime
WON 24, LOST 7, TIED 0

1965–1966 Coach: John "Snooks" Kelley
Captain: Allan Kierstead

N	30	(H) R.P.I.	9	0
D	4	(R) Cornell	1	3—
D	8	(H) Brown	3	0
D	11	(A) Boston U.	2	9—
D	15	(H) Princeton	6	2

Boston Garden Tourney

D	17	(G) Dartmouth	10	1

ECAC Madison Square Tourney

D	19	(N) St. Lawrence	3	5—
D	27	(H) McGill	5	1
D	30	(H) Montreal	3	2
J	2	(H) Loyola	10	2
J	4	(A) Northeastern	2	3—
J	7	(R) Clarkson	0	5—
J	8	(R) St. Lawrence	3	9—
J	12	(H) Harvard	4	7—
J	15	(R) Brown	1	3—
J	28	(H) Colgate	5	4
J	30	(H) Eastern Olympics	1	2—
F	2	(R) Yale	8	0
F	4	(H) Northeastern	5	3

Beanpot Tourney

F	7	(G) Boston U.	4	6—
F	11	(H) Providence	5	4

Beanpot Tourney Finals

F	14	(G) Northeastern	5	3
F	19	(H) Army	6	2
F	22	(H) Dartmouth	6	2
F	26	(H) Boston U.	*4	5
M	1	(R) Providence	14	5
M	5	(R) Colby	10	4

ECAC Tourney

M	8	(R) Cornell	0	9—

*—overtime
WON 17, LOST 11, TIED 0

1966–1967 Coach: John "Snooks" Kelley
Captain: Jerry York

N	30	(H) Yale	12	3
D	3	(H) Boston U.	2	4—
D	7	(R) Brown	6	3
D	10	(R) Princeton	8	4
D	13	(A) Boston U.	3	8—

ECAC Boston Garden Tourney

D	16	(G) Michigan State	3	5—
D	17	(H) Northeastern	6	0
D	22	(H) Eastern Olympics	8	2—
D	27	(H) Loyola	10	3
D	30	(H) McGill	6	2
J	3	(A) Northeastern	2	4—
J	6	(H) Clarkson	6	5
J	11	(R) Harvard	4	*3
J	14	(H) Colby	6	1
J	28	(R) Colgate	6	2
F	1	(H) Cornell	2	3—
F	3	(R) R.P.I.	12	2

Beanpot Tourney

F	9	(G) Northeastern	5	*6—
F	10	(H) St. Lawrence	5	1

Beanpot Tourney Finals

F	13	(G) Harvard	6	*5
F	16	(R) Providence	9	0
F	22	(R) Dartmouth	8	0
F	25	(R) Army	5	2
M	1	(H) Northeastern	1	3—
M	4	(R) Providence	13	2

ECAC Tourney

M	7	(H) Clarkson	9	2
M	10	(G) Cornell	2	12—
M	11	(G) St. Lawrence	6	4

WON 19, LOST 9, TIED 0

1967–1968 Coach: John "Snooks" Kelley
Captain: Steve Dowling

D	6	(H) Brown	5	4
D	9	(H) Harvard	4	3
D	12	(A) Boston U.	3	6—

ECAC Boston Garden Tourney

D	15	(G) Dartmouth	4	1
D	16	(G) Princeton	4	7—
D	19	(H) Loyola	6	1
D	22	(H) McGill	9	4

St. Paul Classic

D	27	(R) Colorado College	5	8—
D	28	(R) Harvard	5	2
D	30	(R) Minnesota–Duluth	5	3
J	3	(R) Yale	6	3
J	5	(H) Princeton	4	*4T
J	9	(H) Dartmouth	7	2
J	12	(A) Northeastern	6	1
J	14	(H) Olympics (1)	2	6—

1968–1969 Coach: John "Snooks" Kelley
Captain: Mike Flynn

J	26	(R) St. Lawrence	7	*8—
J	27	(R) Clarkson	5	2
J	30	(R) Providence	9	3
F	2	(H) Colgate	2	1

Beanpot Tournament

F	5	(G) Harvard	4	6—
F	9	(H) Providence	13	0

Beanpot Finals (3rd)

F	12	(H) Northeastern	6	4
F	16	(H) R.P.I.	5	4
F	22	(R) Cornell	1	3—
F	24	(H) New Hampshire	4	6—
F	28	(H) Boston U.	1	2
M	2	(R) Army	7	1

ECAC Playoffs

M	5	(R) St. Lawrence	7	*6
M	8	(G) Clarkson	6	**5
M	9	(G) Cornell	3	6—

NCAA Tourney, Duluth

M	14	(R) Denver	1	4—
M	16	(R) Cornell	1	6—

*—overtime
**—double overtime
WON 20, LOST 11, TIED 1

1968–1969 Coach: John "Snooks" Kelley
Captain: Mike Flynn

D	4	(H) Yale	5	2
D	7	(R) Princeton	3	2
D	11	(R) Brown	4	1
D	14	(H) Clarkson	7	2
D	17	(R) Harvard	6	5OT

ECAC Christmas Tournament, Boston Garden

D	20	(G) Princeton	6	3
D	21	(G) Cornell	3	6—
D	27	(H) McGill	8	1
D	30	(H) Colorado	7	4

Centennial Tournament, Montreal Forum

J	3	(N) McGill	9	3
J	4	(N) Loyola	4	7—
J	8	(R) Dartmouth	10	2
J	11	(H) Boston Univ.	5	10—
J	24	(R) Colgate	3	2OT
J	28	(H) Cornell	3	4—
J	31	(H) Northeastern	10	2

Beanpot Tourney

F	3	(G) Boston Univ.	2	4—
F	7	(H) St. Lawrence	4	3

Beanpot Finals (3rd)

F	10	(H) Northeastern	6	3
F	14	(R) New Hampshire	3	2
F	17	(R) Providence	7	4
F	19	(R) R.P.I.	5	8—
F	22	(H) Army	5	3
F	26	(A) Boston Univ.	7	3
F	28	(H) Providence	10	1

ECAC Playoffs

M	7	(H) Clarkson	2	4—

WON 19, LOST 7, TIED 0

1969–1970 Coach: John "Snooks" Kelley
Captain: John Sullivan

D	3	(R) Providence	6	5OT
D	5	(H) Princeton	11	3
D	9	(H) Brown	8	3
D	12	(A) Northeastern	7	1
D	17	(H) Harvard	6	5
D	20	(H) Notre Dame	7	3

ECAC Holiday Tourney, Madison Sq. Gdn. (3rd)

D	22	(N) St. Lawrence	6	7—
D	23	(N) R.P.I.	7	1
D	26	(R) Denver	2	6—
D	27	(R) Denver	6	7—OT
D	29	(R) Notre Dame	7	4
J	3	(H) New Hampshire	6	5OT
J	7	(R) Yale	6	4
J	9	(H) Dartmouth	5	2
J	24	(H) Colgate	4	1
J	27	(A) Boston Univ.	3	8—

Beanpot Tourney

F	2	(G) Northeastern	5	0
F	6	(R) R.P.I.	13	6

Beanpot Finals (2nd)

F	9	(G) Boston Univ.	4	5—
F	14	(R) Cornell	3	5—
F	18	(H) Providence	4	3
F	20	(R) Clarkson	5	7—
F	21	(R) St. Lawrence	2	7—
F	25	(H) Boston Univ.	1	8—
F	28	(R) Army	4	0

ECAC Playoffs

M	10	(H) Harvard	5	10—

WON, 16, LOST 10, TIED 0

1970–1971 Coach: John "Snooks" Kelley
Captain: John Powers

D	2	(H) Yale	6	3
D	5	(R) Princeton	8	2
D	8	(R) New Hampshire	4	8—
D	11	(H) Providence	2	7—
D	15	(R) Harvard	0	4—

ECAC Christmas Tournament, Boston Garden (2nd)

D	18	(G) Dartmouth	2	1
D	19	(G) Cornell	2	12—
D	21	(H) Minnesota	5	10—
D	23	(H) McMaster	10	2

St. Louis Tournament (2nd)

D	27	(N) St. Louis	9	5
D	28	(N) Wisconsin	2	7—
D	30	(H) Notre Dame	3	5—
J	2	(H) Pennsylvania	3	5—
J	6	(R) Brown	3	6—
J	9	(H) Boston U.	3	8—
J	13	(R) Dartmouth	5	4
J	26	(H) Clarkson	1	3—
J	29	(H) St. Lawrence	7	4
F	2	(R) Providence	4	6—
F	5	(H) Northeastern	10	3

Beanpot Tournament

F	8	(G) Harvard	4	10—
F	13	(R) Colgate	9	4
F	16	(R) Boston U.	4	9—
F	19	(II) Cornell	2	9—

Beanpot Finals (3rd)

F	22	(G) Northeastern	8	2
F	27	(R) Army	5	2

WON 11, LOST 15, TIED 0

1971–1972 Coach: John "Snooks" Kelley
Captain: Vin Shanley

Duluth Tournament

N	25	(N) Minnesota—Duluth	4	3
N	26	(N) Lake Superior State	2	9—
N	27	(N) Manitoba	2	5—
N	30	(R) Providence	5	2
D	3	(H) Princeton	4	2
D	7	(H) Brown	4	1
D	10	(R) Northeastern	7	8—
D	14	(H) Harvard	4	6—
D	18	(R) Notre Dame	3	14—

ECAC Madison Sq. Gard. Tourney

D	20	(N) Notre Dame	4	7—
D	21	(N) Brown	6	3
D	28	(H) Boston State	9	2
D	30	(H) Dalhousie	5	2
J	4	(H) Providence	3	8—
J	7	(H) New Hampshire	*5	6—
J	14	(R) Boston U.	1	4—
J	26	(R) Cornell	3	10—
J	28	(H) St. Louis	6	4
F	1	(R) Yale	6	10—
F	4	(H) Colgate	3	2

Beanpot Tournament

F	7	(G) Boston U.	2	4—
F	10	(H) Dartmouth	2	4—

Beanpot Finals (3rd)

F	14	(G) Northeastern	5	4
F	18	(R) Clarkson	6	4
F	19	(R) St. Lawrence	5	7—
F	21	(R) Dartmouth	6	5
F	23	(H) Boston U.	7	5
F	25	(H) Army	6	3
F	29	(H) Bowdoin	2	3—
M	4	(R) Pennsylvania	3	8—

*—Overtime
WON 14, LOST 16, TIED 0

1972–1973 Coach: Len Ceglarski
Captain: Bob Reardon

D	6	(R) Brown	4	9—
D	8	(H) Providence	6	5OT
D	13	(R) Harvard	4	6—
D	16	(H) Boston State	13	2

ECAC Christmas Tourn., Boston Garden (2nd)

D	18	(G) Merrimack	4	1
D	20	(G) Dartmouth	5	8—
D	22	(H) Notre Dame	11	4
D	28	(H) New Brunswick	14	2
D	30	(H) New Hampshire	5	2
J	2	(H) Northeastern	8	2
J	5	(H) St. Louis	8	5
J	9	(R) Princeton	7	3
J	13	(H) Boston Univ.	7	5
J	24	(H) Cornell	3	1
J	27	(H) St. Lawrence	13	4
J	30	(H) Yale	6	2
F	2	(R) New Hampshire	7	8—OT

Beanpot Tournament

F	5	(G) Northeastern	9	8OT
F	8	(R) Dartmouth	6	5

Beanpot Finals (2nd)

F	12	(G) Boston Univ.	1	4—
F	16	(H) Clarkson	9	8OT
F	21	(R) Boston Univ.	2	2OT
F	24	(R) Army	5	2
F	28	(H) Bowdoin	5	1
M	2	(R) Providence	8	3

ECAC Playoffs (2nd)

M	6	(H) New Hampshire	4	2
M	9	(G) Pennsylvania	5	3
M	10	(G) Cornell	2	3—

NCAA Tournament Boston (3rd)

M	15	(G) Denver	4	10—
M	17	(G) Cornell	3	1

WON 23, LOST 7, TIED 1

1973–1974 Coach: Len Ceglarski
Captain: Ray D'Arcy

D	2	(H) St. Anselm's	5	4
D	5	(H) Brown	0	3—
D	8	(H) St. Mary's	6	4
D	11	(R) Providence	10	5
D	15	(H) Princeton	11	3
D	21	(H) New Hampshire	4	5—OT

Great Lakes Tournament (3rd)

D	27	(R) Michigan State	5	12—
D	28	(R) Pennsylvania	6	2
D	30	(R) Notre Dame	4	3
J	2	(R) Northeastern	4	7—
J	5	(H) Loyola	5	3
J	8	(H) Harvard	6	5
J	12	(R) Cornell	3	6—
J	15	(H) Boston State	5	3
J	18	(R) Boston U.	2	11—
J	22	(R) Dartmouth	4	5—OT
J	25	(H) St. Louis	5	3
J	29	(R) Yale	7	6OT
F	1	(H) New Hampshire	2	5—

Beanpot Tourney

F	4	(G) Harvard	6	11—
F	7	(H) Dartmouth	4	3

Beanpot Finals (4th)

F	1	(G) Northeastern	3	4—
F	15	(R) Clarkson	2	4—
F	16	(R) St. Lawrence	2	5—
F	20	(H) Boston U.	7	5
F	23	(R) Army	5	4
F	27	(R) Bowdoin	8	4
M	1	(H) Providence	6	3

WON 16, LOST 12, TIED 0

1974–1975 Coach: Len Ceglarski
Mark Riley   Richie Hart

N	24	(H)	Boston State	13	1
D	1	(H)	St. Louis	7	8—
D	3	(R)	Brown	6	6T
D	6	(H)	St. Anselm's	9	3
D	10	(H)	Northeastern	7	4
D	13	(R)	Providence	4	6—
D	22	(H)	Notre Dame	4	7—
D	27	(R)	Denver	5	2
D	28	(R)	Denver	4	10—
D	30	(H)	Providence	7	4

Holiday Festival, Mad. Sq. Gard. (4th)

J	3	(N)	Cornell	7	10—
J	5	(N)	Brown	4	6—
J	7	(R)	Harvard	1	2—
J	11	(R)	New Hamsphire	1	5—
J	15	(H)	Cornell	6	6T
J	18	(H)	Boston U.	3	10—
J	21	(H)	Dartmouth	6	8—
J	24	(H)	St. Lawrence	1	5—
J	28	(H)	Yale	6	2
J	31	(H)	New Hampshire	6	4

Beanpot Tourney

F	3	(G)	Boston U.	3	5—
F	6	(R)	Dartmouth	5	4

Beanpot Finals (4th)

F	10	(G)	Northeastern	3	5—
F	14	(R)	Clarkson	2	4—
F	18	(R)	Boston U.	1	4—
F	21	(H)	Army	9	7
F	26	(H)	Bowdoin	4	1
M	1	(R)	Princeton	4	3

WON 11, LOST 15, TIED 2

1975–76 Coach: Len Ceglarski
Captains: Mark Albrecht
Richie Smith

S	27	(R)	St. Louis	2	4—
S	30	(R)	St. Louis	2	7—
O	2	(H)	Brown	5	4
O	4	(H)	St. Anselm's	10	1
O	7	(H)	New Hampshire	1	5—
O	10	(R)	Providence	5	6—
O	12	(H)	Princeton	11	2
O	20	(H)	Boston State	9	8
O	22	(R)	Notre Dame	5	6—

Blue/Green Invitational, Hanover, NH, (3rd)

N	2	(R)	Dartmouth	2	4—
N	3	(R)	R.P.I.	8	3
N	7	(H)	Harvard	6	6OT
J	10	(R)	Cornell	6	2
J	12	(R)	Northeastern	7	6
J	16	(R)	Boston University	2	4—
J	20	(R)	Harvard	4	7—
J	23	(H)	Vermont	6	5.
J	27	(R)	Yale	11	2
J	30	(H)	New Hampshire	1	5—

Beanpot Tournament

D	2	(G)	Northeastern	5	3
D	5	(H)	Dartmouth	9	7

Beanpot Final

D	9	(G)	Boston University	6	3
D	13	(R)	Clarkson	5	6—OT
F	14	(R)	St. Lawrence	4	5—

F	18	(H)	Boston University	4	6—
F	21	(R)	Army	6	4
F	25	(R)	Bowdoin	4	3
F	27	(H)	Providence	7	5

ECAC Playoffs

M	9	(R)	Boston University	5	6—

WON 16, LOST 13, TIED 1

1976–1977 Coach: Len Ceglarski
Captain: Bob Ferriter

N	23	(H)	Boston State	18	0
N	28	(H)	St. Louis	3	2
N	30	(R)	Brown	7	5
D	3	(H)	Northeastern	4	5—
D	5	(H)	St. Anselm's	9	2
D	8	(R)	Providence	7	4
D	11	(R)	Vermont	3	6—
D	13	(H)	Providence	4	1
D	19	(H)	Notre Dame	4	7—

Syracuse Invitational (1st)

D	28	(N)	Colgate	9	6
D	29	(N)	Cornell	6	4
J	6	(H)	Pennsylvania	7	9—
J	8	(R)	New Hampshire	4	7—
J	11	(H)	Harvard	4	1
J	15	(H)	Cornell	8	5
J	18	(H)	Dartmouth	8	5
J	22	(R)	Boston University	6	6OT
J	25	(H)	Yale	8	3
J	28	(H)	St. Lawrence	10	4
F	1	(H)	New Hampshire	3	6—
F	2	(R)	Dartmouth	4	3

Beanpot Tournament (3rd)

F	7	(G)	Harvard	2	4—
F	10	(H)	Clarkson	3	6—
F	14	(G)	Northeastern	6	4
F	19	(R)	Army	4	2
F	22	(H)	Bowdoin	4	3
F	26	(H)	Boston University	5	6—
M	1	(R)	R.P.I.	4	5—
M	5	(R)	Princeton	3	1

ECAC Playoffs

M	8	(R)	Boston University	7	8—

WON 19, LOST 11, TIED 1

1977–1978 Coach: Len Ceglarski
Captains: Paul Barrett
Rob Riley

N	20	(R)	Pennsylvania	7	6
N	22	(R)	St. Anselm's	10	1
N	29	(H)	Brown	4	3
D	2	(R)	St. Lawrence	7	2
D	3	(R)	Clarkson	5	9—
D	6	(R)	Northeastern	7	6OT
D	9	(H)	Princeton	4	2
D	12	(R)	Harvard	7	0
D	22	(R)	Gustavus Adolphus	7	0
D	23	(R)	Notre Dame	8	4
D	28	(H)	Air Force	6	1
J	3	(R)	New Hampshire	2	7—
J	6	(H)	Colgate	10	2
J	10	(H)	Harvard	11	3

J	14	(R)	Cornell	3	13—
J	17	(H)	Dartmouth	5	4
J	21	(R)	Boston University	3	6—
J	24	(R)	Yale	7	10—
J	28	(H)	R.P.I.	6	5OT
J	31	(R)	Providence	6	3
F	2	(R)	Dartmouth	4	2

Beanpot Tournament

F	6	(G)	Boston University	5	12—
F	16	(H)	Boston University	5	10—
F	21	(R)	Bowdoin	5	2
F	24	(H)	Army	7	4
F	28	(H)	Vermont	2	3—OT

Beanpot Finals (3rd)

M	1	(G)	Northeastern	3	2OT
M	3	(R)	Providence		
M	5	(H)	New Hampshire	4	2

ECAC Playoffs (1st)

M	7	(R)	R.P.I.	7	6OT
M	10	(G)	Brown	6	4
M	11	(G)	Providence	4	2

NCAA Tournament, Providence (2nd)

M	24	(N)	Bowling Green	6	2
M	25	(N)	Boston University	3	5—

WON 24, LOST 9, TIED 0

1978–1979 Coach: Len Ceglarski
Captain: Joe Mullen

N	21	(H)	St. Anselm's	8	1
N	27	(R)	Brown	2	4—
D	1	(R)	Vermont	4	5—
D	5	(H)	Northeastern	5	3
D	8	(H)	Providence	4	2
D	11	(H)	Lowell	0	3—
D	16	(H)	New Hampshire	5	7—
D	22	(H)	Notre Dame	10	5

Auld Lang Syne Classic, Hanover, NH (3rd)

D	30	(N)	Clarkson	5	9—
D	31	(N)	Bowdoin	8	3
J	2	(H)	New Hampshire	3	5—
J	5	(R)	Air Force	11	1
J	6	(R)	Air Force	14	7
J	9	(H)	Harvard	4	5—OT
J	13	(H)	Cornell	4	11—
J	16	(R)	Dartmouth	2	6—
J	20	(R)	Boston University	2	4—
J	24	(H)	Yale	8	5
J	25	(R)	Providence	1	7—
J	28	(R)	St. Lawrence	9	3
F	1	(H)	Dartmouth	8	6

Beanpot Tournament—first round

F	5	(G)	Northeastern	7	2
F	9	(R)	Army	6	2

Beanpot Tournament Finals (2nd)

F	12	(G)	Boston University	3	4—
F	17	(H)	Clarkson	8	6
F	20	(H)	Bowdoin	4	7—
F	23	(R)	Colgate	4	2
F	24	(R)	R.P.I.	7	9—
F	27	(H)	Boston University	5	3
M	2	(R)	Princeton	6	4

WON 16, LOST 14, TIED 0

1979–1980 Coach: Len Ceglarski
Captain: Steve Barger

N	16	(H)	Ohio State	4	5—OT
N	19	(H)	Salem State	8	5
N	26	(H)	St. Anselm's	7	3
N	29	(R)	New Hampshire	5	3
D	3	(H)	Brown	4	4T OT
D	7	(R)	Clarkson	8	4
D	8	(R)	St. Lawrence	7	1
D	11	(H)	Maine	3	6—
D	14	(H)	Princeton	7	5

UNH Tournament (1st)

D	28	(R)	Bowdoin	7	1
D	29	(R)	New Hampshire	8	5
J	4	(R)	Michigan	3	7—
J	5	(R)	Michigan State	5	3
J	9	(R)	Harvard	6	2
J	12	(R)	Cornell	6	5
J	15	(R)	Dartmouth	4	0
J	18	(R)	Boston University	7	6OT
J	22	(R)	Yale	4	2
J	25	(H)	Providence	4	1
J	27	(H)	R.P.I.	8	4
J	31	(R)	Dartmouth	5	6—
F	1	(H)	Colgate	6	3

Beanpot Tournament (first round)

F	4	(G)	Harvard	4	3
F	7	(H)	New Hampshire	4	3

Beanpot Finals (2nd)

F	11	(G)	Northeastern	4	5—OT
F	17	(H)	Northeastern	9	1
F	21	(R)	Maine	6	3
F	23	(R)	Army	9	3
F	25	(H)	Vermont	7	3
M	1	(R)	Providence	2	6—
M	5	(H)	Boston University	4	1
M	8	(R)	Northeastern	8	6

ECAC Playoffs

M	11	(H)	Cornell	1	5—

WON 25, LOST 7, TIED 1

1980–1981 Coach: Len Ceglarski
Captains: Mike Ewanouski,
Mark Switaj

N	7	(R)	Bowling Green	4	3
N	8	(R)	Bowling Green	4	0
N	21	(H)	Merrimack	7	3
N	24	(H)	Holy Cross	8	7
D	3	(R)	Brown	4	4T OT
D	5	(R)	Providence	3	3T OT
D	8	(H)	Maine	3	2
D	11	(R)	Vermont	6	3
D	14	(H)	New Hampshire	2	5—
D	29	(H)	Salem State	6	5OT
J	3	(R)	Princeton	3	6—
J	6	(H)	Harvard	6	2
J	9	(R)	Boston University	6	4
J	13	(R)	Dartmouth	6	1
J	16	(R)	Cornell	6	6T OT
J	20	(H)	Yale	6	1
J	23	(H)	St. Lawrence	3	2
J	26	(R)	Northeastern	5	3
J	29	(R)	Dartmouth	2	1

Beanpot Tournament—first round

F	2	(G)	Boston University	5	2
F	6	(H)	Providence	2	5—

Beanpot Finals (2nd)

F	9	(G)	Harvard	0	2—
F	13	(H)	Clarkson	0	5—
F	17	(R)	Maine	4	1
F	20	(R)	Colgate	3	6—
F	21	(R)	R.P.I.	4	1
F	24	(R)	Boston University	3	5—
F	27	(H)	Army	5	1
M	1	(R)	New Hampshire	4	3OT
M	4	(H)	Northeastern	4	3OT

ECAC Playoffs

M	10	(H)	Providence	2	5—

WON 20, LOST 8, TIED 3

HOCKEY COACHING RECORDS

Name	Seasons	GP	W	L	T	Years
Robert Fowler	2	6	4	2	0	1917–1919
Walter Falvey	1	7	5	1	1	1919–1920
Fred Rocque	5	51	32	16	3	1920–23 & 25–27
Charles Foote	2	28	12	13	3	1923–1925
James Foley	2	18	6	11	1	1927–1929
John Temple	1	9	7	2	0	1942–1943
Joseph Glavin, S.J.	1	3	1	2	0	1945–1946
John A. "Snooks" Kelly	36	759	501	243	15	1932–42 & 46–72
Len Ceglarski	9	273	167	97	9	1972–present

BASKETBALL

1904–1905

Battery H	6	8—
Tufts	23	17
Dartmouth	13	60—
E. Boston Evening HS	4	77—
Andover Academy	10	70—
Co. M. 8th Regt.	27	18
Lowell Tech.	5	16—
Boston U.	13	31—
Battery H	26	17
Lakesides	20	15
Cambridge All Stars	7	36—
Cushing Academy	6	20—
Boston U.	36	5

WON 6, LOST 8

1905–1906

Boston U.	32	17
Chelsea YMCA	29	18
Newport Navy Res.	5	53—
Lakesides	15	42—
Tufts	13	16—
All—Somerville	57	5
Lakesides	14	17—
Battery H	12	14—
Massachusetts State	15	20—
Lowell Technological	1	20—
Andover Academy	27	16
Revere Collegians	16	13
East Boston Evening HS	6	33—
M.I.T.	21	23—
Cambridge All Stars	26	16
Holy Cross	14	35—
Boston University	23	10
Harvard	6	42—
Cushing Academy	14	35—
New Hampshire	7	19—
Tufts	17	30—
Co. M. (Somerville)	26	22
Holy Name Club	14	24—
Holy Cross	20	22—
St. Alphonsus Club	5	24—
E. Boston Evening IIS	6	29—

WON 7, LOST 18

1906–1907

M.I.T.	23	46—
St. Alphonsus A.A.	18	14
Holy Name Society	8	44—
Andover Academy	15	29—

WON 1, LOST 3

1910–1911

M.I.T.	35	46—
Tufts	19	32—
Andover Academy	18	17
Rhode Island	13	33—
New Hampshire	17	53—
Cushing Academy	22	17

WON 2, LOST 4

1916–1917 Coach: Rev. McNally, S.J.

New Hampshire	20	35—
Dean Academy	19	30—
St. Mary's Catholic	32	20
St. Mary's Catholic	16	26—
Mass. Pharm.	29	14

WON 2, LOST 3

1918–1919

Newport Navy St.	36	28
Tufts	26	15
Connecticut	27	45—
Tufts	24	16
Connecticut	42	20

WON 4, LOST 1

1919–1920

Boston University	29	8
Connecticut	13	58—
Tufts	18	43—
Rhode Island	25	12
Boston University	30	20
Tufts	30	25
Rhode Island	19	14
Fordham	28	43—

WON 5, LOST 3

1920–1921 Coach: Luke Urban

Rhode Island	34	26
St. Michael's (Vt.)	29	15
Rhode Island	33	21
Springfield	34	33
Lowell Textile	33	22
Portland A.C.	33	23
Brooklyn Poly.	24	41—
Trinity (Conn.)	20	23—
St. Francis (N.Y.)	27	33—
Springfield	32	39—
Maine	36	27
Holy Cross	26	28—
Holy Cross	23	35—

WON 7, LOST 6

1922–1923 Coach: William Coady

Lowell Tech.	30	26
Holy Cross	32	26
Portland	27	21
Maine	24	28—
Trinity	32	22
Fitchburg State	13	14—
Springfield	19	52—
Springfield	20	28—
Holy Cross	26	35—

WON 4, LOST 5

1923–1924 Coach: William Coady

Fitchburg	22	16
Portland A.C.	45	27
Maine	29	28
Trinity	28	12
Lowell Tech	20	
Holy Cross	21	19
Vermont	14	31—
St. Michael's	45	30
M.I.T.	29	17
Holy Cross	21	25—
Newark A.C.	18	26—

WON 8, LOST 3

1924–1925 Coach: William Coady
Captain: Ed Harrison

Fitchburg	22	13
Maine	40	41—
Fordham	16	46—
Newark A.C.	27	19
Lowell Tech	29	10
Springfield	22	36—
Holy Cross	23	19
Boston University	38	30
Williams	34	50—
Vermont	20	36—
Holy Cross	26	25

WON 6, LOST 5

1945–1946 Coach: Al McClellan
Captain: Jim Sharry

D	13	(H) Manhattan College	44	50—
D	21	(A) U.S. Merchant Marine	53	50
J	10	(H) Villanova	34	38—
J	17	(H) Holy Cross	39	70—
J	22	(A) Dartmouth	35	62—
J	24	(H) Providence	60	47
J	31	(H) New York U.	33	64—
F	5	(A) Andrews (Me.) Amer. L.	30	37—
F	7	(H) St. John's	44	69—
F	9	(H) Amherst	67	38
F	12	(A) Chelsea Naval Hosp.	65	68—
F	14	(H) Holy Cross	46	62—
F	16	(A) R.P.I.	55	68—

WON 3, LOST 10

1946–1947 Coach: Al McClellan
Captain: Jim Sharry

N	30	(H) LaSalle College	76	41
D	9	(A) Siena College	44	39
D	10	(H) Georgetown	56	70—
D	14	(A) Providence	66	49
D	17	(H) Bowling Green St.	54	55—
D	21	(H) Fordham U.	72	50
D	31	(H) Georgia Tech	50	54—
J	7	(H) Brown	57	50
J	14	(A) Andrews (Me.) Ameri. L.	74	30
J	25	(A) St. Anselm's	79	74

J	28	(H) Geneva College	56	46
F	4	(H) Harvard	27	51—
F	6	(A) Colby College	64	67—
F	12	(A) Amherst	65	36
F	15	(A) Ft. Devens	81	53
F	18	(H) Brandley Polytech	56	60—
F	21	(A) Wayne University	43	38
F	22	(A) Michigan State	49	70—
F	25	(H) Holy Cross	48	90—
M	4	(H) Boston U.	57	60—
M	12	(A) Brown	60	57
M	14	(A) Georgetown	54	61—

WON 12, LOST 10

1947–1948 Coach: Al McClellan
Captain: John Letvinchuk

D	9	(A) Rhode Island St.	58	78—
D	15	(H) St. Anselm's	67	61
D	18	(A) American International	66	51
D	20	(H) Harvard	62	50
D	26	(A) Sienna College	50	58—
J	3	(H) Sienna College	32	51—
J	10	(H) Providence	62	43
J	13	(H) Manhattan	66	57
J	28	(A) Tufts	60	50
J	31	(A) Becker College	54	59—
F	1	(A) St. Anselm's	65	57
F	5	(H) Texas Wesleyan	44	61—
F	7	(A) St. Anselm's	45	42
F	10	(H) Bowling Green St.	48	74—
F	14	(A) Ft. Devens	80	50
F	17	(H) Holy Cross	34	45—
F	20	(A) Bates	54	65—
F	21	(A) Colby	56	52
F	24	(A) Providence	51	41
F	28	(A) Holy Cross	41	56—
M	2	(H) Boston U.	58	49
M	3	(H) Ft. Devens	46	43
M	10	(A) Georgetown	46	65—

WON 13, LOST 10

1948–1949 Coach: Al McClellan
Captain: Ray Carr

D	8	(A) Dartmouth	46	48—
D	14	(A) Tufts	66	69—
D	21	(H) Harvard	47	45
J	5	(H) Boston U.	59	53
J	7	(A) New York Ath. Club	54	53
J	8	(A) St. Francis (N.Y.)	52	63—
J	15	(A) Providence	58	63—
J	22	(A) Becker College	63	46
F	3	(H) Manhattan	54	68—
F	5	(A) Holy Cross	39	46—
F	8	(H) Tampa U.	63	52
F	10	(H) Duquesne U.	42	52—
F	17	(A) St. Anselm's	73	65
F	19	(H) Tufts	59	54
F	21	(H) Holy Cross	48	66—
F	23	(H) Providence	63	59
F	26	(H) St. Michael's	44	36
M	5	(A) Canisius	46	63—

WON 9, LOST 9

1949–1950 Coach: Al McClellan
Captain: Tom O'Brien

D	6	(H)	Rhode Island St.	63	46
D	10	(H)	St. Anselm's	72	57
D	13	(H)	Harvard	49	54—
D	17	(A)	St. Michael's	48	56—
D	20	(H)	Loyola (L.A.)	55	53
D	27	(A)	Yale U.	45	33
J	4	(H)	Tufts	61	56
J	7	(A)	Holy Cross	46	93—
J	14	(H)	DePaul U.	55	88—
J	24	(H)	Providence	67	50
J	27	(A)	New York Ath. Club	54	70—
F	2	(H)	C.C.N.Y.	56	64—
F	11	(A)	Seton Hall	42	38
F	14	(H)	Boston U	89	67
F	18	(A)	Villanova	64	61
F	21	(H)	Holy Cross	63	71—
F	25	(H)	Colby	80	60
M	4	(A)	Providence	64	77—
M	6	(H)	LaSalle	61	83—

WON 11, LOST 9

1950–1951 Coach: Al McClellan
Captain: Tom Deegan

D	4	(H)	American International	80	41
D	6	(H)	Arnold College	92	53
D	8	(A)	Rhode Island St.	79	76
D	14	(H)	Boston U.	88	48
D	19	(A)	Harvard	76	48
D	23	(A)	Connecticut	52	56—
J	9	(H)	Providence	84	54
J	11	(A)	C.C.N.Y.	63	59
J	13	(A)	Canisius	54	56—
J	27	(A)	Villanova	67	98—
J	31	(A)	Boston U.	90	65
F	1	(H)	Tufts	65	61
F	3	(A)	Seton Hall	53	67—
F	6	(H)	Springfield	58	50
F	10	(A)	Williams College	47	55—
F	12	(H)	St. Francis (N.Y.)	63	58
F	15	(A)	Dartmouth	54	35
F	17	(A)	Yale	59	64—
F	21	(A)	Holy Cross	48	71—
F	24	(A)	St. Anselm's	57	63—
F	26	(A)	U. Mass	59	43
F	27	(H)	Holy Cross	49	62—
M	2	(A)	New York Ath. Club	68	70—
M	3	(A)	Iona College	49	61—
M	5	(H)	Rhode Island St.	68	54
M	12	(A)	*Bowdoin	56	47
M	13	(A)	*Colby	79	64
M	16	(A)	*Trinity (Ct.)	82	72

*—New England Tourney
WON 17. LOST 11

1951–1952 Coach: Al McClellan
Captain: Tom O'Toole

D	3	(H)	Camp Edwards	84	60
D		(A)	Rhode Island	76	69
D	8	(H)	Stonehill	75	43
D	10	(H)	U. Mass	76	52
D	15	(A)	Connecticut	57	53
D	17	(H)	Boston U.	70	47
D	20	(A)	Harvard	76	63
D	28	(H)	Bucknell	86	64
D	29	(H)	Holy Cross	59	78—
J	5	(A)	Seton Hall	48	80—
J	9	(H)	Rhode Island	83	65
J	11	(H)	Stonehill	68	58
J	21	(H)	Dartmouth	64	51
J	26	(A)	Iona College	61	53
J	28	(H)	Fairfield	75	55
F	1	(A)	Le Moyne College	74	58
F	2	(A)	Canisius	55	65—
F	4	(H)	Tufts	95	64
F	8	(A)	New York Ath. Club	72	64
F	9	(A)	Villanova	67	72—
F	12	(H)	Brandeis U.	96	49
F	16	(A)	Holy Cross	74	80—
F	18	(A)	Boston U.	84	69
F	23	(A)	St. Anselm's	78	58
F	25	(A)	Springfield	84	59
M	1	(A)	Brandeis U.	72	65
M	3	(H)	Holy Cross	64	61

WON 22, LOST 5

1952–1953 Coach: Al McClellan
Captain: John B. Silk

D	4	(A)	Rhode Island	70	82—
D	6	(A)	New York	71	80—
D	12	(A)	Connecticut	51	70—

Boston Invitational Tournament

D	29	(A)	Rhode Island	68	72—
D	30	(A)	Seattle	86	99—
J	7	(H)	Rhode Island	*92	82
J	8	(A)	Dartmouth	54	51
J	12	(H)	Harvard	*70	73—
J	14	(A)	Boston University	73	65
J	14	(A)	Seton Hall	71	92—
J	30	(A)	LeMoyne	59	64—
J	31	(A)	Canisius	71	88—
F	5	(H)	Boston University	98	76
F	11	(A)	Brandeis	91	90
F	14	(A)	Villanova	73	105—
F	16	(A)	Holy Cross	66	87—
F	18	(H)	Stonehill	68	52
F	21	(A)	St. Francis (B)	62	71—
F	24	(A)	St. Anselm's	82	64
F	28	(A)	Holy Cross	60	87—
M	2	(A)	Colby	68	72—
M	4	(A)	Brandeis	71	80—

*—overtime
WON 7, LOST 15

1953–1954 Coach: Don Martin
Captain: John A O'Hara

D	3	(A)	Rhode Island	70	62
D	5	(A)	St. Anselm's	68	64
D	8	(H)	Merrimack	95	54
D	10	(H)	Stonehill	67	47
D	12	(A)	Northeastern	78	58
D	15	(A)	Brandeis	77	74
J	6	(A)	Providence	58	63—
J	9	(A)	Colby	59	50
J	12	(A)	Holy Cross	57	83—
J	16	(A)	U. Connecticut	81	106—
J	29	(A)	Rhode Island	101	103—
F	2	(A)	Holy Cross	77	82—
F	5	(A)	LeMoyne	63	77—
F	6	(A)	Canisius	59	60—
F	9	(A)	Boston University	70	58
F	10	(A)	Harvard	73	52
F	12	(A)	Tufts	60	62—
F	13	(A)	Villanova	52	78—
F	22	(H)	Providence	87	84
F	24	(A)	Stonehill	75	62
F	27	(N)	Boston University	81	88—
M	2	(A)	Brandeis	75	84—

WON 11, LOST 11

1954–1955 Coach: Don Martin
Captain: Philip C. Powell

D	4	(A)	Fairfield	65	76—
D	7	(A)	Rhode Island	63	96—
D	9	(H)	Merrimack	81	64
D	11	(A)	New York	63	80—
D	13	(A)	Connecticut	74	117—
D	16	(A)	Brandeis	81	90—
D	21	(A)	Holy Cross	42	95—
D	28	(A)	Richmond	68	90—
D	29	(A)	Rutgers	78	75
D	30	(A)	Colgate	68	80—
J	8	(A)	Holy Cross	63	102—
J	12	(A)	Providence	65	40
J	15	(A)	Connecticut	76	95—
J	29	(H)	Boston University	58	78—
F	2	(A)	Tufts	63	54
F	4	(A)	LeMoyne	73	82—
F	5	(A)	Canisius	52	71—
F	8	(A)	Harvard	73	70
F	11	(A)	Seton Hall	56	88—
F	12	(A)	Villanova	75	100—
F	14	(A)	Boston University	58	72—
F	19	(A)	Colby	73	94—
F	22	(H)	Providence	69	67
F	24	(A)	Northeastern	84	69
F	28	(A)	Brandeis	98	91
M	1	(A)	St. Anselm's	80	86—

WON 8, LOST 18

1955–1956 Coach: Don Martin
Captain: Patrick M. Cahill. Jr.

D	5	(H)	Suffolk	89	73
D	7	(H)	Stonehill	97	43
D	10	(A)	Williams	69	72—
D	12	(A)	Rhode Island	75	72
D	14	(A)	Dartmouth	48	65—
D	17	(A)	Northeastern	51	62—
D	19	(A)	U. Massachusetts	73	91—
D	29	(H)	Marshall	69	130—
D	30	(H)	Virginia Military	72	70
J	6	(A)	N.Y.A.C.	76	86—
J	7	(A)	Seton Hall	53	68—
J	11	(A)	Boston University	65	80—
J	14	(A)	Connecticut	57	88—
F	3	(A)	LeMoyne	76	92—
F	4	(A)	Canisius	60	90—
F	8	(A)	Brandeis	64	90—
F	11	(A)	Springfield	59	64—
F	13	(A)	Tufts	91	79
F	16	(H)	Providence	51	63—
F	18	(A)	Providence	69	77—
F	25	(A)	Harvard	74	93—
F	27	(A)	St. Anselm's	90	82
F	28	(A)	Boston University	70	94—
M	1	(A)	Holy Cross	75	111—

WON 6, LOST 18

1956–1957 Coach: Don Martin
Captain: Paul J. McAdams

D	1	(H)	Brown	76	58
D	5	(A)	Rhode Island	84	79
D	8	(A)	Brandeis	72	76—
D	12	(A)	Northeastern	63	49
D	15	(A)	Connecticut	87	81
D	18	(A)	Tufts	55	61—
D	21	(A)	St. Peter's	71	83—
D	22	(A)	Seton Hall	76	88—
D	28	(A)	Evansville	76	96—
D	29	(A)	Evansville	60	58
J	5	(A)	Fairfield	75	54
J	9	(H)	Merrimack	91	53
J	11	(A)	N.Y.A.C.	70	74—
J	26	(A)	St. Anselm's	71	90—
J	30	(A)	Massachusetts	68	66
F	2	(H)	Providence	68	55
F	10	(A)	Israeli Olympics	64	59
F	11	(A)	Boston University	64	83—
F	13	(A)	Harvard	86	101—
F	16	(A)	New York University	68	94—
F	18	(H)	Stonehill	94	65
F	20	(H)	Suffolk	102	63
F	23	(A)	Holy Cross	65	89—
F	25	(H)	Boston University	57	56
F	27	(A)	Providence	71	89—

WON 13: LOST 12

1957–1958 Coach: Don Martin
Captain: John P. Harrington, Jr.

D	2	(A)	Rhode Island	73	53
D	7	(A)	Colby	87	66
D	11	(A)	Northeastern	95	82
D	14	(A)	Connecticut	82	68
D	17	(A)	Tufts	78	63
D	19	(A)	Brandeis	92	62
J	2	(A)	Brown	88	78
J	4	(A)	Fairfield	71	64
J	18	(A)	Seton Hall	77	64
J	24	(A)	N.Y.A.C.	76	68
J	25	(A)	St. Peter's	46	58—
J	28	(H)	Massachusetts	71	67
J	30	(A)	Harvard	65	60
F	1	(A)	Marquette	64	80—
F	7	(H)	Stonehill	99	66
F	12	(H)	Providence	65	54
F	19	(H)	Suffolk	82	63
F	22	(A)	Holy Cross	73	78
F	24	(H)	Boston University	60	63—
M	1	(A)	Providence	59	81—
M	5	(A)	Boston University	76	93—

NCAA Tournament
M	11	(1)	Maryland	63	86—

WON 16, LOST 6
1—Madison Square Garden, New York

1958–1959 Coach: Don Martin
Captain: George Gierash

D	2	(A)	Rhode Island	80	67
D	4	(H)	Holy Cross	72	63
D	9	(H)	Northeastern	79	38
D	11	(A)	New York U.	70	81—
D	13	(H)	U. Conn.	81	55
D	15	(H)	Tufts	87	40
D	18	(H)	Brown	67	54
D	20	(A)	Seton Hall	74	66
D	29	(A)	Brown	98	78
D	30	(A)	Providence	60	67—
J	3	(H)	St. Bonaventure	70	82—
J	6	(H)	Fairfield	66	56
J	10	(A)	Georgetown	67	73—
J	13	(H)	Suffolk	73	51
J	17	(H)	Providence	51	49
J	30	(A)	Syracuse	78	71
F	4	(H)	Harvard	63	49
F	6	(A)	Villanova	69	85—
F	7	(A)	Navy	72	78—
F	10	(H)	Brandeis	79	63
F	14	(A)	Providence	44	51—
F	19	(A)	U. Mass	65	68—
F	20	(H)	Detroit	76	62
F	23	(H)	Boston U	55	54
F	26	(A)	Colby	77	73
M	4	(A)	Holy Cross	72	82—

*—overtime
WON 17, LOST 9

1959–1960 Coach: Don Martin
Captain: John Schoppmeyer

D	1	(A)	Brown	75	69
D	5	(A)	Army	81	83—
D	7	(A)	Northeastern	65	63
D	12	(A)	U. Conn	67	84—
D	18	(A)	Pittsburgh	75	66
D	20	(A	Detroit	81	94—

Queen City Tourney, Buffalo
D	26	(A)	Rhode Island	80	85—
D	28	(A)	Wisconsin	82	95—
J	2	(H)	Villanova	67	81—
J	5	(H)	Boston U.	64	81—
J	13	(A)	Fairfield	78	67
J	16	(A)	Providence	56	71—
J	28	(H)	U. Mass	74	51
J	30	(H)	Georgetown	93	77
F	1	(H)	Colby	75	59
F	6	(A)	Holy Cross	68	80—
F	9	(A)	Harvard	86	82
F	13	(H)	Seton Hall	71	88—
F	19	(H)	Providence	56	59—
F	23	(A)	Boston U.	78	82—
F	25	(A)	Brandeis	87	70
F	29	(A)	Tufts	98	76
M	2	(H)	Holy Cross	78	86—
M	4	(H)	Syracuse	77	70

WON 11, LOST 13

1960–1961 Coach: Don Martin
Captain: Frank Quinn

D	3	(H)	Fairfield	83	70
D	6	(A)	Rhode Island	85	79
D	9	(H)	U. Conn	110	96
D	10	(A)	Dartmouth	100	66
D	13	(H)	Harvard	88	61
D	15	(A)	Brown	70	76—
D	17	(A)	Seton Hall	87	105—
J	4	(A)	Boston U.	85	58
J	7	(H)	Providence	65	75—
J	10	(H)	Holy Cross	79	78
J	14	(H)	Navy	71	59
J	28	(H)	Fordham	66	68—
F	1	(A)	Yale	65	69—
F	4	(A)	Army	86	62
F	10	(A)	Georgetown	78	102—
F	11	(A)	St. Bonaventure	69	103—
F	18	(H)	Brandeis	98	89
F	20	(H)	Northeastern	75	54
F	21	(H)	Boston U.	69	59
F	25	(H)	Providence	65	76—
F	27	(H)	Tufts	84	74
M	1	(A)	Holy Cross	75	87—
M	4	(H)	Syracuse	80	78

WON 14, LOST 9

1961–1962 Coach: Don Martin
Captain: Bill Foley

D	1	(H)	Brown	84	65
D	6	(H)	Providence	73	77—
D	9	(A)	U. Conn	71	78—
D	12	(A)	Yale	109	96
D	14	(H)	Fairfield	98	77
D	16	(A)	Maine	104	92
J	6	(A)	Navy	88	79
J	11	(H)	Boston U.	77	70
J	13	(A)	Army	*88	89—
J	26	(H)	Pittsburgh	108	94
J	27	(A)	Canisius	80	108—
J	31	(A)	Northeastern	71	63
F	3	(A)	Holy Cross	82	77
F	8	(A)	Providence	68	70—
F	10	(H)	Georgetown	84	77
F	14	(H)	Brandeis	119	63
F	17	(A)	Fordham	69	65
F	19	(A)	Tufts	86	60
F	23	(H)	Seton Hall	90	86
F	27	(A)	Holy Cross	75	86—
M	3	(H)	Syracuse	72	73—
M	8	(A)	Boston U.	76	63

*—overtime
WON 16, LOST 7

1962–1963 Coach: Frank Power
Captain: Gerry Ward

D	4	(H)	Miami (Fla)	69	72—
D	6	(A)	Harvard	57	45
D	8	(H)	U. Conn	53	63—
Steel Bowl, Pittsburgh					
D	14	(A)	Duquesne	45	57—
D	15	(A)	William & Mary	66	53
Holiday Festival, New York					
D	26	(A)	West Virginia	*64	65—
D	28	(A)	Holy Cross	79	66
D	29	(A)	Pennsylvania	69	71—
J	3	(H)	Dartmouth	50	58—
J	5	(H)	Providence	49	59—
J	10	(A)	Brandeis	80	44
J	12	(A)	Georgetown	58	71—
J	25	(H)	Seton Hall	53	61—
J	26	(H)	Army	42	44—
J	30	(H)	Northeastern	63	43
F	2	(A)	Holy Cross	61	74—
F	7	(H)	Notre Dame	66	74—
F	9	(A)	Fairfield	68	64
Beanpot Tourney					
F	12	(H)	Tufts	64	54
F	15	(H)	Fordham	58	59—
Beanpot Tourney (1st)					
F	18	(H)	Northeastern	59	53
F	22	(A)	Syracuse	54	55—
F	23	(A)	Canisius	61	82—
F	26	(H)	Holy Cross	59	64—
M	2	(H)	Boston U.	59	57

*—overtime
WON 9, LOST 16

1963–1964 Coach: Bob Cousy
Captain: George Fitzsimmons

D	6	(H)	Fairfield	63	69—
D	12	(H)	U. Mass	74	93—
D	14	(A)	U. Conn	81	108—
D	19	(H)	Colby	97	80
D	21	(H)	Los Angeles St.	94	83
Quaker City Tourney, Phil.					
D	27	(A)	St. Bonaventure	74	77—
D	28	(A)	Temple	68	99—
J	4	(A)	Canisius	82	98—
J	7	(H)	Brandeis	95	67
J	23	(A)	Dartmouth	93	62
J	29	(A)	Northeastern	95	84
F	1	(A)	Holy Cross	71	99—
F	4	(A)	Providence	78	102—
F	8	(H)	Army	66	90—
Beanpot Tourney					
F	11	(A)	Northeastern	71	73—
F	15	(A)	Fordham	96	90
Beanpot Tourney (3rd)					
F	17	(A)	Tufts	105	75
F	21	(H)	Georgetown	107	92
F	25	(H)	Holy Cross	84	88—
F	28	(H)	Seton Hall	105	92
M	4	(A)	Boston U.	61	60

WON 10, LOST 11

1964–1965 Coach: Bob Cousy
Captain: George Humann

D	3	(H)	Dartmouth	104	76
D	6	(A)	Georgetown	89	71
D	10	(A)	New York U.	102	84
D	12	(H)	U. Conn	*81	85—
D	15	(H)	Harvard	83	72
Milwaukee Classic					
D	18	(A)	Wisconsin	86	85
D	19	(A)	U.C.L.A.	93	115—
D	21	(A)	St. Mary's (Cal.)	78	62
D	22	(A)	Los Angeles St.	88	104—
Rainbow Classic, Hawaii					
D	26	(A)	Wisconsin	69	70—
D	29	(A)	Hawaii	120	74
D	30	(A)	Utah State	*120	118
J	6	(H)	Providence	79	89—
J	10	(A)	St. Joseph's	71	93—
J	12	(A)	Rhode Island	107	105
J	15	(H)	Colby	89	54
J	29	(A)	Fairfield	96	88
J	30	(A)	Seton Hall	78	73
F	2	(A)	U. Mass	109	97
F	9	(H)	Northeastern	101	90
F	13	(H)	Boston U.	94	86
F	16	(A)	Fordham	89	78
F	20	(A)	Brandeis	81	51
			Holy Cross	95	94
Beanpot Tourney					
F	24	(A)	Boston U.	90	85
F	26	(H)	Phillips 66ers	104	88
Beanpot Tourney (1st)					
M	1	(A)	Northeastern	56	51
M	4	(H)	Holy Cross	111	89
National Invitational					
M	8	(A)	St. John's	92	114—

*—overtime
WON 22, LOST 7

1965–1966 Coach: Bob Cousy
Captain: Ed Hockenbury

D	4	(A)	Dartmouth	107	84
D	7	(H)	Fairfield	93	100—
D	11	(A)	U. Conn	90	74
D	13	(H)	St. Mary's	95	72
D	18	(A)	Notre Dame	93	89
D	21	(H)	Georgetown	87	85
Holiday Festival, New York					
D	27	(A)	Colorado St. U.	86	64
D	28	(A)	Army	92	85
D	30	(A)	Providence	86	91—
J	5	(H)	Rhode Island	99	91
J	8	(H)	New York U.	88	75
J	13	(A)	Northeastern	70	63
J	15	(A)	Providence	77	79—
J	29	(A)	Colby	95	79
F	2	(H)	St. Joseph's	89	107—
F	5	(H)	Holy Cross	98	68
F	8	(H)	U. Mass	101	80
F	12	(A)	Fordham	96	86
F	15	(A)	Boston U	73	62
F	19	(A)	Navy	94	78
Beanpot Tourney					
F	23	(A)	Tufts	94	66
F	25	(H)	Seton Hall	112	77
Beanpot Finals (1st)					
F	28	(A)	Northeastern	85	78
M	5	(A)	Holy Cross	87	83
National Invitational					
M	13	(A)	Louisville	***96	90
M	16	(A)	Villanova	85	86—

***—triple overtime
WON 21, LOST 5

1966–1967 Coach: Bob Cousy
Captain: Willie Wolters

D	1	(H)	Quantico	101	80
D	3	(A)	U. Mass	86	63
D	7	(A)	Fairfield	93	76
D	10	(H)	U. Conn	87	69
D	13	(A)	Harvard	99	81
D	15	(H)	Swedish Nationals	84	65
Boston Garden Tourney					
D	20	(A)	Syracuse	87	75
D	21	(A)	U. Mass	75	67
Sugar Bowl Classic					
D	29	(A)	Utah	88	90—
D	30	(A)	Tennessee	68	61
J	7	(H)	Navy	101	76
J	10	(A)	Northeastern	54	47
J	12	(A)	Duquesne	93	66
J	31	(A)	Seton Hall	90	75
F	4	(H)	Holy Cross	92	74
F	8	(A)	St. Joseph's	83	69
F	11	(H)	Fordham	81	85—
F	14	(A)	Rhode Island	81	71
F	18	(H)	Providence	83	82
F	21	(H)	Boston U.	74	46
F	24	(A)	Georgetown	103	91
F	28	(H)	Canisius	80	76
M	4	(A)	Holy Cross	76	61
NCAA First Round, URI					
M	11	(A)	Connecticut	48	42
NCAA East Reg., Maryland					
M	17	(A)	St. John's	63	62
M	18	(A)	No. Carolina	80	96—

WON 23, LOST 3

1967–1968 Coach: Bob Cousy
Captain: Jim Kissane

D	5	(H)	Dartmouth	116	69
D	9	(A)	Connecticut	76	60
D	13	(H)	Fairfield	96	76
D	17	(H)	St. John's	90	91—

Boston Garden Tournament

D	20	No. Carolina St.	72	55
D	21	Providence	88	70

ECAC Holiday Festival

D	26	Penn State	87	58
D	28	St. John's	57	60—
D	30	Louisville	74	81—
J	6	(A)	Northeastern	83	75
J	13	(A)	Boston Univ.	102	80
J	20	(H)	St. Joseph's	67	76—
J	25	(A)	LeMoyne	90	61
J	27	(A)	U.C.L.A.	77	84—
J	31	(A)	Providence	86	70
F	3	(H)	Holy Cross	82	89—
F	6	(H)	Massachusetts	94	70
F	10	(A)	Fordham	71	79—
F	13	(H)	Rhode Island	125	73
F	17	(H)	Georgetown	103	79
F	21	(H)	Seton Hall	99	65
F	24	(A)	Syracuse	97	74
F	28	(A)	Duquesne	104	88
M	2	(A)	Holy Cross	90	87

NCAA First Round, U.R.I.

M	8	St. Bonaventure	93	102—

WON 17, LOST 8

1968–1969 Coach: Bob Cousy
Captain: Terry Driscoll

D	5	(H)	LeMoyne	86	66
D	7	(H)	Connecticut	105	75
D	10	(H)	Harvard	91	77
D	13	(H)	Villanova	68	78—
D	18	(A)	Fairfield	81	69
D	21	(A)	St. John's	81	85—

Gator Bowl Tournament, Jacksonville, Fla.

D	26	(N)	Georgia	89	83
D	27	(N)	Northwestern	68	77—
J	5	(A)	St. Joseph's	76	74
J	7	(H)	U. Cal.—Irvine	95	79
J	10	(G)	Providence	90	84OT
J	22	(A)	Seton Hall	84	56
J	25	(A)	Canisius	107	73
J	29	(H)	Northeastern	80	69
F	1	(H)	Holy Cross	77	69
F	5	(A)	Massachusetts	78	67
F	8	(H)	Fordham	105	70
F	11	(A)	Rhode Island	70	62
F	15	(A)	Penn State	67	63
F	18	(A)	Georgetown	72	66OT
F	23	(H)	Detroit	99	72
F	25	(H)	Boston University	110	80
M	1	(A)	Holy Cross	80	74
M	5	(H)	Duquesne	93	72

National Invitational Tournament, New York (2nd)

M	16	(N)	Kansas	78	62
M	18	(N)	Louisville	88	83
M	20	(N)	Army	73	61
M	22	(N)	Temple	76	89—

WON 24, LOST 4

1969–1970 Coach: Chuck Daly
Captain: Tom Veronneau

D	2	(A)	Boston University	70	76—
D	6	(H)	Fairfield	69	74—
D	10	(H)	Canisius	70	56
D	13	(A)	Connecticut	72	77—
D	16	(H)	Penn State	63	67—
D	19	(A)	Cornell	78	60
D	20	(A)	LeMoyne	76	56

ECAC Holiday Festival, New York

D	27	(N)	Pennsylvania	65	86—
D	29	(N)	Manhattan	91	84
D	30	(N)	Cincinnati	70	85—
J	6	(A)	Providence	62	65—
J	10	(H)	St. Joseph's	62	60
J	21	(A)	Villanova	68	96—
J	24	(A)	Detroit	67	80—
J	28	(A)	Northeastern	95	64
J	31	(H)	Holy Cross	70	72—
F	3	(H)	Massachusetts	83	76
F	7	(A)	Fordham	71	68
F	11	(H)	Rhode Island	96	79
F	14	(H)	Seton Hall	71	83—
F	17	(H)	Georgetown	79	69
F	22	(A)	Duquesne	72	105—
F	28	(A)	Holy Cross	86	73
M	3	(H)	St. John's	65	71—

WON 11, LOST 13

1970–1971 Coach: Chuck Daly
Captain: Jim O'Brien

Beanpot Tournament

D	1	(N)	Northeastern	62	58
D	4	(A)	Fairfield	59	56

Beanpot Finals (1st)

D	8	(A)	Harvard	73	71

Mountaineer Tourn. W. Va. (4th)

D	11	(N)	Virginia	69	79—
D	12	(N)	Army	61	63—
D	16	(H)	LeMoyne	105	68
D	19	(A)	Penn State	63	66—
D	22	(A)	St. John's	69	66

Charlotte Invitational (2nd)

D	29	(N)	Davidson	72	67
D	30	(N)	LaSalle	63	75—
J	3	(A)	St. Joseph's	70	78—
J	8	(H)	Providence	83	71
J	12	(H)	Connecticut	71	69
J	16	(H)	Holy Cross	73	75—
J	23	(A)	Canisius	67	58
J	28	(A)	Cornell	101	76
J	30	(A)	Seton Hall	73	70
F	3	(A)	Rhode Island	86	80
F	6	(H)	Fordham	80	84—OT
F	9	(A)	Massachusetts	77	85—
F	13	(H)	Boston University	110	62
F	15	(A)	Georgetown	66	67—
F	20	(H)	Detroit	76	80—
F	24	(H)	Duquesne	67	52
F	27	(A)	Holy Cross	69	59
M	3	(H)	Villanova	77	90—

WON 15, LOST 11

1971–1972 Coach: Bob Zuffelato
Captain: Peter Schmid

Beanpot Tournament

D	2	(N)	Boston University	83	85—
D	6	(H)	Vanderbilt	75	82—
D	9	(H)	Canisius	76	58

Beanpot Consolation (3rd)

D	13	(N)	Northeastern	52	51
D	18	(A)	LeMoyne	81	67
D	20	(A)	St. Bonaventure	66	86—

ECAC Quaker City Tourn., Phila. (4th)

D	27	(N)	LaSalle	62	61
D	28	(N)	South Carolina	64	86—
D	30	(N)	Tennessee	60	61—
J	2	(H)	Fairfield	100	78
J	5	(A)	Providence	68	86—
J	8	(H)	St. Joseph's	68	82—
J	12	(A)	Dartmouth	88	93—OT
J	15	(H)	Holy Cross	71	70
J	27	(A)	Duquesne	79	93—
J	29	(A)	Detroit	68	76—
F	2	(H)	Rhode Island	64	63OT
F	6	(A)	Fordham	58	65—
F	9	(H)	Massachusetts	75	74OT
F	12	(H)	Seton Hall	82	71
F	15	(H)	St. John's	70	66
F	19	(H)	Penn State	64	68—
F	21	(A)	Villanova	70	92—
F	26	(A)	Holy Cross	90	77
F	29	(A)	Connecticut	41	39OT
M	4	(H)	Georgetown	78	69

WON 13, LOST 13

1972–1973 Coach: Bob Zuffelato
Captain: Bobby Smith

N	28	(H)	Athletes in Action		
D	5	(A)	Rhode Island	85	75
D	9	(H)	Brown	81	70
D	13	(H)	St. Bonaventure	78	65
D	16	(A)	Penn State	63	65—
D	21	(A)	St. John's	96	95OT
D	23	(A)	Vanderbilt	62	78—
D	26	(A)	Michigan	70	88—
			Villanova	63	65—

ECAC Holiday Festival Madison Square Garden, NY

J	3	(H)	Dartmouth	102	76
J	6	(H)	Villanova	82	81OT
J	8	(A)	Harvard	67	77—

Beanpot Tournament Boston Garden

J	13	(H)	Holy Cross	71	82—
J	15	(A)	Boston University	72	82—

Beanpot Finals, Boston Garden

J	24	(A)	Fairfield	65	69—
J	27	(A)	Canisius	58	78—
J	31	(A)	Providence	64	73—
F	3	(H)	Fordham	75	74
F	7	(A)	Massachusetts	52	76—
F	9	(H)	Merrimack	106	70
F	13	(A)	St. Joseph's	66	78—
F	17	(A)	Georgetown	55	56—
F	20	(A)	LeMoyne	88	68
F	24	(A)	Holy Cross	95	86
F	27	(A)	Connecticut	65	66—
M	3	(A)	Seton Hall	78	76OT

WON 11, LOST 14

1973–1974 Coach: Bob Zuffelato
Captain: Dan Kilcullen

D	4	(H)	Canisius	81	86—
D	8	(A)	Brown	73	71
D	12	(H)	Fairfield	76	68
D	14	(A)	Harvard	68	65
D	22	(A)	Syracuse	88	110—

Maryland Invitational (2nd)

D	28	(A)	Michigan State	94	81
D	29	(A)	Maryland	37	58—
J	3	(A)	LeMoyne	94	75
J	10	(A)	Villanova	81	79OT
J	12	(A)	New Hampshire	57	56OT

Beanpot Tournament (2nd)

J	15	(A)	Northeastern	65	59
J	16	(H)	Boston University	94	95—OT
J	19	(H)	Holy Cross	85	62
J	23	(A)	Providence	77	79—OT
J	26	(H)	Yale	83	72
J	29	(H)	Rhode Island	85	80
F	2	(H)	Fordham	74	64
F	6	(H)	Massachusetts	78	74OT
F	9	(H)	St. Joseph's	81	64
F	13	(H)	St. Francis (Pa.)	86	73
F	16	(H)	Penn State	86	72
F	18	(H)	St. John's	72	80—
F	20	(A)	Dartmouth	94	62
F	23	(A)	Holy Cross	76	79—
F	26	(A)	Connecticut	69	77—
M	2	(H)	Georgetown	92	68

National Invitational Tournament, New York (3rd)

M	17	(N)	Cincinnati	63	62
M	21	(N)	Connecticut	76	75
M	23	(N)	Utah	93	117—
M	24	(N)	Jacksonville	87	77

WON 21, LOST 9

1974–1975 Coach: Bob Zuffelato
Captain: Mel Weldon

D	4	(H)	LeMoyne	113	66
D	7	(H)	Harvard	70	66
D	11	(A)	Rhode Island	88	67
D	14	(H)	Northeastern	103	78
D	21	(A)	St. John's	62	75—

Far West Classic (7th)

D	26	(N)	Arizona State	73	81—
D	28	(N)	Creighton	61	62—
D	30	(N)	Iowa	86	81
J	4	(A)	Penn State	82	71
J	10	(A)	St. Joseph's	97	84

Beanpot Tournament (1st)

J	14	(H)	Boston University	86	78
J	16	(N)	Harvard	86	77
J	18	(H)	Holy Cross	70	77—
J	20	(H)	Dartmouth	61	55
J	22	(A)	Yale	103	78
J	25	(A)	Syracuse	79	73
J	29	(H)	Providence	85	77
F	1	(H)	Fordham	91	74

F	5	(A)	Massachusetts	71	80—
F	8	(H)	Villanova	94	80
F	12	(A)	Fairfield	74	80—
F	15	(A)	Georgetown	82	90—OT
F	22	(A)	Holy Cross	87	77
F	25	(H)	Connecticut	68	67
M	1	(H)	New Hampshire	88	63

ECAC New England Regionals (1st)

M	6	(N)	Connecticut	68	58
M	8	(N)	Holy Cross	69	55

NCAA First Round, Charlotte, NC

M	15	(N)	Furman	82	76

NCAA East Reg., Providence, RI

M	20	(N)	Kansas State	65	74—
M	22	(N)	North Carolina	90	110—

WON 21, LOST 9

1975–1976 Coach: Bob Zuffelato
Captain: Bill Collins

N	30	(H)	Bentley	87	74
D	3	(H)	LeMoyne	87	72
D	6	(A)	Harvard	72	71
D	9	(H)	Rutgers	82	105—
D	13	(H)	Fairfield	78	80—
D	20	(A)	Syracuse	58	59—
D	27	(A)	Vanderbilt	71	75—

Charlotte Invitational (3rd)

D	29	(N)	Clemson	60	80—
D	30	(N)	Hofstra	77	70
J	2	(A)	Connecticut	94	83
J	6	(A)	Dartmouth	68	71—
J	9	(A)	Villanova	70	78—

Beanpot Tournament (3rd)

J	13	(A)	Harvard	65	79—
J	14	(A)	Northeastern	83	82
J	17	(A)	Holy Cross	83	84—
J	21	(H)	St. John's	51	53—
J	24	(H)	Yale	70	56
J	28	(H)	St. Joseph's	56	57—
J	31	(A)	Fordham	77	68
F	4	(H)	Massachusetts	70	77—
F	7	(A)	New Hampshire	61	63—
F	11	(A)	Providence	71	79—
F	14	(H)	Rhode Island	87	79OT
F	18	(A)	St. Francis (Pa.)	78	83—
F	21	(H)	Georgetown	64	70—
F	28	(H)	Holy Cross	77	82—

WON 9, LOST 17

1976–1977 Coach: Bob Zuffelato
Captain: Jeff Jurgens

N	29	(H)	Maine—Orono	99	87
D	1	(H)	New Hampshire	74	71
D	4	(H)	Harvard	75	71
D	7	(H)	Syracuse	54	67—

Colonial Classic (4th)

D	11	(N)	Providence	67	77—
D	12	(N)	Massachusetts	71	94—
D	18	(A)	St. Joseph's	62	65—

Milwaukee Classic (4th)

D	27	(N)	Wisconsin	66	74—
D	28	(N)	Clemson	76	128—

Pillsbury Classic (3rd)

D	30	(N)	Montana	73	84—
D	31	(N)	Cornell	74	70OT
J	12	(A)	LeMoyne	79	89—
J	15	(A)	Rutgers	92	102—
J	19	(H)	Northeastern	68	66
J	22	(H)	Holy Cross	84	90—
J	25	(A)	Yale	70	64
J	27	(H)	Connecticut	66	83—
J	30	(H)	Villanova	85	89—
F	2	(A)	Massachusetts	69	85—
F	5	(H)	Fordham	77	76OT
F	9	(A)	Rhode Island	58	85—
F	12	(A)	Holy Cross	92	112—
F	15	(H)	Dartmouth	80	74
F	19	(A)	Georgetown	69	87—
F	23	(A)	St. John's	69	92—
F	26	(A)	Fairfield	76	101—

WON 8, LOST 18

1977–1978 Coach: Tom Davis
Captains: Bennifield,
Cobb, Sweeney

N	27	(H)	LeMoyne	99	70
N	30	(A)	New Hampshire	77	87—
D	3	(A)	Harvard	84	70
D	6	(H)	Fairfield	79	76

First Union Invitational (3rd)

D	9	(N)	UNCC	61	79—
D	10	(N)	East Carolina	86	75
D	13	(H)	Stonehill	92	67

All—College Tournament (3rd)

D	27	(N)	Oklahoma City	77	71
D	29	(N)	Arizona State	96	105—
D	30	(N)	Miami of Ohio	81	76
J	4	(H)	St. Joseph's	81	79
J	7	(A)	Villanova	76	102—
J	14	(H)	St. John's	54	76—
J	17	(A)	Northeastern	94	75
J	19	(H)	Merrimack	89	79
J	21	(A)	Dartmouth	73	58
J	24	(A)	Holy Cross	76	82—

Colonial Classic (3rd)

J	27	(N)	Massachusetts	64	84—
J	28	(N)	Connecticut	101	72
F	1	(H)	Georgetown	81	76
F	4	(A)	Fordham	114	93
F	14	(H)	Rhode Island	82	84—
F	19	(A)	Providence	74	92—
F	22	(A)	Connecticut	76	74OT
F	25	(A)	Syracuse	80	97—
F	27	(H)	Holy Cross	98	99—OT

WON 15, LOST 11

1978–1979 Coach: Tom Davis
Captains: Ernie Cobb
& Jim Sweeney

N	27	(H)	Stonehill	89	76
N	30	(H)	Bentley	83	79
D	3	(A)	LeMoyne	93	70
D	6	(H)	Providence	83	64
D	10	(H)	New Hampshire	78	65
D	12	(H)	Vermont	126	89
D	16	(N)	Harvard	86	83
D	21	(A)	St. Mary's (CAL.)	79	81—
D	23	(A)	UCLA	81	103—

Rainbow Classic, Hawaii (5th)

D	28	(N)	Purdue	54	82—
D	29	(N)	Harvard	83	78
D	30	(N)	Tennessee	74	72
J	6	(H)	Northeastern	80	68
J	10	(A)	Rhode Island	78	91—
J	12	(H)	Baltimore	92	72
J	15	(H)	St. Anselm's	95	76
J	17	(H)	Connecticut	78	77
J	20	(H)	Holy Cross	89	87OT
J	23	(H)	Villanova	83	75

Colonial Classic (1st)

J	26	(N)	Massachusetts	82	70
J	27	(N)	Connecticut	78	77
F	3	(H)	Fordham	71	64
F	6	(A)	St. John's	76	85—
F	10	(A)	Holy Cross	96	98—
F	13	(H)	Dartmouth	66	56
F	15	(H)	Merrimack	105	73
F	17	(A)	Georgetown	81	84—
F	21	(H)	Boston University	99	84
F	24	(A)	Fairfield	81	93—

ECAC New England Regionals, Providence, RI

M	1	(N)	Connecticut	74	91—

WON 21, LOST 9

1979–1980 Coach: Tom Davis
Captain: Jim Sweeney

N	30	(H)	Bentley	95	77
D	2	(H)	LeMoyne	86	57
D	4	(H)	Fairfield	77	53
D	11	(A)	Seton Hall	82	61

Industrial National Classic, Providence (3rd)

D	21	(N)	Duke	64	70—OT
D	22	(N)	Stanford	97	89

ECAC Holiday Festival (2nd)

D	26	(N)	Goergetown	75	74OT

D	28	(N)	St. John's	70	78—
J	3	(A)	Villanova	67	86—
J	5	(H)	New Hampshire	97	69
J	7	(H)	Biscayne	107	75
J	10	(A)	Connecticut	71	83—
J	12	(A)	Fordham	60	47
J	16	(H)	St. John's	63	66—
J	19	(H)	Georgia Tech	40	37
J	22	(H)	Rhode Island	65	57
J	24	(H)	Merrimack	87	63
J	26	(H)	Stonehill	89	77
J	30	(H)	Georgetown	92	97—OT

Colonial Classic (1st)

F	1	(N)	Harvard	74	62
F	2	(N)	Holy Cross	92	83
F	5	(H)	Brown	60	49
F	9	(H)	Holy Cross	69	72—
F	16	(A)	Providence	57	55
F	20	(A)	Northeastern	76	67
F	23	(H)	Syracuse	77	85—

The BIG EAST Championships, Providence

F	28	(N)	Connecticut	68	79—

National Invitational Tournament

M	6	(H)	Boston University	95	74
M	10	(A)	Virginia	55	57—

WON 19, LOST 10

1980–1981 Coach: Tom Davis
Captain: Chris Foy

N	30	(H)	Bentley	93	67
D	2	(H)	New Hampshire	72	58
D	6	(H)	Fordham	79	69
D	10	(A)	Brown	70	56
D	13	(A)	Villanova	71	74—

Music City Tournament (1st)

D	29	(N)	Penn State	74	67
D	30	(N)	Vanderbilt	87	72
J	3	(A)	Providence	98	71
J	7	(A)	Vermont	65	56
J	10	(A)	Georgetown	55	57—
J	14	(H)	Connecticut	58	57
J	17	(H)	Merrimack	109	79
J	21	(H)	Syracuse	66	63
J	24	(H)	Seton Hall	72	68OT
J	26	(H)	Villanova	73	60

Colonial Classic (1st)

J	30	(N)	Boston University	57	52
J	31	(N)	Holy Cross	48	43
F	2	(A)	St. John's	71	76—
F	4	(H)	Lowell	114	54

F	7	(A)	Connecticut	76	71
F	11	(H)	Providence	70	55
F	14	(A)	Holy Cross	74	86—
F	18	(H)	Georgetown	53	49
F	21	(H)	St. John's	59	58
F	25	(A)	Syracuse	86	90—
F	28	(H)	Seton Hall	64	57

BIG EAST Tournament

M	5	(N)	Providence	65	67—

NCAA First Round, Tuscaloosa, Al

M	13	(N)	Ball State	93	90
M	15	(N)	Wake Forest	67	64

NCAA Mideast Regional, Bloomington, Ind

M	20	(N)	St. Joseph's	41	42—

WON 23, LOST 7

1981–1982 Coach: Tom Davis

Bentley	86	58
Stonehill	83	67
Villanova	75	97—
Brown	84	69
New Hampshire	82	50
Fairfield	79	73(2 OT)
Virginia Tech	70	75—
Texas Tech	78	84—
Villanova (A)	53	54—
Georgetown (A)	51	67—
Connecticut (A)	58	59—
Providence	62	59
Seton Hall	82	71
Syracuse (A)	80	62
Rhode Island (A)	46	44
Northeastern	87	77
Merrimack	95	59
St. John's	70	71—
Connecticut	59	67—
Providence (A)	78	71
Holy Cross	102	81
Georgetown	80	71
St. John's (A)	90	81
Syracuse	88	77
St. Anselm's	101	45
Seton Hall (A)	92	74
Syracuse	94	92
Villanova	71	74—
San Francisco	70	66
DePaul	82	75
Kansas State	69	65
Houston	92	99—

WON 22, LOST 10

BASKETBALL COACHING RECORDS

COACH	—SEASONS—		W	L	PCT
William Coady	1922–25	4	21	21	.500
Bob Cousy	1963–69	6	117	38	.755
James Crowley	1907	1	1	3	.250
Chuck Daly	1969–71	2	26	24	.520
Tom Davis	1977–	4	78	37	.678
Higgins	1906	1	7	18	.280
Don Martin	1954–62	9	110	103	.516
Al McClellan	1946–53	8	83	81	.506
Rev. McNally, S.J.	1917	1	2	3	.400
Frank Power	1962–63	1	10	16	.385
Luke Urban	1920–21	2	14	8	.636
Bob Zuffelato	1971–77	6	83	80	.509
unknown	1905, 1911	2	8	12	.400

Major and Minor Sports Letterwinners

BOSTON COLLEGE LETTERWINNERS: FOOTBALL

1893

Edward Almeida, Frederick Beering, Stephen Bergin, John Brewin, Frank Brick, John Carey, Frank Carney, Timothy Collins, Frank Crawford, Owen Davis, Robert Does, Joseph Drum, Maurice Flynn, Albert Gleason, Edward Moore, Edward Murphy, Albert Macdonald, John McCusker, John Prendergast, Charles Reade, Timothy Sweeney, Bernard Wefers (Captain), Michael White.

1894

John Brewin, Frank Brick, Frank Carney, Joseph Collins, Robert Croker, Owen Davis, Herman Dierkas, Robert Does, Maurice Flynn (Captain), Joseph Gary, Albert Gleason, Harry Grainger, James Laudrigan, Edward Moore, Edward Murphy, Albert Macdonald, Joseph McGarry, John Prendergast, Timothy Sweeney, Joseph Walsh, Arthur White, Joseph Williams, Edward Grainger, Charles Reade.

1895

John Brewin (Captain), Frank Brick, James Cahill, Frank Carney, Robert Croker, Owen Davis, Herman Dierkes, Robert Does, Maurice Flynn, Albert Gleason, Thomas Grady, Edward Grainger, Harry Grainger, William Holland, James Landrigan, William Long, John Merill, Edward Moore, Edward Murphy, Albert Macdonald, John Prendergast, Charles Reade, Timothy Sweeney, Thomas Vahey, Joseph Walsh, Arthur White, John Winslow.

1896

John Brewin, Frank Brick, James Cahill, Robert Croker. Thomas Grady, Edward Grainger, William Holland, William Kelliher, James Landrigan, William Long, William Lyons, Benjamin Merrill, John Merrill, Albert Macdonald, Hugh McGrath, James O'Connell, John Prendergast, Edward Ryan, Thomas Vahey, Joseph Walsh (Captain), Arthur White.

1897

Benjamin Bowles, James Cahill, Robert Croker, Thomas Grady, Edward Grainger, Harry Grainger, William Holland, John Hurley, William Kelliher, Charles Kiley, William Koen, James Landrigan, William Long, Dennis Maguire, Frank Martin, Benjamin Merrill, John McDermott, Hugh McGrath, James O'Connell, Edward Ryan, Joseph Walsh, Arthur White (Captain).

1898

James Hart, William Holland, William Kelliher, John Kelley, Joseph Kenney, Charles Kiley, William Koen (Captain), William Long, Timothy Murphy, Humphrey McCarron, John McDermott, Hugh McGrath, James O'Connell, Daniel O'Connor, Joseph Reilly, Charles Richards, Alexander Rorke, Patrick Sullivan, William Toohig.

1899

James Hart, William Kelliher, John Kelly, Joseph Kenney, Charles Kiley (Captain), William Koen, Timothy Murphy, Humphrey McCarron, William McCarthy, Cornelius McCusker, John McCusker, John McDermott, Frank McGrath, Hugh McGrath, Daniel O'Connor, Joseph Reilly, Charles Richards, Alexander Rorke, William Sheehan, John Sullivan, Patrick Sullivan.

1900: No Team

1901

William Chesterman, Herman Cramer, Walter Fogarty, Thomas Foley, John Ford, James Kendrigan, Joseph Kenney (Captain), William Koen, Fred Lafferty, John Lane, Daniel Lucey, Timothy Murphy, Charles McCarthy, Cornelius McCusker, John McCusker, John McDermott, John Riley, Alexander Rorke, Patrick Sullivan.

1902

Herman Cramer, Drowley, Fitzpatrick, John Greene, Joseph Kenney, Henry Lang, Leary, Daniel Lucey, Cornelius McCusker, John McCusker, John Riley, John Rodina, Patrick Sullivan (Captain), Michael Sweeney, Edward Tevlan, Geoffrey Whalen.

1903–1907: No Team

1908

William Bailey, John Churchward, Frank Cummings, Matthew Doyle, Thomas Fitzpatrick, Patrick Flaherty, Florence Gillis, Vincent Greene, Francis Harrington, Edward Hartigan, Joseph Lynch, Walter O'Keefe, Thomas Parle, George Pearce (Captain), Edward Ryan, Leo Supple, Henry Tatton, James Welch.

1909

William Bailey, James Barron, John Churchward, Frank Cummings, John Donahue, Matthew Doyle, Aloysius Finn, Patrick Flaherty, Florence Gillis, Vincent Greene, Francis Harrington, Edward Hartigan, Martin Hunt, Daniel Hurld, George Leonard, Joseph Lynch, George Pearce (Captain), Edward Ryan, Thomas Shaughnessy, Leo Supple, James Welch.

1910

James Barron, John Churchward, Frank Cummings, William Dacey, Patrick Dawson, Frederick Doyle, Matthew Doyle, Matthew Duggan, Aloysius Finn, Patrick Flaherty, James Gallagher, Florence Gillis, Vincent Greene, Henry Halligan, Edward Hartigan (Captain), Henry Hartigan, Irving Heath, Leslie Heath, Walter Hickey, Martin Hunt, Daniel Hurld, George Leonard, Thomas McIntyre, O'Brien, Martin O'Connor, George Tattan, James Welch.

1911

Edmund Brandon, James Brennan, John Burke, Patrick Dawson, Frederick Fallon, Aloysius Finn, George Fitzgerald, James Gallagher, Ernest Gioiosa, Henry Halligan, John Hartigan (Co-Captain), Thomas Heagney, Irving Heath, Leslie Heath, Walter Hickey, Daniel Hurld (Co-Captain), James Linnehan, Charles Mahoney, Walter Mullan, Peter McGrath, Martin O'Connor, Robert O'Keefe, Richard Rogers, George Tattan, Robert White.

1912

Edmund Brandon, James Brennan, John Burke, George Casey, Lawrence Conley, Leo Daley, Patrick Dawson, James Duffy, Frederick Fallon, George Fitzgerald, William Fleming, James Gallagher, Thomas Gavin, John Hartigan (Captain), Roy Heffernan, Daniel Hurld, Charles Hurley, John Keohane, Edward Killion, James Linnehan, William McCarthy, Peter McGrath, Daniel O'Connor, Martin O'Connor, Robert O'Keefe, Frank Roche, Frank Rogers, Richard Rogers, Joseph Sheehan, Frank Woods.

1913

Edmund Brandon, James Brennan, John Burke, Leonard Carolan, George Casey, Thomas Cronin, Leo Daley (Captain), Patrick Dawson, Joseph Dee, James Drummey, James Duffy, John Fitzgerald, William Fleming, Thomas Gavin, Charles Hurley, George Kenney, John Keohane, Edward Killion, James Linnehan, George Meehan, George MacDonald, Daniel McKnight, William McCarthy, Peter McGrath, Daniel O'Connor, Frank Roche, John Rogers, John Sullivan, John Wall.

1914

Alex Anderson, Edmund Brandon, John Burke, George Casey, Roger Conway, Thomas Cronin, Leo Daley, Joseph Dee, James Duffy, Maurice Dullea, Charles Fitzgerald, John Fitzgerald, Stephen Fitzgerald, William Fleming, Thomas Gavin, John Kirk, James Linnehan (Captain), John Maloney, Vincent Murray, William McCarthy, John McCarty, Francis McKenna, James Regan, Frank Roche, James Rooney, John Sullivan, Thomas Twetchell.

1915

Edward Austin, Francis Bowen, Charles Brady, Roger Conboy, Thomas Craven, Joseph Curry, Leo Daley, Joseph Dee, Thomas Dee, James Duffy (Captain), Maurice Dullea, Walter Falvey, Charles Fitzgerald, Stephen Fitzgerald, William Fleming, Jon Kirk, John Lowney, Bennett Murray, Vincent Murray, John McCarty, Francis McKenna, Joseph McKenzie, Robert O'Brien, James Regan, James Rooney, Henry Tonry, Francis Wall.

1916

Edward Austin, Joseph Brickley, Michael Callahan, Walter Collins, Robert Curley, Joseph Curry, William Davidson, Thomas Dee, Maurice Dullea (Captain), Walter Falvey, Charles Fitzgerald, James Fitzpatrick, Edward Foy, Edward Grabowski, Frank Hanlon, Frank Harrigan, John Kirk, John Lowney, John Lyons, James Morrissey, Bennett Murray, Vincent Murray, John McCarty, Francis McKenna, Joseph McKenzie, John McNamara, Robert O'Brien, Thomas Scanlan, John Shea, John Sullivan, Charles Tierney, Raymond Trowbridge, Louis Urban, Christopher Vachon, Joseph White.

1917

Hugh Bond, William Cashin, Walter Collins, Philip Corrigan, Joseph Curry, Thomas Dee, Walter Falvey, Charles Fitzgerald (Captain), James Fitzpatrick, Edward Foy, Clarence Halloran, Frank Hannon, Leroy Higginson, Frank Horrigan, John Kirk, John Lyons, Edward Madden, Frank Morrissey, James Morrissey, Bennett Murray, John McNamara, William Niland, John Ring, Paul Ryan, Thomas Scanlan, John Shea, John Sheehan, Louis Smith, John Sullivan, Carl Swanson, Louis Urban, George White, George T. White, Joseph White.

1918

Francis Bowler, John Brawley, William Bridges, Charles Brophy, Walter Collins, John Connell, Philip Corrigan, James Crowley, Arthur Cusick, James Doyle, Edward Egan, Patrick Egan, Norman Fermoyle, Patrick Flaherty, Raymond Gent, Frank Hannon, Matthew Heaphy, John Lyons, Frank Morrissey (Captain), James Morrissey, George Mullen, Leo McElaney, Frank Ryan, Paul Ryan, Thomas Swan, George Young.

1919

Walter Comerford, Philip Corrigan, James Doyle, James Fitzpatrick, Edward Foy, Clarence Halloran, John Heaphy, Matthew Heaphy, Leo Hughes, William Kelleher, George Kelley, Walter La Plante, John Lyons, Edward Madden, Joseph Meredith, Frank Morrissey, David Mullen, John McClokey, Leo McElaney, Cornelius O'Brien, Nelson O'Brien, John Ring, Paul Ryan, John Sheehan, Louis Smith, Thomas Swan, Louis Urban, Joseph White.

1920

Walter Comerford, Philip Corrigan, James Doyle, Raymond Duffy, Lemuel Dunbar, James Fitzpatrick, Edward Foy, John Heaphy, William Kelleher, George Kelly, James Kennedy, James Liston, Walter Matthews, Joseph Meredith, Frank Morrissey, David Mullen, John McCloskey, Charles McGahan, Cornelius O'Brien, Nelson O'Brien, Benjamin Roderick, Thomas Swan, Herbert Treat, Louis Urban (Captain), Frank Wilson.

1921

John Beaver, Walter Comerford (Captain), John Corcoran, Charles Darling, Charles Donnelian, George Dowd, James Doyle, William Doyle, Raymond Duffy, Francis Elbery, James Foley, James Hickey, Leo Hughes, William Kelleher, George Kelley, John Keohane, Joseph Kozlowsky, James Liston, Walter Matthews, William Melley, Joseph Meredith, Arthur McManus, Nelson O'Brien, Raymond Paton, Stephen Patten, Edward Phillips, John Pyne, John Reardon, Allen Smullen, Frank Wilson.

1922

Joseph Aleckna, John Beaver, Frank Colbert, Walter Comerford, John Corcoran, William Crean, William Cronin, Charles Darling, John Donahue, Charles Donnellan, George Dowd, William Doyle, Raymond Duffy, Francis Elbery, James Foley, Edward Harrison, John Heaphy, James Hickey, Leo Hughes, Arthur Johnson, William Kelleher (Captain), John Keahane, Stephen Koholinski, Joseph Kozlowski, Walter Matthews, William Molloy, William McManus, Grattan O'Connell, Albert O'Neal, Raymond Paton, Stephen Patten, Edward Philips, John Reardon, Harold Ward, Frank Wilson.

1923

John Beaver, Frank Colbert, Frank Corcoran, William Crean, John Cronin, William Cronin, Charles Darling (Captain), John Donahue, Charles Donnellan, George Dowd, William Doyle, Raymond Duffy, Lemuel Dunbar, Francis Elbery, Edward Harrison, Edward Hickey, Leo Hughes, Arthur Johnson, John Keahane, Stephen Kobolinski, Joseph Kozlowski, Philip Larkin, Daniel Linehan, Walter Matthews, William Melley, Owen Murphy, Joseph McKenney, Arthur McManus, John McNamara, Thomas O'Brien, Grattan O'Connell, William Ohrenberger, Albert O'Neal, Stephen Patten, John Reardon, Frank Sullivan, Harold Ward, Frank Wilson.

1924

Joseph Aleckna, Frank Colbert, William Crean, John Cronin, William Cronin, Charles Darling, David Dillon, John Donahue, Francis Dower, William Doyle, Albert Dumas, Lemuel Dunbar, Michael Durant, Francis Elbery, Joseph Fitzgerald, Thomas Gemelli, William Green, Richard Hardy, Edward Harrison, James Higgins, Arthur Johnson, John Keahane, Stephen Kobolinski, Joseph Kozlowski (Captain), Philip Larkin, James Logue, Anthony Martin, William Melley, Owen Murphy, Joseph McKenney, Arthur McManus, Fred McMenimen, John McNamara, Thomas O'Brien, Grattan O'Connell, William Ohrenberger, Albert O'Neal, Stephen Patten, John Reardon, Frank Sullivan, Harold Ward, Martin Whelan, John Kelleher.

1925

Joseph Aleckna, Irwin Beach, John E. Clinton, Frank Colbert, William Crean, Patrick Creeden, John Cronin, William Cronin, David Dillon, Edward Donahue, John Donahue (Captain), Francis Dower, Albert Dumas, Michael Durant, Joseph Fitzgerald, Thomas Gemelli, William Green, William Hafferty, Richard Hardy, Edward

Harrison, James Hickey, James Higgins, John Kennedy, Bernard Kilroy, John Kilroy, Stephen Kobolinski, Philip Larkin, James Logue, John Mahoney, Anthony Martin, Joseph Mirley, Owen Murphy, Warren McGuirk, Joseph McKenney, Fred McMenimen, John McNamara, Grattan O'Connell, William Ohrenberger, Albert O'Neal, Donald Sheehan, Thomas Smith, Frank Sullivan, Alfred Weston, Martin Whelan, George Wilczewski, John Kelleher.

1926

Joseph Aleckna, Irwin Beach, Edward Bond, John E. Clinton, Francis Corcorochio, Patrick Creeden, John Cronin, David Dillon, Edward Donahue, Francis Dower, Bernard Duffy, Albert Dumas, Michael Durant, Joseph Fitzgerald, Thomas Gemelli, Richard Gorman, William Green, William Hafferty, Richard Hardy, Maurice Harris, Edward Herman, James Higgins, John Kennedy, Bernard Kilroy, John Kilroy, Philip Larkin, Mortimer Lenane, James Logue, Frank Lyons, John Mahoney, Anthony Martin, Warren McGuirk, Joseph McKenney (Captain), Fred McMenimen, John McNamara, Thomas O'Brien, William Ohrenberger, Donald Sheehan, Thomas Smith, Frank Sullivan, Alfred Weston, Martin Whelan, George Wilczewski, John Kelleher.

1927

Irwin Beach, Edward Bond, John E. Clinton, John Convery, Francis Corcorochin, Patrick Creeden, David Dillon, John Divenati, Edward Donahue, Francis Dower, Bernard Duffy, Michael Durant, Joseph Fitzgerald, Thomas Gemelli, Richard Gorman, William Green, William Hafferty, Edward Herman, John Kennedy, Bernard Kilroy, John Kilroy, Mortimer Lanane, James Logue, Frank Lyons, John Mahoney, Joseph Mirley, Charles Murphy, Warren McGuirk, Fred McMenimen, Thomas O'Brien (Captain), Donald Sheehan, Thomas Smith, Alfred Weston, George Wilczewski, John Kelleher.

1928

Edward Aaron, Anders Anderson, Ceslaus Antos, Edward Bond, Austin Brosnan, Henry Buckley, James Cochrane, George Colbert, John Convery, Arthur Conway, Francis Corcorachio, Patrick Creeden, Michael Curran, Frank DiPesa, John Divenuti, John Dixon, Edward Donahue, Bernard Duffy, Edward Gibbons, Richard Gorman, William Hafferty, Edward Herman, Thomas Horne, John Kennedy, Bernard Kilroy, John Kilroy, Frank Lyons, John Mahoney, Ralph Mallet, John Marr, George Mason, Joseph Mirley, Albert Morelli, Charles Murphy, Joseph McDonald, Warren McGuirk (Captain), Edward O'Brien, Thomas O'Brien, George O'Connell, Henry Plausse, Alvin Ricci, Joseph Shea, Donald Sheehan, Thomas Smith, Joseph Sullivan, Michael Vadoklys, Alfred Weston, Martin Whelan, George Wilczewski, John Young.

1929

Edward Aaron, Anders Anderson, Ceslaus Antos, William Bennett, Edward Bond, Austin Brosnan, Henry Buckley, Daniel Cahill, Charles Callery, James Cochrane, George Colbert, John Convery, Arthur Conway, Francis Corcorachio, Michael Curran, Peter Davis, Frank DiPesa, John Divenuti, John Dixon, Henry Downes, C. Flynn Fraser, Charles Frazer, Edward Gallagher, Edward Gibbons, Bertram Gleason, James Heggis, Edward Herman, Thomas Horne, Joseph Kelley, William Kelly, Daniel Larkin, Ralph Mallet, John Marr, George Mason, Fred Meier, Joseph Mirley, John Maloney, Albert Morelli, Charles Murphy, Joseph McDonald, Thomas O'Brien, George O'Connell, Henry Plausse, Paul Raftery, Alvin Ricci, Emil Romanowski, Joseph Shea, Edward Stewart, Joseph Sullivan, Michael Vadoklys, Bartholomew Welch, John Young.

1930

Edward Aaron, Anders Anderson, Ceslaus Antos, William Bennett, John Brennan, Henry Buckley, Daniel Cahill, Raymond Callen, Charles Callery, Peter Chesnulevich, James Cochrane, George Colbert, John Warren, Arthur Conway, Philip Couhig, Michael Curran, Christopher Cutler, Peter Davis, Frank DiPesa, John Divenuti, John Dixon (Captain), Henry Downes, Glynn Fraser, Edward Gallagher, Edward Gibbons, Richard Gorman, James Heggis, Thomas Horne, Joseph Kelley, Daniel Larkin, Ralph Mallet, John Marr, George Mason, Fred Meir, John Maloney, Albert Morelli, Louis Musco, Thomas O'Brien, George O'Connell, Matthias O'Malley, Joseph Orlanski, Paul Raftery, Richard Reynolds, Alvin Ricci, Marco Romano, Emil Romanowski, Joseph Ryder, Joseph Shea, Edward Stewart, Joseph McDonald, John Niedziocha, Joseph Sullivan, Flavio Tosi, Michael Vadoklys, George Taylor, Bartholomew Welch, Maurice Whalen, John Young.

1931

William Bennett, Thomas Blake, William Boehner, John Brennan, Daniel Cahill, Raymond Callen, Charles Callery, William Carr, Peter Chesnulevich, Matthew Connolly, Philip Couhig, Christopher Cutler, Peter David, Charles Donohue, John Dougan, Henry Downes, Alphonse Ezmunt, Glynn Fraser, Charles Frazer, John Frectos, Edward Gallagher, Bertrom Gleason, Raymond Harrington, James Heggis, Stanley Jundzil, Edward Kelley, Joseph Kelley (Captain) Walter Kelley, Joseph Killilea, Daniel Larkin, James Lillis, Frank Maloney, Fred Meir, John Maloney, Louis Musco, John Niedziocha, Matthias O'Malley, Robert Ott, Henry Plausse, Harold Ramsey, Richard Reynold, Mario Romano, Emil Romanowski, Joseph Ryder, Gerald Slamin, Edward Stewart, Gregory Sullivan, George Taylor, John Warren, Maurice Whalen.

1932

Edward Anderson, Thomas Blake, William Boehner, John Brennan, Raymond Collin, William Carr, Peter Chesnulevich, Matthew Connolly, Gordon Connor, David Couhig. Philip Couhig (Captain), David Cowhig, Joseph Curran, Robert Curran, Christopher Cutler, Charles Donohoe, Paul Donohoe, John Dougan, William Duffy, Alphonse Ezmunt, John Freitas, Bertram Gleason, Raymond Harrington, Stanley Jundzil, Edward Kelley, Joseph Killilea, James Lillis, Alfred Luppi, Frank Maloney, Bernard Moynahan, Louis Musco, John Neidziocha, Edward O'Brien, Henry Ohrenberger, Matthias O'Malley, Joseph Orloski, Robert Ott, Richard Reynolds, Mario Romano, Joseph Ryder, Gerald Slamin, Gregory Sullivan, George Taylor, Flavio Tosi, John Warren, Maurice Whalen, Randolph Wise.

1933

Edward Anderson, Earl Avery, Thomas Blake, Thomas Brennan, William Carr, Gordon Connor, David Couhig, David Cowhig, Joseph Curran, Robert Curran, Paul Donohoe, John Dougan, Edward Driscoll, William Duffy, Alphonse Ezmunt, William Fenlow, Paul Flaherty, John Freitas, Edward Furbush, Theodore Galligan, Raymond Harrington, Stanley Jundzil, Edward Kelley, Joseph Killilea, James Lillis, Alfred Luppi, Frank Maloney (Captain), Fred Moore, Bernard Moynahan, Edward O'Brien, Henry Ohrenberger, Joseph Oliaski, Robert Ott, Neal Owens, Harold Ramsey, William Ryan, Gerald Slamin, Gregory Sullivan, Flavio Tosi, Dimitri Zaitz.

1934

Edward Anderson, Earl Avery, Thomas Brennan, Robert Cash, John Conlon, David Couhig (Captain), David Cowhig, Joseph Curran, Robert Curran, Nicholas Dergay, Andrew Dominick, Paul Donohoe, Edward Driscoll, William Duffy, William Fenlon, Atilio Ferdenzi, Paul Flaherty, Edward Furbush, Theodore Galligan, Oscoe Gilman, William Hurley, Joseph Keaney, Vincent Keough, Alfred Luppi, George Mahoney, Fred Moore, Bernard Moynahan, Edward O'Brien, Joseph O'Brien, Henry Ohrenberger, Neal Owens, Alexander Pszenny, William Ryan, Peter Shannon, Paul Sweeney, Paul Toomey, Albert Tortolini, Joseph Walsh, Dimitri Zaitz.

1935

Arthur Allen, Earl Avery, Hugo Blandari, Thomas Brennan, Walter Bryan, Thomas Buckeley, James Cahill, Robert Cash, Henry Chiarini, John Conlan, Nicholas Dergay, Anthony DiNatale, Andrew Dominick, Edward Driscoll, William Fenlon, Atilio Ferdenzi, Paul Flaherty, Edward Furbush, Theodore Galligan, Oscoe Gilman, Thomas Guinea, William Hurley, John Janusas, Joseph Keaney, Vincent Keough, John Killion, James Kissell, Jan Kozlowsky, Walter Lepeisha, George Mahoney, Fred Moore, John Morris, Joseph O'Brien (Captain), Thomas G. O'Callaghan, Neal Owens, Raymoned Perrault, Alexander Pszenny, William Ryan, Peter Shannon, Paul Sweeney, Paul Toomey, Albert Tortolini, Joseph Walsh, Dimitri Zaitz.

1936

Arthur Allen, Andrew Bismarck, Hugo Blandori, Walter Bryan, Thomas Buckeley, James Cahill, Robert Cash, Henry Chiarini, John Conlon, Frank Connelly, John Connolly, Richard Cummings Nicholas Dergay, Anthony DiNatale, Andrew Dominick, Atilio Ferdenzi, William Flynn, Oscoe Gilman, Fella Gintoff, Thomas Guinea, William Holland, Albert Horsfall, William Hurley, John Janusas, Ira Jivilikian, Joseph Keaney, Vincent Keough, John Killion, James Kissell, Jan Kozlowski, Andrew Lentini, Walter Lepeisha, George Mahoney, John Morris, John Murphy, John Murray, Daniel McFadden, Joseph O'Brien, Thomas O'Callaghan, Raymond Perrault, Alexander Pszenny (Captain), Peter Shannon, Paul Sweeney, Paul Toomey, Albert Tortolini, Joseph Walsh, Ralph Worth.

1937

Arthur Allen, Vito Ananis, Roger Battles, Andrew Bismarck, Hugo Blandari, Walter Bryan, Thomas Buckley, James Byrne, James Cahill, Henry Chiarini, Peter Cignetti, Frank Connelly, John Connolly, Richard Cummings, Anthony DiNatale (Captain), James Fitzgerald, William Flynn, Fella Gintoff, Thomas Guinea, Richard Harrison, William Holland, Albert Horsfall, John Janusas, Ira Jivilikian, Louis Kedhart, John Killion, James Kissell, Jan Kozlowski, Andrew Lentini, Walter Lepeisha, David Lucey, John Morris, John Murphy, John Murray, Charles McCarthy, Daniel McFadden, Thomas O'Callaghan, Raymond Perrault, Leo Reardon, George Ryan, Ernest Schwotzer, Edward Swenson, Ralph Worth.

1938

Arthur Allen, Vito Ananis, Roger Battles, Andrew Bismarck, James Byrne, Peter Cignetti, Frank Connelly, John Connolly, Edward Cowhig, Richard Cummings, James Fitzgerald, William Flynn (Captain), Frank Galvani, Fella Gintoff, Chester Gladchuck, Eugene Goodreault, William Griffin, Richard Harrison, William Holland, Albert Horsfall, Ira Jivilikian, George Kerr, Louis Kidhardt, Andrew Lentini, David Lucey, Alexander Lukachik, Thomas Mahon, Joseph Manzo, Louis Montogmery, John Murphy, John Murray, Charles McCarthy, Daniel McFadden, Charles O'Rourke, Thomas Powers, Leo Reardon, George Ryan, Ernest Schwotzer, Edward Swenson, Anthony Tassinari, Henry Toczylowski, David White, Henry Woronicz, Ralph Worth, John Yauckoes, Joseph Zabilski.

1939

Vito Ananis, James Byrne, Peter Cignetti, Ronald Corbette, Edward Cowhig, Frank Davis, James Fitzgerald, Frank Galvani, Terrence Geoghegan, Chester Gladchuck, Eugene Goodreault, William Griffin, Richard Harrison, Robert Jauron, George Kerr, Louis Kidhardt, Adolph Kissell, Steven Levinitis, David Lucey, Alex Lukachick, Joseph Mahon, Francis Maznicki, Louis Montgomery, Alfred Morro, Charles McCarthy, Justin McGowan, Charles O'Rourke, Adolph Pasink, Thomas Powers, George Ryan, Ernest Schwotzer (Captain), Leo Strumski, Edward Swenson, Anthony Tassinari, Henry Toczylowski, David White, John Yauckoes, Edward Zabilski, Joseph Zabilski.

1940

Walter Boudreau, Rocco Canale, Harry Connolly, Ronald Corbett, Donald Currivan, Frank Davis, Albert Fiorentino, Frank Galvani, Terrence Geoghegan, Chester Gladchuck, Eugene Goodreault, William Griffin, Michael Holovak, Robert Jauron, George Kerr, Adolph Kissell, Steven Levinitis, Carl Lucas, Alex Lukachick, Thomas Mahon, Joseph Manzo, Francis Maznicki, Louis Montgomery, Thomas Moran, Alfred Morro, Justin McGowan, Ralph Nash, Fred Naumetz, Charles O'Rourke, Adolph Pasink, Thomas Powers, Joseph Repko, Leo Strumski, Anthony Tassinari, Henry Toczylowski (Captain) David White, Theodore Williams, Henry Woronicz, John Yauckoes, Edward Zabilski, Joseph Zabilski.

1941

James Benedetto, Lindon Blanchard, Walter Boudreau, Gilbert Bouley, Rocco Canale, William Connery, Harry Connolly, Donald Currivan, Pasquale Darone, Edward Doherty, John Dubzinski, Albert Fiorentino, Charles Furbush, Terrence Geoghegan, Michael Holovak, Robert Jauron, Joseph King, Adolph Kissell, Edward Lambert, Steven Levanitis, Carl Lucas, Edward Mahoney, Francis Maznicki, Thomas Moran, Alfred Morro (Captain), Justin McGowan, Ralph Nash, Fred Naumetz, Angelo Nicketakis, Peter Prezekop, William Quinn, Joseph Repko, Angelo Sisti, Leo Strumski, Albert Twoomey, Theodore Williams, Henry Woronicz, Edward Zabilski.

1942

Walter Boudreau, Gilbert Bouley, Laurent Bouley, William Boyce, Thomas Brennan, Edward Burns, Rocco Canale, Howard Chisholm, William Commane, William Connery, Harry Connolly, Donald Currivan, Pasquale Darone, Edward Doherty, John Dubzinski, Albert Fiorentino, Edward Fiorentino, Charles Furbush, John Furey, Mario Giannelli, Michael Holovak (Co-Captain), John Killilea, Joseph King, John Kissell, Edward Lambert, Bernard Lanoue, Chester Lipka, Carl Lucas, Robert, Mangene, Fred Naumetz (Co-Captain), Victor Palladino, Peter Prezekop, Joseph Repko, Angelo Sisti, Joseph Tobin, Emmanuel Zissis.

1943

David Aznovoorian, Peter Baleyko, Kevin Burke, James Cahill, Robert Campbell, Edward Doherty (Captain), George Donelan, Walter Fitzgerald, Albert Gould, David Hoar, James Lennon, William Morro, William McCarthy, William S. McCarthy, Charles McCoy, Hugh O'Brien, Francis Panaro, Alfred Peters, Donald Shea, Stanley Tomozewski.

1944

Peter Baleyko, Burt Barrett, John Callahan, Thomas Carney, James Casey, Brendan Conway, Thomas Daily, George Donelan, Thomas Eden, Joseph Elliott, Charles Englett, Edward Fredenzi, William Ferguson, Mario Fortunato, John Griffin, William Hogan, Paul Kelley, Edmund Kehoe, Robert Lawier, William McCarthy, Paul Murphy, Robert Owens, John Rabbett, Eugene Ratto, William Reardon, Louis Sammartino,. Robert Schoenfield, Thomas Seymour, C. Sullivan, Thomas Sullivan, Albert Twomey, Edward Walsh.

1945

Charles Bennett, Thomas Carney, James Casey, Cosmo Caterino, Silvio Conte, Edward Cronin, William DeRosa, George Donelan, Thomas Eden, Joseph Elliott, William English, Edward Ferdenzi, John Graham, Stephen Helstowski, Peter Kalafatas, Eugene Kevit, Edward King, Joseph King, Thomas Lamb, Robert Lawler, Armond Longval, John Maloney, James McMorrow, Henry Michaelewicz, Louis Mroz, Paul Murphy, John Muse, Eugene Nash, John O'Donnell, Robert Owens, Victor Palladino, Henry Pelletier, John Queenan, Matthew Ruggiero, Louis Sammartino, Veto Stasunas, Edward Sullivan, Louis Sullivan, Albert Twomey.

1946

James Benedetto, Thomas Brennan, Edward Burns, Anthony Cannava, Arthur Cesario, Robert Chouinard, Edward Clasby, Pasquale Darone, Wilfred DeRosa, Joseph Diminick, Arthur Donovan, John Farrell, John Furey, Mario Gianelli, Albert Gould, Edward Kennedy, John Killelea, Edward King, Joseph King, John Kissell, Joseph Kulis, Bernard Lanoue, Chester Lipka, Robert Mangene, Angelo Nicketakis, Robert Palladino, Victor Palladino, Donald Panciera, Dominic Papaleo, Maurice Poissant, William Quinn, Angelo Sisti, Alfred Songin, Arthur Spinney, Ernest Stautner, Albert Twomey, Emmanuel Zissis.

1947

James Benedetto, Walter Boverini, Thomas Brennan, Anthony Cannava, Richard Caruso, Arthur Cesario, Robert Chouinard, Edward Clasby, Wilfrd DeRosa, Joseph Diminick, Arthur Donovan. John Farrell, John Furey, James Gallagher, Mario Giannelli, Benjamin Giordano, Stanley Goode, Albert Gould, Kenneth Hughes, Edward Kennedy, Edward King, John Kissell, Joseph Kulis, Bernard Lanoue, Chester Lipka, William McCarthy, William Morro, Alfred Murray, Angelo Nicketakis (Captain), Roy Norden, George Osganian, Robert Palladino, Victor Palladino, Dominic Papaleo, Maurice Poissant, Armando Provitola, Eugene Ratto, John Ring, Alfred Songin, Arthur Spinney, Ernest Stautner, Stephen Stuka, Edward Walsh, Matthew Walsh, John Wisniewski.

1948

Walter Boverini, Thomas Brennan, Anthony Cannava, Robert Chouinard, Edward Clasby, Philip Coen, Sahag Dekagian (Manager), Albert DeRobbio, Wilfred DeRosa, Joseph Diminick, Arthur Donovan, John Farrell, Leonard Flaherty, John Furey (Captain), Stanley Goode, Albert Gould, Joseph Gould, John Harbison, Kenneth Hughes, Edward Kennedy, Joseph Kulis, Bernard Lanoue, Chester Lipka, William Malloy, William McCarthy, Alfred Murray, Roy Norden, George Osganian, Robert Palladino, Dominic Papaleo, Maurice Poissant, John Ring, Edward Songin, Arthur Spinney, Ernest Stautner, Stephen Stuka.

1949

Walter Boverini, Anthony Cannava, Robert Chouinard, Edward Clasby, Philip Coen, Francis Cousineau, Joseph Diminick, Arthur Donovan, John Farrell, Leonard Flaherty, Stanley Goode, Albert Gould, Joseph Gould, John Harbison, Kenneth Hughes, Michael LaRocco, William Malloy, William McCarthy, Douglas Millette, Alfred Murray, Roy Norden, Robert Palladino, Dominic Papaleo, James Parsons, Edward Petela, Charles Pinette, Maurice Poissant, John Ring, Michael Roarke, William Scholz, Edward Songin, Arthur Spinney (Captain), Anthony Stathopoulos, Ernest Stautner, George Tarasovich, John Wisniewski.

1950

Pasquale Cacace, Robert Callahan, Philip Coen (Captain), Joseph Coffey, Robert Cote, Roy Delaney, Albert DeRobbio, Michael Doohan, John Doran, Joseph Gould, John Harbison, Leo Kraunelis, Henry Maznicki, Richard McBride, John McCauley, John McKinnon, Michael Mikulics, Douglas Millette, Miles Murphy, Henry O'Brien, Paul O'Brien, James Parsons, Edward Petela, Charles Pinette, George Pollinger, John Quinlan, Robert Richards, Michael Roarke, Alfred Schmitz, Thomas Seymour, Anthony Stathopoulos, Daniel Sullivan, John Sullivan, Francis Tanner, John Toppa, Edward Wall.

1951

Joseph Ahearn, Robert Baggett, Daniel Brosnahan, Pasquale Cacace, Robert Callahan, Richard Charlton, Joseph Coffey, Robert Cote, Charles Crowley, Michael Doohan, John Doran, William Emmons, Robert Flanagan, John Irwin, Thomas Izbicki, Joseph Johnson, James Kane, Richard McBride, John McCauley, John McKinnon, John Miller, Michael Mikulics, Donald Morgan, Frank Morze, Richard Nicolo, Henry O'Brien, Charles Pinette, John Parker, George Pollinger, Robert Richards, Michael Roarke (Captain), Gilbert Rocha, Alfred Schmitz, Anthony Stathopoulos, John Sullivan, Paul Sullivan, Thomas Sullivan, John Toppa, Edward Wall, Richard Zotti.

1952

Joseph Ahearn, Robert Baggett, Daniel Brosnahan, Pasquale Cacace, Richard Chartlton, Joseph Coffey. James Coghlin, Robert Cote, Michael Doohan, William Emmons, Robert Flanagan, Louis Florio, Harold Hanewich, John Irwin, Thomas Izbicki, Joseph Johnson, James Kane, David Keelan, Francis Marr, Joseph Mattaliano, John McCauley, John McKinnon, Michael Mikulics, Donald Morgan, Frank Morze, Henry O'Brien, John Parker, George Pollinger, Gilbert Rocha, Harry Stathopoulos, William Stuka, Francis Tanner, John Toppa (Captain), Eward Wall, Richard Zotti.

1953

Leonard Andrusaitis, Robert Baggett, Daniel Brosnahan, Richard Charlton, James Coghlin, Paul Craig, Edward DeSilva, Emerson Dickie, Louis Florio, Francis Furey, Richard Gagliardi, Harold Hanewich, Joseph Hines, John Irwin, Thomas Izbicki, Joseph Johnson (Captain), James Kane, George Lovett, Thomas Magnarelli, Francis Marr, Joseph Mattaliano, Dorick Mauro, John McDonnell, John Miller, Frank Morze, Richard Myles, John Parker, Richard Pearce, Clifford Poirier, Emiddio Petrarca, John Regan, Gilbert Rocha, Alvini St. Pierre, William Stuka, Richard Zotti.

1954

Leonard Andrusaitis, Valentino Bertolini, James Coghlin, Francis Cousineau, Edward DeSilva, Emerson Dickie, John Doherty, William Donlan, Francis Furey, Richart Gagliardi, Harold Hanewich Joseph Hines, Thomas Izbicki, James Kane, David Keelan, George Lovett, Richard Lucas, Thomas Magnarelli, Joseph Mattaliano (Captain), Dorick Mauro, John McDonnell, John Miller, Frank Morze, Mario Mozzillo, Richad Myles, Emiddio Petrarca, Clifford Poirier, John Poskus. Antonio Quintiliani, John Regan, Alvini St. Pierre, Henry Sullivan, Bernard Teliszewski, James Tiernan.

1955

William Alves, Leonard Andrusaitis, Valentino Bertolini, Francis Cousineau, Edward DeSilva, Emerson Dickie, John Doherty, William Donlan, William Fitzpatrick, Anthony Folcarelli. Francis Furey, Joseph Gabis, Richard Gagliardi, Joseph Hines, Alexander Kulevich, Richard Lucas, Dorick Mauro, Thomas Meehan, John Miller (Captain), Richard Myles, Richard Pearce, Emiddio Petrarca, Lawrence Plenty, John Poskus, Antonio Quintiliani, Richard Reagan, Thomas Rice, Henry Sullivan, Thomas Sullivan, Bernard Teliszewski.

1956

Donald Allard, William Alves, Leon Bennett, Stephen Bennett, Valentino Bertolini, James Colclough, John Connelly, James Cotter, Edware DeGraw, John Doherty, William Donlan, John Flanagan, Anthony Folcarelli, Joseph Gabis, Francis Gallagher, Jerome Havrda, Alexander Kulevich, Thomas Lane, George Larkin, Richard Lynch, George Mancini, Kevin McIntyre, Thomas Meehan, Alan Miller, Robert Murphy, Lawrence Plenty, Antonio Quintiliani, Richard Reagan, Ralph Rogers, Henry Sullivan (Captain), Raymond Sullivan, Thomas Sullivan, Bernard Teliszewski, James Tiernan, John Wissler.

1957

Anthony Abraham, Donald Allard, Harrison Ball, Leon Bennett, William Brown, Francis Casey, James Colclough, John Connelly, James Cotter, Edward DeGraw, James Duggan, John Flanagan, Joseph Gabis, Jerome Havrda, Vincent Hogan, Clement Kacergis, Alexander Kulevich, Thomas Lane, George Larkin, Richard Lynch, George Mancini, Thomas Meehan, Alan Miller, Francis Moretti, Robert Murphy, James O'Brien, William O'Brien, Lawrence Plenty. Donald Seager, Raymond Sullivan, Thomas Sullivan (Captain), Donald Tosi.

1958

Anthony Abraham, Donald Allard, John Amabile, Gerald Bartush, Leon Bennett, Stephen Bennett, Robert Branca, William Brown Harry Ball, Francis Casey, Thomas Casey, James Colclough, James Cotter, Edward DeGraw, James Duggan, Lawrence Eisenhauer, John Flanagan, Donald Gautreau, Frederick Glynn, Jerome Havrda, Vincent Hogan, Robert Keresey George Larkin (Captain), Robert LeBlanc, George Mancini, Alan Miller, Frank Moretti, James Murphy, James O'Brien, Ross O'Hanley, Robert Perrault, Clifford Poirier, William Robinson, Frank Robotti, Jeffrey Sullivan, Donald Tosi.

1959

Anthony Abraham, John Amabile, Harrison Ball, John Buckley, William Byrne, Francis Casey (Captain), James Connolly, Ronald Dyer, Lawrence Eisenhauer, Richard Gill, Frederick Glynn, Vincent Hogan, Vincent Hurley, Robert Keresey, Louis Kirouac, Karl

203

Krikorian, Anthony LeRosa, Robert LeBlanc, Jeffrey Linehan, John McDonald, George McHugh, Francis Moretti, James Murphy, James O'Brien, Ross O'Hanley, Robert Perreault, William Robinson, Frank Robotti, Joseph Sikorski, Daniel Sullivan, James Sullivan, Donald Tosi, George Van Cott.

1960

John Amabile, Domenic Antonellis, John Buckley, William Byrne, Eugene Carrington, Louis Cioci, Harry Crump, Jerome Donovan, Henry Downes, Lawrence Eisenhauer, William Fitzpatrick, John Flanagan, Carl Fleigner, Guy Garon, Donald Gautreau, Richard Gill, Frederick Glynn (Captain), Arthur Graham, Thomas Hall, Joseph Hutchinson, John Janas, Clem Kacergis, Louis Kirouac, Harry Kushigian, Robert LeBlanc, John McGann, George McHugh, Robert Perrault, William Robinson, Frank Robotti, Joseph Sikorski, Daniel Sullivan, Michael Tomeo, George Van Cott, Lionel Gagnon, Robert Sullivan.

1961

Domenic Antonellis, John Barrett, John Buckley, William Byrne, Phil Carlino, Gene Carrington, Louis Cioci, Bart Connelly, Harry Crump, Joseph DiGuglielmo, Jerome Donovan, Henry Downes, William Fitzpatrick, William Flanagan, Carl Fleigner, Guy Garon, Donald Gautreau, Arthur Graham, Thomas Hall, Lawrence Hines, Joseph Hutchinson, Gerard Jakubczak, John Janas, Louis Kirouac, John McGann, John McGourthy, William McKenney, David O'Brien, C., Murray Regan, Peter Shaughnessy, John Shields, Joseph Sikorski, (Captain), Robert Smith, Daniel Sullivan, John Sullivan, Michael Tomeo, George Van Cott, David Yelle, Karl Krikorian, John Concannon.

1962

Domenic Antonellis, John Barrett, Ralph Bello, Phil Carlino, Gene Carrington, Louis Cioci, John Concannon, Bart Connelly, Richard Cremin, Harry Crump, John Daly, Frank DeFelice, Jerome Donovan, Henry Downes, Walter Dubzinski, Francis Fitzgibbons, John Flanagan, William Fitzpatrick, William Flanagan, John Fleming, Carl Fleigner, John Frechette, Phil Gallagher, Guy Garon, Gerard Gillis, Arthur Graham (Captain), Frank Grywalski, Thomas Hall, Charles Henry, Lawrence Hines, Joseph Hutchinson, John Janas, Emil Kleiner, Harry Hushigian, Joseph Lukis, John McGann, James McGowan, John McGourthy, William McKenney, Steve Murray, David O'Brien Charles Regan, Robert Shann, Peter Shaughnessy, John Shields, Robert Smith, John Sullivan, Gary Testa, Michael Tomeo, John West, James Whalen, David Yelle.

1963

John Barrett, Henry Blaha, Robert Budzinski, Edward Butler, Philip Carlino, John Concannon, Richard Capp, Bart Connelly, Richard Cremin, William Cronin, Frank DeFelice, Martin DiMezza, Walter Dubzinski, Francis Fitzgibbons, John Flanagan, John Frechette, Leonardo Gonsalves, Frank Grywalski, Kenneth Kiriocopoulos, Harry Kushigian, John Leone, Joseph Lukis (Captain), Lawrence Marzetti, James McGowan, Donald Moran, Stephen Murray, William Risio, Robert Ryan, William Schoeck, Robert Shann, Peter Shaughnessy, Charles Smith, Thomas Tobin, John Walsh, James Whalen.

1964

Henry Blaha, Robert Budzinski, Edward Butler, James Chevillot, Richard Cremin, William Cronin (Captain) Frank DeFelice, Martin DiMezza, Edward Foley, John Frechette, Ron Gentili, Frank Gry-

walski, Daniel Hosteller, Robert Hyland, Emil Kleiner, Gordon Kutz, John Leone, Edmund Lipson, Lawrence Marzetti, James McGowan, Donald Moran, Stephen Murray, Michael O'Neill, David Pesapane, Richard Powers, David Reardon, William Risio, Robert Ryan, Thomas Sarkisian, William Schoeck, Robert Shann, Charles Smith, William Stetz, Gary Testa, John Walsh, James Whalen.

1965

John Blair, Henry Blaha, Alan Borsari, Robert Budzinski, Richard Capp, Thomas Carlyon, Richard DeLeonardis, Paul Della Villa, Martin DiMezza, Joseph DiVito, William Donovan, Terry Erwin, Mike Evans, Edward Foley, Nicholas Franco, James Garofalo, Ronald Gentili, Paul Gramling, Daniel Hostetter, Robert Hyland, Gordon Kutz, James Chevillot, William Ladewig, John Leone, Edmund Lipson, Lawrence Marzetti, Brendan McCarthy, Michael O'Neill, Len Persin, Ronald Persuitte, David Pesapane, Richard Powers, Joseph Pryor, William Risio, Robert Ryan, Thomas Sarkisian, Douglas Shepard, Charles Smith (Captain), William Stetz, Arthur Stratton, Richard Taylor, Michael Violante, John Williamson.

1966

Gary Andrachik, David Bennett, John Blair, Alan Borsari, Thomas Carlyon, Richard Collins, Harry Connors, Richard DeLeonardis, Paul Della Villa, Joseph DiVito, John Egan, Terry Erwin, William Evans, Barry Gallup, James Garofalo, Alphonse Giardi, James Grace, John Gurry, Kerry Horman, Robert Hyland, John Kane, James Kavanagh, Richard Kroner, Leo Kruger, Gordon Kutz, William Ladewig, Edmund Lipson (Captain), Joseph Marzetti, Brendan McCarthy, Michael Nevard, Michael O'Neill, Leonard Persin, Ronald Persuitte, Jerry Ragosa, John Salmon, Thomas Sarkisian, Douglas Shepard, William Stetz, Michael Violante.

1967

Gary Andrachik, Dave Bennett, Alan Borsari, Robert Bouley, Jim Catone, Skip Coppola, Mondell Davis, Joe DiVito (Captain), Jim Duffy, John Egan, Terry Erwin, Mike Evans, Mike Fallon, John Fitzgerald, Bob Gallivan, Barry Gallup, Jim Garofalo, Jim Grace, John Hazlin, Kerry Horman, Carter Hunt, Mike Johnson, Jim Kavanagh, Steve Kives, Dick Kroner, Bud Kruger, Bill Ladewig, George Lavoie, Chris Markey, Joe Marzetti, Gary Matz, Brendan McCarthy, Jim McCool, Ed McDonald, Joe McDonald, John McGovern, Paul Murphy, Mike Nevard, John O'Connell, Len Persin, Ron Persuitte, Harry Pierandri, Bill Rabadan, Bob Racioppi, Jerry Ragosa, Mike Robertson, John Salmon, Doug Shepard, Dave Thomas, Jim Toupal, Dan Zailskas.

1968

Gary Andrachik (Captain), Dave Bennett, Bob Bouley, Jim Catone, Paul Cavanagh, John Cookson, Mike Corrigan, Walt Cullen, Joe Cunningham, Gary Dancewicz, Larry Daniels, Mondell Davis, Paul Della Villa, John Egan, Mike Fallon, Gene Ferris, John Fitzgerald, Fran Fleming, Bernie Galeckas, Bob Gallivan, Barry Gallup, George Gill, Dick Gill, Jim Grace, Gary Guenther, Frank Harris, Kerry Horman, Mike Johnson, Jim King, Steve Kives, Dick Kroner, Rich Kurowski, Mike Lardner, George Lavole, Joe Marzetti, Jim McCool, Jim Milham, Joe McDonald, Jim O'Reilly (Mgr), Jim O'Shea, Bill Rabadan, Jerry Ragosa, Ed Ransford, Mike Robertson, John Salmon, Dave Thomas, Tom Uzdavinis, Fred Willis, Dan Zailskas.

1969

Ted Anderson, Kent Andiorio, John Bonistali, Robert Bouley, John Brennan, Gregory Broskie, Norman Cavallaro (Mgr), James Catone, Steven Cipot, Kevin Clemente, Eugene Comella, Joseph Coppola, John Craigen, Walter Cullen, Gary Dancewicz, James Darcy, Mondell Davis, Albert Dhembe, Gregg Dziama, Michael Fallon, John R. Fitzgerald, George Gill, Gary Guenther, Frank Harris, Michael Johnson, Stephen Kirchner, Stephen Kives, John Kline, Richard Kurowski, Michael Lardner, James McCool (Capt), Edward McDonald, Joseph McDonald, Peter McHugh, David McKay, John Michaels, James Millham, Michael Mucci, John O'Hagen, William O'Neill, James O'Shea, William Perry, William Rabadan, Edward Ransford, Edward Rideout, Lucien Silva, Richard Tataronis, William Thomas, Charles Toczylowski, Michael Whitney, Frederick Willis.

1970

Chuck Anadore, Kent Andiorio, Ralph Angel, Greg Aungst, Chris Baker, Bill Balmat, Larry Berridge, Charlie Blank, John Bonistalli, Tom Bougus, John Brennan, Greg Broskie, Steve Cipot, Kevin Clemente, Gene Comella, Joe Coppola (Tri-Captain), Mike Corrigan, Gary Dancewicz, Al Dhembe, Jim Dunn, Gregg Dziama, Dave Ellison, John Fitzgerald, Greg Fleck, George Gill, Chet Gladchuk, Gary Guenther, Frank Harris (Tri-Captain), Gary Hudson, Ed Hurley, John Kelly, Chris Kete, Steve Kirchner, John Kline, Bill Knox, Rich Kurowski, Jim Jozier, Mark LeBrecque (Mgr), John McElgunn, John Michaels, Larry Molloy, Mike Mucci, John O'Hagen, Jim O'Shea, Bill Perry, Ed Prisco, Ed Ransford, Ed Rideout, Ray Rippman, Orrie Scarminach, Lou Silva, Steve Sperandio (Mgr), Bill Thomas, Mike Vernezze, Fred Willis (Tri-Captain), Jeff Yeates.

1971

Chuck Anadore, Kent Andiorio, Greg Aungst, Phil Bennett, Larry Berridge, Tom Bougus, Greg Brand, Mel Briggs, Greg Broskie, Gordie Browne, Dave Bucci, Steve Cipot, Kevin Clemente (Co-Captain), Jim Combs, Tom Condon, Steve Corbett, Dave Danker, Al Dhembe, Gregg Dziama, Dave Ellison, Greg Fleck, Chet Gladchuk, Pete Hajjar (Manager), Steve Hegedus, Gary Hudson, Ralph Hudson, Chris Kete, Steve Kirchner, John Kline, Al Krevis, John Laurenzo, Dennis McCleary, John McElgunn, Steve Macinsky, Gary Marangi, Tom Marinelli, Larry Molloy, Mike Mucci, Bill O'Neil, Ed Prisco, Ed Rideout, Ray Rippman (Co-Captain), Dennis Rozum, Bob Rush, Orrie Scarminach, Don Schneider, Pat Sgambati, Lu Silva, Frank Smith, Tom Sokol, Dave Soroko, Burt Stevens, Jim Stewart, Tom Szocik, Bill Thomas, Joe Waters, Jeff Yeates.

1972

Chuck Anadore, Greg Aungst, Phil Bennett, Pat Bentzel, Larry Berridge, Paul Boudreau, Greg Brand, Mel Briggs, Gordie Browne, Dave Bucci (Co-Captain), John Bykowski, Jim Combs, Tom Condon, Steve Corbett, Gary Cottet, Dave Danker, Dan Delatorre (Manager), Art Driscoll, Dave Ellison (Co-Captain), Mike Esposito, Chet Gladchuk, Ned Guillet, John Halcovich, Bob Howatt, Ralph Hudson, John Kelly, Chris Kete, Steve Kolbe, Ken Ladd, Chris Leber, Alex MacLellan, Gary Marangi, Paul Martin, John McElgunn, Dennis McCleary, Larry Molloy, John Murphy, Brad Newman, John O'Hagan, Bill O'Neill, John Petersen, Howie Richardson, Bob Rush, Dan Schneider, Pat Sgambati, Frank Smith, Dave Soroko, Fred Steinfort, Burt Stevens, Tony Sukiennik, Joe Sullivan, Martin Toczlowski, Frank Vasile, Tom Vine, Jeff Yeates.

1973

Rick Aloi, Keith Barnette, Phil Bennett, Greg Brand, Mel Briggs, Gene Brown, Gordie Browne, Mark Burlingame, Brian Clemente, Jim Combs (Tri-Captain), Jerry Concannon, Tom Condon (Tri-Captain), Steve Corbett, Peter Cronan, Kevin Cunniff, Art Driscoll, Mike Esposito, Joe Glandorf, Ned Guillet, John Halcovich, Byron Hemingway, Terry Henninger, Bob Howatt, Al Krevis, Mike Kruczek, Ken Ladd, Chris Leber, Chuck Lee, Tom Lopezzo (Manager), Don Macek, Alex MacLellan, Jack Magee, Gary Marangi (Tri-Captain), Tom Marinelli, Paul Martin, Dan Mullen (Manager), John Murphy, Charlie O'Donoghue, Gary O'Hagan, John Petersen, Howie Richardson, Dennis Rozum, Bob Rush, Steve Scialabba, Pat Sgambati, Bill Smith, Frank Smith, Fred Steinfort, Bill Stempsey (Manager), Burt Stevens, Tony Sukiennik, Joe Sullivan, Steve Turner, Tom Vine, Bob Watts, Dave Zumbach.

1974

Dave Almeida, Steve Anzalone, Keith Barnette, Gene Brown, Glenn Capriola, Brian Clemente (Co-Captain), Jerry Concannon, Peter Cronan, Kevin Cunniff, Kelly Elias, Mike Esposito (Co-Captain), Joe Glandorf, Mike Godbolt, Byron Hemingway, Al Krevis, Mike Kruczek, Ken Ladd (Co-Captain), Tom Lynch, Don Macek, Alex MacLellan (Co-Captain), Jack Magree, Steve Manni, Tom Marinelli, Paul Martin, John Maxwell, Tony Melchiorre, Bob Moore, Chuck Morris, Brian Murdock, John Murphy, Paul Murphy, Gary O'Hagan, Bill Paulsen, Joe Pendergast, Don Petersen, John Petersen, Rich Ramirez, Howie Richardson, Steve Schindler, Steve Scialabba, Rich Scudellari, Bill Smith, Fred Steinfort, John Strollo, Earl Strong, Steve Turner, Jim Walton, Bob Watts, Dave Zumbach.

1975

Rick Aloi, Dave Almeida, Steve Anzalone, Keith Barnette, Gene Brown, Dennis Buchanan, Glen Capriola, Peter Cronan, Kevin Cunniff, Kelly Elias, Ed Finn, Clint Gaffney, Joe Glandorf, Mike Godbolt, Byron Hemingway, Jeff Kaufman, Mike Kruczek (Captain), Pete LaBoy, Tom Lynch, Don Macek, Steve Manni, John Maxwell, Paul McCarty, Tony Melchiorre, Tom Miller, Bob Moore, Chuck Morris, Paul Murphy, Bill Ohrenberger, John O'Leary, Chuck Pascale, Bill Paulsen, Joe Pendergast, Don Petersen, Rich Ramirez, Mike Rawlings, Steve Schindler, John Schmeding, Steve Scialabba, Fred Smerias, Fred Steinfort, Earl Strong, Bob Thayer, Bob Walsh, Jim Walton, Bob Watts.

1976

Dave Almeida, Steve Anzalone, Jerry Baroffio, Joe Bremer, Anthony Brown, Gene Brown, Dennis Buchanan, Mike Campolieta, Glen Capriola, Dan Conway, Peter Cronan (Captain), Kevin Cunniff, Jeff Dziama, Kelly Elias, Ed Finn, Clint Gaffney, Mike Godbolt, Neil Green, Byron Hemingway, Junior Hogan, Mike Jackson, Jeff Kaufman, John Kelliher, Jack Kent, Pete LaBoy, Tom Lynch, John Maxwell, Mike Mayock, Paul McCarty, Tony Melchiorre, Bob Moore, Tim Moorman, Paul Moran, Chuck Morris, J.R. Mullen, Paul Murphy, Joe O'Brien, Bill Ohrenberger, Bill Paulsen, Joe Pendergast, Don Petersen, Roger Reddick, Paul Remillard, Jim Rourke, Steve Schindler, John Schmeding, Rich Scudellari, Jim Sheridan, Fred Smerias, Ken Smith, Joe Staub, Bob Thayer, Bob Walsh, Jim Walton, Bob Watts, Dave Zumbach.

1977

Vinny Allen, Doug Alston, Peter Blute, Ike Bogosian, Anthony Brown, Greg Cantone, Tom Carr, John Cassidy, Peter Cassidy, Bill Chaplick, Jim Conroy, Dan Conway, Mike Curry, Jeff Dziama, Kelly Elias (Tri-Captain), Matt Funchion, Clint Gaffney, Steve Giordano, Mike Godbolt, Neil Green, Mike Gunn, Al Haggen, Izear Hogan, Dave Johnson, Jeff Kaufman, Cyril Keniry, Jack Kent, Ed Kulas, Pete LaBoy, Ed Logue, Jerry Madden, Paul McCarty, Bob Moore (Tri-Captain), Tim Moorman, Chuck Morris, Paul Murphy, Joe O'Brien, Bill Ohrenberger, Jay Palazola, Pete Palmiero, Dave Poirier, Roger Reddick, Lewis Reynolds, Rives Robertson, Mark Roopenian, Jim Rourke, Jeff Ryan, John Schmeding, Rich Scudellari (Tri-Captain), Jim Sheridan, Tim Sherwin, Mike Siegel, Fred Smerias, Ken Smith, Jerry Stabile, Joe Staub, Karl Swanke, Ziggy Szczawinski, Jim Walton.

1978

Doug Alston, Kevin Benjamin, Anthony Brown, Jim Budness, Dennis Buchanan, Greg Cantone, Tom Carr, John Cassidy, Mark Ciruolo, Dan Conway, John Cooper, Dan Cordeau, Mike Curry, Rich Dyer, Jeff Dziama, Joe Ferraro, Clint Gaffney, Neil Green, Mike Gunn, Rich Hajjar (Manager), Junior Hogan, Dave Johnson, Russell Joyner, Jeff Kaufman, Cyril Keniry, Jack Kent, Ed Kulas, Bill Leary, Steve Lively, Jerry Madden, Mike Mayock, Paul McCarty (Tri-Captain), Tim Moorman, Casey Muldoon, Mike Murphy (Manager), Joe Nash, Jack O'Brien, Bill Ohrenberger, Jay Palazola, Dave Poirier, Gerry Raymond, Lew Reynolds, Robert Rikard, Mark Roopenian, Jim Rourke, Jeff Ryan, Bernie Sales, Dennis Scala, Jim Sheridan, Tim Sherwin, Mike Siegel, Fred Smerias (Tri-Captain), Jerry Stabile, Bill Stephanos, Greg Storr, Karl Swanke, John Toppa, Bob Walton, Lee Wezenski, Matt Wozniak.

1979

Doug Alston, Jack Belcher, Ray Bequet, Kevin Benjamin, Jim Budness, Greg Cantone, Tom Carr, Mark Ciruolo, Dan Conway, John Cooper, Vic Crawford, Kevin Dempsey, Rich Dyer, Jeff Dziama (Co-Captain), Joe Ferraro, Clint Gaffney, Shelby Gamble, Steve Giordano, Mike Gunn, Junior Hogan, Kevin Jez, Russell Joyner, Cyril Keniry, Jack Kent (Co-Captain), Ed Kulas, John Loughery, Mike Mayock, Greg Michalec, Steve Moriarty, Casey Muldoon, Joe Nash, Scott Nizolek, Jay Palazola, Junior Poles, John Ray, Gerry Raymond, Lew Reynolds, Robert Rikard, Mark Roopenian, Jeff Ryan, John Schmeding (Co-Captain), Tim Sherwin, Jon Schoen, Leo Smith, Jerry Stabile, Bill Stephanos, Greg Storr, Karl Swanke, Bob Walton, Skip Zabilski.

1980

Doug Alston, Kevin Bailey (Manager), Craig Beal, Jack Belcher, Kevin Benjamin, Bob Biestek, Brian Brennan, Ed Broderick, Jim Budness, Mark Ciruolo, John Cooper, Vic Crawford, Steve De-Ossie, Rich Dyer, Joe Ferraro, Shelby Gamble, John Gonet, Mike Grant, Mike Gunn, Doug Guyer, Russ Joyner, Cyril Keniry, Gary Kowalski, Brian Krystoforski, Steve Lively, Eddie Lord, John Loughery, Mike Mayock (Co-Captain), Greg Michalec, Steve Moriarty, Casey Muldoon, Joe Nash, Scott Nizolek, Roy Norden, Junior Poles, George Radachowsky, Gerry Raymond, Lew Reynolds, Rob Rikard, Mark Roopenian, Jon Schoen, Paul Shaw, Mike Sheppard, Tim Sherwin (Co-Captain), Leo Smith, Jerry Stabile, Bill Stephanos, Greg Storr, Rob Swanke, Bob Vissers, Brian Waldron, Matt Walker.

1981

Steve Andrien, Craig Beal, Jack Belcher, Kevin Benjamin, Bob Biestek, Brian Brennan, Ed Broderick, Howard Brown, Jim Budness, Roger Cattelan, Pat Cooney, John Cooper, Vic Crawford, Steve DeOssie, Rich Dyer, Joe Ferraro, Tom Fitzpatrick, Doug Flutie, John Gonet, Doug Guyer, Scott Harrington, Peter Holey, Kevin Jez, Russ Joyner, Gary Kowalski, Brian Krystoforski, Steve Lively, John Loughery, Steve Lubishcer, Steve Moriarty, Joe Nash, Scott Nizolek, Ray Norden, Dave Paulik, David Pereira, Gerard Phelan, Junior Poles, George Radachowsky, John Ray, Gerry Raymond, Glenn Reagan, Rob Rikard, Todd Russell, Dennis Scala, Jon Schoen, Paul Shaw, Mike Sheppard, Leo Smith, Greg Storr, Stephen Strachan, Rob Swanke, Toney Thruman, Geoff Townsend, Bob Vissers, Ed Von Nessen, Brian Waldron, Paul Zdanek, Eric Shulman, Manager.

LETTERWINNERS: BASKETBALL

1945–1946

Robert Bidwell, Robert Fitzgerald, James Harrington, Philip Kenney, Thomas Lamb, Gerald Levinson, Robert Quirk, Edward Ryan, James Sharry (Capt.), Albert Toomey, Robert Woolf.

1946–1947

Daniel Bricker, Raymond Carr, James Harrington, Francis Higgins, Philip Kenney, John Letvinchuk, Elmore Morganthaler, Edward Ryan, James Sharry (Capt.), Morton Stagoff, Emil Strug, Robert Woolf.

1947–1948

Robert Bidwell, Daniel Bricker, Raymond Carr, Robert Fitzgerald, Francis Higgins, Philip Kenney, John Letvinchuk (Capt.), Gerald Levinson, Thomas Meade, Thomas O'Brien, Edward Ryan, Morton Stagoff, Emil Strug, Robert Woolf.

1948–1949

Daniel Bricker, Raymond Carr (Capt.), Thomas Deegan, Robert Fitzgerald, Francis Gaffney, Ronald Hickey, Francis Higgins, Philip Kenney, Gerald Levinson, Thomas Meade, Thomas O'Brien, Morton Stagoff, Robert Woolf.

1949–1950

Thomas Deegan, Francis Duggan, Richard Fitzgerald, Francis Gaffney, Ronald Hickey, John Moran, James Norton, Thomas O'Brien (Capt.), Timothy O'Connell, Thomas O'Toole, John Silk, Stanley Sincoski, Harold Kirby.

1950–1951

Thomas Deegan (Capt.), Francis Duggan, Richard Fitzgerald, Francis Gaffney, Ronald Hickey, John Moran, James Norton, Timothy O'Connell, Thomas O'Toole, John Silk, Stanley Sincoski, Harold Kirby.

1951–1952

Anthony Daukas, Francis Duggan, William Gauthier, John Moran, James Norton, Timothy O'Connell, John O'Hara, Thomas O'Toole (Capt.), John Silk, Stanley Sincoski, John Whelpley.

1952–1953

Ronald Bielicki, James Cashman, John Cox, Thomas Cullinane, Anthony Daukas, John O'Hara, Philip Powell, Louis Shurtleff, John Silk (Capt.), Stanley Sincoski.

1953–1954

Daniel Burns, Patrick Cahill, Thomas Cullinane, Anthony Daukas, John O'Hara (Capt.), Philip Powell, Louis Shurtleff, Richard Skeffington Jr.

1954–1955

Thomas Aldrich, James Brosnahan, Patrick Cahill, Thomas Cullinane, Richard Dunn, Stanley Kieon, Paul McAdams, Robert McGurkin, Philip Powell (Capt.), Leo Power, Louis Shurtleff, Richard Skeffington, Jr.

1955–1956

Ronald Bielicki, George Bigelow, Fred Bortolussi, James Brosnahan, Patrick Cahill (Capt.), John Harrington, Paul Lyons, Paul McAdams, Leo Power, Richard Skeffington, Jr.

1956–1957

George Bigelow, Fred Bortolussi, Richard Dunn, George Giersch, John Harrington, Robert Latkany, Paul Lyons, Joseph Manning, Paul McAdams (Capt.), John McGrath, William Powers.

1957–1958

George Giersch, John Harrington (Capt.), Robert Latkany, Paul Lyons, John Magee, John McGrath, James Power, John Schoppmeyer, Rudy VonBurg.

1958–1959

Charles Chevalier, Raymond Falvey, George Giersch (Capt.), John Magee, John McGrath, James Power, Francis Quinn, John Schoppmeyer.

1959–1960

William Donovan, Raymond Falvey, Brian Fitzpatrick, William Foley, James Hooley, John McAuliffe, Vincent McKeever, John Schoppmeyer (Capt.), Joseph Sikorski.

1960–1961

Robert Boberg, Charles Carr, Charles Chevalier, Robert DeGrass, William Donovan, Brian Fitzpatrick, William Foley, James Hooley, Jerome Power, Francis Quinn (Capt.), Gerald Ward.

1961–1962

Robert Boberg, Charles Carr, Charles Chevelier, William Donovan, William Foley (Capt.), James Hooley, Jerome Power, Gerald Ward.

1962–1963

Robert Boberg, Charles Carr, John Ezell, George Fitzsimmons, Robert Furbush, George Humann, Robert Madigan, John Mastropolo, James Nelson, David Reynolds, Frank Richichi, Gerald Ward (Captain).

1963–1964

John Austin, Charles Chaney, John Ezell, George Fitzsimmons (Capt.), Robert Furbush, Edward Hockenbury, George Humann, Robert Madigan, James Nelson, Manuel Papoula, Jerome Power, Robert Ward.

1964–1965

John Austin, Edward Carter, Charles Chaney, John Ezell, Douglas Hice, Edward Hockenbury, George Humann (Capt.), Tom Kelly, James Nelson, Manuel Papoula, Robert Rossi, Robert Ward, Willie Wolters.

1965–1966

Steve Adelman, John Austin, Charles Chaney, Douglas Hice, Ed Hockenbury (Capt.), Stephen Kelleher, James Kissane, Jack Kvancz, Edward Rooney, Robert Rossi, Willie Wolters.

1966–1967

Steve Adelman, Terry Driscoll, Billy Evans, Barry Gallup, Jim Halton, Douglas Hice, Steve Kelleher, Jim King, Jim Kissane, Jack Kvancz, Tom Pacynski, Ed Rooney, Willie Wolters (Capt.).

1967–1968

Steve Adelman, Edward Carter, Dennis Doble, Edward Driscoll, Robert Dukiet, William Evans, Steven Kelleher, James King, James Kissane (Capt.), Jack Kvancz, Raymond LaGace, Michael Marks, Thomas Pacynski, Edward Rooney, Peter Sollene, Thomas Verroneau.

1968–1969

Vin Costello, Don Crosby, Dennis Doble, Jim Downey, Terry Driscoll (Capt.), Mike Dunn, Billy Evans, Frank Fitzgerald, Ray LaGace, Jim O'Brien, Greg Sees, Pete Sollenne, Tom Veronneau.

1969–1970

Vin Costello, Dennis Doble, Jim Downey, Bob Dukiet, Mike Dunn, Frank Fitzgerald, Jim O'Brien, Pete Schmid, Greg Sees, Pete Sollenne, Tom Veronneau (Capt.).

1970–1971

Rick Bolus, Vin Costello, Mike Dunn, Frank Fitzgerald, Dave Freitag, Scott Hay (Mgr.), Jim O'Brien (Capt.), Peter Schmid, Greg Sees, Bob Smith, Dave Walker.

1971–1972

Tom Anstett, Rich Bolus, Terry Budny (Mgr.), Dave Freitag, Dan Kilcullen, Jere Nolan, Mark Raterink, Jim Phelan, Peter Schmid (Capt.), Bobb Smith, Dave Walker.

1972–1973

Tom Anstett, Richie Burke, Bob Carrington, Dave Freitag, Dan Kilcullen, Will Morrison, Jere Nolan, Mark Raterink, Bobby Smith (Capt.), Willie Taylor, Dave Ulrich, Dave Walker.

1973–1974

Paul Berwanger, Mitch Buonaguro, Bob Carrington, Bill Collins, Jeff Jurgens, Dan Kilcullen (Capt.), Will Morrison, Jere Nolan, Mark Raterink, Syd Sheppard, Mike Shirey, Frank Tracey, Mel Weldon.

1974–1975

Jeff Bailey, Paul Berwanger, Mitch Buonaguro, Bob Carrington, Bill Collins, Jeff Jurgens, Herrick Lengers, Will Morrison, John O'Brien, Syd Sheppard, Mike Shirey, Frank Tracey, Mel Weldon (Capt.).

1975–1976

Jeff Bailey, Michael Bowie, Bob Carrington, Ernie Cobb, Bill Collins (Capt.), James Jackson, Tom Meggers, Will Morrison, John O'Brien, Mike Shirey.

1976–1977

Bob Bennifield, Louis Benton, Michael Bowie, Ernie Cobb, Jeff Jurgens, (Capt.), Rick Kuhn, Tom Meggers, John O'Brien, Jeff Roth, Mike Shirey, Jim Sweeney.

1977–1978

Carl Baldwin, Bob Bennifield (Tri-Capt.), Michael Bowie, Vin Caraher, Tim Chase, Ernie Cobb (Tri-Capt.), Chris Foy, Rick Kuhn, Tom Meggers, Kevin O'Brien (Mgr.), Dave Prokopchak, Jeff Roth, Jim Sweeney (Tri-Capt.), Jack Uhlar.

LETTERWINNERS: HOCKEY

1917–1918

Edmund Burke, Philip Corrigan, Edward Enright, Walter Falvey (Captain), James Fitzpatrick, Frank Morrissey, Florence O'Connell, Paul Ryan, George White.

1918–1919

Philip Corrigan, Thomas Dooley, Walter Falvey (Captain), Bernard Healy, Frank Morrissey, James Morrissey, Donald McCloskey, Edmund O'Brien, Florence O'Connell, John White.

1919–1920

John Curry, Edmund Garrity, Bernard Healy, Frank Morrissey (Captain), Leonard Morrissey, Donald McCloskey, Edmund O'Brien, Louis Urban.

1920–1921

John Curry, Edmund Garrity, Joseph Haggerty, Leo Hughes (Captain), Frank Morrissey, Leonard Morrissey, Donald McCloskey, Edmund O'Brien, Louis Urban.

1921–1922

John Culhane, John Curry, Charles Donnellan, John Fitzgerald, James Foley, Edmund Garrity, Leo Hughes (Captain), Leonard Morrissey.

1922–1923

John Culhane, John Curry, Charles Donnelan, John Fitzgerald, James Foley, Edmund Garrity (Captain), Henry Groden, Frank Mahoney, Leonard Morrissey, William Morrissey, Edward Mullowney, George O'Brien.

1923–1924

John Culhane, Charles Donnellan, John Fitzgerald (Captain), Pierce Fitzgerald, James Foley, Arthur Gorman, Henry Groden, Arthur Johnson, Frank Mahoney, William Mahoney, William Morrissey, Edward Mullowney, George O'Brien.

1978–1979

Joe Beaulieu, Mike Bennett, Michael Bowie, Vin Carahar, Dwan Chandler, Tim Chase, Ernie Cobb (Co-Capt.), Ron Crevier, Jan Dabrowski (Mgr.), Chris Foy, Chris Jantzen, Rick Kuhn, Tom Meggers, Rich Shrigley, Jim Sweeney (Co-Capt.).

1979–1980

Burnett Adams, John Balgey, Joe Beaulieu, Mike Bennett, Bobby Bonanno (Mgr.), Vin Caraher, Dwan Chandler, Tim Chase, Ron Crevier, Chris Foy, Jeff Nocera, Rich Shrigley, Jim Sweeney (Capt.).

1980–1981

Burnett Adams, John Bagley, Joe Beaulieu, Dwan Chandler, Vin Caraher, Tim Chase, Martin Clark, Chris Foy (Capt.), Peter Krause, Jay Murphy, Jeff Nocera, Tim O'Shea, Rich Shrigley.

1981–1982

Burnett Adams, Michael Adams, John Bagley, John Chander, Martin Clark, Ron Crevier, John Garris, Tony Kinsley, Jay Murphy, Tim O'Shea, Stu Primus, Mark Schmidt, Rich Shrigley, Terrence Talley.

1924–1925

Cornelius Cronin, John Culhane (Captain), Eugene Fitzgerald, John Fitzgerald, Joseph Fitzgerald, Pierce Fitzgerald, James Foley, Arthur Gorman, Henry Groden, Arthur Johnson, John Kelleher, Frank Mahoney, William Mahoney, William Morrissey, Edward Mullowney, George O'Brien.

1925–1926

Cornelius Cronin, Michael Dee, John Drummond, John Dunn, Eugene Fitzgerald, Joseph Fitzgerald, Leon Fitzgerald, Pierce Fitzgerald, Arthur Gorman, Henry Groden (Captain), Arthur Johnson, John Kelleher, John Kelley, Frank Mahoney, William Mahoney, Arthur Morrissey, William Morrissey, John Martin, Edward Mullowney, Robert McGovern, Perley Payson, Nicholas Tedesco.

1926–1927

Cornelius Cronin (Captain), Michael Dee, John Drummond, John Dunn, Joseph Fitzgerald, Leon Fitzgerald, Pierce Fitzgerald, Lawrence Gibson, John Groden, Edmund Kelleher, John Kelleher, John Kelley, John Martin, Arthur Morrissey, Robert McGovern, Perley Payson, Nicholas Tedesco.

1927–1928

Michael Dee, Joseph Fitzgerald (Captain), Leon Fitzgerald, Lawrence Gibson, John Groden, Edmund Kelleher, John Kelleher, John Martin, Arthur Morrissey, Perley Payson, Lawrence Sanford, Edward Sliney, Nicholas Tedesco.

1928–1929

John Fitzgerald, Lawrence Gibson, Edward Goggin, John Groden, Lawrence Haran, Edmund Kelleher, John Marr, John Martin, Arthur Morrissey (Co-Capt.), Lawrence Sanford, Caleb Soully, Edward Sliney, Nicholas Tedesco (Co-Capt.).

1930–1931

No team.

1932–1933
Thomas Blake, Lawrence Cadigen, Edward Conaty, Herbert Crimlisk, Charles Downey, William Dunne, Raymond Funchion, Harold Groden, William Hogan (Captain), Francis Liddell, Owne Mullaney, Justin McCarthy, Douglas MacDonald, Gregory Sullivan, Randolph Wise.

1933–1934
Ralph Ambrose, Herbert Crimlisk, Charles Downey, Raymond Funchion (Captain), Edward Furbush, Harold Groden, Francis Liddell, Fred Moore, Joseph O'Dowd, Timothy Ready, Randolph Wise, Joseph Zibbell.

1934–1935
Ralph Ambrose, John Burgess, John Conlon, Anthony DiNatale, Raymond Funchion, Harold Groden, Francis Liddell (Captain), Fred Moore, Peter Murphy, Thomas McDermott, Joseph O'Dowd, Timothy Ready, Charles Sampson, Thomas Sharkey, Joseph Walsh, Joseph Zibbell.

1935–1936
John Burgess, John Conlon, James Davis, William Flynn, Joseph Hartigan, John Janusas, Thomas McDermott, Peter Murphy, Joe Powers, William Prior, Mario Roscio, Thomas Sharkey, Joseph Walsh.

1936–1937
Raymond Coyne, James Davis, Ralph Dougherty, George Fallon, William Flynn, Joseph Hartigan (Captain), Alfred Horsfall, John Janusas, Frank Lowery, Paul Moore, George Norberg, Thomas O'Callahan, Joe Powers, William Prior, Mario Roscio.

1937–1938
Raymond Coyne, James Davis, Ralph Dougherty, George Fallon, William Flynn, Joseph Hartigan (Captain), Alfred Horsfall, John Janusas, Frank Lowery, Paul Moore, George Norberg, Thomas O'Callahan, William Prior, Mario Rosco.

1938–1939
Thomas Ahearn, John Buckley, Raymond Coyne, Walter Cuenin, Ralph Dougherty, George Fallon, William Flynn, John Hayes, Alfred Horsfall, Frank Lowry, Joseph Maguire, Paul Moore (Captain), John McLaughlin, George Norberg, John Pryor.

1939–1940
James Boudreau, John Buckley, Walter Cuenin, Ralph Dougherty (Captain), Joseph Maguire, Robert Mee, Ralph Powers, John Pryor, Hugh Sharkey, Charles Sullivan.

1940–1941
Lawrence Babine, Walter Boudreau, Raymond Chaisson, Walter Cuenin, Elphege Dumond, Nicholas Flynn, Laurent Houle, Joseph Maguire, George Malone, Robert Mee, Ralph Powers, John Pryor (Captain), Hugh Sharkey, Albert Skene, Charles Sullivan.

1941–1942
Lindon Blanchard, Walter Boudreau, Edward Burns, Philip Carey, Raymond Chaisson, Harry Crovo, John Cunniff, Elphege Dumond, James Edgeworth, Walter Fitzgerald, Nicholas Flynn, Laurent Houle, George Malone, John Murphy, Ralph Powers (Captain), Hugh Sharkey, Albert Skene, Charles Sullivan.

1942–1943
Walter Boudreau (Captain), Edward Burns, Philip Carey, Harry Crovo, John Cunniff, James Edgeworth, Walter Fitzgerald, Nicholas Flynn, John Harvey, Joseph Kraatz, John Murphy, Albert Skene.

1944–1945
No team.

1946–1947
Bernard Burke, Edward Burns, John Corcoran, Norman Daily, James Fitzgerald, John Gallagher, John Harvey, Warren Lewis, Robert Mason, John Murphy (Captain), Joseph McCusker, John McIntire, Edward Songin, Giles Threadgold.

1947–1948
Bernard Burke, John Corcoran (Co-Captain), Norman Daily, Walter Delorey, James Fitzgerald, John Gallagher, Vincent Harding, John Kelley, Warren Lewis, Robert Mason (Co-Captain), Joseph McCusker, John McIntire, Edward Songin, Frederick Talbot, Giles Threadgold.

1948–1949
Bernard Burke (Captain), William Byrne, Leonard Ceglarski, Norman Dailey, Walter Delorey, James Fitzgerald, John Gallagher, Francis Harrington, Warren Lewis, Frederick Mahler, Joseph McCusker, John McIntire, Jack Mulhern, Frank Shellenback, Edward Songin, Frederick Talbot, Giles Threadgold, William Walsh.

1949–1950
Lawrence Brennan, Edward Casey, Leonard Ceglarski, Walter Delorey, Francis Harrington, George Lewis, Joseph McCusker, John McIntire, Peter Maggio, John Mulhern, Francis Shellenback, Edward Songin (Captain), George Sullivan, Giles Threadgold, William Walsh.

1950–1951
Lawrence Brennan, Edward Casey, Wellington Burnett, Joseph Carroll, Leonard Ceglarski, George Costa, William Emmons, John Hansbury, Francis Harrington, Joseph Hosford, Leo Kraunelisk, Peter Maggio, Donald McIver, Edward Emery, Joseph Morgan, John Mulhern, Francis O'Grady, Sherman Saltmarsh.

1951–1952
Robert Babine, Wellington Burnett, John Canniff, Joseph Carroll, George Costa, James Duffy, Edward Emery, William Emmons, Robert Gallagher, John Hansberry, Joseph Hosford, Robert Kiley, Peter Maggio (Captain), William Maguire, Joseph Morgan, Francis O'Grady, Sherman Saltmarsh.

1952–1953
Robert Babine, Wellington Burnett (Captain), Joseph Carroll, James Cisternelli, Joseph Colleran, Richard Dempsey, William Emmons, Robert Kiley, William Maguire, Donald McIver, Francis O'Grady, Sherman Saltmarsh, Robert Siblo, Norbert Timmons.

1953–1954
Robert Babine (Captain), John Canniff, Edward Carroll, James Cisternelli, Richard Dempsey, Charles D'Entremont, Gerald Forgues, Richard Gagliardi, Robert Kiley, William Maguire, Francis Quinn, Robert Siblo, Paul Smith, Basil Vassil.

1954–1955
Paul Bilafer, Paul Carey, Edward Carroll, Joseph Celeta, Richard Dempsey (Captain), Charles D'Entremont, William Donlan, Edward Emery, Donald Fox, Richard Gagliardi, William Leary, Carl Marino, Richard Michaud, Joseph Moylan, Francis Quinn, Paul Sheehy, James Tiernan.

1955–1956
John Cadagan, Edward Carroll (Captain), Myles Cassidy, Charles D'Entremont, Gerald Forgues, Donald Fox, Richard Gagliardi, Richard Kane, William Leary, Carl Marino, Richard Michaud, Joseph Moylan, Alvan Pitts, Francis Quinn, Paul Sheehy, Paul Smith, James Tiernan.

1956–1957
Edmond Bunyon, John Cadagan, Myles Cassidy, Joseph Celeta, Edward Coakley, Donald Fox, Joseph Jangro, Richard Kane, William Leary, Thomas Mahoney, Carl Marino, Richard Michaud, Joseph Moylan (Captain), Alvin Pitts, David Sheehan, Paul Sheehy.

1957–1958
Robert Boyle, Edmond Bunyon, John Cadegan (Captain), Myles Cassidy, John Cusack, Joseph Jangro, Richard Kane, Robert Leonard, John Madden, Thomas Mahoney, Donald O'Neil, Alvan Pitts, David Pergola, Edward Smith, Ronald Walsh.

1958–1959
Robert Boyle, John Cusack, William Daley, Clark Duncan, Robert Famiglietti, Owen Hughes, Joseph Jangro (Captain), James Logue, Robert Leonard, Thomas Martin, John Madden, Donald O'Neil, David Pergola, Richard Riley, Robert Rudman, Edward Smith, Ronald Walsh.

1959–1960
John Cusack, William Daley, Charles Driscoll, Clark Duncan, Robert Famiglietti, Owen Hughes, Robert Leonard, Thomas Martin, Michael Mullowney, Charles McCarthy, David Pergola, Robert Pons, Richard Riley, Robert Rudman, Edward Smith (Captain), Ronald Walsh.

1960–1961
Paul Aiken, John Callahan, William Daley, Charles Driscoll, Robert Gamglietti, Kenneth Giles, George Grant, William Hogan, Owen Hughes, John Leetch, James Logue, Francis Larkin, Thomas Martin (Captain), Charles McCarthy, Edward Sullivan.

1961–1962
Paul Aiken, John Callahan, Charles Driscoll, David Duffy, Kenneth Giles, George Grant (Captain), William Hogan, Thomas Latshaw, John Leetch, Paul Lufkin, Charles McCarthy, Roderick O'Connor, Edward Sullivan, John Warren.

1962–1963
Paul Aiken (Captain), Thomas Apprille, Edward Breen, John Callahan, Edward Downes, David Duffy, Peter Flaherty, Kenneth Giles, William Hogan, Francis Kearns, John Leetch, Paul Lufkin, John Marsh, Norman Nelson, Edward Sullivan, Ralph Toran.

1963–1964
Thomas Apprille (Captain), John Cunniff, Edward Downes, David Duffy, Philip Dyer, Peter Flaherty, Francis Kearns, Alan Kierstead, Thomas Latshaw, Paul Lufkin, Tom Lufkin, John Marsh, Edward McElaney, John Moylan, James Mullen, Ralph Toran.

1964–1965
Edward Breen, Arthur Byrne, Robert Cornish, John Cunniff, Edward Downes (Captain), Philip Dyer, Peter Flaherty, Frederick Flavin, Richard Fuller, Woodrow Johnson, Francis Kearns, Alan Kierstead, Frederick Kinsman, Robert Kupka, Richard Leetch, John Moylan, James Mullen, Patrick Murphy, Ralph Toran, Jeremiah York.

1965–1966
David Allen, Gordon Clarke, Jeffrey Cohen, Robert Cornish, John Cunniff, Stephen Dowling, Philip Dyer, Richard Fuller, Paul Hurley, Woodrow Johnson, Alan Kierstead (Captain), Robert Kupka, Thomas Lufkin, John Moylan, James Mullen, Patrick Murphy, Jeremiah York.

1966–1967
David Allen, Raymond Bastarache, Gordon Clarke, Stephen Cedorchuk, Jeffrey Cohen, Stephen Dowling, Michael Flynn, Richard Fuller, Paul Hurley, Woodrow Johnson, Frederick Kinsman, Robert Kupka, Barry MacCarthy, George McPhee, James Prevett, William Putnam, Michael Robertson, Jeremiah York (Captain).

1967–1968
Kevin Ahearn, Dave Allen, Ray Bastarache, Steve Cedorchuk, Gordie Clarke, Jeff Cohen, Steve Dowling (Captain), Mike Flynn, Barry MacCarthy, George McPhee, Jack O'Neill, Jim Prevett, Willy Putnam, Paul Schilling, Tim Sheehy, John Snyder, John Sullivan, Charlie Toczlowski.

1968–1969
Kevin Ahearn, Raymond Bastarache, Stephen Cedorchuk, Michael Flynn (Captain), Paul Hurley, Barry MacCarthy, George McPhee, William Putnam, Paul Schilling, Timothy Sheehy, Timothy Smythe, John Sullivan; Charles Toczylowski, Frederick Willis.

1969–1970
Kevin Ahearn, Jim Barton, John Burnett, Don Callow, Jack Cronin, Scott Godfrey, Tom Mellor, Pete Morse, John Powers, Paul Schilling, Vin Shanley, Tim Sheehy, Tim Smythe, John Snyder, John Sullivan (Captain), Charlie Toczylowski.

1970–1971
Charlie Ahern, Jim Barton, Harvey Bennett, Don Callow, Jack Cronin, Scott Godfrey, Bob Haley, Neil Higgins, Kevin Horton, Joe Keaveney, Ed Kenty, Kevin Kimball, Ray Lawrence, Tom Maguire (Mgr.), Tom Mellor, Len Nolan, Randi Picard, John Powers (Captain), Bob Reardon, Vin Stanley, Mike Sico.

1971–1972
Charlie Ahern, Harvey Bennett, Bill Butler (Mgr.), Bob Conceison, Bob Cooper, Jack Cronin, Ray D'Arcy, Ed Donahue (Mgr.), Joe Fidler, Scott Godfrey, Ed Hayes, Neil Higgins, Ed Kenty, Kevin Kimball, Jim King, Chuck Lambert, John Monahan, Tom Murray, Len Nolan, Tom Parlato, Bob Reardon, Vin Shanley (Captain), Harvey Taylor, Ned Yetten.

1972–1973

John Baier, Harvey Bennett, Ray D'Arcy, Jim Doyle, Joe Fidler, Rich Hart, Neil Higgins, Ed Kenty, Kevin Kimball, Jim King, Chuck Lambert, Tom Mellor, John Monahan, Mike Powers, Bob Reardon (Captain), Mark Riley, Richie Smith, Ned Yetten.

1973–1974

Mark Albrecht, Dave Annecchiarico, John Baier, Ray D'Arcy, Jim Doyle, Joe Fernald, Bob Ferriter, Rich Hart, Jim King, Chuck Lambert, Mike Martin, John Monahan, Tom Murray, Mark Riley, Leo Scarry, Richie Smith, Bill Wilkens, Bud Yandle, Ned Yetten.

1974–1975

Mark Albrecht, Dave Annecchiarico, Paul Barrett, Joe Fernald, Bob Ferriter, Tim Flynn, Rich Hart (Co-Capt.), Mike Martin, Dan McDonough, Paul O'Neil, Ed Reardon, Dale Redmond, Mark Riley (Co-Capt.), Rob Riley, Richie Smith, Terry Smith, Tom Songin, Tom Sullivan, Bill Wilkens, Kerry Young, Mark Rudnick (Mgr.).

1975–1976

Mark Albrecht (Co-Capt.), Dave Annecchiarico, Joe Augustine, Paul Barrett, Kevin Bartholomew, Brian Driscoll, Joe Fernald, Bob Ferriter, Brendan Glynn, Skip House, Jack Lowry, Mike Martin, Dan McDonough, John McGuire, Joe Mullen, Ed Reardon, Rob Riley, Paul Skidmore, Richie Smith (Co-Capt.), Tom Songin, Tom Sullivan, Bill Wilkens, Kerry Young, Joe Boyle (Mgr.).

1976–1977

Dave Annecchiarico, Charlie Antetomaso, Bill Army, Joe Augustine, Paul Barrett, Brian Burns, Joe Fernald, Bob Ferriter (Captain), Skip House, Bill Kennedy, Walt Kyle, Mike Martin, Dan McDonough, John McGuire, Joe Mullen, Ed Reardon, Rob Riley, Paul Skidmore, Tom Songin, Bill Wilkens, Kerry Young, Kevin Murphy (Mgr.).

1977–1978

George Amidon, Charlie Antetomaso, Bill Army, Joe Augustine, Steve Barger, Paul Barrett (Co-Capt.), Brian Burns, Joe Casey, Mike Cronin, Brian Driscoll, Mike Ewanouski, Paul Hammer, Bobby Hehir, Skip House, Bill Kennedy, Walt Kyle, Rob McClellan, John McGuire, Joe Mullen, Rob Riley (Co-Capt.), Paul Skidmore, Mark Switaj, Jim Pretat (Mgr.).

1978–1979

George Amidon, Charlie Antetomaso, Bill Army, Peter Arnold, Steve Barger, Brian Burns, Joe Casey, Jeff Cowles, Brian Driscoll, Doug Ellis, Mike Ewanouski, Paul Hammer, Jack Harrington, Bobby Hehir, Otto Marenholz, Joe Mullen (Capt.), Mark Murphy, Billy O'Dwyer, Jim Pretat (Mgr.)., Mark Richardson (Mgr.), Gary Sampson, Paul Skidmore (Alt. Capt.), Jeff Smith, Mark Switaj, Tom Wright.

1979–1980

George Amidon, Charlie Antetomaso, Bill Army, Steve Barger (Captain), Lee Blossom, Brian Burns (Alt. Capt.), Jeff Cowles, Doug Ellis, Mike Ewanouski (Alt. Capt.), Paul Hammer, Bobby Hehir, Joe McCarran, Gordie Moore, Mark Murphy, Bob O'Connor, Billy O'Dwyer, Mike O'Neil, Fran Rockett (Mgr.), Gary Sampson, Jeff Smith, Mark Switaj, Jerry Welch, Chris Wray, Tom Wright.

1980–1981

George Amidon, Peter Arnold, Lee Blossom, Jim Chisholm, Jeff Cowles, Doug Ellis, Mike Ewanouski (Co-Captain), Dan Griffin, Paul Hammer, Bobby Hehir (Alternate Captain), Jack Hurley (Manager), Otto Marenholz, Joe McCarran, Rob McClellan, Billy McDonough, Todd Mishler, Robin Monleon, Gordie Moore, Mark Murphy, Bob O'Connor, Billy O'Dwyer, Mike O'Neil, Ed Rauseo, Gary Sampson, Jeff Smith, Billy Switaj, Mark Switaj (Co-Captain), Chris Wray, Tom Wright.

1981–1982

Doug Ellis, Jeff Smith, Joe McCarran, George Boudreau, Jim Chisholm, John Hanlon, Tom Wright, Jeff Cowles, Mike O'Neil, Gary Sampson, Jim Herlihy, Billy O'Dwyer, Billy McDonough, Joe Siddall, David Livingston, Ed Rauseo, Gordie Moore, Otto Marenholz, Chris Wray, Peter Arnold, Lee Blossom, Tim Mitchell, Chris Delaney, Gerry Dunne, Robin Monleon, Dan Griffin, Mark Murphy, Todd Mishler, Bob O'Connor, Billy Switaj.

Major Sports' Individual Records

FOOTBALL

Rushing yardage

Play—91, Ed Walsh, 1944, v. Brooklyn
Game—253, Phil Bennett, 1972, v. Temple
Season—1289, Mike Esposito, 1973, eleven games
Career—2759, Mike Esposito, 1972–74, 28 games

Touchdowns

Game—six players tied with four (Glen Capriola, '75; Keith Barnette, '74; Phil Bennett, '73; Tom Magnarelli, '54; Ed Petela, '49; Chuck Darling, '24)
Season—22, Keith Barnette, 1974, eleven games
Career—34, Keith Barnette, 1973–75, 32 games

Passing yardage

Play—92, Don Allard, 1957, v. Navy
Game—374, Frank Harris, 1968, v. Army
Season—2073, Ken Smith, 1977, nine games
Career—4555, Frank Harris, 1968–70, 28 games

Passes attempted

Game—57, Frank Harris, 1968, v. Army
Season—257, Ken Smith, 1977, nine games
Career—655, Frank Harris, 1968–70, 28 games

Passes completed

Game—37, Frank Harris, 1968, v. Army
Season—149, Ken Smith, 1977, nine games
Career—366, Frank Harris, 1968–70, 28 games

Touchdown passes thrown

Game—five, Ken Smith, 1977, v. Army
Season—19, Frank Harris, 1969, nine games
Career—44, Frank Harris, 1968–70, 28 games

Passes intercepted

Game—six, Frank Harris, 1970, v. Penn State
Season—20, Ken Smith, 1977, nine games
Career—45, Frank Harris, 1968–70, 28 games

Pass completion percentage

Season—68.9, Mike Kruczek, 1974
Career—66.8, Mike Kruczek, 1973–75

Pass receptions

Game—12, Luke Urban, 1919, v. Rutgers
Season—46, Barry Gallup, 1968, nine games
Career, 113, Dave Zumbach, 1973–76, 34 games

Pass reception yardage

Play—92, Tom Joe Sullivan, 1957, v. Navy
Game—165, Jim Whalen, 1963, v. Air Force
Season—823, Art Graham, 1962, ten games
Career—1521, Dave Zumbach, 1973–76, 34 games

Touchdown passes caught

Game—three, Pete LaBoy, 1977, v. Army
Season—two tied with eight (Mel Briggs, '72; John Bonistalli, '69)
Career—twelve, Mike Roarke, 1949–51, 28 games

Interceptions made

Game—eight tied with three (Jim Budness, '79; Kelly Elias, '76; Ned Guillet, '73; Gary Dancewicz, '69; Jim King, '68; Hank Blaha, '63; Bob Flanagan, '51; Harry Downes, '29)
Season—two tied with eight (John Salmon, '68; Ed Clasby, '48)
Career—17, John Salmon, 1966–68, 29 games

Interception on return yardage

Play—100, Don Allard, 1956, v. Brandeis
Game—136, Jim McGowan, 1962, v. Texas Tech (two interceptions)
Season—182, Jim McGowan, 1962, ten games (seven interceptions)
Career—209, John Salmon, 1966–68, 29 games (17 interceptions)

Touchdowns scored off interceptions

Game—two tied with two (Jim McGowan, '62; Ed Doherty, '43)
Season—two tied with three (Jim McGowan, '62; Ed Doherty, '43)
Career—two tied with three (Jim McGowan, 1962–64; Ed Doherty, 1941–43)

Kickoff returns made

Game—eight, Dave Bennett, 1968, v. Army
Season—25, Ed Rideout, 1969, nine games
Career—39, Mel Briggs, 1971–73, 33 games

Kickoff return yardage

Play—two tied with 100 yards (Mike Esposito, '73; Joe Diminick, '48)
Game—214, Dave Bennett, 1968, v. Army
Season—557, Ed Rideout, 1969, nine games (25 returns)
Career—867, Mel Briggs, 1971–73, 33 games (39 returns)

Kickoff return average yardage

Season (minimum eight returns)—27.5, Dave Bennett, 1968, nine games
Career (minimum twelve returns)—26.6, Dave Bennett, 1966–68, 29 games

Punt returns made

Game—two with six (Dick Zotti, '52; Dick McBride, '51)
Season—22, Gary Hudson, 1971, eleven games
Career—43, Ed Rideout, 1969–71, 27 games

Punt return yardage

Play—90, Ed Rideout, 1970, v. VMI
Game—131, Ed Rideout, 1970, v. Holy Cross
Season—272, Ed Rideout, 1971, ten games (fifteen returns)
Career—442, Ed Rideout, 1969–70, nineteen games (28 returns)

Punt return average yardage

Season (minimum ten returns)—18.1, Ed Rideout, 1971, eleven games
Career (minimum 15 returns)—16.6, Dick Zotti, 1951–53, 27 games

Punts attempted

Game—12, John Cooper, 1980, v. Navy
Season—58, Bill Robinson, 1950, ten games
Career—196, Jim Walton, 1974–78, 44 games
Longest—two tied with 77 yards—(John Cooper, 1980, v. Navy; Jim Walton, 1976, v. Florida State)

Punt yardage average

Game (minimum four per game)—two tied with 51.0 (Jim Walton, 1975, v. Temple; Walton, '75, v. Army)
Season (minimum 20 per season)—44.3, Jim Walton, 1975 (49 punts)
Career (minimum 50 per career)—42.3, Jim Walton, 1974–77, 44 games (196 punts)

Extra points completed

Game—two tied with ten (Fred Steinfort, '74; Ed Petela, '49)
Season—42, Fred Steinfort, 1974, eleven games
Career—119, Fred Steinfort, 1972–75, 44 games

Field goals made

Game—two tied with three (John Cooper, '80, Villanova, Army, Air Force; Fred Steinfort, '73, Navy).
Season—16, John Cooper, 1980, eleven games
Career—32, Fred Steinfort, 1972–76, 44 games
Longest—55 yards, Fred Steinfort, 1974, v. Tulane

Total points scored

Game—34, Ed Petela, 1949, v. Holy Cross (4 TDs, 10 PATs)
Season—134, Keith Barnette, 1974, eleven games (22 TDs, 1 PAT)
Career—215, Fred Steinfort, 1972–75, 44 games (96 FGS, 119 PATs)

HOCKEY

Goals scored

Game—six, John Pryor, 1939, v. Cornell
Season—two tied with 34 (Jack Mulhern, 1948–49; Joe Mullen, 1977–78)
Career—110, Joe Mullen, 1975–79

Goals-per-game average

Season—2.07, Ray Chaisson, 1940–41
Career—1.94, Ray Chaisson, 1939–41

Hat tricks

Season—six, Paul Hurley, 1966–67
Career—two tied with eight (Ray Chaisson, 1939–41; Warren Lewis, 1947–50)

Assists

Game—seven, Jack Mulhern, 1948, v. Devens State
Season—45, Tom Mellor, 1972–73
Career—two tied with 111 (Tom "Red" Martin, 1958–61; Tim Sheehy, 1967–70)

Points

Game—two tied with eleven (John Pryor, 1939, v. Cornell; Ray Chaisson, 1939, v. Cornell—yes, the same game)
Season—74, Billy Daley, 1960–61
Career—212, Joe Mullen, 1975–79

Points-per-game average

Season—4.14, Ray Chaisson, 1940–41
Career—3.72, Ray Chaisson, 1939–41

Saves in goal

Game—82, Tim Ready, 1936, v. Princeton
Season—841, Al Pitts, 1957–58
Career—2761, Paul Skidmore, 1975–79

Shutouts

Season—four, Jack Fitzgerald, 1924–25
Career—eleven, Jack Fitzgerald, 1922–25

Goals-against average (stat kept only since 1932)

Season—2.20, Jim Logue, 1960–61
Career—2.74, Tom Aprille, 1961–64

Penalty minutes

Game—17, Allan Kierstead, 1963, v. Toronto
Season—90, Joe Augustine, 1976–77
Career—196, Joe Augustine, 1975–78

BASKETBALL

Total points scored

Game—49, John Austin, 1964, v. Georgetown
Season—673, John Austin, 1964–65, 29 games
Career—1849, Bob Carrington, 1973–76

Field goals made

Game—20, Jim Hooley, 1962, v. Brandeis
Season—263, Bob Carrington, 1974–75, thirty games
Career—778, Bob Carrington, 1973–76

Field goal percentage

Game—90.0, Martin Clark, 1981, v. Providence
Season—68.7, Tom Veronneau, 1968–69, 28 games
Career—64.6, Tom Veronneau, 1967–70

Free throws made

Game—17, John Austin, 1964, v. Georgetown
Season—211, John Austin, 1964–65, 29 games
Career—525, John Austin, 1963–66

Free throw percentage

Game—1.000, John Bagley, 1981, v. Villanova (16–16)
Season—85.7, Jim Sweeney, 1978–79, thirty games
Career—81.3, Jim Sweeney, 1976–80

Scoring average

Season—29.2, John Austin, 1963–64, 21 games
Career—29.2, John Austin, 1963–66

Rebounds

Game—31, Terry Driscoll, 1969, v. Fordham
Season—498, Terry Driscoll, 1968–69, 28 games
Career—1071, Terry Driscoll, 1966–69

Rebounding average

Season—19.0, Phil Powell, 1954–55, 26 games
Career—13.9, Terry Driscoll, 1966–69

Assists

Game—18, Jim O'Brien, 1970, v. LeMoyne
Season—276, Billy Evans, 1966–67, 26 games
Career—669, Billy Evans, 1966–69

Games played

Career—105, Vin Caraher, 1978–81

Boston College Hall of Fame

1970 RECIPIENTS

Frank Cavanaugh—Football coach, 1919–1926
Harold Connolly '53—Track
Bob Cousy—Basketball coach 1964–1969
John P. Curley '13—Graduate manager of athletes, 1925–1956
Don Currivan—Football
Billy Daley '61—Hockey, Golf
Chuck Darling '25—Football, Baseball
Gilmour Dobie—Football coach, 1936-1938
Arthur Donovan '50—Football
Henry Downes '32—Football, Baseball
James Driscoll '22—Track
Jimmy Fitzpatrick '21—Football, Baseball, Basketball, Hockey
Chester Gladchuck '41—Football
Gene Goodreault '41—Football
Art Graham '63—Football, Baseball
Nathaniel J. Hasenfus '22—Athletic Historian
Mike Holovak '43—Football, Football coach, 1951–1959
Frank Jones—Trainer, 1927–1962
John A. "Snooks" Kelley '28—Hockey, Hockey coach, 1933–1972
George Kerr '41—Football
Frank Leahy—Football coach, 1939–1940
Joe McKenney '27—Football, Baseball, Track, Football coach, 1928–1934
Warren McGuirk '29—Football
Charlie Murphy '30—Football, Baseball
Charlie O'Rourke '41—Football
Eddie Pellagrini—Baseball coach, 1957–1972
Jack Ryder—Track coach, 1919–1952
Rev. Frank Sullivan, S.J. '21—Founder, BC Varsity Club
Luke Urban '21—Football, Basketball, Baseball, Hockey
Gerry Ward '63—Basketball
Bernie Wefers '96—Track, Football
Al Weston '29—Football, Baseball

1971 RECIPIENTS

Paddy Creedon '30—Baseball, Football
James "Sonny" Foley '25—Baseball, Hockey, Football
William J. Flynn '39—Football, Hockey, Baseball, Athletic Director 1957–present
Jack Heaphy '23—Football
Leo Hughes '24—Hockey, Football
Joe Kozlowsky '25—Football
Tom "Red" Martin '61—Hockey, Baseball
Frank "Monk" Maznicki '43—Football, Baseball
Francis "Cheese" McCrehan '25—Baseball
Tom O'Brien '50—Basketball
Grattan O'Connell '26—Football, Basketball
Larry Sanford '30—Hockey
Dimitri Zaitz '37—Track, Football

1972 RECIPIENTS

John Austin '65—Basketball
Ray Chaisson '42—Hockey
Henry (Luke) McCloskey '27—Track
Mike Roarke '52—Baseball, Football
Tom Scanlan '20—Varsity Club President 1942-1946
Art Spinney '50—Football
Joe Zabilski '41—Football, Track

1973 RECIPIENTS

Bernie Burke '49—Hockey
Chuck Chevalier '62—Basketball, Baseball
Jack Concannon '64—Football, Baseball

Bill Gilligan '40—Head Track coach, 1953–1978
Bernie O'Kane '09—Track, Basketball, Baseball
Andy Spognardi '33—Baseball
Ernie Stautner '50—Football

1974 RECIPIENTS

Len Ceglarski '51—Hockey, Baseball
Phil Corrigan '21—Football, Baseball, Track, Hockey
Terry Driscoll '69—Basketball
Dick Gill '38—Track
Jim Kavanaugh '68—Track, Football
Hank Toczlowski '41—Football

1975 RECIPIENTS

Frank Power '50—Basketball Coach
Ross O'Hanley '60—Football
John Fiore '66—Track
Billy Evans '69—Basketball
Tim Sheehy '70—Hockey
Eddie Mullowney '21—Baseball

1976 RECIPIENTS

Eddie Gallagher '32—Football, Baseball
John Dixon '32—Football, Baseball
Al Morro '42—Track, Football
Tim Ready '36—Hockey, Baseball
Dan Sullivan '62—Football
Jim O'Brien '71—Basketball

1977 RECIPIENTS

Wally Boudreau '43—Football, Hockey, Baseball
George Colbert '32—Football, Basketball
Joe Ingoldsby '27—Track, Tennis
Eddie Miller '57—Baseball, Director of Sports Publicity, 1960–1974.
Tom O'Toole '52—Basketball
Al Ricci '32—Football, Baseball, Track
Fred Willis '71—Football

1978 RECIPIENTS

John Cunniff '66—Hockey
D. Leo Daley '14—Football
Rev. Maurice V. Dullea, S.J. '17—Football,
Larry Eisenhauer '61—Football
Bill McKillop '27—Track
Bob Niemiec '61—Baseball
John Silk '53—Basketball

1979 RECIPIENTS

Msgr. Jim Doyle '22—Football
Billy Hogan '63—Hockey
Jim Hooley '62—Basketball
Joe Morgan '53—Baseball
Bill Ohrenberger '27—Football
Louis Welch '25—Track
John Yauckoes '41—Football

1980 RECIPIENTS

Gil Bouley '44—Football
Jack Cronin '27—Football
Mike Esposito '75—Football
Hon. John C. Fitzgerald '25—Hockey
Til Ferdenzi '37—Football
Larry Jeffers '68—Track
Tom Mellor '73—Hockey
Ernie Schwotzer '40—Football
Willie Wolters '67—Basketball
Frank Zeimetz '39—Track

1981 RECIPIENTS

Dr. Al Branca '39—Founder of Blue Chips
Rev. Bill Commane '43—Baseball
Tony Daukas '54—Basketball
Dr. Tom Davis—Coach of Basketball 1977–1982
Mary Kay Finnerty '76—Swimming, Field Hockey
Keith Francis '76—Track
Joe Johnson '54—Football
Mike Kruczek '76—Football
Warren Lewis '50—Hockey

1982 RECIPIENTS

Tony Comerford '23—Football
John Fitzgerald '70—Football
Johnny Freitas '33—Football
Sara Groden '76—Swimming
Jim Kissane '68—Basketball
Joe Manzo '41—Football
Jack McDonald '73—Track
Jack Mulhern '51—Hockey
Hugh "Duffy" O'Regan '21—Baseball
Fordie Pitts '54—Golf
Flavio Tosi '34—Football
Jerry York '67—Hockey

216

Index

AAU hockey championship
(1942), 64
Adams, Michael, 120, 121
Adelman, Steve, 107, 111
AIAW (Association of
Intercollegiate Athletics
for Women), 161
Aiken, Paul, 74
Alcindor, Lew, 107
Allard, Don, 28
Allard, Ed, 152
Alumni Field, 10, 12; *ills. 12, 28, 127*
Alumni Stadium, 13, 152–3
Amateur Athletic Union (AAU):
hockey championship (1942), 64
Amick, Mickey, 140
Aprille, Tommy, 75
Army, Billy, 83
Army, *vs.* BC:
in football, 28, 29, 33, 36, 51
in hockey, 58
Ashworth, Dick, 173
Augustine, Joe, 80, 81, 82; *ill. 82*
Austin, John, 105, 106, 107, 111; *ill. 106*

Babine, Bobby, 68–9
Bagley, John, 115, 119, 120, 121, 122–3; *ills. 117, 119*

Bapst, Rev. John, 3
Barnette, Keith, 39, 40
Barton, Jim, 70
Baseball, 124–43
Eastern Collegiate
Championship, 132
fields, 126, 127, 136
Holy Cross rivalry, 125, 126, 127, 129, 130, 132, 133, 135, 136; *ill. 125*
junior varsity established, 130
NCAA championships, 132–3, 135, 136, 140–42
Pellagrini-coached teams
(1958–   ), 133–43
post-World War I era, 128–31
post-World War II era, 131–33
teams:
(1870s, first), 125
(1919), 128; *ill. 128*
(1929), 129
(1949), 132–3; *ill. 133*
(1953), 133–4
(1961), 136; *ill. 137*
(1967), 140–42
Basketball, 86–123
Cousy coaching era (1963–69), 105–11
Davis coaching era (1977–82), 114–22
DePaul game (March 1982),

121; *ill. 119*
early varsity era (1919–25), 89–91
Holy Cross rivalry, 88, 90, 91, 93, 94, 96, 98, 99, 100, 101, 104, 113, 120
invention of game, 86–7
letterwinners (list), 206–208
NCAA tournament, 97, 99, 107, 109, 113, 120–21, *ill. 119*
NIT tournament:
(1965), 106
(1969), 111
(1974), 112–13
playing facilities, 88, 91, 92, 93, 98, 99, 100
point-shaving allegations
(1981), 118–20
postwar varsity era (1945–   ), 91–123
records:
coaching, *table 197*
individual, 214
team, by year, *table 190–97*
roughness, physical contact, 87–8
teams:
(1904–05, first), 87
(1950–51), 97–8; *ill. 98*
(1964–65), 106

(1967–68), 107, 109
(1968–69), 109–11; ill. 110
women's, 165
Basset, Ted, 173
Baylor University, Waco, Tex.,
vs. BC:
in football, 15; ill. 16
Beaudreau, Walter, 21
Beanpot Basketball Tournament,
105
Beanpot Hockey Tournament, 70
(1952), 68, 70
(1953), 68–9
(1955), 69
(1956), 69
(1957), 72
(1960), 74
(1961), 74
(1963), 75
(1965), 75
(1969), 77
(1979), 82
(1982), 85
BC MVPs, 70
trophy, ill. 71
Bent, George (Lefty), 131
Bentley College Invitational
basketball tournament
(1975), 165
Berwanger, Paul, 112, 113
Bicknell, Jack, 49–52; ill. 50
Big East Conference:
basketball, 102, 115
Fall Tennis Tournament, 173
women's basketball
tournament, 165
Blossom, Lee, 83, 85
Boston Arena, 57, 58, 72, 92
Boston Bruins, 59
Boston Celtics, 92, 94
Boston College:
Athletic Club, 5
Chestnut Hill site, 10, 12
colors, athletic, 7
"Eagles" team name, 15
early athletic history, 3–5
founding of, 2–3
gymnasium (erected 1870s), 4;
ill. 4
Hall of Fame, 215–16
Harrison Ave. site, 3; ill. 3
letterwinners, 199–211

mascot (golden eagle), 34–5;
ills. 34, 35
teams' and coaches' records,
tables 175–97
Boston Garden, 92
Boston Intercollegiate Hockey
League, 56
Boston Olympics (hockey team),
63
Boston Patriots, 29
Boston Red Sox, 126, 127, 130
Boston University, vs. BC:
in basketball, 98
in hockey, 58, 62, 63, 65, 67,
79, 81–3, 98. See also
Beanpot Hockey
Tournament
in soccer, 169
in track, 143
Boudreau, George, 83, 85
Boudreau, Wally, 64
Bougus, Tom, 37
Boursaud, Rev. Edward V., 5
Bowie, Mike, 113
Brand, Rev. Leo J., SJ, 5
Braz, Fernando, 156
Brazilian, John (the Sheik), 141;
ill. 140
Brennan, James, 144
Brennan, John, 173
Brewster, Ben, 164, 168–9,
170–71; ill. 168
Brick, Frank (Plinthos), 6, 7
Bricker, Danny, 92, 93, 96
Brickley, Charles, 11
Brosnahan, Jimmy, 99
Brosnahan, Johnny, ill. 133
Brosnahan, Rev. Timothy, 53
Broughton, Frank, 173
Brown, Richard D., 2
Brown, Walter, 68, 70, 74, 92,
105
Brown University, Providence,
R.I., vs. BC:
in hockey, 54
Bruins, 59
Buckley, Ed, 135
Buckley, John, 132
Budness, Jim, 49; ill. 50
Bullman, Neil, 87
Bunker, Charlie, 136
Burke, Bernie, 65, 67, 171–2; ills.

61, 73
Burtnett, Wellington (Wimpy), 68
Bykowsky, John, 155
Byrne, Jim, ill. 132

Caffrey, Jim, 146
California. University, at Los
Angeles (UCLA), vs. BC:
in basketball, 106, 107, 109
in soccer, 170
Campbell, Siobhan, 163, 164
Capriola, Glen, 40; ill. 41
Caraher, Vin, 114, 115
Carey, Phil, 64
Carrington, Bob (Smooth), 112,
113; ill. 112
Carroll, Andy, 90
Carroll, Ed, 69, 172
Casell, Jimmy 90
Cavanaugh, Francis W. (the Iron
Major), 15–17; ill. 15
Cavanaugh, Thomas F., 146; ill.
147
CCNY, vs. BC:
in basketball (1951), 96–7
Ceglarski, Len, 60, 65, 67, 74; ill.
61
as coach, 79–85; ill. 79
Celtics, 92, 94
Chaisson, Ray, 63; ill. 64
Chandler, Dawn, 115, 118,
120–21
Cheers, college, 7–8
Chevalier, Chuck, 100, 101, 136;
ill. 104
Chlebek, Ed, 47–9; ill. 48
Churchward, Johnny, 88
Cisternelli, Jim, 133
Clark, Martin, 115, 121
Clasby, Ed, ill. 133
Coady, William (Bill), 90; ill. 90
Cobb, Ernie, 113, 115, 118
Colbert, George, 130; ill. 130
Colclough, Jim, 28; ill. 43
College World Series:
(1949), 132–3
(1953), 135
(1960), 136
(1961), 137
(1967), 140–42
Collins, Bill, 112, 113
Collins, Eddie, ill. 133

Collins, Rev. Patrick H., *ill. 131*
Colors, athletic, 7
Concannon, Dave, 130
Concannon, Jack, 30, 136; *ills. 27, 31, 42*
Concannon, Joe, 83
Connolly, Harold (Hal), 149, 150, 152; *ills, 151, 152*
Connolly, Mickey, 21, 91; *ill. 23*
Corcoran, Fred J., 171
Corcoran, John, 87
Correa, John, 173
Corrigan, Phil, 128
Cotton Bowl game (1940), 20–21
Counsell, Peter, 165
Courtney, Joe, 10
Cousy, Bob, 94–5; *ills. 94, 95*
    as BC coach (1963–69), 105–11; *ills. 108, 110*
    as Holy Cross player, 93, 96
Creedon, Patrick, 17
Cronin, Bill, 30; *ill. 31*
Cronin, Cornelius (Tubber), 59
Cross-country running, 145
    women's varsity, 164
Crowley, Bob, 171
Crowley, James, 88
Crump, Harry, 29, 30
Cunis, Bill, 136, 142
Cunniff, John, 75; *ill. 75*
Cunningham, Bill, 19
Curley, John (Jack), 16, 18, 19
Curry, Arthur, 144
Curry, Joe, 89
Curtin, John, 89

Dachos, Tom, 142
Daley, Bill, 70, 73, 74; *ill. 73*
Daley, D. Leo, 17
Daley, Frank, 148
Daley, Kathleen, 166; *ill. 165*
Daly, Chuck, 111
Darling, Chuck, 15–16, 128; *ills. 17, 34, 129*
Dartmouth College, Hanover, N.H., *vs.* BC:
    in hockey, 57, 61, 62, 63, 65, 67, 74, 76
Daukas, Tony, 98; *ill. 97*
Daunt, Jerry, 132
Davis, Emerson, 169
Davis, Dr. Tom, 114–22, 123; *ill.*

114
Debating society, 127
DeBettancourt, Doug, 172
Deegan, Tom, 96; *ill. 96*
D'Elia, Ryder, 169
Dempsey, Bill, 145
Dempsey, Dick, 69
D'Entremont, Chuck, 69
DePaul University, Chicago, Ill., *vs.* BC:
    in basketball, 93, 121; *ill. 119*
Desnoyers, George (Dizzie), 153; *ill. 154*
Devitt, Rev. E. I., SJ, 6
Dixon, Johnny, 17–18
Dobie, Gilmour (Gil), 18–19; *ill. 18*
Dominick, Joe, 25
Doneski, Harvey, 141
Donovan, Arthur, 25; *ill. 43*
Dooley, Charley, 171
Doran, Mike, *ill. 168*
Dorfman, Peter, 170
Downes, Harry, 18
Downey, Walter, 146
Driscoll, James W., 127
Driscoll, James W. (Jake), 145, 146; *ill. 145*
Driscoll, Terry, 107, 110, 111; *ill. 109*
Duff, Jim, 153
Duffy, Bob, 130
Duffy, Hugh, 129
Duggan, Matt, 88
Dukiet, Bob, 110; *ill. 109*
Dullea, Rev. Maurice, 10, 25
Dumond, Al, 63; *ill. 64*
Dunn, Dick, 99

Eagle(s):
    as mascot, 34–5; *ills. 34, 35*
    as team name, 15
EAIAW (Eastern Association of Intercollegiate Athletics for Women), 161
    Eastern Regional competition, 164
Egan, Col. Dave, 20
Eisenhower, Larry, 29
Elias, Kelly, 44, 46; *ill. 45*
Ellis, Doug, 82, 83
Enos, Maureen, 165

Enright, Eddie, 56
Ernst, Harry, 171
Esposito, Mike (Espo), 37, 39; *ill. 38*
Evans, Billy, 107, 110, 111
Ewing, Patrick, 120

Falla, Bill, 153
Falvey, Walter, 56
Farkouh, Gordie, 171
Farrington, Joe, 171
Farrow, Jon, 170
Fenway Park, Boston:
    for football, 13; *ills. 13, 28*
Ferdenzi, Tilly, 91
Ferriter, Dick, 131
Field hockey (women's), 164
Finnerty, Mary Kay, 163; *ill. 162*
Fiore, John, 153; *ill. 154*
Fitzgerald, David, 87
Fitzgerald, Dick, 96; *ill. 96*
Fitzgerald, Frank, 110, 111
Fitzpatrick, Jimmy, 11, 14, 15, 89, 127–8; *ills. 11, 128*
Flanagan, Bob, 133
Florescu, Nick, 173
Flutie, Doug, 51–2; *ill. 51*
Flying wedge, 7
Flynn, Bill, 173
Flynn, Larry, 153
Flynn, Mike, 77
Flynn, William J. (Bill):
    as athletic director, 13, 28, 29, 30, 39, 44, 47, 48, 49, 72, 104–05, 111, 114, 118, 119, 121–2, 123, 125, 136, 159, 163; *ill. 122*
    as football player, *ill. xvi*
    as hockey player, 63
Flynn Recreation Complex, 159–60, 163, 173
    dedication (1979), *ill. xvi*
Foley, Jim (Sonny), 58, 59; *ill. 57*
Football, 3, 5, 6–52
    Cotton Bowl game (1940), 20–21
    danger, violence of, 5, 7, 9
    "flying wedge" tactic, 7
    Holy Cross rivalry, 8, 10, 15, 20, 22, 24, 26, 27, 28, 33, 36, 49, 52
    letterwinners (list), 198–206

Orange Bowl game (1943), 25
playing fields, 6, 8, 10, 12–13,
     28; ills. 12, 13
professional players from BC
     (list), 42
records:
     coaching, table 81
     individual, 212–13
     team, by years, table 175–81
Sugar Bowl game (1941), 22–3
teams and seasons:
     (1893–1912), 6–10
     (1913–41), 10–11, 14–23
     (1941–59), 24–9
     (1959–68), 29–32
     (1968–82), 32–52
For Boston (fight song), xv, 1, 5, 8
Foster's Cadets (drill team), 3
Foy, Chris, 114
Francis, Keith, 155; ill. 155
Fraser, Bill, 169
Friel, Gerry, 107; ill. 108
Funchion, Ray, 62

Gallagher, Mike, 142
Galligan, Ted, 91
Gammons, Peter, 37
Gannon, John, 89
Garris, John, 120
Gasson, Rev. Thomas Ignatius,
     SJ, 9, 10, 12, 55, 87
Gately, Paul, 89
Gavitt, Dave, 102
Georgetown University,
     Washington, D.C., vs. BC:
     in basketball, 100, 106, 113,
          114, 120
Gianelli, Mario, 25
Giersch, George, 99, 100; ill. 100
Gildea, Tom, 128
Gill, Richard, 148
Gilligan, Bill, 143, 149, 152–6,
     164; ills. 152, 154
Gilvey, Bob, 153
Gintoff, Fella, 91
Giulotti, Joe, 39
Gladchuk, Chet, 19, 21, 91
Golf, 171–2
Goodreault, Gene, 19, 21–2; ill.
     22
Gostyla, Alfred (Skip), 167
Grace, Dick, 171

Graham, Art, 29, 30, 136; ill. 42
Greater Boston Intercollegiate
     track meet:
     (1960), 153
     (1963), 153
Greater Boston League (GBL),
     133
     soccer title:
     (1978), 169
     (1980), 170
     (1981), 170
Green, Neil, 44; ill. 45
Grimes, Bill, 20
Groden, Sara, 160, 161, 163; ill.
     162
Groden, Tom, 161; ill. 161

Haggerty, Frank, 173
Hall of Fame (BC), 215–16
Halloran, Leo, 127
Hamel, Gerry, 136
Harris, Frank (Red), 33, 36
Hart, Jim, 10
Hartigan, Joe, 63
Harvard University, Cambridge,
     Mass., vs. BC:
     in baseball, 132
     in football, 11, 25
     in hockey, 56, 57–8, 64–5,
          68–9, 75. See also Beanpot
          Hockey Tournament
Hasenfus, Nathaniel J. (Nat), vii,
     xi, xv–xvi
     on baseball, 125
     on basketball, 87, 88, 89, 90, 91
     on football, 6, 12, 32
     on track and field, 143
Haskell, Richard (R. D.), 172
Haubrich, Jane, 166
Hazard, Phil, 155
Hefferle, Ernie, 29, 34
Heinsohn, Tommy, 98, 99
Henriksen, Olaf, 128
Hockenbury, Ed, 106, 107
Hockey. See Field hockey; Ice
     hockey
Hogan, Billy, Jr., 74, 75; ill. 75
Hogan, William (Bill), 62; ills. 73
Holland, James (Dutch), 89
Holovak, Mike, 21, 24, 25, 26–9;
     ills. 22, 27
Holy Cross College, Worcester,

Mass., vs. BC, 8
     in baseball, 125, 126, 127, 128,
          129, 130, 132, 133, 135,
          136; ill. 125
     in basketball, 88, 90, 91, 93,
          94, 96, 98, 99, 100, 101,
          104, 113, 120
     in football, 8, 10, 15, 20, 22,
          24, 26, 27, 28, 33, 36, 49,
          52
     in golf, 171
     in hockey, 59, 65
     in swimming, 163
     in tennis, 173
     in track and field, 143, 146,
          149
Hooley, Jim, 100, 101, 104; ill.
     101
Horton, Tom, 156
Howe, Irv, 149
Hughes, Leo, 56; ill. 57
Hughes, Owen, 73, 75
Hurley, Paul, 76, 77
Hurley, Thomas J., 5
     For Boston, 5, 8
Hussey, Frank, 148

Ice hockey, 53–85
     AAU championship (1942), 64
     Beanpot Tournament, 68–70,
          71, 72, 74, 75, 77, 82, 85
     Boston University rivalry, 58,
          62, 63, 65, 67, 79, 81–3, 98
     chosen over ice polo, 54
     Dartmouth rivalry, 57, 61, 62,
          63, 65, 67, 74, 76
     Harvard rivalry, 56, 57–8,
          64–5, 68–9, 75
     Kelley era (1928–42, 1946–72),
          57–79
     letterwinners (list), 208–11
     Madison Square Garden
          dedication tournament
          (1925), 58–9
     NCAA championships:
          (1948), 65
          (1949), 65, 67
          (1950), 67
          (1954), 69
          (1956), 69
     records:
          coaching, table 190

individual, 212–13
   team, by years, *table 181–90*
rinks and ponds, 53, 54, 55,
   56, 72
roughness, danger, 56
teams and seasons:
   (1896–97, first), 53–4; *ill. 54*
   (1922–23), 58; *ill. 57*
   (1948–49), 65, 67; *ill. 68*
   (1955–56), 69
"Independents" (basketball team),
   91
Ingoldsby, Joe, 148
Injuries. *See* Safety
Intercollegiate Association of
   Amateur Athletes of
   America (IC4A) annual
   track and field meet
   (1901), 144

Jack Ryder Track, 153
Jangro, Joe, 73
Jauron, Bob, 21, 91
Jeremiah, Eddie, 68, 74; *ill. 61*
Johnson, Mike, 155
Jones, Frank (Jonesy), 16; *ill. 135*
Joy, Bill (Hiker), 10; *ill. 14*
Joyce, John, 152

Kamp, Ike, 89
Kane, Jimmy, 27; *ill. 27*
Kavanaugh, Jim, 153; *ill. 154*
Kelley, Jack, 67, 79
Kelley, John (Snooks), 55–6; *ill.
   60*
   as golf coach, 171
   as hockey coach (1928–42,
      1946–72), 59–79; *ills. 61*
   achievements, 60–61
   500th victory, 79; *ill. 61*
Kelly, John, 9
Kenney, Joseph, 10; *ill. 8*
Kenney, Phil, 92
Kenty, Ed, 78; *ill. 78*
Kickham, Ed, 148
Kiley, Bob, 69
Kinchla, Dick, 171
King, Edward J., 25, 132; *ills. xvi,
   26*
King, Ralph, 149; *ill. 149*
Kissell, John, 21, 25, 91
Kitley, Bill, 140

Kramer, Murray, 21
Krevis, Al, 39
Kruczek, Mike, 39, 40–41; *ill. 38*
Kryzovic, John, 152
Kuhn, Rick, 118, 120
Kvancz, Jack, 119

Lacrosse (women's), 163–4
Lang, Gyorgy, 167
Lanney, Rob, 156; *ill. 156*
Lavigne, Michael, 164
Leahy, Frank, 19–23, 29, 40; *ill.
   19*
Leahy, Fred, 131; *ill. 132*
LeBlanc, Steve, 170
Leetch, Jack, 74, 75
Lermond, George, 148
Letterwinners (list), 199–211
Levinson, Gerry, 132, 133
Lewis, Warren, 65, 67
Linnehan, Jim, 10
Liston, James, *ill. 15*
Lochiatto, Pat, 152
Logue, Jim, 73
Lojek, John, 169
Low, Jim, 149
Loyola, St. Ignatius of, 1–2; *ill. 2*
Lucas, Carl, 21
Lusk, Marty, 169
Lyons, Rev. Charles, 10
Lyons, Joseph, 87
Lukachik, Al, 21
Luongo, Rod, 142
Lynch, Ann Marie, 164

MacDonald, Mike, 173
Mackey, Kevin, 115
Madison Square Garden, New
   York, N.Y., dedication
   hockey tournament (1925),
   58–9
Magdalenski, Dave, 172
Magee, John, 99, 100
Maguire, Fred, 131–3; *ill. 132*
Mahoney, Patrick, J., 146; *ill. 147*
Mahoney, Steve, 11
Manley, Connie, 89
Marangi, Gary, 37, 39
Margo (eagle mascot), 34–5; *ill.
   35*
Marinelli, Tom, 39
"Maroons" (basketball team), 91

Marso, Charlie, 131
Martin, Bob (Beaver), 136; *ill.
   137*
Martin, Donald (Dino), 98
Martin, Tom (Red), 72–3, 74; *ill.
   73*
Marzetti, Joe, 32
Mascot (golden eagle), 34–5; *ills.
   34, 35*
Maxwell, Rev. Joseph R. N., SJ,
   13, 28, 72
Maznicki, Monk, 91
McAdams, Paul, 99
McAllister, Bob, 152
McAuliffe, Maureen, 165
McCarthy, Brendan, 30; *ill. 31*
McCarthy, Charles, 144
McCarthy, Charlie, 10
McCloskey, Henry F. (Luke), 148
McCrehan, Frank (Cheese), 128,
   129, 130–31; *ill. 130*
McDonald, Jack, 155–7, 164, 166
McDonald, Joe, 152
McElroy, Rev. John, SJ, 2–3
McElroy, Tom, 169–70; *ill. 170*
McGovern, Patricia, 165
McGowan, Justin, 149
McGrath, Jack, 135
McGuiness, Henry, 87
McHugh, Rev. Patrick, SJ, 73
McHugh Forum, 72–3
McIntire, John, 67
McKenley, Herbert H., 149
McKenney, Joe, 13, 17–18
McKillop, William T., 146; *ill.
   147*
McKinnon, Bob, 133, 135
McLaughlin, Rev. Edward, J. 34
McLaughlin, Raymond, 172
McLellan, Al (the General), 92,
   93, 94
McMahon, Jim, 153
McNally, Rev. Paul, SJ, 89
McNamara, Jack, 153
McNulty, Hugh, 129
Meagher, Tom, 155
Meara, Bob, 142
Megan, Carolyn, 163
Meggers, Tom, 113
Mellor, Tom, 77, 78
Military service and athletics, 11,
   24–5, 65, 89, 127, 131

Miller, Jim, 29–32; *ill. 31*
Monahan, D. Leo, 47
Monahan, Joe, 127
Monan, Rev. J. Donald, SJ, 44; *ill. xvi*
Moncewicz, Fred, 130
Montgomery, Lou, 20, 21, 23; *ill. 21*
Mooney, Frank, 90
Morgan, Joe, 133, 134; *ill. 134*
Morganthaler, Elmore, 92–3; *ill. 93*
Morrison, Wil, 112, 113
Morrissey, Arthur, 59
Morrissey, Frank, 56
Morro, Al, 148–9
Mulcahy, Stephen, 87
Mullan, Rev. W. J. Read, SJ, 8–9, 12, 55, 87
Mullen, Joe, 80, 81, 82, 83; *ill. 81*
Murphy, Charley, 17
Murphy, Jay, 115, 121; *ill. 118*
Murphy, Peter, 63
Murray, Mark, 155
Mwaura, Frank, 167
Myers, Denny, 24–6; *ill. 24*

Nagle, William, 7
Naismith, Dr. James, 86–7
Nash, Ralph, 21
Nason, Jerry, 30
National Basketball Association (NBS), 91–2
National Collegiate Athletic Association (NCAA):
 baseball championships, 132–3, 135, 136, 140–42
 basketball championships, 97, 99, 107, 109, 113, 120–21; *ill. 119*
 and football, 9, 11
 hockey championships, 65, 67, 69, 75, 81–2
National Invitational Tournament (NIT):
 (1965), 106
 (1969), 111
 (1974), 112–13
Navy, *vs.* BC:
 in football, 28, 29, 30, 32
NCCA. *See* National Collegiate Athletic Association

Nelson, Dave, 155
New England Intercollegiate League, 63
 golf championships, 171
 tennis championships, 173
 track and field championships, 146
Niemiec, Bob, 136
NIT:
 (1965), 106
 (1969), 111
 (1974), 112–13
Nolan, Jere, 112, 113
Nolan, Walter, 146
Norris, Bill, 153
Notre Dame University, West Bend, Ind., *vs.* BC:
 in football (1975), 40–41; *ill. 41*

O'Brien, Bill, 140, 141; *ill. 140*
O'Brien, Jimmy, 110, 111
O'Brien, Tom, 92, 93, 96
O'Connell, George, 173
O'Connell, Joseph F., 6
O'Conner, John, 173
O'Connor, Bob, 84, 85
O'Day, Hank, 129
O'Dwyer, Billy, 82, 83, 85; *ill. 84*
O'Grady, Francis, 70
O'Kane, Bernie, 127, 144
O'Leary, Bob, 153
O'Neil, Ed, 141
O'Neil, Edward J., 172
O'Neill, Paul, 80
Orange Bowl game (1943), 25
O'Rourke, Charley, 19, 20, 21, 22–3, 91; *ills. 22, 23*
O'Shea, Jim, 33
O'Shea, Tim, 115
O'Toole, Tommy, 98; *ill. 96*

Pacynski, Tom, 107
Pagliuca, Jerry, 131
Papadellis, Lou, 169, 170
Patriots, 29
Pellagrini, Eddie, 124
 as coach, 135–45; *ills. 135, 141*
Penn Relays:
 (1921), 146
 (1924), 146
 (1927), 148
Pfeiffer, John, 169

Pitts, Al, 72
Pitts, Fordie, 172
Plotzke, Margo, 165; *ill. 166*
Poirier, Cliff, 28, 30
Powell, Phil, 99
Powell, Dr. Theresa, 158–9
Power, Frank, 92, 93, 96, 98, 99, 104, 105, 106, 110, 111, 115; *ill. 108*
Powers, Ralph, 64

Quinn, Ed, 153
Quirk, Bob, 132

Ramisch, Frank, 89
Raterink, Mark, 112, 113
Ravanis, George, 142
Rawson, Larry, 153
Ready, Tim, 62, 131
Recreational Complex (RecPlex), BC, 159–60, 163, 173
Red Sox, 126, 127, 130
Reilly, Joseph, 10
Rensselaer Polytechnic Institute (RPI), Troy, N.Y., *vs.* BC:
 in hockey, 69, 74
Ricci, Al, 148
Rideout, Eddie, 37
Rinella, Jim, 153
Ripp, Mary Beth, 163
Roarke, Mike, 133, 136; *ill. 133*
Roberts, Vin, 171, 173
Roberts Center, BC, 100, 153
Robertson, Mike, 140
Robinson, Bill, 136
Rockne, Knute, 19, 20
Rocque, Fred, 59; *ill. 57*
Rovegno, Eddie (the Eagle), 35
Ruane, Bill, 142
Ruggiero, John, 133, 135
Ryder, Jack, 143, 145–9; *ills. 145, 147*
Ryder Track, 153

Safety:
 in basketball, 87–8
 in football, 7, 9
 in hockey, 56
Salmon, John, 140, 141
Saltmarsh, Sherman (Whip), 68
Samir, Vincent, 153
Sanford, Lawrence, 59

Sarkisian, Tom, 141
Sarni, Jim, 79
Sarno, Amerino (Moody), 25
Scanlon, Tom, 127
Schaeffer Stadium, Boston, 40;
  ill. 13
Schilling, Paul, 77
Schneider, Don, 155
Scully, Mike, 153
Shea, Cmdr. John J., 137
Shea Field, BC, 136; *ill. 138*
  dedication (May 1961), 136; *ill.*
  138
Sheehy, Tim, 70, 76–8; *ill. 77*
Shrigley, Rich, 115, 120, 121; *ill.*
  116
Silk, John, 96, 98; *ill. 97*
Skeffington, Dick, 98–9
Skidmore, Paul, 70, 80, 81, 82
Slattery, Jack, 129
Small, Nancy, 166
Smith, Ken, 44, 46–7; *ills. 45, 46*
Smith, Richie, 70, 80, 81; *ills. 71,*
  80
Snyder, Tom, 77
Soccer, 167–71
  fields, 167–8
  GBL title:
    (1978), 169
    (1980), 170
    (1981), 170
  women's, 164–5
Songin, Ed (Butch), 25, 29, 60,
  65, 67; *ill. 67*
Songin, Tom, 80
Spinney, Art, 25; *ill. 43*
Stagoff, Morton, 92, 93, 96
Stautner, Ernie, 25
Steinfort, Fred, 37, 39, 40
Stewart, Greg, 142
Sugar Bowl game (1941), 22–3
Sullivan, Billy, 20
Sullivan, Dennis J., 4, 125
Sullivan, Jimmy, 172
Sullivan John (Joe), 146
Sullivan, Mary Ellen, 161, 163
Sullivan, Pat, 158
Sullivan, Peter, 88
Sullivan, Tommy Joe, 27
Supple, James, 87
Swanke, Karl, 156
Sweeney, Jim, 114, 118

Sweeney, Joseph (Red), 149
Swimming and diving (women's),
  161, 163; *ills. 160, 161,*
  162
Switaj, Mark, 82, 83
Syracuse University, Syracuse,
  N.Y., *vs* BC:
  in basketball, 120–21

Taylor, Jim, 149
Tedesco, Nick, 59
Temple, John, 64
Temple, Johnny, 133, 135; *ill.*
  135
Tennis, 172–3
  women's, 164
Tessier, Lucien, 153
Texas. University, Austin, *vs.* BC:
  in football, 39, 41, 43; *ills. 45*
Thomas, Bill, 37
Thompson, Thamie; *ill. 162*
Threadgold, Giles, 67; *ill. 61*
Tobin, Bill, 171
Tocylowski, Charlie, 77
Tocylowski, Henry, 19, 21; *ills.*
  22, 23
Track and field, 143–57
  first intramural meet (1885),
    143
  first varsity team (1890s), 143
  New England Intercollegiate
    Championship, 146
  "Open" meet (March 1897),
    144
  relay teams:
    (1921), 146
    (1924), 146; *ill. 147*
    (1930), 148
    (1956), 152
    (1961), 153
    (1963), 153
  stars:
    of the 1960s, 153
    of the 1970s, 155–6
  tracks for, 144, 146, 152–3, 155
  women's varsity, 164
Treseler, Fred, 164

UCLA, *vs.* BC:
  in basketball, 106, 107, 109
  in soccer, 170
U.S. Military Academy, West

Point, N.Y., *vs.* BC:
  in football, 28, 29, 33, 36, 51
  in hockey, 58
U.S. Naval Academy, Annapolis,
  Md., *vs.* BC:
  in football, 28, 29, 30, 32
University of Texas, Austin, *vs.*
  BC:
  in football, 39, 41, 43; *ills. 45*
Urban, Louis J. (Luke), 11, 14,
  15, 89, 128; *ills. 11, 128*

Veronneau, Tom, 110, 111
Violence in sports:
  basketball, 87–8
  football, 5, 7, 9
  hockey, 56
Volpone, Charlie, 172

Walsh, Rev. Michael P., SJ, *ill.*
  139
Ward, Gerry, 101, 104, 105; *ill.*
  101
Watson Rink, Harvard
  University, 72
Wefers, Bernie, 6–7, 143–4
Welch, Louis R., 146; *ill. 147*
Weldon, Mel, 113
Westerkamp, Hans, 169
Weston, Al, 17, 129
Whalen, Jim, 29
Williams, Gary, 122; *ill. 122*
Willis, Fred, 33, 36; *ill. 36*
Woicik, Mike, 155
Wolters, Willie, 106, 107
Women's sports, 158–66
  basketball, 165; *ill. 166*
  cross-country running, 164
  facilities for, 159–60
  federal legislation on, 160
  financial aid for athletes, 165
  lacrosse, 163–4
  soccer, 164–5
  swimming and diving, 161,
    163; *ills. 160, 161, 162*
  tennis, 164
  track and field, 164
  varsity status for teams, 160,
    163
WRA (Women's Recreational
  Association), 158–9

Yale University, New Haven, Ct.,
   vs. BC:
   in football, 11, 14–15
   in hockey, 65, 80
Yauckoes, John, 19
Yetten, Ned, 142
York, Jerry, 76

Yukica, Joseph Michael (Joe),
   32–3, 36–7, 39–41, 44–7;
   ill. 33
Yurewicz, Johnny, *ill. 133*

Zabilski, Joe, 148
Zailowsky, Chuck, 153

Zailskas, Dan, 141
Zaitz, Dimitri, 148
Zeimetz, Frank, 148
Zuffelato, Bob, 112–14
Zumbach, Dave, 37, 40, 41